DEFENCES IN UNJUST ENRICHMENT

This book is the second in a series of essay collections on defences in private law. It addresses defences to liability arising in unjust enrichment. The essays are written from a range of perspectives and methodologies. Some are doctrinal, others are theoretical, and several offer comparative insights. The most important defence in this area of the law, change of position, is addressed in detail, but many other defences are treated too, as well as the interrelations between these defences within the law of unjust enrichment. The essays offer novel claims and ways of looking at problems in this challenging area of legal study.

Volume 2 in the series Hart Studies in Private Law: Essays on Defences

Hart Studies in Private Law: Essays on Defences

The series offers a systematic treatment of defences in private law as a connected field. It addresses tort law, unjust enrichment, contract law and equity, in that order. Its aim is to contribute to this theoretically challenging and practically important, yet understudied, area of the law. The essays that constitute each of the collections in this series are written by some of the world's leading judges and scholars. They bring together insights from several jurisdictions, including civilian jurisdictions. The series is of value to academics and practitioners alike.

Defences in Unjust Enrichment

Edited by
Andrew Dyson
James Goudkamp
and
Frederick Wilmot-Smith

•HART•
PUBLISHING
OXFORD AND PORTLAND, OREGON
2018

Hart Publishing
An imprint of Bloomsbury Publishing Plc

Hart Publishing Ltd
Kemp House
Chawley Park
Cumnor Hill
Oxford OX2 9PH
UK

Bloomsbury Publishing Plc
50 Bedford Square
London
WC1B 3DP
UK

www.hartpub.co.uk
www.bloomsbury.com

Published in North America (US and Canada) by
Hart Publishing
c/o International Specialized Book Services
920 NE 58th Avenue, Suite 300
Portland, OR 97213-3786
USA

www.isbs.com

First published in hardback, 2016
Paperback edition, 2018

British Library Cataloguing-in-Publication Data
A catalogue record for this book is available from the British Library.

ISBN: PB: 978-1-50992-110-2
HB: 978-1-84946-725-4

Library of Congress Cataloging-in-Publication Data

Defences in unjust enrichment / Edited by Andrew Dyson, James Goudkamp and Frederick Wilmot-Smith.
pages cm. – (Hart studies in private law : essays on defences)

Includes index.

ISBN 978-1-84946-725-4 (hardback : alk. paper) 1. Unjust enrichment—Great Britain.
2. Restitution—Great Britain. 3. Defense (Civil procedure)—Great Britain.
I. Dyson, Andrew, editor. II. Goudkamp, James, 1980– editor.
III. Wilmot-Smith, Frederick, 1986– editor.

KD1924.D46 2016 346.4102'9—dc23
2015036600

Typeset by Compuscript Ltd, Shannon

Foreword

The law of restitution for unjust enrichment has come a long way since its origins in the 16th century writ of *indebitatus assumpsit*. The ancient idea of making restitution when one has been unfairly enriched at the expense of another was traditionally captured by a collection of fact-specific categories that allowed recovery. In recent decades, spurred by the academic writings of Goff and Jones, these categories have been replaced by a unified conceptual framework.

With the publication of this second of four volumes, the editors of *Defences in Unjust Enrichment* are making good on their promise to develop a comprehensive understanding of private law defences as a whole, and build and cultivate an international network of experts in the field.

This collection of essays brings clarity to the conceptual structure of claims in unjust enrichment. The essays review core doctrinal elements of the law of unjust enrichment, including its scope. But they also provide scholarly treatment of the different answers that can be made to claims in unjust enrichment. A theme that emerges is the continuing relevance of the debate between denials—ie, allegations that a claimant has failed to establish one of the ingredients of her action—and defences proper—ie, a defendant's recognition that the elements of a claim are made out, coupled with an assertion that restitution is nevertheless unavailable. What is at stake here is the epistemological status of defences in private law. The essays also deal with the constitutive elements and scope of doctrines like 'enrichment owed', 'change of position', 'illegality' and 'bona fide purchase'. They examine the effects of the age of minority on defences, the availability of defences between victims of a common fraud, and restitution of money paid as tax that is not due. Where appropriate, the authors look for insight in the law of common law jurisdictions from around the world, and to the civil law tradition.

The matters discussed in these essays are not only of interest to scholars. They will help lawyers to advise their clients, and courts to ensure that the common law keeps pace with changes in the fabric of society. As Lord Reed aptly points out in the closing chapter of this book, in this area of the law, 'much of the case law predates the modern development of unjust enrichment as a category, and lacks the clarity and coherence of scholars' explanatory theories' (p 310). Essays like the ones in this collection help make sense of this challenging area of law.

I commend the authors and editors on an impressive achievement which will, undoubtedly, assist in further developments in the law of restitution. Theirs is a valuable contribution to the dynamic legal thinking that characterises the common law tradition.

The Right Honourable Beverley McLachlin, PC
Chief Justice of Canada

Preface

This book is the second part of an investigation into defences in private law. The present volume explores defences to unjust enrichment claims. Two further volumes are planned, on contract and equity.

The chapters in the present volume were delivered at a workshop at All Souls College, Oxford in January 2015. We are grateful, first and foremost, for the support of All Souls College, which provided both the setting for the proceedings and significant financial support. The workshop could not have gone ahead without the further financial assistance of the Oxford Law Faculty and the University of Oxford's John Fell OUP Research Fund.

Discussions at the workshop were greatly enriched by the contributions of several observers—including Chief Justice McLachlin, Lord Hoffmann, Lord Sumption, Sir Launcelot Henderson, Professor Andrew Burrows, Mr Frank McArdle, Professor Robert Stevens and Professor Reinhard Zimmermann—and we would like to thank everyone who attended. Finally, Melody Ihuoma's assistance was invaluable throughout the organisation process.

For their assistance in helping to turn the workshop papers into the chapters that feature in this volume, we are grateful to Jodi Gardner, Paolo Ronchi, Jocelyn Teo and Mengfei Ying. We are indebted to Hart Publishing for their editorial assistance. Finally, we are doubly grateful to Chief Justice McLachlin for supporting the series from its inception, and in particular for generously agreeing to write the foreword to this book.

Andrew Dyson
James Goudkamp
Frederick Wilmot-Smith

1 February 2016
Oxford

Table of Contents

Contributors

Elise Bant is a Professor at Melbourne Law School, University of Melbourne.

Robert Chambers is a Professor of Private Law at King's College London.

Andrew Dyson is an Assistant Professor in Private Law at the London School of Economics and Political Science.

James Goudkamp is a Fellow of Keble College, Oxford and an Associate Professor of Law at the University of Oxford. He is also an Academic Fellow of the Inner Temple, an Honorary Senior Research Fellow at the Faculty of Law, University of Western Australia and an Honorary Principal Fellow at the Faculty of Law, University of Wollongong. James is a barrister at 7 King's Bench Walk.

Birke Häcker is a Senior Research Fellow at the Max Planck Institute for Tax Law and Public Finance, Munich and a Fellow of All Souls College, Oxford.

Dennis Klimchuk is an Associate Professor of Philosophy at the University of Western Ontario.

Andrew Kull is a Distinguished Senior Lecturer at the School of Law, University of Texas.

Sonja Meier is a Professor of Law at the University of Freiburg.

Charles Mitchell is a Professor of Law at University College London.

Ajay Ratan is a barrister at Blackstone Chambers.

The Rt Hon Lord Reed is a Justice of the Supreme Court of the United Kingdom.

Helen Scott is a Professor of Private Law at the University of Cape Town.

Lionel Smith is the Sir William C Macdonald Professor of Law at the Faculty of Law, McGill University and Professor of Private Law at the Dickson Poon School of Law, King's College London.

Graham Virgo is a Fellow in Law at Downing College, Cambridge and Professor of English Private Law at the University of Cambridge.

Frederick Wilmot-Smith is a Prize Fellow at All Souls College, Oxford.

Table of Cases

Australia

British Virgin Islands

Canada

Eastern Africa

European Court of Justice

Germany

Ireland

Jamaica

New Zealand

Singapore

South Africa

United Kingdom

United States of America

Table of Legislation

Israel

New Zealand

United Kingdom

United States of America

Table of Conventions

Table of Restatements

1

Defences in Unjust Enrichment: Questions and Themes

ANDREW DYSON, JAMES GOUDKAMP AND FREDERICK WILMOT-SMITH

1. INTRODUCTION

THIS BOOK IS the second in a series of four that is concerned with defences to liability arising in private law. We felt, and still feel, that the topic has not received the attention that it deserves.[1] We are not alone in holding this view.[2] By contrast, defences have dominated the research agendas of many scholars of the criminal law.[3] The asymmetry in attention to defences in these different fields is striking in part because of the apparent parallels between the two domains. For instance, the distinction in private law between causes of action and defences arguably mirrors that between offences and defences in the criminal law.[4]

[1] In our first collection, on tort law defences, we observed that defences are rarely discussed in the theoretical literature, citing J Oberdiek (ed), *Philosophical Foundations of the Law of Torts* (Oxford, Oxford University Press, 2014) as an illustration. In a similar vein, there are no chapters on defences in R Chambers, C Mitchell and J Penner (eds), *Philosophical Foundations of the Law of Unjust Enrichment* (Oxford, Oxford University Press, 2009).

[2] eg, Ross Grantham and Charles Rickett write: 'The integration of defences into the normative justification for liability is something that has been overlooked in most areas of the private law': R Grantham and C Rickett, 'A Normative Account of Defences to Restitutionary Liability' (2008) 67 *CLJ* 92, 103 fn 57. Similarly, Graham Virgo observes: 'In the field of private law, much work has been done to describe, explain and rationalise different causes of action. Whilst some excellent work has also been done as regards the analysis of specific defences, notably change of position and passing on as defences to claims in unjust enrichment, surprisingly little work has been done to analyse defences in private law more generally': G Virgo, 'Book Review' (2015) 74 *CLJ* 160, 160.

[3] See, eg, HLA Hart, *Punishment and Responsibility: Essays in the Philosophy of Law* (Oxford, Oxford University Press, 1968) chs 2, 4 and 8; GP Fletcher, *Rethinking Criminal Law* (Boston, Little, Brown & Co, 1978) chs 7, 9–10; J Gardner, *Offences and Defences: Essays in the Philosophy of Criminal Law* (Oxford, Oxford University Press, 2007) chs 4–9.

[4] Nevertheless, few theorists with expertise in both criminal law and private law have considered the possibility of cross-fertilisation. There are, of course, exceptions. The influence of Hart's work on criminal law defences is visible in his seminal account of the concept of defeasibility, in which he considered defences in private law: HLA Hart, 'The Ascription of Responsibility and Rights' (1949) 49 *Proceedings of the Aristotelian Society* 171.

Our first book examined defences to tort claims.[5] The present volume deals with defences to claims in unjust enrichment. The next two books will concern defences to contractual claims and claims in equity respectively. Part of the reason why we undertook to produce a series of books was that we believe there is merit in thinking about private law defences as a whole.[6] The workshop at which the chapters published here were originally presented, and the chapters themselves, confirms that that belief was, and remains, justified. The same questions that had arisen in our exploration of tort law defences frequently recurred in the unjust enrichment defences workshop. In this introductory chapter, we review several of these questions. We also set out how our contributors seek to answer them.

2. TWO QUESTIONS ABOUT DEFENCES

In this section we discuss two important controversies about defences: the first is what a defence actually is; the second is the justification for a legal system recognising defences. We discuss the first of these questions by reference to the distinction between denials and defences.

2.1. Distinguishing Denials and Defences

2.1.1. Preliminaries

At the first workshop, on tort law defences, it was clear that there was no consensus as to the meaning of the term 'defence'. Indeed, one of the chapters in the collection on tort defences concerned itself exclusively with the definition of the concept.[7] It reveals that scholars understand the term in numerous different ways and that disagreements between scholars in this regard are vigorous and multi-faceted, with several orthogonal debates breaking out. There seemed to be fewer disagreements at the unjust enrichment workshop on this particular point. However, this harmony may be illusory: when the question was approached in terms of denials and defences (ie, how are defences distinct from denials?), alliances seemed to be much shakier.

In our chapter in the first book on tort law defences, we considered the distinction between denials and defences at some length.[8] The distinction

[5] A Dyson, J Goudkamp and F Wilmot-Smith (eds), *Defences in Tort* (Oxford, Hart Publishing, 2015).

[6] For more details regarding the project generally, see A Dyson, J Goudkamp and F Wilmot-Smith, 'Central Issues in the Law of Tort Defences' in Dyson, Goudkamp and Wilmot-Smith (n 5) 3–5.

[7] L Duarte d'Almeida, 'Defining "Defences"' in Dyson, Goudkamp and Wilmot-Smith (n 5).

[8] Dyson, Goudkamp and Wilmot-Smith (n 6) 6–8.

aims to separate two kinds of response that a defendant might make to a claim: a denial is an assertion that the cause of action is incomplete;[9] a defence accepts that the cause of action is complete, but argues that liability should be reduced or eliminated on account of some other consideration (although some scholars consider rules that merely reduce liability not to be defences but a *tertium quid*).[10] Difficult issues regarding this distinction that we identified included: whether there is indeed a conceptual distinction between denials and defences; and, if there is a distinction, the identification of the different characteristics of denials and defences.

Several contributors endorse the distinction between denials and defences in this volume.[11] For instance, Klimchuk says:[12]

> We can ask, first, whether change of position works to deny that an element of the cause of action in unjust enrichment has been made out, or whether instead it serves to reduce the defendant's liability notwithstanding that the elements of the cause of action have been made out.

However, although the distinction is evidently seen to be of vital import by contributors who recognise it—for example, both Helen Scott and Dennis Klimchuk dedicate substantial parts of their chapters to the proper classification of two doctrinal rules by reference to it—our contributors seem as a whole to assume the distinction is unproblematic. In our earlier work, we suggested some reasons to doubt whether the distinction is indeed trouble-free.[13] We want to highlight three problems with which scholars who endorse the distinction must, in our view, grapple: first, we discuss some disagreement about the nature of the distinction between denials and defences; next, we ask whether the law of unjust enrichment recognises the distinction; and, finally, we consider whether the distinction is exhaustive of the rules that comprise the law of unjust enrichment.

2.1.2. *What Kind of Distinction is it?*

There appeared to be some disagreement amongst our contributors about the nature of the distinction between denials and defences. In her contribution,

[9] This is perhaps insufficiently nuanced. A defendant might raise a *partial* denial. For instance, a defendant might accept that she has been unjustly enriched at the claimant's expense, but deny that she has been enriched to the extent of the objective measure. We observe that debate exists as to whether such a contention should be characterised as a partial denial ('subjective devaluation') or a defence ('change of position'). See, in particular, *Sempra Metals Ltd (Formerly Metallgesellschaft Ltd) v Inland Revenue Commissioners* [2007] UKHL 34; [2008] 1 AC 561, 606 [119] (Lord Nicholls); *Benedetti v Saiwiris* [2013] UKSC 50; [2014] AC 938, 987–88 [118] (Lord Reed JSC).

[10] See, eg, J Goudkamp, *Tort Law Defences* (Oxford, Hart Publishing, 2013) 6.

[11] Ch 12, p 280; ch 3, p 54 *et seq*; ch 8, p 171. *Cf* ch 9, p 196 fn 7.

[12] Ch 4, p 69. See, further, Meier's definition of a defence, at ch 11, p 259, as 'a fact that is able to extinguish an otherwise given cause of action'.

[13] Dyson, Goudkamp and Wilmot-Smith (n 6) 7.

Elise Bant argues that understanding the defence of change of position 'as an aspect of the general enrichment enquiry' (ie, as part of the cause of action) would be 'contrary to the vast preponderance of authority that conceives of and treats the defence as having a role independent of the elements of the primary claim'.[14] Although Bant is here concerned with the possible changes to the substantive rules of change of position which might have to be made if change of position were thought of as a denial, the passage suggests one way in which the distinction between denials and defences can be understood: as one that the law itself draws. On this analysis, in other words, the boundary of the distinction between denials and defences is to be settled by legal authorities.

Compare Bant's analysis with that offered by Helen Scott. Scott writes that 'the distinction between actions and defences, and more specifically denials and defences, turns on substantive arguments about the definition of torts'.[15] Although Scott is talking about the law of torts here, the context makes it clear that her claim in this regard is not confined to that branch of private law. Scott adds that the task of deciding whether some doctrine is 'extrinsic to the claimant's action' is 'an exercise informed by doctrinal and moral arguments specific to the unjust enrichment context, not instrumental arguments of relatively general application'.[16] All this suggests that the classification of a doctrine as a defence or a denial is not a *mere* function of authority; instead, it depends in part on normative arguments extrinsic to the law (even if these arguments must, for whatever reason, be local 'to the unjust enrichment context'). Scott does not, we take it, mean to suggest that the question is whether there are good normative reasons to employ the distinction—we are here concerned with definition, not justification.[17] Instead, she suggests that normative arguments cannot be avoided in the description of the distinction between denials and defences.[18]

2.1.3. Does the Law of Unjust Enrichment Recognise the Distinction?

The next problem concerns whether the distinction between denials and defences, howsoever understood, is recognised in the law of unjust enrichment. It is salutary here to recall certain statements defining the cause of

[14] See ch 7, p 140.
[15] See ch 3, p 53.
[16] ibid p 54.
[17] We address the issue of justification in 2.2.
[18] There are interesting parallels here with well-known debates in general jurisprudence concerning the nature of conceptual analysis. See, eg, HLA Hart, *The Concept of Law*, 2nd edn (Oxford, Clarendon Press, 1994) 244; JM Finnis, *Natural Law and Natural Rights* (Oxford, Oxford University Press, 1980) ch 1. *cf* Dworkin's claim that 'the flat distinction between distinction and evaluation' has 'enfeebled legal theory': R Dworkin, *A Matter of Principle* (Cambridge MA, Harvard University Press, 1985) 148.

action in unjust enrichment. In a widely endorsed passage, Lightman J stated:[19]

> It is now authoritatively established that there are four essential ingredients to a claim in restitution:
>
> i) a benefit must have been gained by the defendant;
> ii) the benefit must have been obtained at the claimant's expense;
> iii) it must be legally unjust, that is to say there must exist a factor (referred to as an unjust factor) rendering it unjust, for the defendant to retain the benefit;
> iv) there must be no defence available to extinguish or reduce the defendant's liability to make restitution.

Taken literally, this would show that the law of unjust enrichment does not distinguish denials and defences. The fourth ingredient that Lightman J mentions brings defences within his definition of an action in unjust enrichment in negative form.[20] The absence of defences is, in other words, one of the elements of the action.[21]

Attempts to fold defences into the cause of action have been made not only in relation to definitions of a cause of action in unjust enrichment but also in connection with individual 'defences'. Consider, for example, the fact that one prominent way of understanding the change of position 'defence' is to see it as concerned with 'disenrichment' and hence with the enrichment element of the action. Peter Birks argued that this 'defence' '[attacks the element of] "enrichment at the expense of the claimant."'[22] So conceived, the change of position 'defence' is not, it would seem, 'external' to the cause of action. Given the prominence of the change of position 'defence', this logic might lead one to think that the law of unjust enrichment does not recognise any defences. Perhaps some legal systems have reached that position already. For instance, Helen Scott, in her contribution in this volume, suggests that 'South African law may embody that mythical system ... in which all liability rules have been assimilated to the elements of the action,

[19] *R (Rowe) v Vale of White Horse DC* [2003] EWHC 388 (Admin); [2003] 1 Lloyd's Rep 418, 421 [11].

[20] *cf* the more circumspect remarks of Lord Clarke JSC in *Benedetti v Sawiris* [2013] UKSC 50; [2014] AC 938, 955 [10]: 'a court must first ask itself four questions'.

[21] For a thorough theoretical consideration (and rejection) of the thesis that there is no distinction between defences and denials, see L Duarte d'Almeida, *Allowing for Exceptions: A Theory of Defences and Defeasibility in Law* (Oxford, Oxford University Press, 2015).

[22] P Birks, *Unjust Enrichment*, 2nd edn (Oxford, Oxford University Press, 2005) 207. Birks' commitment to this view is unclear. Elsewhere he made remarks that are inconsistent with viewing the change of position doctrine as striking at the enrichment element of an action in unjust enrichment. See ibid 207, where Birks spoke of defences as 'trumping the injustice of the defendant's enrichment'. For elaboration of Birks' position in this regard, see J Goudkamp and C Mitchell, 'Denials and Defences in the Law of Unjust Enrichment' in C Mitchell and W Swadling (eds), *The Restatement Third: Restitution and Unjust Enrichment* (Oxford, Hart Publishing, 2013) 144.

rendering defences (or at least defences specific to the law of enrichment) superfluous'.[23]

These remarks raise many important questions. Is the law of unjust enrichment best understood without considering defences? Or is there some reason why the concept of defences—howsoever understood—is important to our understanding of the terrain? More generally, should such an approach—whereby defences are folded into the cause of action—be applied to the legal system as a whole? Or is there something wrong with such a system? We will return to this last question later, when we consider the point of formulating legal rules as defences.[24] For now, however, we want to highlight another reason to examine the law of unjust enrichment through the prism of this distinction between defences and denials: it casts light on a well-known debate concerning the basis of the law of unjust enrichment. Unjust enrichment lawyers customarily distinguish 'unjust factors' systems from 'absence of basis' systems.[25] Under the former system, a claimant's success depends upon her showing that an enrichment was transferred under the influence of an 'unjust factor', such as a mistake. In the latter, a claimant's success depends upon her demonstrating that the enrichment was transferred without legal basis. These systems may view particular doctrines, in terms of the divide between denials and defences, differently. Consider, for example, the well-recognised rule that 'to the extent that a payment made under a mistake discharges a contractual debt of the payee, it cannot be recovered'.[26] Lawyers who endorse the 'unjust factors' approach sometimes interpret this 'enrichment owed' doctrine as a defence.[27] This seems to have been how Robert Goff J understood the doctrine. In *Barclays Bank Ltd v WJ Simms* his Lordship wrote:[28]

> If a person pays money to another under a mistake of fact which causes him to make the payment, he is prima facie entitled to recover it as money paid under a mistake of fact ... His claim may however fail if ... the payment is made for good consideration, in particular if the money is paid to discharge, and does discharge,

[23] See ch 3, p 64.

[24] See 2.2.2.

[25] The literature on these different approaches is voluminous. See, eg, A Burrows 'Absence of Basis: The New Birksian Scheme' in A Burrows and A Rodger (eds), *Mapping the Law: Essays in Memory of Peter Birks* (Oxford, Hart Publishing, 2006) 33; S Meier, 'No Basis: A Comparative View' in A Burrows and Lord Rodger (eds), *Mapping the Law: Essays in Memory of Peter Birks* (Oxford, Oxford University Press, 2006) 343; R Stevens 'Is There a Law of Unjust Enrichment?' in J Edelman and S Degeling (eds), *Unjust Enrichment in Commercial Law* (Sydney, Law Book Co, 2008) 11.

[26] *Fairfield Sentry Ltd v Migani* [2014] UKPC 9; [2014] 1 CLC 611 (PC (BVI)) 619 [18] (Lord Sumption JSC). In his contribution to the present volume, Andrew Kull examines restitution between successive fraud victims, which gives rise to similar issues.

[27] C Mitchell, P Mitchell and S Watterson, *Goff & Jones: The Law of Unjust Enrichment*, 8th edn (London, Sweet & Maxwell, 2011) ch 29.

[28] *Barclays Bank Ltd v WJ Simms* [1980] QB 677 (QBD) 695.

> a debt owed to the payee (or a principal on whose behalf he is authorised to receive the payment) by the payer or by a third party by whom he is authorised to discharge the debt.

If one endorses the view that any payment 'under a mistake of fact', *regardless of whether it discharges a liability*, is prima facie sufficient for restitution, enrichment owed—or the 'good consideration' doctrine—naturally falls to be considered at a later stage.

By way of contrast, in her chapter in the present volume, Helen Scott suggests that under an absence of basis system:[29]

> The claimant cannot make out even a prima facie case without pleading the absence of liability ... and, at least in cases involving an apparent contractual or other obligation, without proving the non-existence or invalidity of that obligation.

In this way, the proper classification of the enrichment owed doctrine feeds into one of the most heated questions in the academic debate on the law of unjust enrichment. Indeed, the proper classification of the doctrine may turn on the following question: does the fact that the enrichment was owed defeat a prima facie injustice, as the unjust factors view might hold?[30] Or does it instead demonstrate that there was no injustice at all, as the absence of legal ground view might hold? We hope that this shows that examining the distinction between denials and defences, and seeing whether it is instantiated in the law of unjust enrichment, is vitally important if we are to understand the law as a whole.

2.1.4. Is the Distinction Exhaustive?

The final question that we will discuss regarding the distinction between denials and defences is whether it is exhaustive (that is, does it encompass every plea a defendant might make to resist a claim in unjust enrichment?). One might conclude that there are doctrines in the law of unjust enrichment that cannot properly be categorised as pertaining to either the denials or defences categories. The doctrine of illegality is arguably such a rule.[31] Although many—including Graham Virgo in his contribution to

[29] See ch 3, p 65.

[30] *cf*, however, A Burrows, 'Good Consideration in the Law of Unjust Enrichment' (2013) 129 *LQR* 329, 331: 'The importance of a mistaken payment being made for good consideration is not that this constitutes a defence but that this means that the payment is being made under a contract so that, unless the contract is invalid, there is no prima facie right to restitution'. If this is correct, the distinction between the supposedly rival systems arguably becomes very difficult to make out.

[31] We do not consider here the possibility of illegality as a cause of action in unjust enrichment. For discussion, see W Swadling, 'The Role of Illegality in the English Law of Unjust Enrichment' in D Johnston and R Zimmerman (eds), *Unjustified Enrichment: Key Issues in Comparative Perspective* (Cambridge, Cambridge University Press, 2002).

this volume[32]—regard the doctrine of illegality as a defence, consider Lord Sumption JSC's claim that:[33]

> [A]lthough described as a defence, it is in reality a rule of judicial abstention. It means that rather than regulating the consequences of an illegal act (for example by restoring the parties to the status quo ante, in the same way as on the rescission of a contract) the courts withhold judicial remedies, leaving the loss to lie where it falls.

This passage suggests that Lord Sumption would not regard the distinction between denials and defences as being exhaustive. His Lordship explicitly states that illegality is not a defence, but nor does he appear to understand it as a denial. In similar fashion, Ross Grantham and Charles Rickett argue that:[34]

> The need to incorporate the defences into the overall normative justification of unjust enrichment does not, of course, rule out the existence of defences that reflect policy considerations external to the law of unjust enrichment or even the private law as a whole. As is the case with contractual and tortious liabilities, issues such as illegality and excessive delay in bringing proceedings offer reasons to deny liability, but these factors are not central to the logic or extent of liability.

If there are indeed such doctrines, how should they be classified? Is illegality the sole example, or are there other similar doctrines, as Grantham and Rickett seem to suggest?

2.1.5. Conclusion

Attempts to distinguish denials from defences are regarded by some as arid conceptualism. We hope that we have shown this not to be the case. There are important theoretical questions at the heart of the distinction, and a proper understanding of the distinction and its application in the law is vital to questions as basic as the foundation of the law of unjust enrichment. Our remarks have perhaps raised more questions than they have answered, but this only goes to show the amount of work that remains to be done in this field.

[32] See ch 8, p 171: 'If a claimant seeks restitution for unjust enrichment, the fact that the claim is tainted by illegality will operate as a defence.'

[33] *Les Laboratoires Servier v Apotex Inc* [2014] UKSC 55; [2015] AC 430, 445 [23]. *cf Jetivia SA v Bilta (UK) Ltd (in Liquidation)* [2015] UKSC 23; [2015] 2 WLR 1168, where Lord Sumption at 1187 [60] calls judicial abstention the 'policy' (rather than the rule?) and, at 1187 [55], where he says: 'It is convenient to call this the illegality defence, although the label is not entirely accurate for it also applies to a very limited category of acts which are immoral without being illegal.'

[34] Grantham and Rickett (n 2) 94.

2.2. The Rationale of Defences

There may, of course, be numerous reasons why a legal system might employ defences.[35] In this subsection we will examine the rationale of defences from two angles. First, we will consider two reasons why the law of unjust enrichment might limit the circumstances in which claimants can recover and note that the difference between these reasons may have practical consequences. In this discussion, we want to remain agnostic as to whether recovery is limited by way of a defence or by modification of the elements of the cause of action. Accordingly, we will refer to such control devices as 'exceptions'. Second, we will ask whether the law should formulate exceptions as *defences* (rather than through more precise definition of the cause of action).

2.2.1. Two Reasons for Recognising Exceptions

In his contribution to this volume, Graham Virgo writes that:[36]

> Most of the defences to claims in unjust enrichment focus on the relationship between the claimant and the defendant, and are normatively related to the principle of corrective justice. That is not the case with the defence of illegality, which is influenced by external considerations of public policy rather than securing justice between the parties.

Many judges and scholars would accept Virgo's claim that the illegality doctrine is unconcerned with justice between the parties.[37] For example, Lord Mansfield said in *Holman v Johnson* that the doctrine 'is founded in general principles of policy, which the defendant has the advantage of, contrary to the real justice, as between him and the plaintiff'.[38] Lord Sumption JSC endorsed Lord Mansfield's understanding in *Les Laboratoires Servier v Apotex Inc.* His Lordship remarked that the illegality doctrine 'is in the nature of things bound to confer capricious benefits on defendants some of whom have little to be said for them in the way of merits, legal or otherwise'.[39] We have already noted[40] Lord Sumption's view that the

[35] For a list of possible rationales, see Goudkamp and Mitchell (n 22) 146–50.

[36] See ch 8, p 165 (footnotes omitted).

[37] *cf*, in this respect, Chief Justice McLachlin's contribution to the previous collection on tort law defences, in which she argued that the doctrine of illegality is founded on corrective justice: B McLachlin, 'Weaving the Law's Seamless Web: Reflections on the Illegality Defence in Tort Law' in Dyson, Goudkamp and Wilmot-Smith (n 5). This claim arguably commits her to the proposition that the doctrine of illegality is concerned with interpersonal justice rather than with broader societal concerns.

[38] *Holman v Johnson* (1775) 1 Cowp 341, 343; 98 ER 1120, 1121.

[39] *Les Laboratoires Servier v Apotex Inc* (n 33) 440 [13]. *cf* his Lordship's remark that 'the defence [ought not to be extended] far more widely than anything warranted by the demands of justice': *Jetivia SA v Bilta (UK) Ltd (in Liquidation)* (n 33) 1192 [70]. It is unclear whether 'justice' here refers to interpersonal justice or to some other concept.

[40] See the text accompanying n 33 above.

illegality doctrine is 'in reality a rule of judicial abstention'.[41] This view is related to the proposition that the doctrine is unconcerned with realising interpersonal justice. Instead, the justification for the illegality doctrine is, for Lord Sumption, a 'principle of consistency'.[42] When achieving interpersonal justice would undermine the consistency (or 'integrity', in the language of McLachlin J in *Hall v Hebert*)[43] of the legal system, the interest in consistency is prioritised. Consistency is achieved by judicial abstention.

It is not our purpose to engage with the merits of these rival accounts of the doctrine of illegality. Instead, we want to draw attention to the fact that the passages in the previous paragraph suggest that there are at least two general reasons why a legal system might recognise an exception to a liability rule: first, in order to take account of the concerns of justice between the parties; and, second, to uphold the integrity of the legal process itself. We believe that these reasons may have consequences for the rules of pleading. Virgo claims that the doctrine of illegality's 'public policy foundations' explains why 'illegality may defeat a claim even though it has not been pleaded'.[44] This implies that rules concerned with upholding the integrity of the legal system can be considered by the court on the court's own motion.

Another potential consequence of the distinction between inter-party justice exceptions and integrity-based exceptions relates to the breadth of application of the exception in question. As Lionel Smith observes in his chapter in this collection: 'Some defences are available to more than one cause of action. Illegality is an example.'[45] In *Vellino v Chief Constable of Greater Manchester* Sedley LJ said '[the illegality doctrine] applies across the board'.[46] If the illegality doctrine seeks to uphold the integrity of the legal system, the doctrine's application to numerous causes of action is unsurprising: such a doctrine should be available (if desired) whenever a cause of action is capable of undermining that integrity. Interpersonal defences do not appear to have such broad applicability. For example, the doctrine of contributory negligence is available to some actions in tort (such negligence) but not others (such as trespass[47] and deceit).[48] Quite how important

[41] *Les Laboratoires Servier v Apotex Inc* (n 33) 445 [23].

[42] ibid 446 [24].

[43] *Hall v Hebert* [1993] 2 SCR 159 (SCC) 176.

[44] See ch 8, p 177. Virgo is correct that illegality can be raised by the court *proprio motu:* Law Commission, *The Illegality Defence: A Consultative Report* (Law Com Consultation Paper 189, 2009) 133 [7.22]; *Ferguson v John Dawson & Partners (Contractors) Ltd* [1976] 1 WLR 1213 (CA) 1218.

[45] See ch 2, p 45.

[46] *Vellino v Chief Constable of Greater Manchester* [2001] EWCA Civ 1249; [2002] 1 WLR 218, 228 [44]. 'We do not consider that the public policy that the court will not lend its aid to a litigant who relies on his own criminal or immoral act is confined to particular causes of action': *Clunis v Camden and Islington Health Authority* [1998] QB 978 (CA) 987.

[47] *Co-Operative Group (CSW) Ltd v Pritchard* [2011] EWCA Civ 329; [2012] QB 320.

[48] *Standard Chartered Bank v Pakistan National Shipping Corp (Nos 2 and 4)* [2002] UKHL 43; [2003] 1 AC 959.

this apparent distinction is remains to be seen, but it is certainly worthy of further inquiry.

2.2.2. Why Use Defences?

Would there be anything wrong with what Helen Scott terms the 'mythical system ... in which all liability rules have been assimilated to the elements of the action'?[49] Some scholars seem to think that there would be. For instance, in her contribution Elise Bant considers the change of position defence and warns of 'the danger—realised in some cases—that, by focusing on the extent to which a defendant's assets remain swollen by her receipt the defence will come to be treated simply as an aspect of the general enrichment enquiry'.[50] Bant here assumes that there would be something wrong with a system which assimilated change of position to an aspect of the cause of action. However, what, exactly, would be wrong with such a system?[51] Why should a legal system not fold exceptions into the elements of the action in order to create Scott's postulated 'mythical system'? In other words, why should the law seek to respond to the reasons for exceptions to rules by way of *defences*?

To understand an interesting—but, we think, ultimately flawed—answer to this question, notice that the cause of action in unjust enrichment is very expansive. In most cases, it is complete on receipt of the enrichment—for instance, when money is paid to the defendant by mistake.[52] The upshot of this is that the cause of action in unjust enrichment imposes not only strict liability (that is, liability that arises irrespective of whether the defendant was at fault) but also what might be called 'passive liability'.[53] By passive liability, we mean liability that arises irrespective of the defendant's participation in, or perhaps even irrespective of the defendant's awareness of, the facts on which the claim is based.[54] This 'unilaterality', ie, the creation of 'a right against someone who had no hand in bringing about the matter she

[49] See ch 3, p 64.

[50] See ch 7, p 140.

[51] Bant's reason is that it would restrict the ambit of change of position to situations where the defendant is 'disenriched', ie, loses what the law would class as an enrichment at the cause of action stage: see text to n 14. We are unconvinced by this; the law *could* recognise a doctrine with the same ambit at the cause of action stage.

[52] *cf* subsequent failures of consideration: *Guardian Ocean Cargoes Ltd v Banco do Brasil* [1994] 2 Lloyd's Rep 152 (CA).

[53] S Smith, 'A Duty to Make Restitution' (2013) 26 *Canadian Journal of Law and Jurisprudence* 157, 170: 'the subject of the duty may be entirely innocent, even passive'.

[54] There is a debate in the literature about whether the defendant comes under a duty or merely a liability when the cause of action is complete: ibid. However, no one questions whether the cause of action is complete on receipt; the debate concerns what the consequence of that conclusion is (or ought to be).

now bears a responsibility to set aright', gives rise to a puzzle: how can such a rule be justified?[55]

It has been argued that defences can justify an expansive cause of action. For example, in *Lipkin Gorman v Karpnale Ltd* Lord Goff opined that:[56]

> [T]he recognition of change of position as a defence should be ... beneficial [because it] ... will enable a more generous approach to be taken to the recognition of the right to restitution, in the knowledge that the defence is, in more appropriate cases, available.

Several contributors to this volume endorse the view, as Dennis Klimchuk puts it, that 'restitution for unjust enrichment should never make defendants worse off'.[57] Meeting that promise is widely understood to be the purpose of the change of position defence. There is some debate in the chapters about whether the appropriate baseline for being 'worse off' is historical, as Bant argues,[58] or counterfactual, as Ratan argues.[59] An historical baseline seeks to ensure that the defendant is not worse off than the position she *was in* before the defective transfer; a counterfactual baseline seeks to ensure that the defendant is not worse off than the position she *would have been* in some specified possible world.[60] But prior to this debate, these commentators all appear to agree with the claim that the existence of the change of position defence helps to justify the cause of action in unjust enrichment.[61]

This argument is difficult to assess as it has never been developed in detail. It may state no more than a conditional: if you have defences, they can justify causes of action. However, in relation to change of position, Lord Goff

[55] D Klimchuk, 'The Normative Foundations of Unjust Enrichment' in R Chambers, C Mitchell and J Penner (eds), *Philosophical Foundations of the Law of Unjust Enrichment* (Oxford, Oxford University Press, 2009) 86.

[56] *Lipkin Gorman v Karpnale Ltd* [1991] 2 AC 548 (HL) 581. See also Birks (n 22) 40; Grantham and Rickett (n 2) 93.

[57] See ch 4, p 72. See, further, Ratan, ch 5, p 88; Chambers, ch 6, pp 117–19; Bant, ch 7, pp 139 and 148; Kull, ch 10, pp 237–38.

[58] See ch 7, p 139: the defendant should not be placed in a worse position than she occupied prior to her receipt. See, further, S Smith, 'The Restatement of Liabilities in Restitution' in C Mitchell and W Swadling (eds), *The Restatement Third: Restitution and Unjust Enrichment* (Oxford, Hart Publishing, 2013) 231.

[59] See ch 5, p 87: 'a counterfactual comparison is embedded at the core of the change of position doctrine'.

[60] Amongst counterfactualists, many have claimed that the appropriate possible world is the one where the defendant did not receive the enrichment; Ratan, in his chapter, argues that it is the one where there was no defect in the claimant's intention.

[61] On a counterfactual account, like Ratan's, the specification of the appropriate counterfactual may well be bound up with the question of what problem the cause of action in unjust enrichment seeks to remedy. He claims that to discover the appropriate counterfactual for the change of position defence, we would ideally: 'delve into the normative theory of unjust enrichment. The pertinent question would be: which counterfactual baseline figures in the most compelling moral justification for the imposition of unjust enrichment liability? The baseline adopted in that fundamental debate could then be doctrinally implemented by the change of position defence'. See ch 5, p 109.

does appear to commit to more than a conditional. His Lordship implies that the defence will allow the law to vindicate some good that it could not realise through manipulation of the cause of action alone. How can this be so? Why could the law not, for instance, develop causes of action which are capable of justification without the need for defences—or which distinguish between 'appropriate cases' at the cause-of-action stage? One thought, which has occurred to a number of scholars, is that defences may help to finesse legal rules in a manner which cannot be done by modifying the content of the cause of action or which can be done only with great impracticality. For instance, Peter Birks opined:[62]

> It has become apparent in recent years that the fine tuning of the law of unjust enrichment will fall to the [defences stage]. Restrictive interpretations of the cause of action have been relaxed as defences have begun to take the strain ... [T]he new strategy will do more sensitive justice.

Andrew Burrows appears to be attracted to this idea. He writes that: 'Rather than the courts placing arbitrary restrictions on liability, the scope of restitution is now more satisfactorily and openly controlled by the defences'.[63] Burrows' suggestion appears to be that attempting to control the circumstances in which liability arises at the cause-of-action stage would be less 'satisfactory'. However, what reason is there to accept that this is the case? In Birks' terms, why does recognising defences permit the law of unjust enrichment to 'do more sensitive justice'? In Burrows' language, why does the law of unjust enrichment dispose of cases 'more satisfactorily and openly' than it would if there were no defences and all relevant issues were treated as asking whether a cause of action exists?

Perhaps the idea is that it would be too cumbersome to define a cause of action with sufficient specificity to account for all exceptions. In his chapter in this collection, Lionel Smith highlights Joseph Raz's analysis on the individuation of norms.[64] Raz writes that: 'It is possible to devise principles of individuation which guarantee that every rule includes all its qualifications and that no rules ever conflict with each other.'[65] For example:[66]

> The criminal law includes a rule prohibiting assault. This rule is qualified by various other laws. Assault is permitted in self-defense, in carrying out lawful orders, in cases of necessity ... One might wish to claim ... that no statement of the law against assault is a complete description of that law unless it enumerates all these qualifications. One may claim that the qualifying laws are not separate laws but only parts of the law prohibiting assault.

[62] Birks (n 22) 40.

[63] A Burrows, *The Law of Restitution*, 3rd edn (Oxford, Oxford University Press, 2011) 523.

[64] J Raz, 'Legal Principles and the Limits of Law' (1972) 81 *Yale Law Journal* 823, 825–34.

[65] ibid 831.

[66] ibid.

However, Raz asserts that: 'To do so would be to accept a very misguided doctrine of the individuation of laws.'[67] The laws we would have, on such a system, would be 'enormously complex. They [would] also be very repetitive, having much of their content in common (the doctrine of self-defense, for example, will be a part of each of the criminal laws)'.[68] Instead, therefore, 'we should adopt a doctrine of individuation which keeps laws to a manageable size, avoids repetition, minimizes the need to refer to a great variety of statutes and cases as the sources of a single law'.[69]

Smith suggests that these passages 'may also go a long way in helping us to understand why some elements should be classified as defences, rather than as parts of a cause of action'.[70] He does not develop this idea. There are perhaps two distinct reasons to reduce complexity in the legal system. First, a pragmatic reason: less complexity makes the legal system easier for officials to manage. Second, a rule of law reason: by reducing complexity in this way, the law may be more intelligible and accessible. Both of these reasons may have intriguing implications for defences as a whole: they suggest that, where possible, the law should favour general defences, applicable to multiple causes of action, rather than a plethora of specific defences.

A related argument in support of recognising defences, which is particularly relevant to the law of unjust enrichment, concerns burdens of proof.[71] It might be contended that defences allow the law to allocate burdens efficiently and/or fairly.[72] For example, imagine a system which required claimants to prove the surviving enrichment in an unjustly enriched defendant's hands in order to recover. The defendant is likely to have all of the evidence relevant to the claim (certainly, it is plausible to think that defendants will be much more likely to have access to the relevant evidence than claimants); if a claimant were required to prove the ultimate enrichment in the defendant's hands, she would have to make invasive and possibly wasteful inquiries into the defendant's actions.[73] These considerations perhaps

[67] ibid.

[68] ibid.

[69] ibid 832.

[70] See ch 2, p 38, fn 50.

[71] There is also a debate about the role of proof in constituting what *is* a defence. For example, Helen Scott in her chapter in this collection writes: 'there remains a close correspondence between defences and the burden of proof' (see ch 3, p 53). We have previously contended that questions of definition must be kept distinct from the consequence of a definition: Dyson, Goudkamp and Wilmot-Smith (n 6) 5–6. See, further, L Duarte d'Almeida (n 21) 133.

[72] Some scholars define defences as rules in respect of which the defendant carries the onus of proof. We have set this definition to one side for the purposes of these remarks.

[73] *cf* R Epstein, 'Pleadings and Presumptions' (1973) 40 *University of Chicago Law Review* 556, 580. Epstein doubts the strength of this point. He contends, inter alia: 'whenever the question of access is crucial, there are better techniques available for handling it [than by way of the allocation of the burden of proof] ... discovery procedures can largely eliminate the problem of unequal access. Under most modem systems, pre-trial discovery rules enable each party to obtain from his adversary all relevant evidence, regardless of whether it is admissible at trial'.

explain why most legal systems require the defendant to produce evidence of expenditure. We doubt whether this point about access to evidence is a compelling reason for recognising defences. Instead of a change of position defence, could the law not, in a system which incorporated all defences as negative elements of the cause of action, avoid the difficulty involved in requiring the claimant to make invasive/wasteful inquiries into the defendant's actions by putting the defendant to proof in respect of the enrichment element of the cause of action?

3. THEMES ACROSS PRIVATE LAW

3.1. The Unity of a Defence

John Gardner has argued that self-defence to criminal liability might be both justificatory and excusatory. For Gardner, a defendant is justified in acting in self-defence if the defendant had an undefeated reason to exercise defensive force and the defendant acted for that reason. By contrast, in Gardner's view, a defendant is excused in exercising defensive force where she mistakenly believed that there was an undefeated reason to use defensive force.[74] Since (at least in England) the defence of self-defence is granted both to defendants who were justified and to defendants who were excused, in Gardner's terms,[75] he is committed, we believe, to the proposition that there are justificatory and excusatory versions of the defence of self-defence.[76] In a similar vein, Paul Robinson suggests that in some jurisdictions in the US, there may be two separate criminal law defences conflated under the heading of self-defence: one justificatory and the other excusatory.[77] Within the law of unjust enrichment, illegality can operate as a defence and to disable a defence. In the first context, a claimant might be barred from raising the fact of an illegal agreement and so may not be able to make good her claim (for example, for a failure of condition);[78] in the second context, a defendant's putative change of position defence can be barred if the act relied upon

[74] For more detail in this regard, see Gardner (n 3) ch 5.

[75] See the Criminal Justice and Immigration Act 2008 (UK), s 76.

[76] Incidentally, Gardner does not adopt this position about only self-defence. We understand him as extending this view to the criminal law's network of defences generally. He writes: 'in general no excuse is accepted into the criminal law which is not also a partial justification, and no justification is accepted which is not also a partial excuse' (Gardner (n 3) 113).

[77] PH Robinson, 'Criminal Law Defenses: A Systematic Analysis' (1982) 82 *Columbia Law Review* 199, 240: 'A jurisdiction may properly provide a "self-defense" justification and a "self-defense" excuse' (footnote omitted).

[78] *Berg v Sadler and Moore* [1937] 2 KB 158 (CA).

is itself illegal.[79] One might therefore argue that there is more than one illegality defence within the law of unjust enrichment.[80]

In his chapter in the present volume, Ajay Ratan resists a possible splintering of the change of position defence, arguing that the doctrine encompasses both pre- and post-receipt detriment.[81] Conversely, Dennis Klimchuk suggests that a unitary defence cannot be found. He considers change of position in the context of both reliance and non-reliance-based expenditures, and concludes that the doctrine 'collects two defences'.[82] Klimchuk's reason for saying there are two defences is that he believes one to be a denial (of enrichment) and the other 'is akin to but not quite a denial'.[83] This account is different again from Elise Bant's contribution, which holds there to be common ground between reliance and non-reliance-based cases.[84]

The assumption that change of position is unitary may also underpin part of Lionel Smith's analysis. Smith asks: 'Is unjust enrichment a single cause of action, or a principle that unifies many causes of action?'[85] Relevantly for present purposes, he considers whether thinking about defences can assist in answering that question. He argues that the fact the defence of change of position is unavailable to certain claims, such as *Woolwich* claims for restitution of unlawfully levied taxes,[86] 'strongly suggest[s] that the claim being made is, in an important way, a *different claim* from the claims which are susceptible to the defence'.[87] He reasons that: 'If [two claims] were based on the same cause of action—in the sense of the same normative justification—then surely the defence, whatever it is, would be potentially available in both situations.'[88] Our only point is that this argument depends upon a proper individuation of the defence, such that it can be said that the same

[79] *Barros Mattos Junior v MacDaniels Ltd* [2004] EWHC 1188 (Ch); [2005] 1 WLR 247. For a comment, sensitive to the distinctions defences require, see A Tettenborn, 'Bank Fraud, Change of Position and Illegality: The Case of the Innocent Money-Launderer' [2005] *Lloyd's Maritime and Commercial Law Quarterly* 6, 8.

[80] For a similar argument in the tort context, see Goudkamp (n 10) 61–62. It should be noted that whether or not there is more than one illegality defence in the law of unjust enrichment depends on whether an exception to a defence properly can be characterised as a defence: in the second context, the doctrine of illegality operates not as a defence to an action, but by preventing a defence from biting.

[81] See ch 5, pp 99–102.

[82] See ch 4, p 85.

[83] ibid.

[84] See ch 7, pp 151–55.

[85] See ch 2, p 29.

[86] *Woolwich Equitable Building Society v Inland Revenue Commissioners* [1993] AC 70 (HL).

[87] See ch 2, p 45 (emphasis in original). Smith does not specify what he means by a defence being 'unavailable'. Is a defence 'unavailable' if it is, for example, bound to fail on the facts? Surely not: there are mistaken payments where the defendant immediately becomes aware of the mistake; no change of position defence would then be possible. Instead, a defence is 'unavailable' if some aspect of the cause of action disqualifies the defence.

[88] ibid. He adds: the 'availability of the same defence to more than one kind of claim does not imply that they rest on the same cause of action'.

defence applies to different situations. Debates about the unity of causes of action are well known, as Smith describes in his chapter. Analogous questions arise at the defence stage: how unified must a doctrine be in order for it to count as *a* defence rather than one among many?

How should scholars approach this question? In his chapter, Smith attempts to explain in virtue of what one cause of action is distinct from another. He claims that:[89]

> The correct level of generality for the definition of causes of action is one that neither lumps together juridically distinct justifications for legal recourses, nor pointlessly distinguishes between different ways in which the same justification may be activated.

This is undoubtedly question begging—it depends, for example, upon our being able to identify which justifications are 'juridically distinct'—but it is a start. However, can it serve as a template for thinking about defences? Do the same concerns that affect the unity of causes of action affect the unity of defences? These questions are not tackled in this volume, but they are undoubtedly important for future work in this field.

Why, specifically, are they important? Beyond their theoretical interest, they can have practical implications. For example, a perennial question in the law of unjust enrichment concerns the interrelation between estoppel and change of position,[90] and a number of lawyers—both scholars and judges—have tried to assimilate one doctrine into the other. Andrew Burrows has argued that 'the injustice that estoppel is concerned to prevent is entirely, and more appropriately, achieved by another defence, namely change of position'.[91] The recognition of change of position, it follows, swallows up estoppel as a defence to claims in unjust enrichment. In *Australian Financial Services and Leasing Pty Ltd v Hills Industries Ltd* Gageler J took the opposite view.[92] His Honour said that: 'There is much to be said for treating the defence of change of position ... as a particular application of [estoppel] doctrine.'[93] Burrows' argument depends upon an evaluation of the normative foundations of the two doctrines and concludes that the purpose of the estoppel defence is achieved more sensitively by change of position; Gageler J's argument depends upon an ability to individuate defences (such that one defence can be said to be a class of another defence). These arguments therefore turn on prior questions about how to identify the purposes of defences and how to distinguish defences on this basis.

[89] ibid p 39.

[90] For a detailed discussion, see E Bant, *The Change of Position Defence* (Oxford, Hart Publishing, 2009) ch 2, 224–30.

[91] Burrows (n 63) 558.

[92] *AFSL v Hills Industries* [2014] HCA 14; (2014) 307 ALR 512. The case is discussed in detail by Elise Bant in ch 7, pp 136–38.

[93] *AFSL v Hills Industries* (n 92) 559 [155].

3.2. Defences and Commensurability

Two things are commensurable if they can be measured by a common metric; they are incommensurable if they cannot.[94] Commensurability—or, rather, incommensurability—is important to several questions in the law of unjust enrichment (and, indeed, private law generally) and is hence a topic that deserves further attention.[95] Peter Birks argued that: 'All the defences [to claims in unjust enrichment] work by trumping the injustice of the defendant's enrichment.'[96] Birks' explanation of how defences operate seems here to invoke competing claims of justice, which are surely commensurable. Contrast this with Birks' claim that the change of position defence exists in order to:[97]

> [R]econcile the interest in obtaining restitution of unjust enrichment with the competing interest in the security of receipts. There is a general interest in our being free to dispose of wealth which appears to be at our disposition. The defence avoids the need to sterilize funds against the danger of unsuspected unjust enrichment claims.

From this passage, it is clear that Birks did not see the interests in play regarding change of position as having a common currency; the interest in security of receipts is not one of justice.

These comments raise several important questions. One such question is whether it is logically possible for incommensurable considerations to be weighed. Another is whether concerns regarding incommensurability are more acute depending on where in the law of unjust enrichment they arise. In her contribution, Helen Scott seems to suggest that we should be less worried about incommensurability when it arises in connection with defences than where the incommensurable factors are confined to the cause of action stage. She rejects Andrew Burrows' claim that the good consideration doctrine overrides the injustice at the cause of action stage:[98] 'In order for the defendant's entitlement to the benefit to "override" or "outweigh" the claimant's mistake, these two considerations would have to

[94] For elaboration, see J Raz, *The Morality of Freedom* (Oxford, Oxford University Press, 1986) 342.

[95] The philosophical literature on incommensurability is vast, but the subject is surprisingly under-examined in the legal context, especially so, it seems, in private law. Public lawyers have been more attentive to the topic: see, eg, FJ Urbina, 'Incommensurability and Balancing' (2015) 35 *OJLS* 575.

[96] Birks (n 22) 207.

[97] ibid 209.

[98] See A Burrows, 'Good Consideration in the Law of Unjust Enrichment' (2013) 129 *LQR* 328; A Burrows, 'Is There a Defence of Good Consideration?' in C Mitchell and W Swadling (eds), *The Restatement Third: Restitution and Unjust Enrichment* (Oxford, Hart Publishing, 2013) 174.

be commensurable.'[99] From these remarks, we might derive the following claim: the law cannot meaningfully weigh up two incommensurable goods when those goods are found within the cause of action stage. However, she does not doubt that the good consideration doctrine 'overrides' in this fashion and accepts it is rational for it to form part of the law. Her objection is to placing it within the cause of action stage. She suggests that it must instead come at a later stage. It follows that Scott does not appear to think that the incommensurability objection applies equally at the defences stage. We doubt that this is so, though the point deserves more attention.

Other scholars and judges appear to agree that the law can balance incommensurable goods at the defence stage. Within unjust enrichment, Elise Bant has argued that having a child can count as a relevant change of position, notwithstanding the fact that it cannot (she says) be understood in terms commensurable with the concept of enrichment.[100] Beyond the law of unjust enrichment, consider a case where a court reduces a claimant's damages due to her contributory negligence. Lord Reed JSC has argued that: 'The court is not comparing like with like.'[101] His Lordship explains that the '[defender] has acted in breach of a duty (not necessarily a duty of care) which was owed to the pursuer; the pursuer, on the other hand, has acted with a want of regard for her own interests'.[102] On this analysis, it follows that 'the blameworthiness of the pursuer and the [defender] are incommensurable'.[103] Notice, however, that Lord Reed does not conclude that the apportionment exercise is impossible;[104] instead, it leads his Lordship to the view that appellate courts would rarely interfere with a finding concerning apportionment as 'a variety of possible answers can legitimately be given'.[105]

This disagreement casts light on a prominent debate within the law of illegality. On one view, the law should aim to balance a number of competing policies—the need to deter, to do inter-party justice, to ensure that the integrity of the law is upheld etc—in a fact-specific inquiry. For example, in *Parkingeye Ltd v Somerfield Stores Ltd* Toulson LJ said: 'in the area of illegality, experience has shown that it is better to recognise that there may be conflicting considerations and that the rules need to be developed and

[99] See ch 3, p 59 (footnotes omitted).

[100] Bant (n 90) 132–33.

[101] *Jackson v Murray* [2015] UKSC 5; [2015] 2 All ER 805, 813 [27]. *Jackson* is discussed in J Goudkamp, 'Apportionment of Damages for Contributory Negligence: Appellate Review, Relative Blameworthiness and Causal Potency' (2015) 19 *Edinburgh Law Review* 367.

[102] *Jackson v Murray* (n 101) 813 [27].

[103] ibid.

[104] *cf* on this same point R Stevens, 'Contributory Fault—Analogue or Digital?' in Dyson, Goudkamp and Wilmot-Smith (n 6) 259. See also R Stevens, *Torts and Rights* (Oxford, Oxford University Press, 2007) 310.

[105] *Jackson v Murray* (n 101) 813 [28].

applied in a way which enables the court to balance them fairly'.[106] One objection that might be raised against balancing a range of factors is that it yields unpredictable outcomes. For instance, in *Apotex* Lord Sumption JSC said that the Court of Appeal's approach in the instant case 'was a process, discretionary in all but name, whose outcome would have been exceptionally difficult for either party's advisers to predict in advance'.[107] Is this a problem? One participant at the workshop suggested that, insofar as the illegality defence was designed in part to deter wrongdoing, *less* certainty about its application could be a virtue, not a vice![108]

Perhaps a more powerful objection is that a balancing approach is conceptually confused, like asking a judge to 'gauge whether three metres or 16 gallons is greater'.[109] In *Saunders v Edwards* Bingham LJ seemed to suggest that in applying the doctrine of illegality, it was relevant to consider the unlawfulness of the claimant's act on the one hand and the quantum of the claimant's loss on the other.[110] The apparent purpose of this examination was to ensure that the denial of a claim for illegality did not result in the infliction of punishment on the claimant that was out of all proportion to the gravity of her wrongdoing. But if these two factors—unlawfulness and the magnitude of the loss that would be left uncompensated if the defence of illegality applied—are incommensurable, does it make sense to ask the court to reach a 'proportionate' conclusion about how they are to be balanced?[111] It was perhaps this concern that prompted Graham Virgo to suggest that there is a 'danger that [an approach that requires the court to weigh a host of policy considerations] collapses from a principled exercise of judicial discretion into the exercise of arbitrary choice, potentially even returning to the old public conscience test'[112] espoused in *Tinsley v Milligan*.[113] Whether this is indeed a problem depends upon what constitutes a 'principled exercise of judicial discretion'. Virgo does not define this concept. The question is: can a discretion be exercised in a principled fashion when the goods in

[106] *Parkingeye Ltd v Somerfield Stores Ltd* [2012] EWCA Civ 1338; [2013] QB 840, 853 [54]. See also his Lordship's remarks in *Jetivia SA v Bilta (UK) Ltd (in Liquidation)* (n 33) 1225 [173]. For discussion, see Virgo, ch 8.

[107] *Les Laboratoires Servier v Apotex Inc* (n 33) 444 [21].

[108] We are reminded in this regard of a claim made in PH Robinson, 'Criminal Law Defenses: A Systematic Analysis' (1982) 82 *Columbia Law Review* 199, 272. Robinson argues that 'vagueness and ambiguity in [certain defenses] may serve the useful purpose of deterring undesirable conduct by persons who in fact qualify for the defense'.

[109] R Stevens, 'Contributory Fault' (n 104) 259.

[110] *Saunders v Edwards* [1987] 1 WLR 1116 (CA) 1133. See, further, *Cross v Kirkby* The Times, 5 April 2000 (CA) [53]; *Clarke v Clarke* [2012] EWHC 2118 (QB) [30].

[111] For the language of proportionality (and a position endangered by incommensurability objections), see A Burrows, *A Restatement of the Law of Unjust Enrichment* (Oxford, Oxford University Press, 2012) s 28(3)(c). Burrows proposes that the law of illegality should produce a result that is proportionate to myriad considerations.

[112] See ch 8, p 192.

[113] *Tinsley v Milligan* [1994] 1 AC 340 (HL).

question are incommensurable? Virgo seems to think so. He advocates a 'middle way' between the two approaches canvassed. We should, he claims, recognise:[114]

> [T]he public policy dimension of the illegality defence as a starting point for its application, but then moderate ... this by reference both to how illegality is defined and to various recognised mechanisms which can be analysed as involving both countervailing policy considerations and the need to consider the justice of the case as between the parties. This involves the exercise of judicial discretion in a principled way.

It should be clear that this approach is possible only if incommensurable goods can be balanced: it involves more factors, not fewer. We do not have the space to reach a considered view on these various claims. Our concern here has been to highlight the issue, and we hope that private law scholars will in the future consider the topic in greater detail.

3.3. The Merits of a Comparative Perspective?

Several contributions in this volume make use of comparative law. For instance, Sonja Meier examines bona fide purchase in the context of both English and German law; Helen Scott considers the distinction between unjust factor and absence of basis systems through the lens of 'enrichment owed'; and Lionel Smith surveys not only a number of common law jurisdictions, but also a civilian perspective on his question.[115] Even those contributors who do not adopt an overtly comparative analysis do analyse the law from numerous jurisdictions. Birke Häcker looks at German and US law on minority as well as England and Wales; Elise Bant considers authorities from Australia and England and Wales on change of position; and Andrew Kull examines both US and English and Welsh authorities.

This approach has found favour in many common law courts. Judges often cite comparative material.[116] Lord Neuberger of Abbotsbury PSC recently said:[117]

> As overseas countries secede from the jurisdiction of the Privy Council, it is inevitable that inconsistencies in the common law will develop between different jurisdictions. However, it seems to us highly desirable for all those jurisdictions to

[114] See ch 8, p 192.

[115] See ch 2, pp 34–35, 48.

[116] For a recent survey of the use of foreign decisions by the House of Lords and Supreme Court, see A Burrows, 'The Influence of Comparative Law on the English Law of Obligations' in A Robertson and M Tilbury (eds), *The Common Law of Obligations: Divergence and Unity* (Oxford, Hart Publishing, 2015).

[117] *FHR European Ventures LLP v Cedar Capital Partners LLC* [2014] UKSC 45; [2015] AC 250.

> learn from each other, and at least to lean in favour of harmonising the development of the common law round the world.

Comparative law has been vital to the development of the law of unjust enrichment, and its defences. In *Kleinwort Benson v Lincoln CC* the House of Lords abolished the rule that mistakes of law would not ground a claim in unjust enrichment. Lord Goff said:[118]

> I have referred to the fact that the mistake of law rule has already been abrogated in other common law jurisdictions, either by legislation or by judicial decision. This material is, of course, well known to lawyers in this country, and has, I know, been studied by all members of the appellate committee, not of course for the first time, and is regarded with great respect.

And in *Lipkin Gorman v Karpnale Ltd*, as part of his argument in favour of the recognition of the change of position defence, his Lordship said: 'The principle is widely recognised throughout the common law world ... The time for its recognition in this country is, in my opinion, long overdue.'[119]

This harmony of academic and judicial approaches is striking for at least two reasons. First, academics rarely agree with each other, let alone with the judiciary, about the proper role of history, philosophy and economics in legal reasoning; why is there such agreement on the use of comparative material? Second, not everyone *does* agree with this use of comparative material. The most famous disagreements on this point have been on the US Supreme Court in the context of constitutional interpretation.[120] For instance, in *Roper v Simmons* Kennedy J's plurality opinion referred to the United Nations Convention on the Rights of the Child (a treaty the US has not ratified).[121] A number of Justices have argued that such citation is illicit. Thomas J has protested that: 'While Congress, as a *legislature*, may wish to consider the actions of other nations on any issue it likes, this Court's Eighth Amendment jurisprudence should not impose foreign moods, fads, or fashions on Americans.'[122] On that basis, Scalia J has called the use of foreign law 'dangerous';[123] indeed, 'the basic premise of the [US Supreme] Court's argument—that American law should conform to the laws of the rest of the world—ought to be rejected out of hand'.[124] The context of this debate is obviously quite far removed from the law of unjust enrichment, but we think that parallel issues arise.

[118] *Kleinwort Benson v Lincoln City Council* [1999] 2 AC 349 (HL) 373.

[119] *Lipkin Gorman v Karpnale Ltd* (n 56) 579.

[120] See generally RJ Delahunty and J Yoo, 'Against Foreign Law' (2005) 29 *Harvard Journal of Law & Public Policy* 291. Essentially the same debate broke out in the Australian High Court at around the same time. See M Kirby, 'The Citation of Foreign Decisions in Constitutional Adjudication: The Relevance of the Democratic Deficit' (2009) 43 *Suffolk University Law Review* 117.

[121] *Roper v Simmons* 543 US 551 (2005) 571.

[122] *Foster v Florida* 537 US 990, 991 n 1 (2002) (Thomas J) (emphasis in original).

[123] *Lawrence v Texas* 539 US 558 (2003) 598.

[124] *Roper v Simmons* (n 121) 624.

This harmony—and discord—prompts a number of questions. Our interest here is to raise perhaps the most obvious, but also the most important, question: what is the merit of a comparative analysis? At one point in his chapter, Lionel Smith points out that: 'Neither a claim in German law nor a source of obligation in French or Quebec law is defined entirely in terms of primary facts.'[125] One might respond: so what? Why is it that this discovery is an *important* discovery? More specifically, why should a court ever look to foreign law in formulating its own rules? We will consider three possible justifications.

The first possible justification of a comparative approach is the notion that it is not really comparative; a 'comparative approach' in reality involves looking to a common set of rules. For example, in the context of constitutional jurisprudence, Jeremy Waldron has argued that courts can draw on supranational legal norms, an *ius gentium*.[126] Closer to our topic, Lord Hailsham LC in *Broome v Cassell & Co Ltd (No 1)* (a case about the availability of exemplary damages in private law) said that he viewed 'with dismay the doctrine that the common law should differ in different parts of the Commonwealth'.[127] Why? One possible reason is that Lord Hailsham regarded divergence as a betrayal of the very nature of the common law—the gist of the common law is that it is *common* to multiple legal system. A similar argument is put forward by Robert Stevens, who claims that:[128]

> Our common law [of torts] is the embodiment of our rights one against another. At the margin these rights are, as a matter of morality, underdetermined, and one of the justifications for private law is that it provides the determinacy which individual reflection cannot provide. At the margin some divergence between different systems is understandable and not a source of concern. However, it should be and is a source of grave concern if the judges of one common law system embark on radical change based upon a novel conception of what the law of torts is.

A second possible explanation is epistemic. The basic idea would be that foreign courts are a source of wisdom from which to draw. A caricature of this view would suppose that whatever rule is most widely endorsed has the prima facie case to being the best rule.[129] According to this caricature, the determination of the rule that should be adopted in any given context

[125] See ch 2, p 35.

[126] J Waldron, *'Partly Laws Common to All Mankind': Foreign Law in American Courts* (New Haven, Yale University Press, 2012).

[127] *Broome v Cassell & Co Ltd (No 1)* [1972] AC 1027 (HL) 1067 (Lord Hailsham LC). *cf Broome v Cassell & Co Ltd (No 1)* [1972] AC 1027 (HL) 1127 (Lord Diplock). For discussion, see J Harris, 'The Privy Council and the Common Law' (1990) 106 *LQR* 574.

[128] R Stevens, 'The Divergence of the Australian and English Law of Torts' in S Degeling, J Edelman and J Goudkamp (eds), *Torts in Commercial Law* (Sydney, Law Book Co, 2011) 62.

[129] Perhaps it is not *such* a caricature: the theory might be supported by something like Condorcet's theorem, applied writ large.

should be decided according to a popularity contest. Stevens endorses a moderate version of this thesis when he says:[130]

> Being inconsistent with other legal systems does not of course necessarily demonstrate that English law is wrong and other systems are right. However, being out of step with a large number of other systems should give pause for thought.

A final reason why courts and academics might look to other jurisdictions is second order.[131] There may be incidental benefits of legal systems adopting the same rule on some matter. For example, the preamble to the Rome I Regulation asserts that:[132]

> The proper functioning of the internal market creates a need, in order to improve the predictability of the outcome of litigation, certainty as to the law applicable and the free movement of judgments, for the conflict-of-law rules in the Member States to designate the same national law irrespective of the country of the court in which an action is brought.

This is said to be 'necessary for the proper functioning of the internal market'.[133] These propositions are taken to be self-evident; no empirical evidence is provided to support them. Whether this is justified is not a question we seek to answer here. Our only point is that this is a plausible form of argument in favour of studying comparative law: to discover what the law is in a different jurisdiction, and then to adopt a similar rule so as to achieve these incidental benefits.

There may be additional reasons why a comparative approach is appropriate. Whatever the reasons are, it is important that they be stated clearly as they will determine the nature of the comparative inquiry. It may be more appropriate for any given court to look to the jurisprudence of certain jurisdictions than of other jurisdictions. For example, Lionel Smith writes that he would be 'doubtful of [a] scheme' that would 'threaten ... to cut common law Canada off from the rest of the common law world'.[134] We take it that his doubt would be less acute if there was the threat of cutting common law Canada off from a civilian jurisdiction (assuming there were harmony between the systems at the start of the story). Why, though, should common law countries have any priority? This will depend on the reason for the comparative inquiry. If the rationale is that there is a common law, the reason is self-evident. If the rationale is epistemic, there is no a priori reason to give more weight to common law traditions. But if the rationale is the indirect benefits harmonisation brings, there may be more reason to harmonise with

[130] R Stevens, 'The Contracts (Rights of Third Parties) Act 1999' (2004) 120 *LQR* 292, 315.
[131] For more of such arguments in the context of international trade, see Harris (n 127) 596–99.
[132] Rome I, Recital (6).
[133] ibid Recital (1).
[134] See ch 2, pp 49–50.

other common law jurisdictions insofar as (for example) those jurisdictions are ones with which England has most trading links. This picture has been complicated of late. Perhaps for this reason, Lord Reed says:[135]

> Nor is it only common law jurisdictions which should be considered. Particularly at a time when steps have begun to be taken towards some degree of harmonisation of private law across the European Union, it can sometimes be helpful also to consider civilian approaches.

4. THE STRUCTURE OF THE BOOK

In *Defences in Tort*, we divided the chapters into general and specific. We have not replicated this structure in this book. Part of the reason for this is that some of the most general chapters, such as Dennis Klimchuk's inquiry into the nature of change of position, deal with specific defences. Nevertheless, we have attempted to group together those chapters which we suggest should be read sequentially, such as the various contributions on the change of position defence. We close with an interesting and provocative chapter by Lord Reed. Lord Reed gave an important opinion in *Benedetti v Saiwiris*.[136] His Lordship was struck by the extent to which argument in the case revolved around academic interpretations of the law. His chapter here sets out his thoughts on the interrelation between academic work and practice—and thus casts light over the book and project as a whole. What is the point of academic work?[137] Should it appeal to judges and practitioners?[138]

[135] See ch 13, p 316.

[136] *Benedetti v Saiwiris* [2013] UKSC 50; [2014] AC 938. See G Virgo, 'Evaluating Enrichment' (2013) 72 *CLJ* 508.

[137] A famous cynical and entertaining reply to this question is given in F Rodell, 'Goodbye to Law Reviews' (1936) 23 *Virginia Law Review* 38.

[138] For different answers to this question, see M Kirby, 'Welcome to Law Reviews' (2002) 26 *Melbourne University Law Review* 1; and J Gava, 'Law Reviews: Good For Judges, Bad for Law Schools' (2002) 26 *Melbourne University Law Review* 560.

2

Defences and the Disunity of Unjust Enrichment

LIONEL SMITH*

1. INTRODUCTION

THE RECENT HISTORY of the common law of unjust enrichment can be presented as a story of revolution—or, perhaps more accurately, as a story of a series of rebellions. The first shot was fired in Philadelphia, with the publication in 1937 of the *Restatement of Restitution*.[1] The next action took place in Ottawa in 1954, when common law Canada followed the US lead and accepted the autonomous existence of this body of law.[2] The English story is more complex. The first edition of *Goff & Jones on Restitution* was published in 1966,[3] Birks' groundbreaking *Introduction to the Law of Restitution* in 1985[4] and acceptance of unjust enrichment by the House of Lords occurred in 1991.[5]

* For helpful comments, I thank Elise Bant, Andrew Burrows, Niamh Connolly, Tatiana Cutts, Eric Descheemaeker, Alexandra Popovici, Irit Samet, Robert Stevens, Frederick Wilmot-Smith and particularly Reinhard Zimmermann. I acknowledge with gratitude the financial support of the Social Sciences and Humanities Research Council of Canada.

[1] American Law Institute, *Restatement of the Law of Restitution: Quasi-Contracts and Constructive Trusts* (St Paul, MN, American Law Institute Publishers, 1937). For the prior history, the indispensable account is A Kull, 'James Barr Ames and the Early Modern History of Unjust Enrichment' (2005) 25 *OJLS* 297.

[2] *Deglman v Guaranty Trust Co of Canada* [1954] SCR 725 (SCC). Both the facts and the Court's decision took place in Ottawa.

[3] R Goff and G Jones, *The Law of Restitution*, 1st edn (London, Sweet & Maxwell, 1966). The current edition, with new editors and a significantly changed title, is C Mitchell, P Mitchell and S Watterson, *Goff & Jones: The Law of Unjust Enrichment*, 8th edn (London, Sweet & Maxwell, 2012).

[4] P Birks, *An Introduction to the Law of Restitution* (Oxford, Clarendon Press, 1985); with endnotes and corrections, P Birks, *An Introduction to the Law of Restitution*, rev edn (Oxford, Clarendon Press, 1989).

[5] *Lipkin Gorman (A Firm) v Karpnale Ltd* [1991] 2 AC 548 (HL). Many scholars doubt that this was actually an unjust enrichment case (for example, G Virgo, *The Principles of the Law of Restitution*, 2nd edn (Oxford, Oxford University Press, 2006) 570; L Smith, 'Simplifying Claims to Traceable Proceeds' (2009) 125 *LQR* 338, 338–40). Even if this is correct, however, it does not touch the revolutionary character of the decision.

What was so revolutionary about these developments? The principal element of the revolution was unification: the unification, under a single and general conceptual framework, of what had previously been understood as a multiplicity of disparate claims. In *White v Central Trust Co*, La Forest JA (as he then was) said:[6]

> As I have tried to indicate the well recognized categories of unjust enrichment must be regarded as clear examples of the more general principle that transcends them. We are currently in a similar position with regard to unjust enrichment as we are in relation to negligence where we have for some time been abandoning recourse to particularized duties in favour of a generalized duty to one's neighbour, although the process has not yet proceeded as far in the case of restitution.

Later, in *Peel (Regional Municipality) v Canada*, McLachlin J (as she then was) said, on behalf of the majority:[7]

> The concept of restitution for unjust enrichment in the common law world has evolved over the past century from a collection of fact-specific categories in which recovery was permitted, toward a body of law unified by a single set of coherent rules applicable to all cases ...
>
> The tripartite principle of general application which this court has recognized as the basis of the cause of action for unjust enrichment is thus seen to have grown out of the traditional categories of recovery. It is informed by them. It is capable, however, of going beyond them, allowing the law to develop in a flexible way as required to meet changing perceptions of justice.

And yet ... 'la révolution dévore ses enfants'.[8] Even some of those who considered themselves revolutionaries asked whether unification had gone too far. One of the first debates related to cases of gain-based remedies for wrongful actions. Because these cases are about taking away gains, not compensating losses, they were considered part of 'restitution' in the first *Restatement* and in the early English commentaries. But many took the view that gain-based remedies for wrongful actions were part of the law of wrongs, which by definition stands apart from the law of unjust enrichment. On this view, 'restitution', or giving *back*, is different in an important way from 'disgorgement', or giving *up*, and bringing both together under the label 'restitution' only invites confusion.[9] Others thought that gain-based

[6] *White v Central Trust Co* (1984) 7 DLR (4th) 236 (New Brunswick CA) 246–47.

[7] *Peel (Regional Municipality) v Canada* [1992] 3 SCR 762, 784, 788 (SCC).

[8] J Mallet du Pan, *Considérations sur la nature de la révolution de France* (London, Emmanuel Flon, 1793) 80 (paginations of this pamphlet differ and the original spelling is 'enfans').

[9] L Smith, 'The Province of the Law of Restitution' (1992) 71 *Canadian Bar Review* 672; J Edelman, *Gain-Based Damages: Contract, Tort, Equity and Intellectual Property* (Oxford, Hart Publishing, 2002) 36–41.

remedies for wrongful conduct are cases of restitution, but not restitution for unjust enrichment.[10] This is a debate that continues.

More recently, there have been signs of another counter-revolution. Some traces of it appeared as far back as 1995, when Peter Watts argued that property claims and services claims are governed by different principles.[11] At that time, this was a reactionary position, because one of the main precepts of the revolution was that there was only one principle against unjust enrichment. More recent scholarship has brought this issue to the fore.[12] In my view, these developments are likely to lead to a serious reassessment of the unity of unjust enrichment.[13]

This chapter aims to make a small contribution to this debate, partly by asking the question the other way around. Does the law of defences help us to understand whether, and to what extent, the law of unjust enrichment is a unity?

Apart from the Introduction and Conclusion, this chapter features two sections. The intermediate goal is to address a question that has been addressed by many authors: is unjust enrichment a single cause of action or a principle that unifies many causes of action? In order to reach a view on that question, section 2 asks what we mean by the label 'cause of action'. Section 3 then applies this argument to the case of unjust enrichment and concludes that the better view is that there are multiple causes of action within the domain of unjust enrichment, although they have not been adequately articulated. The defences that exist in unjust enrichment assist in reaching this conclusion. The Conclusion then presents a view of what might usefully be the next steps in analysing what are the causes of action within the common law of unjust enrichment.

2. WHAT IS A CAUSE OF ACTION?

2.1. Judicial Definitions

What is unjust enrichment? Is it a 'principle' or is it a cause of action? In order to answer this question, we must first think a little bit about what a cause of action is.

[10] P Birks, 'Misnomer' in WR Cornish et al (eds), *Restitution: Past, Present and Future: Essays in Honour of Gareth Jones* (Oxford, Hart Publishing, 1998) 1; A Burrows, *The Law of Restitution*, 3rd edn (Oxford, Oxford University Press, 2010) 9–12; Virgo (n 5) 9–11.

[11] P Watts, 'Restitution—A Property Principle and a Services Principle' [1995] *Restitution Law Review* 49.

[12] R Chambers, 'Two Kinds of Enrichment' in R Chambers, C Mitchell and J Penner (eds), *Philosophical Foundations of Unjust Enrichment* (Oxford, Oxford University Press, 2009) 242; B McFarlane, 'Unjust Enrichment, Rights and Value' in D Nolan and A Robertson (eds), *Rights and Private Law* (Oxford, Hart Publishing, 2012) 581.

[13] Other contributions that aim to assess the unity or otherwise of unjust enrichment (although not from the perspective of 'transfer of rights' claims versus 'increases of value'

The abolition of the forms of action in the nineteenth century led to the emergence of the modern concept of the cause of action.[14] The forms of action were far more isolated, one from another, than today's jurists sometimes realise. In modern terms, they each had their own civil procedure: their own rules for getting the defendant into court, their own rules for how facts were proved, their own rules for what orders the court could make and so on.[15] The elimination of the forms of action could be described as the creation of a unified law of civil procedure. This allowed jurists to see, in a sense for the first time, the substantive law unclouded by rules of procedure.[16] And it led to the rise of a new concept: that of the cause of action. The abolition of the forms of action was not understood to modify the substantive law; whatever had been actionable before should still be actionable, and what had not been, should not be. The old question was whether one or another 'action' would 'lie'. Stripped of the procedural rules of the forms of action, the question became, what counts as a legally actionable grievance? And this was understood to mean, what *facts* constitute a legally actionable grievance?

The phrase 'cause of action' is an old one and, like most terms of art, it started out as something else: an expression whose words had their ordinary meanings. In a case of 1617, we read that the court held that 'the plaintiff had just cause of action upon his counter-bond'.[17] This phrase does not speak of a 'cause of action' as a concept, but only says that the claimant had a good cause, or justification, to bring a successful action in debt; that is, the old *form of action* in debt. While the forms of action survived, a cause of action meant the foundation of an action. But 'cause of action' survived the abolition of the forms of action because grievances have to be classified and

claims) include R Stevens, 'Is There a Law of Unjust Enrichment?' in S Degeling and J Edelman (eds), *Unjust Enrichment in Commercial Law* (Sydney, Thomson Reuters, 2008) 11; and L Smith, 'Unjust Enrichment: Big or Small?' in S Degeling and J Edelman (eds), *Unjust Enrichment in Commercial Law* (Sydney, Thomson Reuters, 2008) 35. It may be significant that both chapter titles end with question marks. There are also those who have been wholly sceptical of the utility of the idea of unjust enrichment; see the discussion in Burrows (n 10) 31–35.

[14] For more detail, see L Smith, 'Common Law and Equity in R3RUE' (2011) 68 *Washington and Lee Law Review* 1185, 1189–93.

[15] In Milsom's characteristically evocative language: 'If one tries to imagine a Prosser or a Winfield early in the sixteenth century sitting down with all the year books on his table to write a textbook, the product would have been scrappy: as it were a lot of blank pages with scattered single assertions about things like beating epileptics and pulling down houses to halt the spread of fires. But such an enterprise would not have entered anyone's head. The nearest you could sensibly get would be a book arranged by kinds of action, under each of which would be set out cases showing what pleas had and had not been found acceptable.' SFC Milsom, *A Natural History of the Common Law* (New York, Columbia University Press, 2003) 12–13. In the last sentence, Milsom alludes to the genre of common law literature known as the 'abridgement'.

[16] This cannot be pressed too far; in particular, land law was different. The elaboration of the law relating to estates and future interests in land evolved long before, and stood apart to a large extent (but not entirely) from procedural considerations.

[17] *Abbots v Johnson* (1617) 3 Bulstrode 233, 235; 81 ER 197, 198.

like cases have to be treated alike. It became a term of art in the nineteenth century, prompted in part by its use in statutes that defined the jurisdiction of inferior courts. One of the best-known judicial definitions, arising in that context, is that given by Brett J (as he then was) in *Cooke v Gill*: '"Cause of action" has been held from the earliest time to mean every fact which is material to be proved to entitle the plaintiff to succeed—every fact which the defendant would have a right to traverse.'[18]

More recently, the Supreme Court of Canada said:[19]

> A cause of action has traditionally been defined as comprising every fact which it would be necessary for the plaintiff to prove, if disputed, in order to support his or her right to the judgment of the court: *Poucher v. Wilkins* (1915), 33 O.L.R. 125 (C.A.). Establishing each such fact (sometimes referred to as material facts) constitutes a precondition to success.

Both quotations state that the elements of a cause of action are facts.[20] They also state that proof of each of them is necessary for success. Both quotations imply that when all of the elements are proven, success follows, subject only to defences. In logical terms, the elements of the cause of action are individually necessary and collectively sufficient to establish the cause of action.

2.2. Complications

However, this is not as simple as it looks. There are at least two complications. One is that in some cases, the elements of a cause of action might not seem so close to the primary facts (the facts proven by evidence). We may say that a claimant attempting to establish a defendant's liability for negligent harm has to establish that he was owed a duty of care. The presence of a duty of care is a legal conclusion, not a primary fact.[21] The courts have sought to identify the factual elements that must be proven to support this conclusion: the claimant must show that it was reasonably foreseeable that

[18] *Cooke v Gill* (1872–73) LR 8 CP 107, 116. There were earlier non-statutory examples of the phrase being used in this jurisdictional context, in disputes regarding which county was the appropriate venue for trial; see, for example, *Neale v Nevill* (1816) 6 Taunt 565; 128 ER 1155.

[19] *Danyluk v Ainsworth Technologies Inc* [2001] SCC 44; [2001] 2 SCR 460 [54].

[20] See also *Letang v Cooper* [1965] 1 QB 232 (CA), in which Diplock LJ, as he then was, said (at 242–43): 'A cause of action is simply a factual situation the existence of which entitles one person to obtain from the court a remedy against another person.' See also DM Walker, *The Oxford Companion to Law* (Oxford, Clarendon Press, 1980) sv 'cause of action': 'The fact or set of facts which give a person a right to bring an action.'

[21] In *Danyluk* (n 19), the Court went on to say that 'the existence of an employment contract is a material fact common to both the ESA [Employment Standards Act] proceeding and to the appellant's wrongful dismissal claim in court'. I would say that the existence of a contract is an intermediate legal conclusion that is part of a cause of action in breach of contract, but the contract arises from facts.

the actions of the defendant would cause injury to person or property.[22] The standard of care that is associated with a duty of care is also a legal conclusion, drawn differently depending on the facts of the case.

Overall, to establish liability for negligence, several elements need to be proven, including the presence of a duty of care and its breach. So the ultimate conclusion—that a cause of action has been established and thus that there is liability, subject to defences—depends on intermediate conclusions that are legal, not factual. What this means is that, contrary to the impression given by the classical definitions of 'cause of action', the articulation of the elements of a cause of action may include not only primary facts, but also intermediate legal conclusions. On the other hand, it must always be possible to articulate which facts will establish the required intermediate legal conclusions.[23] In this sense, it should always be possible to 'unpack' the intermediate legal conclusions and thus to state all elements of the cause of action in terms of the facts that must be proved.

The other complication relates to what might be called the level of generality at which we define causes of action. In order to avoid setting that level too low, the facts that have to be proven must be defined generically. The cause of action in battery requires physical contact with the claimant, but it can be with a hand, a hammer or a haddock. Absolutely nothing would be gained, and the law would make itself slightly ridiculous, if it were to distinguish between hammer-battery and haddock-battery. Worse, it would be positively unjust if the legal principles were different for the two situations. Nor is this an idle comment. This is exactly the structure of the argument that led to the position that despite the historically separate evolution of the common counts, the modern law should admit no relevant distinctions between cases of unjust enrichment by transfer of property, and unjust enrichment by the performance of valuable services or the improvement of property.[24] Again, this is the issue that is on the table when it is

[22] It seems clear that other things are needed to establish a duty not to cause pure economic loss; I do not venture into those waters here. But it is worth pointing out that while the present text suggests that the law of unjust enrichment has been subjected to a too-enthusiastic process of unification, this is also what many commentators think happened to the law of liability for negligence since *Donoghue v Stevenson* [1932] AC 562 (HL). See, for example, K Crawley and S Van Praagh, '"Academic Concerns"—Caring about Conversation in Canadian Common Law' (2011) 34 *Dalhousie Law Journal* 405.

[23] In *Unjust Enrichment*, 2nd edn (Oxford, Oxford University Pres, 2005), Peter Birks argued that the English law of unjust enrichment had changed from requiring plaintiffs to prove reasons for restitution to an approach based on 'absence of legal basis'. At 116–17, he constructed a metaphorical pyramid (with primary facts at the bottom and intermediate legal conclusions higher up) to provide a 'limited reconciliation' between the two approaches. This exercise reflects the same point I am making: even if the conditions of liability be expressed as including intermediate legal conclusions (such as 'absence of legal basis'), it must be possible to articulate what facts will establish those intermediate conclusions.

[24] The scholarship mentioned above, at nn 11 and 12 and the accompanying text, incorporates counter-arguments to contend that there are normatively significant differences between a transfer of rights and a conferral of pure value.

asked whether libel and slander are, or should be, separate causes of action or rather different ways of committing a single cause of action,[25] and when it is asked whether a claimant who is directly injured by the careless action of a defendant can sue in trespass to the person or only in negligence.[26]

But it also seems important not to define 'cause of action' at too high a level of generality. One influential author has said: 'A tort is a species of wrong. A wrong is a breach of a duty owed to someone else.'[27]

It seems clear that even though this generic description of 'wrong' is accurate, it would be a mistake to say that there is a cause of action called 'wrong' or 'legal wrong' that includes all torts, all equitable wrongs, breaches of contract and perhaps more. The formulation 'a wrong is a breach of a duty owed to someone else' is true, but does not purport to identify a cause of action. It is too general; there are too many duties and too many ways to breach them. Nor, one level of generality down, is 'tort' a cause of action.

If this is obviously correct, the implication is less clear. What is the appropriate level of generality for a cause of action?

2.3. Comparative Perspectives

Particularly in relation to the first complication—whether a cause of action is made up solely of facts—we may gather some insight from comparative inquiry.

Although care must be taken not to oversimplify, one can find a parallel in the civil law to the common law's transition from the forms of action to the more modern idea of causes of action. In the institutional structure of Roman law, all of private law was divided into persons, things and actions.[28] How actions related to the rest of the law, however, was not entirely obvious. The Roman *actio*, like the common law *form* of action, included procedural elements.[29] Shortly after the *Institutes* of Justinian were promulgated, Theophilus, one of the compilers of the *Institutes*, authored a paraphrase of them in Greek. In explaining the relationship between obligations and actions, he famously said that 'obligations are the mothers of actions'.[30]

[25] In 1975, the Faulks Committee (Report of the Committee on Defamation, Cm 5909, 1975) recommended the abolition of the distinctions between libel and slander.

[26] Compare *Cook v Lewis* [1951] SCR 830 (SCC) 839 with *Letang* (n 20).

[27] R Stevens, *Torts and Rights* (Oxford, Oxford University Press, 2007) 2.

[28] Gaius, *Institutes*, 1.8, extracted in Justinian's *Digest*, 1.5.1; Justinian, *Institutes*, 1.2.12.

[29] E Metzger, 'Actions' in E Metzger (ed), *A Companion to Justinian's Institutes* (Ithaca, NY, Cornell University Press, 1998) 208–10, 214–17; HF Jolowicz, 'Obligatio and Actio' (1952) 68 *LQR* 469, 469–71; see also B Windscheid, *Lehrbuch des Pandektenrechts*, vol 1 (Frankfurt am Main, Literarische Anstalt, 1891) § 44; Italian translation, B Windscheid, *Diritto delle pandette*, vol 1 (C Fadda and PE Bensa (trans), Turin, Unione Tipografico-Editrice, 1901) § 44.

[30] Theophilus, *Paraphrase*, 3.13, discussed in Jolowicz (n 29) 473; Metzger (n 29) 217; R Zimmermann, *The Law of Obligations: Roman Foundations of the Civilian Tradition* (Cape Town, Juta and Co, 1990) 28.

HF Jolowicz explained that for centuries, the dominant view among jurists of Roman law was that in the series persons–things–actions, the subject of obligations belonged to the law of actions.[31] It is only relatively recently that obligations are rather understood to belong, in that series, to the law of things, being incorporeal things.[32]

Another difficulty with the dictum of Theophilus, of course, is that many actions are real actions, which are born of real rights, not of obligations. And so it is perhaps not surprising that for centuries, there has been a wide sense of 'action' that includes the real actions and a narrower sense that is related to obligations, to claims, to what is owed; this narrow sense fits much better with the dictum of Theophilus.[33] If we are to consider all of the actions, both real and personal, then it must be the case that they have a variety of juridical foundations.[34]

In the civilian tradition, the evolution that freed substance from procedure—that freed the proceeding in court from the legal relationships that gave rise to it—started much earlier than in the common law, although one could argue that it was not completed until the age of codification that began in earnest in the nineteenth century.[35] It also played out differently in different places. In France and Quebec, for example, the modern law of obligations is concerned with the classification of 'sources of obligations';[36] such classifications date back to the Roman sources, but they stand apart from the law of actions.[37] Interestingly, however, in those jurisdictions, there

[31] Jolowicz (n 29) 471–74; see also Zimmermann (n 30) 24–30.

[32] P Stein, 'The Quest for a Systematic Civil Law' (1995) 90 *Proceedings of the British Academy* 147, 158: 'Obligations have been the joker in the pack of civil law categories.' On obligations as things, a concept that can be seen in the *Institutes* of Gaius (n 28) (2.12, 2.14, extracted in Justinian's *Digest*, 1.8.1.1) and of Justinian (n 28) (2.2.1), see also Zimmermann (n 30) 26; P Birks, 'Definition and Division: A Meditation on *Institutes* 3.13' in P Birks (ed), *The Classification of Obligations* (Oxford, Clarendon Press, 1997) 1, 7–9; in more detail, see G Gretton, 'Ownership and its Objects' (2007) 71 *Rabels Zeitschrift* 802; F Giglio, 'Pandectism and the Gaian Classification of Things' (2012) 62 *University of Toronto Law Journal* 1.

[33] The argument often revolved around the definition of action in Justinian's *Institutes*, 4.6.pr: 'actio autem nihil aliud est, quam ius persequendi iudicio quod sibi debetur'. Almost the same words appear in the *Digest*, 44.7.51 (Celsus). One English translation is P Birks and G McLeod (trans), *The Institutes of Justinian* (Ithaca, NY, Cornell University Press, 1987) 129: 'An action is nothing but a right to go to court to get one's due.' This translation is apt to include real actions, but the words 'quod sibi debetur' could also be understood more narrowly, to mean 'what is owed to one', a sense that points to personal claims. See, for example, the translation and discussion in Jolowicz (n 29) 474–78, discussing different interpretations of this definition 'endlessly through the ages' (475).

[34] WW Buckland, 'Cause of Action: English and Roman' (1943) 1 *Seminar* 3.

[35] Zimmermann (n 30) 27–28, discusses how this process was under way in Justinian's time. See also Stein (n 32), who tells the story in some detail.

[36] See the French Code civil, art 1370; Civil Code of Québec, art 1372, and see the title before art 1482: 'Certain other sources of obligations.' See also J Hallebeek, 'Unjust Enrichment as a Source of Obligation: The Genesis of a Legal Concept in the European Ius Commune' [2002] *Restitution Law Review* 92.

[37] Zimmermann (n 30) 10–24; Birks (n 32); P Birks, *The Roman Law of Obligations* (E Descheemaeker (ed), Oxford, Oxford University Press, 2014) 16–23.

remains some discussion of the law in terms of actions, both in relation to real rights and in the law of obligations.[38]

The evolution of German law has been somewhat different. Windscheid proposed the concept of *Anspruch*, usually translated as 'claim', as a way of identifying the abstract juridical foundation of actions in court.[39] This won wide acceptance and was taken up into the BGB and as a general concept of German private law. In the English translation of § 194(1) of the BGB that is published by the German Ministry of Justice, *Anspruch* is: 'The right to demand that another person does or refrains from an act.'[40] What is important is that the concept applies both to personal and to real rights. A right of ownership, for example, is composed of a multitude of negative claims; in the case of infringement, however, such as where someone else is in possession of the thing owned, a positive claim against that person arises that is distinct from the right of ownership.[41]

What does this tell us about whether causes of action need to be defined, as the classic common law definitions would have it, in terms of facts? Neither a claim in German law nor a source of obligation in French or Quebec law is defined entirely in terms of primary facts. German law, indeed, is extremely careful about the relationship between the primary facts, and the claims that may arise from them.[42] A claim, as defined above, arises

[38] French and Quebec books on property law speak frequently in terms of actions: *action en revendication, action pétitoire, action possessoire, action confessoire de servitude, action négatoire de servitude, action en bornage* and so on. See, for example, P Malaurie and L Aynès, *Les biens*, 6th edn (Paris, Defrénois, 2015); D-C Lamontagne, *Biens et propriété*, 7th edn (Cowansville, Les Éditions Yvons Blais, 2013). These systems, in classifying property as movable or immovable, hold that *actions* (and not merely rights) whose object is immovable count as immovable property, while those whose object is movable count as movable property: Code Civil, arts 526, 529; Civil Code of Québec, arts 904, 907. As for the continued reference to actions in the law of obligations, see R Sefton-Green, 'Why are Remedies Not a Legal Subject in Civilian Law?' in A Popovici, L Smith and R Tremblay (eds), *Les intraduisibles en droit civil* (Montreal, Les Éditions Thémis, 2014) 255, 262–63.

[39] Windscheid (n 29) §§ 43–44. Windscheid developed the concept earlier and more thoroughly in B Windscheid, *Die Actio des römischen Zivilrechts vom Standpunkte des heutigen Rechts* (Düsseldorf, Scientia-Verlag, 1856).

[40] German Civil Code, BGB, www.gesetze-im-internet.de/englisch_bgb.

[41] Windscheid (n 29) § 43(1), (2); see also the explanation, with reference to more recent scholarship, in C Witz, *Droit privé allemand: Actes juridiques, droits subjectifs* (Paris, Litec, 1992) § 608. There is an interesting parallel with Birks' analysis of rights to restitution arising from pre-existing ownership in Birks, 'Misnomer' (n 10) 1, 21–26. In explaining the vindication of rights of ownership, he concluded that when one person is in possession of another's thing, an obligation to make restitution arises, but not from unjust enrichment; it arises from the 'mere receipt of another's thing' (24). He refused to say that such a claim can be understood simply as the direct enforcement of the pre-existing right of ownership, characterising that right as 'inert' (22). In French and Quebec law, revendication is understood as the direct enforcement of a real (proprietary) right.

[42] For what follows, I have relied on Witz (n 41) §§ 609–18. There are discussions in English of modes of legal reasoning in the German system in F Schmidt, 'The German Abstract Approach to Law' (1965) 9 *Scandinavian Studies in Law* 131 and BS Markesinis, W Lorenz, and G Dannemann, *The Law of Contracts and Restitution: A Comparative Introduction* (Oxford, Clarendon Press, 1997) 13–19, but these do not explain claims/*Ansprüche*.

from a norm: in particular, a claim-norm or *Anspruchnorm*, which may also be called a claim-foundation or *Anspruchgrundlage*. This is a norm that explicitly or implicitly announces that certain facts will yield a certain legal consequence; here, a claim. Given the right facts, a syllogistic form of reasoning can then permit the inference that a claim arises (subject to applicable defences).[43]

The common law's definition of a cause of action in terms of facts seems simply to run together a number of elements that are logically distinct. Of course, the facts are crucial, but they are not normative. The common law's idea of a cause of action, although it is defined in terms of facts, also includes the normative element that attaches a juridical consequence to those facts. What is more, the common law's idea of a cause of action also stands for that juridical consequence, which is usually a legal right.[44] In other words, the common law runs together three things that logically could, and perhaps should, be separated.

This can be illustrated with the tort of battery. If a cause of action is 'every fact which it would be necessary for the plaintiff to prove' in order to succeed,[45] then we are not surprised to see battery defined as 'the intentional infliction upon the body of another of a harmful or offensive contact'.[46] But a concatenation of facts is just that; to say that the law gives a cause of action upon the occurrence of those facts is to say something other than that certain facts occurred. It is to say that the law attaches consequences to the occurrence of those facts; that is, it attaches the *same* consequence to *any* occurrence of those facts. And to say that A has a cause of action in battery against B is to say that A has a right against B; that is, that the law *has attached* those consequences in this particular case.

This seems to give us an answer to the first complication. The common law's articulation of causes of action in terms of facts is part of the story, but not all of it. A purely factual understanding captures neither the *general* phenomenon of the law's attachment of juridical consequences to facts of that kind, nor the *particular* attachment of such consequences in a given

[43] Witz (n 41) § 618 discusses the contribution of H Motulsky, *Principes d'une réalisation méthodique du droit privé: la théorie des éléments générateurs des droits subjectifs* (Paris, Sirey, 1948), who essentially argued (with almost no reference to German law) for the adoption of the same mode of reasoning in French law. Motulsky and some of his contemporaries developed the idea of *situation juridique*, being a set of facts to which the law attaches consequences including the creation of rights. This leaves some mark on the doctrine (see the literature cited in J Rochfeld, *Les grands notions du droit privé*, 2nd edn (Paris, Presses Universitaires de France, 2013) 195), but the idea of *situation juridique* does not form a fundamental element of French legal thought.

[44] Not every cause of action may be thought to generate a right or claim against another litigant. A claim for the rectification of a contract may be an example of one that does not. It is not necessary to explore this here.

[45] *Danyluk* (n 19).

[46] *Bettel v Yim* (1978) 20 OR (2d) 617 (SC).

case. And yet the idea of cause of action includes both of these. For this reason, there is nothing exceptionable about the fact that some causes of action are described with elements that are actually intermediate legal conclusions from primary facts. That is just a slightly more complicated example of the same logical structure.[47]

2.4. Starting from Scratch

The second complication was the question of the level of generality for the definitions of causes of action. I argued above that the concept of 'cause of action' includes different logical structures. One of them is what in German law is called a claim-norm: a general norm that will attach legal consequences to certain facts. This is our concern. This is the part that is general, and therefore for which we have to select an appropriate level of generality. Facts do not have any level of generality; they are just facts. The conclusion that A holds a right against B is normative, in the relation between A and B, but it is not a general norm, and so again it lacks any level of generality.

Earlier, I claimed that 'tort' is not a cause of action. One could, however, define it as such: just as battery can be committed with a hand or a haddock, one could create a giant definition of 'tort' that included all the ways in which one can commit a tort. To explain why this would be a pointless exercise, we can draw some insight from Raz's analysis of the individuation of laws.[48] His study addresses the following question: which approach should we adopt in order to decide what is 'a' law? For example, if we wish to say that the laws within a legal system, properly understood, never conflict, we would have to describe many laws in a complicated and repetitive way. This is because every law would need to be defined in such a way that it incorporated, as part of its strictures, all of the defences and analogous considerations that might disapply the law. For example, almost every one of the laws that articulates a crime that is an offence against the person would have to include an articulation of the defence of self-defence. This would be repetitive, complicated and counterintuitive. Raz says:[49]

> Instead we should adopt a doctrine of individuation which keeps laws to a manageable size, avoids repetition, minimizes the need to refer to a great variety of statutes and cases as the sources of a single law, and does not deviate unnecessarily

[47] Witz (n 41) § 611 explains how German jurists understand some claim-norms to articulate both the relevant facts and the juridical consequence; more commonly, however, claim-norms make reference to other norms (that specify either the relevant facts or the juridical consequence), so that a chain of reasoning is required in order to decide whether the requirements of the original claim-norm are fulfilled.

[48] J Raz, 'Legal Principles and the Limits of Law' (1972) 81 *Yale Law Journal* 823, 825–34.

[49] ibid 832.

> from the (admittedly hazy) common sense notion of a law. Such a doctrine of individuation will result in a greater number of laws which interact with one another, modifying and qualifying each other. This approach is closer to the way lawyers ordinarily think about the law, and also illuminates important connections among laws. It focuses attention on the fact that certain groups of laws are affected by certain other laws stipulating doctrines such as self-defense, necessity, etc., while others are not. In short, such a doctrine of individuation better explains the systematic interrelations between various parts of the legal system.

I suggest that a similar approach to causes of action will also help us to understand the interrelations between parts of the legal system.[50]

The pressure against making causes of action 'too big', like the ridiculous example of the cause of action in 'tort', is that this would disable us from making distinctions that we rightly wish to make between and among causes of action. To take one point to which I will return, we may wish to make some claims subject to a certain defence, but not others. Or we may wish to have defences that operate differently in relation to different claims: longer or shorter limitation periods, for example. We may wish to differentiate in relation to other elements of adjectival law, such as rules on jurisdiction and choice of law.[51] In relation to different claims, we might have different rules for the assessment of damages[52] or for proof of causation.[53] And why might we wish any of these things? Why might we have different rules as between two different torts, or as between a tort claim and an unjust enrichment? The answer must be because we think that the interests in play are not all the same.[54] They are all legally protected, but not necessarily in exactly the same ways.[55]

Another point is that a claimant may have multiple causes of action arising out of the same facts and, in the common law, generally speaking, it is the claimant, and not the defendant or the law or the court, who decides which one shall be relied upon. Indeed, subject to various limiting principles, a claimant may be able to rely upon more than one cause of action arising out of the same facts. This may be important to the claimant precisely because the causes of action have the kinds of differences we have just described.

[50] It may also go a long way in helping us to understand why some elements should be classified as defences rather than as parts of a cause of action.

[51] G Panagopoulos, *Restitution in Private International Law* (Oxford, Hart Publishing, 2000), Part II.

[52] For discussion of the different measures of damages as between conversion and detinue, a distinction of enduring significance in many jurisdictions, see *General and Finance Facilities Ltd v Cooks Cars (Romford) Ltd* [1963] 1 WLR 644 (CA).

[53] Lord Hoffmann, 'Causation' (2005) 121 *LQR* 592.

[54] In using the word 'interests', I deliberately avoid the word 'rights'. A tort may be a violation of a right (n 27). But a claim in unjust enrichment, to take only that example, does not involve a wrong.

[55] In relation to torts, see Stevens (n 27) 88–91, positing an explanation as to why some torts are actionable per se while others are not.

Particularly in the common law, the definition of causes of action may be influenced by history.[56] But history apart, the appropriate level of generality for a cause of action is not arbitrary. It is not simply by convention or choice or pure convenience or aesthetics that we say 'tort' is not a cause of action. There is a substantive reason that the same facts may give rise to multiple causes of action and that different causes of action may be governed by different principles in private international law, and may be vulnerable to different defences and so on. If we had a single cause of action called 'tort', our list of the facts that satisfy the norm would have to include the facts that constitute all torts. This would disenable us from drawing distinctions between and among what we see, in the actual law, as different torts. It would also disenable us from saying that two torts had been committed in relation to a single set of facts. So, conversely, the reason for being more specific is that each cause of action includes a justification for liability. To be more precise, if we focus on the part of the cause of action that is a claim-norm, each claim-norm *is* a justification for liability. Once we see that, it makes sense that one set of facts may generate two or more causes of action, while another set of facts may generate only one, or none. It also makes sense that if there is more than one cause of action, there is a possibility of cumulation (perhaps with an eventual requirement of election) because there are multiple juridical justifications for the creation of different recourses.

This leads to an answer to the question, albeit one that can only be stated in an abstract way, rather like Raz's solution for the individuation of laws. A cause of action identifies a set of facts that are individually necessary and collectively sufficient to generate a legal recourse. The correct level of generality for the definition of causes of action is one that neither lumps together juridically distinct justifications for legal recourses, nor pointlessly distinguishes between different ways in which the same justification may be activated. To make that more concrete, in relation to particular causes of action, we have to be precise about what exactly justifies liability in different situations. We have to think about whether one case is different from another only in the sense that the same claim-norm has been activated by a different set of facts, or rather whether the normative justification for liability is a different one.

[56] I say 'particularly in the common law' because there has never been a moment of comprehensive codification. At the same time, many civil codes bear clear influences of Romanist systems for individuating claims (such as art 1491 of the Civil Code of Québec, which is recognisably based on the Roman *condictio indebiti*). In the common law, the distinction between libel and slander was mentioned above (text at n 25). A decision that there is really only one tort of defamation might be based in part on a conclusion that the distinctions between libel and slander are artefacts of history, without normative significance in the modern world.

3. IS UNJUST ENRICHMENT A CAUSE OF ACTION?

3.1. A Variety of Opinions

There has been some debate about whether unjust enrichment is a cause of action or rather a 'principle' that belongs, presumably, to a higher level of generality. The Supreme Court of Canada has described it as a cause of action:[57]

> As a general matter, the test for unjust enrichment is well established in Canada. The cause of action has three elements: (1) an enrichment of the defendant, (2) a corresponding deprivation of the plaintiff, and (3) an absence of juristic reason for the enrichment...

A number of Canadian scholars have followed suit.[58] And in courts up and down the country, 'unjust enrichment' is routinely pleaded as a cause of action. However, the matter is not entirely clear. In *Kingstreet Investments Ltd v New Brunswick (Department of Finance)*,[59] the Court suggested that the recovery of undue taxes occurs under a cause of action that stands apart from the unjust enrichment claims that operate between citizens. In the light of this and other developments,[60] Robert Chambers has said that: 'The broad category of unjust enrichment now includes several different causes of action in Canada.'[61]

In other common law jurisdictions, the matter is also unclear. Some English cases suggest there is a single cause of action. In *Rowe v Vale of White Horse DC*, Lightman J said:[62]

> It is now authoritatively established that there are four essential ingredients to a claim in restitution:
>
> (i) a benefit must have been gained by the defendant;
> (ii) the benefit must have been obtained at the claimant's expense;

[57] *Garland v Consumers' Gas Co* [2004] SCC 25; [2004] 1 SCR 629 [30]. See also the quotation from *Peel* (text at n 7). Many other examples could be given.

[58] Smith (n 9); M McInnes, *The Canadian Law of Unjust Enrichment and Restitution* (Toronto, LexisNexis Canada, 2014) 81–83. More ambivalent is P Maddaugh and J McCamus, *The Law of Restitution*, looseleaf edn (Toronto, Canada Law Book, 2005) [2:300].

[59] *Kingstreet Investments Ltd v New Brunswick (Department of Finance)* [2007] SCC 1; [2007] 1 SCR 3.

[60] Particularly *BMP Global Distribution Inc v Bank of Nova Scotia* [2009] SCC 15; [2009] 1 SCR 504, in which recovery of money paid by mistake was analysed without reference to unjust enrichment.

[61] R Chambers, 'The Presumption of Resulting Trust: *Nishi v Rascal Trucking Ltd*' (2014) 51 *Alberta Law Review* 667, 675. In Smith (n 13), I tried to make a similar argument. See also S Smith, 'Unjust Enrichment: Nearer to Tort Than Contract' in R Chambers, C Mitchell and J Penner (eds), *Philosophical Foundations of Unjust Enrichment* (Oxford, Oxford University Press, 2009) 181, 208: 'The various forms of unjust enrichments resemble torts in their heterogeneity.'

[62] *Rowe v Vale of White Horse DC* [2003] EWHC 388 (Admin); [2003] 1 Lloyd's Rep 418 [11], approved in *Chief Constable of the Greater Manchester Police v Wigan Athletic AFC Ltd* [2008] EWCA Civ 1449; [2009] 1 WLR 1580 [38], [54], [62].

(iii) it must be legally unjust, that is to say there must exist a factor (referred to as an unjust factor) rendering it unjust, for the defendant to retain the benefit;
(iv) there must be no defence available to extinguish or reduce the defendant's liability to make restitution.

On the other hand, it is still common in England for lawyers to plead 'money had and received to the use of the plaintiff',[63] which suggests a resistance to unification into a single cause of action. Birks considered unjust enrichment to be a single 'causative event', but this did not lead him to think of it as a single cause of action.[64] Virgo takes the same line.[65] Other commentators do not commit themselves on this issue.[66]

The casuistic structure of the *Restatement of the Law Third: Restitution and Unjust Enrichment*[67] reveals an understanding in which unjust enrichment is an overarching principle, not a cause of action. Causes of action are not clearly identified, but the structure of the work, with dozens of articles providing multiple bases of liability, suggests that there are many. In Australia, the High Court has sometimes embraced unjust enrichment and sometimes recoiled from it; for the moment, it would be a courageous lawyer indeed who argued that there is a cause of action in unjust enrichment in that jurisdiction, and the mere suggestion that the phrase identifies a useful juridical concept may attract disapproval in some quarters.[68]

[63] See, for example, *Armstrong DLW GmbH v Winnington Networks Ltd* [2012] EWHC 10 (Ch); [2013] Ch 156. Note the statement in *Goff & Jones*, 8th edn (n 3) 15: 'it would be desirable for claimants to abandon the old language of the forms of action when pleading claims in unjust enrichment'.

[64] This is certainly true in Birks (n 4). Note the plural in the title of P Birks, 'The Independence of Restitutionary Causes of Action' (1990) 16 *University of Queensland Law Journal* 1, repeated in the subtitle 'Independent Restitutionary Causes of Action' for the section at 13–21. This approach is also clearly articulated in P Birks, *Restitution: The Future* (Sydney, Federation Press, 1991) 1: 'failure of consideration is a specific cause of action within the still somewhat less familiar genus "unjust enrichment"'.

The new approach in Birks (n 23) was arguably motivated by an effort to provide a more intellectually convincing unity for the subject (see Stevens (n 13)). There are hints in the book that suggest a new view that there is only one cause of action in unjust enrichment: see, for example, 'the cause of action' at 40, 207, in sentences that suggest a reference to all of unjust enrichment. And yet elsewhere (274–75) he speaks in the plural of the 'reasons' why an enrichment must be given up. See, however, Stevens (n 13, 21 fn 42), suggesting that the text retains elements from earlier drafts.

[65] Virgo (n 5) 61 states that unjust enrichment is a principle and not a cause of action. On the other hand, while he deprecates the language of the old common counts, he does not say what the causes of action are, except that they are 'the recognised grounds of restitution'. This implies that mistake and duress would found distinct causes of action, while a transfer of rights by mistake and a conferral of services by mistake would give rise to the same cause of action.

[66] *Goff & Jones*, 8th edn (n 3) 5–7; Burrows (n 10) 26–28. Note, however, A Burrows, *A Restatement of the English Law of Unjust Enrichment* (Oxford, Oxford University Press, 2012) 26, suggesting a line more like Virgo's (n 5): 'If one does describe unjust enrichment as a cause of action, it must be understood that one is talking about a cause of action in a very general sense.'

[67] American Law Institute, *Restatement of the Law Third: Restitution and Unjust Enrichment*, 2 vols (St Paul, MN, American Law Institute Publishers, 2011) 4–6.

[68] See Burrows (n 10) 35–43.

3.2. A Variety of Approaches

I suggested above that it matters, in practical terms, whether unjust enrichment contains one or many causes of actions. Different causes of actions may be subject to different adjectival rules (such as rules of private international law) and may be susceptible to different defences. As for the theoretical importance of the question, it seems self-evident for those seeking to analyse the nature and structure of the law of unjust enrichment.

The obvious logical sequence for thinking about defences in this context would be to start from causes of action and then to decide which defences might properly be available to which causes of action. In this field, however, we are in a state of some confusion. We don't know whether we have one cause of action or many. If we have many, we don't know how to order and distinguish them. There are several possibilities for thinking about, and ordering, what might be the causes of action in unjust enrichment in the common law.

Traditionalists might wish to preserve old pleading categories, like 'money had and received', 'money paid to the defendant's use' and so on. These were different ways of establishing that a money debt had arisen by operation of law. But it is not obvious that they correspond to the modern concept of a cause of action: a set of facts that are individually necessary and collectively sufficient to generate a legal recourse. For one thing, they do not correspond to modern distinctions between consensual and non-consensual sources of obligations. Each of the common counts (of which there were seven at the abolition of the forms of action)[69] was a subspecies of *indebitatus assumpsit*. Each alleged that a debt arose, with a supporting justification. Some of these justifications (as in account stated, goods sold and work done) were generally consensual and so in the modern law would probably belong to the law of contractual obligations.[70] Some were usually extracontractual, like money had and received and money paid to the defendant's use.[71] And some could be either, like *quantum meruit*.[72] For another thing, the counts were tied to pleading fictions: each presented a justification for a debt, followed by the allegation of a fictional promise by the defendant to pay the debt, for which the consideration (being past) was also fictional. The goal of allowing the allegation of the fictional promise (which the defendant could not deny) was procedural. It allowed the claimant who could establish a debt (whether consensual or non-consensual) to avoid the form of action (not cause of action)

[69] JH Baker, *An Introduction to English Legal History*, 4th edn (London, Butterworths, 2002) 348.

[70] Although sometimes they were used to enforce non-consensual obligations: JH Baker, 'The History of Quasi-contract in English Law' in WR Cornish, et al (eds), *Restitution: Past, Present and Future: Essays in Honour of Gareth Jones* (Oxford, Hart Publishing, 1998) 37, 47–48.

[71] Again there are counter-examples of the enforcement of voluntary undertakings: ibid 44–45, 48–49.

[72] ibid 42–44.

in debt, and instead to sue in *indebitatus assumpsit*, a subspecies of *assumpsit*, which was itself a subspecies of the form of action in trespass.[73] The common counts, tied up with the forms of action and crossing between contract and unjust enrichment, seem ill-suited to be a basis of modern analysis.

Leaving aside those old categories, some authors assume that the causes of action would fall into the series of 'reasons for restitution': mistake, compulsion, failure of consideration or failure of basis and so on. But this is not at all obvious. The series has a long pedigree; however, we should remember that it started not as a list of reasons for restitution, but as a list of justifications for the bringing of a claim in money had and received.[74] If money had and received is a poor candidate for a modern cause of action, then this list is off to a bad start. In its origin, it could only apply to claims arising from payments of money. Using it for other claims—such as claims for services or improvements of property—involves an assumption, which might or might not be warranted, that it is properly applicable to such cases. In other words, using it as the basis of a set of causes of action might bring cases together that should not be brought together. Conversely, it might lead to the separate treatment of cases that should be considered as falling under a single cause of action in modern terms.

Given the complexity of the historical skeletons in the closet, the best solution might be an original analysis drawn out of the modern understanding of the cause of action as a set of facts that are individually necessary and collectively sufficient to justify a legal recourse. A careful application of that understanding might well lead us to the recognition of multiple causes of action in unjust enrichment, in a sequence that has very little to do with anything found in the history of the subject.

Let me give two examples of what I mean. If, as some authors have suggested,[75] the fundamental normative reasons for allowing restitution are different in cases involving a transfer of rights and in cases involving the improvement of property or the rendering of services, then we would expect that each of these two situations would generate its own cause of action (or possibly more than one if there were relevant sub-distinctions). Conversely, it might be that the normative reasons are common to the two kinds of case and that such differences in the scope of liability as may arise are based on factual differences that can be addressed by elements of a common cause of action.[76] I do not express a view on this question here.

[73] The form of action in debt allowed the defendant to defend by 'waging his law'; that is, by swearing he did not owe the debt, and producing 11 others to swear that the defendant was telling the truth. Debt did not allow trial by jury, which was the main reason that claimants sought to use *indebitatus assumpsit* instead. In 1602, it was established that every debt 'imported' a promise to pay the debt; this fictional promise allowed the form of action in debt to be sidelined without any overt change in the law. See Baker (n 69) 341–45.

[74] *Moses v Macferlan* (1760) 2 Burr 1005, 1012; 97 ER 676, 681.

[75] See Watts (n 11) and McFarlane (n 12).

[76] What I mean by this obscure sentence is this. Some would argue that a defendant cannot be liable for an improvement to the value of his property which that defendant neither

The second example is that in terms of normative reasons for allowing restitution, there seems to be a fundamental distinction between cases in which the claimant's consent to an enrichment was somehow impaired—mistake, compulsion, failure of basis and so on—and cases in which the claimant has a claim to recover a transfer *regardless of whether* the claimant consented to it. Examples of the latter include claims to recover undue taxes from public authorities and claims by public authorities to recover public monies or other resources improperly paid out.[77] They may also include claims to recover voidable preferences in bankruptcy, claims to recover overpaid legacies and claims to recover improper distributions of corporate assets in a winding-up.[78] They may further include cases of 'legal compulsion'. This label suggests a group of cases that can be aligned with claims arising from duress; however, in 'legal compulsion' cases, the operative principle is not an impairment of consent, but rather an ordering of liabilities, through legal principles, as primary, secondary or coequal.[79] And they may also include cases in which the best interpretation of a statutory provision is that it requires restitution to the claimant.[80] In all of these cases, it seems that any impairment of the claimant's consent to the enrichment is irrelevant to recovery. These cases can be seen to rest on independent justifications for recovery in unjust enrichment; in other terms, it seems, they are separate causes of action from those based

requested nor acquiesced in: see, for example, E Weinrib, 'Correctively Unjust Enrichment' in R Chambers, C Mitchell and J Penner (eds), *Philosophical Foundations of Unjust Enrichment* (Oxford, Oxford University Press, 2009) 31. This is one reading (of several) of the famous shoe-cleaning dictum of Pollock CB in *Taylor v Laird* (1865) 25 LJ Ex 329, 332; 156 ER 1203. On the other hand, one could argue that in a case involving the transfer of rights, the defendant must have accepted the transfer if he did not disclaim or reject it when he became aware of it. It is not only gifts, but any transfer of rights, that can be disclaimed or rejected. See J Edelman and E Bant, *Unjust Enrichment in Australia* (Oxford, Oxford University Press, 2006) 104, which also discusses non-liability where a defendant was disenriched before becoming aware of the enrichment. A defendant who does not reject a transfer when he becomes aware of it (and still has it) has accepted it, in a stronger way than a defendant who simply becomes aware that his property has been improved. It is conceivable, then, that acceptance is required for liability in both categories of case, but that the factual elements needed to establish acceptance would be analysed very differently.

[77] The best-known case is *Auckland Harbour Board v R* [1924] AC 318 (PC (NZ)). I say 'other resources' because there are also cases that address the applicability of this reasoning to mistaken under-charging for electricity by public entities: *Maritime Electric Co v General Dairies Ltd* [1937] AC 610 (PC (Can)); *Kenora (Town) Hydro Electric Commission v Vacationland Dairy Co-operative Ltd* [1994] 1 SCR 80 (SCC).

[78] For an argument that relates these claims to one another, see L Smith, 'Unjust Enrichment, Property, and the Structure of Trusts' (2000) 116 *LQR* 412, 442–43.

[79] See, for example, *Stimpson v Smith* [1999] Ch 340 (CA): a co-surety is entitled to contribution regardless of whether it paid under legal pressure, even if it paid 'voluntarily' in the sense that it was not legally liable to pay. What matters is that the liabilities among co-sureties are coequal in degree.

[80] The final element of the list in *Moses* (n 74) is '... an undue advantage taken of the plaintiff's situation, contrary to laws made for the protection of persons under those circumstances'. The other elements of the list all go to the claimant's consent.

on defects in consent.[81] This would mean, at least, that a claimant might be able to choose between causes of action where the different causes of action have different susceptibilities to defences.[82]

3.3. Can Defences Help?

Working out a set of causes of action that make up the law of unjust enrichment from first principles will be difficult, partly because many of the relevant issues are contested. In this section I have a more modest aim, which is to ask to what extent defences can assist in such a project.

Some defences are available to more than one cause of action. Illegality is an example. The availability of the same defence to more than one kind of claim does not imply that they rest on the same cause of action. The converse question that arises is this: if a defence is available to one claim but not available to another claim, does this show that these claims are actually based on separate causes of action? If they were based on the same cause of action—in the sense of the same normative justification—then surely the defence, whatever it is, would be potentially available in both situations.

If that is right, then we can learn something about the issues with which I am concerned by looking at defences. The defence of change of position is the characteristic defence in unjust enrichment. It provides crucial protection to the interests of defendants, and in so doing it allows the scope of potential liability to expand beyond what would otherwise be acceptable.[83]

Everyone seems to agree that the defence should not be available to a state authority that collects an undue tax, at least where the claimant relies on the absence of authority for the collection.[84] This is because allowing the defence would be inconsistent with constitutional principles.[85] This seems absolutely correct, but arguably its significance has been underestimated. The central defence in unjust enrichment is not available in these cases. Does that not strongly suggest that the claim being made is, in an important way, a *different claim* from the claims which are susceptible to the defence?

[81] Smith (n 13).

[82] *Deutsche Morgan Grenfell Group plc v IRC* [2006] UKHL 49; [2007] 1 AC 558. In *Kingstreet* (n 59), the Supreme Court of Canada held to the contrary that the 'public law' claim to recover undue taxes excluded any 'private law' claim based on mistake. See L Smith, 'Public Justice and Private Justice: Restitution after Kingstreet' (2008) 46 *Canadian Business Law Journal* 11.

[83] See, for example, Birks (n 4) 414–15.

[84] E Bant, *The Change of Position Defence* (Oxford, Hart Publishing, 2009) 203–04; Burrows (n 10) 550. *Goff & Jones*, 8th edn (n 3) 701 argues that the defence of change of position should not be available to a public authority in respect of a claim to recover undue tax, even if the claim is based on mistake.

[85] For the same reason, in *Kingstreet* (n 59), the Supreme Court of Canada rejected the defence of 'fiscal chaos' that it had arguably recognised earlier as one available to public authorities.

The same phenomenon is arguably present in other unjust enrichment claims that are not based on defects in the claimant's consent. There have been suggestions that change of position is not available to claims to recover voidable preferences in bankruptcy[86] or to claims to recover overpaid legacies.[87] Again, it is difficult to see that the defence could apply in cases of 'legal compulsion'. If the claimant discharges a debt for which the defendant was primarily liable, would it make sense for the defendant to be able to reduce its liability through change of position?

Take another case. The traditional category of 'failure of consideration' has often been distinguished from recovery arising from mistake or undue pressure on the ground that while mistake and pressure involve vitiations of the claimant's consent, failure of consideration involves a valid but conditional consent, followed by a failure of the condition.[88] Some scholars have argued that the defence of change of position is or might be unavailable in cases based on failure of consideration. This is often said to be because the defendant in such a case is aware that the enrichment is conditional, and therefore in changing her position, she takes the risk of having to repay the full amount. This might be the correct explanation if this were a context-specific inquiry, in which different facts would sometimes allow the defence and sometimes not.[89] On another view, the defence is excluded as a matter of law for a whole category of claim.[90] If this were correct, it would suggest that that category of claim is different, in an important way relating to its justification, from those claims that are susceptible to the defence. It suggests that it is founded on a different cause of action.

4. CONCLUSION

4.1. Do We Need Causes of Action in Unjust Enrichment?

In my view, we still do not understand the structure of the common law of unjust enrichment. Perhaps the first question in logical sequence is whether we still care about causes of action, as the common law understands that term. Is it important to be able to spell out the claims claimable in terms of

[86] *Principal Group Ltd v Anderson* (1997) 147 DLR (4th) 229 (Alberta CA); D Sheehan, 'Change of Position in Insolvency' (2003) 63 *CLJ* 41.

[87] *Goff & Jones*, 8th edn (n 3) 699.

[88] See, for example, Birks (n 4) chs VI ('Non-voluntary Transfer I: Vitiation') and VII ('Non-voluntary Transfer II: Qualification)'.

[89] This is the approach in Bant (n 84) 197–98 and in Burrows (n 10) 546–47.

[90] See Stevens (n 13) 32: 'The conditionality of the payment rules out the application of the defence.' See also the detailed comparative study in P Hellwege, 'Unwinding Mutual Contracts: *Restitutio in Integrum* v. the Defence of Change of Position' in D Johnston and R Zimmermann (eds), *Unjustified Enrichment: Key Issues in Comparative Perspective* (Cambridge, Cambridge University Press, 2002) 243, which argues that change of position, as such, is not available to parties who are unwinding a bilateral contract.

the primary facts that are individually necessary and collectively sufficient to give rise to those claims? In my view, it is. Lawyers have to plead facts; even when they plead legal conclusions, they have to plead the supporting facts.[91] So they have to know which facts generate claims and which facts support points of law.

Perhaps unjust enrichment is somehow different. As a field of law, it has defining characteristics. One of these is that it involves the creation of liabilities that arise not by consent but by operation of law; but that, at the same time, are not founded on wrongdoing. We might say, in short, that it responds to injustices that are not wrongful.[92] And one might say that some of these injustices are created by the law itself, or would be created if it were not for the law of unjust enrichment.[93] If unjust enrichment has a 'second order vacuum filling role',[94] then perhaps it can only be expressed in juristic and not in factual terms.

I am doubtful of this. There is nothing wrong with expressing the overall role or function of unjust enrichment in purely juristic terms, just as we might say that the private law of wrongs is about breaches of private law duties. But we have to do more than describe the genus; we have to describe the species. In my view, there is still a lot of work to do in articulating the various causes of action that fall within unjust enrichment.

4.2. What are They?

This final section is in the nature of an agenda for future research. It does not present a scheme of causes of action in unjust enrichment, but makes some suggestions as to what such a scheme might look like. To begin, we return to German law. The English translation of § 812(1) of the BGB that is published by the German Ministry of Justice reads:[95]

> A person who obtains something as a result of the performance of another person or otherwise at his expense without legal grounds for doing so is under a duty to

[91] Here are two provisions from Ontario's *Rules of Civil Procedure*, RRO 1990, r 194, which I would imagine are not unusual in the common law world:

> 25.06 (1) Every pleading shall contain a concise statement of the material facts on which the party relies for the claim or defence, but not the evidence by which those facts are to be proved.
>
> (2) A party may raise any point of law in a pleading, but conclusions of law may be pleaded only if the material facts supporting them are pleaded.

[92] L Smith, 'Restitution: The Heart of Corrective Justice' (2001) 79 *Texas Law Review* 2115; D Klimchuk, 'The Structure and Content of the Right to Restitution for Unjust Enrichment' (2007) 57 *University of Toronto Law Journal* 661.

[93] McFarlane (n 12) 608.

[94] Stevens (n 13) 33. See also L Smith, 'Property, Subsidiarity and Unjust Enrichment' in Johnston and Zimmermann (n 90) 588, 610–13.

[95] German Civil Code, BGB (n 40). For another English translation, see the German Law Archive at: www.iuscomp.org/gla/statutes/BGBrest.htm.

> make restitution to him. This duty also exists if the legal grounds later lapse or if the result intended to be achieved by those efforts in accordance with the contents of the legal transaction does not occur.

Roman law did not have a general enrichment action.[96] This paragraph was intended to create one.[97] One might have thought that this provision, in the light of its generality, was intended to create a single claim. The idea of 'performance' (*Leistung*) has a technical meaning in German law; it refers to the deliberate conferral of an enrichment with a specific purpose in mind (such as discharging a debt).[98] One might think that that this concept was placed in the background in relation to the first sentence of § 812(1) because the liability arises whether or not the benefit was conferred through a performance: 'Why should it be useful to distinguish between two cases of which the one merely comprises whatever is not covered by the other?'[99] And, indeed, the initial interpretation of the provision was that it did not draw a juridical distinction between the two cases.[100] But this is not how the provision is understood today. Through scholarly analysis of § 812(1), the concept of performance has become something like the *summa divisio* of most of the German law of unjust enrichment. This interpretation, which is now almost universally accepted, leads to the position that there are four different claims (*Ansprüche*) in § 812(1).[101]

The reason for telling this story is that this position was not reached by a simple exercise of textual interpretation of a particular codal disposition; rather, it was based on an argument that there is a significant normative difference between cases that involve a performance and cases that do not.[102]

[96] Zimmermann (n 30) 838–84.

[97] ibid 887–88. It was not, however, intended to subsume all enrichment claims, as subsequent provisions in the BGB make clear. The idea of a 'general enrichment action' can be ambiguous; when it is used in relation to § 812(1), it implies a starting point; one turns to more specific provisions only if § 812(1) does not provide a solution. In other systems, however, what looks like a general enrichment action is, on the contrary, residuary, and can only be deployed when no other provision is apt. See R Zimmermann, 'Unjustified Enrichment: The Modern Civilian Approach' (1995) 15 *OJLS* 403, 417; Smith (n 94) 588. This is certainly true of arts 1493–94 in the Civil Code of Québec, which correspond to the *actio de in rem verso* that has been recognised in French jurisprudence, but which remains uncodified there. Note, however, the draft *ordonnance* published on 25 February 2015, www.textes.justice.gouv.fr/textes-soumis-a-concertation-10179/reforme-du-droit-des-contrats-27897.html. This will reform the French law of obligations and will codify the *actio de in rem verso*.

[98] Zimmermann (n 30) 889–90; R Zimmermann and J du Plessis, 'Basic Features of the German Law of Unjustified Enrichment' [1994] *Restitution Law Review* 14, 25–26; G Dannemann, *The German Law of Unjustified Enrichment and Restitution* (Oxford, Oxford University Press, 2009) 23–25.

[99] Zimmermann and du Plessis (n 98) 25.

[100] Zimmermann (n 30) 888; Dannemann (n 98) 22–23.

[101] There is one that applies where there has been a performance, and three possible claims where there has not been. See Zimmermann and du Plessis (n 98) 25–30; for more detail, see Dannemann (n 98) chs 2–5.

[102] Zimmermann and du Plessis (n 98) 25.

Indeed, one German author suggests that it reflects 'the nature of things'.[103] But it is not only German scholars who think so. The distinction has had an important influence on civilian writers working in uncodified systems. In his treatise on the Scots law of unjustified enrichment, Evans-Jones also finds the *summa divisio* between enrichment by deliberate conferral and other kinds of enrichment.[104] So too does Visser in his treatise on South African law.[105]

Recent contributions suggest that the idea of performance, or something like it, has started to make inroads into the common law. McInnes, in his important new book, proposes some novel categories within unjust enrichment, including 'non-participatory transfers' and 'non-purposive transfers', to supplement the Supreme Court of Canada's scheme based on absence of juristic reasons.[106] McInnes describes non-participatory transfers as a sub-category of non-purposive transfers.[107] A non-participatory transfer is a case in which the defendant unilaterally abstracts wealth from the claimant without the claimant's participation; one of McInnes' examples is the finding of property belonging to another.[108] The wider category of non-purposive transfers comprises those in which the claimant did not purposefully enrich the defendant. One of McInnes' examples is the claimant's improvement of the defendant's property under a mistake as to ownership, the claimant thinking the property is hers. But although one might think that McInnes' idea of purposive transfer is similar to the idea of performance that is found in German law, it is actually quite different. As we have seen, in German law different norms apply depending upon whether or not there was a performance. For McInnes, all cases are governed by the same norms; a non-purposive transfer is simply a case in which it is abundantly clear that there is no juristic reason for the transfer. McInnes' discussion of non-purposive transfers aims to show that the scheme adopted by the Supreme Court of Canada can be applied to every case.

Personally, I remain doubtful of that scheme, and not only because it threatens to cut common law Canada off from the rest of the common law

[103] See Zimmermann (n 97) 415 fn 77, quoting Lorenz (my translation).

[104] R Evans-Jones, *Unjustified Enrichment*, vol 1 *Enrichment by Deliberate Conferral: Condictio* (Edinburgh, W Green, 2003) and vol 2, *Enrichment Acquired in Any Other Manner* (Edinburgh, W Green, 2013).

[105] D Visser, *Unjustified Enrichment* (Cape Town, Juta and Co, 2008). The divisions within pt II are 'enrichment by transfer', 'imposed enrichment' and 'enrichment by invasion of rights'.

[106] McInnes (n 58) especially chs 5 and 6. Birks (n 23) 154–55 had earlier proposed the category of 'non-participatory enrichments', although he noted (at 160) that in his scheme, this category was not normatively distinct. As we will see, this is also true for McInnes.

[107] McInnes (n 58) 251.

[108] I do not here address the difficult question whether the solution of such a case lies exclusively in the claims that protect pre-existing property rights rather than in the law of unjust enrichment. See L Smith, 'Tracing' in A Burrows and Lord Rodger of Earlsferry (eds), *Mapping the Law: Essays in Memory of Peter Birks* (Oxford, Oxford University Press, 2006) 119.

world. Such a scheme can help us to understand the law at a high level of generality, but when we come to the fine detail of the all the various types of claims which are available, we find that it cannot be made to work. At least, it requires such a large number of exceptions and qualifications that we have moved into a lower level of generality, closer to the causes of action.[109] To give one example of what I mean, an obligation to confer an enrichment is said to be a juristic reason that justifies the conferral of that enrichment.[110] And yet there are clear counterexamples. A claimant may confer a benefit while legally obliged to do so under a valid and subsisting contract; if that contract is later discharged (prospectively) for breach or by frustration, a claim in unjust enrichment is possible. We may say *very broadly* that there was no juristic reason, but at the level of detail, we have to be more precise. The question whether there was an obligation does *not* finally resolve the question whether a benefit conferred pursuant to that obligation can be retained by the defendant. At a high level of generality, 'juristic reason' can usefully be defined in a rather circular way: a factor that justifies enrichment.[111] This is comparable to saying that a tort is a breach of a duty arising by operation of law. Both are accurate as high-level descriptions, but neither is likely to solve particular cases.

The reason this matters is that a high-level description cannot usefully be applied to a set of proven facts to draw legal conclusions. That is the role of causes of action and, in particular, of the part of the cause of action that I have called a claim-norm. The identification of those claim-norms will therefore help in analysing claims, in pleading them and in deciding them. The Supreme Court of Canada's scheme could, however, turn out to be important in another way if it points towards a better ordering of the causes of action within unjust enrichment.

I have made a similar suggestion about defences. The law relating to defences helps us to see that the field of unjust enrichment contains a range of claims, each normatively related, but with varying details. This insight will, in turn, help us to make sense of a range of puzzles. Here I mention only one such puzzle. There is a large body of Canadian common law on the division of property (in the broad sense of rights) upon the termination of cohabitational relationships. Some of these cases were foundational to the law of unjust enrichment in Canada;[112] paradoxically, these cases have always revealed features that set them apart from the basic structure of

[109] See L Smith, 'Demystifying Juristic Reasons' (2007) 45 *Canadian Business Law Journal* 281.

[110] See *Garland* (n 57) [44].

[111] S Meier, 'Unjust Factors and Legal Grounds' in Johnston and Zimmermann (n 90) 37, 54: 'Finally assigning benefits to a recipient is exactly the function of a legal ground.'

[112] Especially *Pettkus v Becker* [1980] 2 SCR 834 (SCC) and *Peter v Beblow* [1993] 1 SCR 980 (SCC).

unjust enrichment as the restitution of unjust transfers.[113] More recently, the Supreme Court of Canada articulated a new doctrine of 'joint family venture' to explain the basis for property division, while retaining the language of unjust enrichment.[114] One way to understand this is that the doctrine of joint family venture provides a baseline for the proper division of wealth at the time of trial, being a baseline other than the one that normally applies in unjust enrichment: that is, the pre-transaction holdings. Because this new baseline is non-consensual, an unjustified deviation from it could be characterised as an unjustified enrichment on the one hand and an unjustified corresponding deprivation on the other.

If so, this would reveal another type of claim within the genus of unjust enrichment, being a claim founded on different interests from those at play in a typical mistaken payment case. Moreover, it would also arguably reveal a case of unjust enrichment that does not lead to restitution, in the sense that it does not lead to a return to pre-transaction holdings. Beyond the Canadian context, it might be that the same argument applies in relation to claims to contribution or subrogation, which may operate to adjust the parties to a legally justified position that is not the same as their pre-transaction holdings.[115]

The work of spelling out the claims within the category of unjust enrichment, in terms of specific causes of action, lies largely in the future. My suggestion is that a sound scheme may treat as fundamental certain distinctions that are only recently attracting the attention of common lawyers. These include the distinction between cases arising from a performance and those that do not; between cases involving the transfer of rights and those involving the enhancement of the value of the defendant's existing rights; and between cases involving defects in the claimant's consent and those in which the enrichment is considered unjust for other reasons.

113 L Smith et al, *The Law of Restitution in Canada: Cases, Notes and Materials* (Toronto, Emond Montgomery, 2004) 359–63.

114 *Kerr v Baranow* [2011] SCC 10; [2011] 1 SCR 269.

115 I suggested above (n 79 and text) that these cases are not founded on a defective intention on the part of the claimant.

3

Defence, Denial or Cause of Action? 'Enrichment Owed' and the Absence of a Legal Ground

HELEN SCOTT

1. DEFENCES AND DENIALS

THE DISTINCTION BETWEEN defences and denials proposed by James Goudkamp in his recent book *Tort Law Defences* is an extremely useful analytical tool in the hands of tort lawyers.[1] According to his typology, the term 'defence' refers to a rule that, when enlivened, results in a verdict for the defendant even though all the ingredients of the tort in which the claimant sues are present.[2] By contrast, a denial is a plea by the defendant that one of the elements of the tort in which the claimant sues is absent; it does not introduce into the proceedings any issue that the claimant will not already have put in contention.[3] Thus, the definition of tort defences is for Goudkamp a substantive rather than a procedural question, in the sense that it does not turn on the distribution of the burden of proof between the parties.[4] Admittedly, there remains a close correspondence between defences and the burden of proof: it is almost always for the defendant to plead and prove a defence.[5] Nevertheless, according to his typology, the distinction between actions and defences, and more specifically denials and defences, turns on substantive arguments about the definition of torts.

[1] J Goudkamp, *Tort Law Defences* (Oxford, Hart Publishing, 2013).
[2] ibid 2.
[3] ibid.
[4] ibid 3–4. *cf* E Descheemaeker, 'Tort Law Defences: A Defence of Conventionalism' (2014) 77 *MLR* 493, especially 497–99.
[5] Goudkamp (n 1) 47.

The distinction between denials and defences has now been extended by James Goudkamp and Charles Mitchell to the law of unjust enrichment.[6] As in the context of tort, here the term 'denial' refers to any argument by the defendant that liability should not be imposed because one or more of the elements of the claimant's action is missing,[7] whereas the term 'defence' refers specifically to a rule enabling the defendant to be wholly or partly relieved of liability which is independent of or extrinsic to the claimant's action.[8] Here, too, defences are defined independently of the distribution of the burden of pleading and proof.[9] Under the heading 'Rationalising the Distinction between Actions and Defences', Goudkamp and Mitchell discuss a number of possible justifications for the existence of defences in the law of unjust enrichment.[10] These are all more or less instrumental arguments and all five are general in nature, appropriate not only to the unjust enrichment context but also to tort.[11] Goudkamp and Mitchell claim, further, that: 'If the distinction between actions and defences is justifiable, the rationale or rationales that support it may bear upon how rules that govern liability should be classified.'[12] In other words, these general, instrumental arguments may also inform the classification of particular legal institutions either as elements in the claimant's action or as defences.

However, at the risk of lapsing into circularity, it seems that if Goudkamp's definition of defences is correct, then the basis for characterising a particular legal institution as a defence must be whether the institution in question is indeed judged to be extrinsic to the claimant's action. This is surely an exercise informed by doctrinal and moral arguments specific to the unjust enrichment context, not instrumental arguments of relatively general application.[13] We ask ourselves whether our account of the institution is consistent with judicial dicta, whether it coheres with other features of the law of unjust enrichment as a whole, and whether an account of the claimant's action which excludes the institution in question is convincing in light of the law's internal values. Thus, the recognition of the distinction between actions and defences, and denials and defences in particular, assists

[6] J Goudkamp and C Mitchell, 'Denials and Defences in the Law of Unjust Enrichment' in C Mitchell and W Swadling (eds), *The Restatement Third: Restitution and Unjust Enrichment* (Oxford, Hart Publishing, 2013) ch 6.

[7] ibid 137.

[8] ibid 137–38. Again, as in the case of tort, it is admittedly the case that rules that qualify as defences in the second sense must generally be pleaded and proved by the defendant, limitation being a notable exception: see ibid 138.

[9] ibid 137–39.

[10] ibid 146–50.

[11] *cf* the high degree of overlap between the justifications listed by Goudkamp and Mitchell in ibid and those listed by Goudkamp (n 1) 36–41.

[12] Goudkamp and Mitchell (n 6) 149.

[13] *cf* R Grantham and C Rickett, 'A Normative Account of Defences to Restitutionary Liability' (2008) 67 *CLJ* 92, especially 94–96.

in answering fundamental questions about the nature of claims in unjust enrichment. It forces us to think carefully about the normative basis of such claims.

2. IS 'ENRICHMENT OWED' A DEFENCE OR A DENIAL IN ENGLISH LAW?

These introductory remarks lead directly to the central question addressed by this chapter, namely whether a plea that a particular benefit was owed to the defendant under a valid contractual, statutory or other legal obligation constitutes a defence or a denial according to the English law of unjust enrichment. In the introductory chapter of *Unjust Enrichment in South Africa Law: Rethinking Enrichment by Transfer*, published in 2013, I make the following broad claim:[14]

> The first category [of unjust factors] reflects the idea that the impoverished party did not mean to transfer the benefit in question: that its conferral was in some sense involuntary. Mistake occupies a central position within this family of unjust factors. According to Birks' approach, mistake is itself the plaintiff's cause of action: the vitiation of his intent in making the transfer is the reason why it must be returned. The presence of a valid contract, statutory obligation or other relationship of indebtedness, such as a judgment debt, has the effect of blocking restitution. However, according to prevailing orthodoxy, this is simply a defence (or a range of defences) by means of which the recipient can defeat this prima facie claim. It enjoys no analytical significance in itself.

A footnote to the sentence in which it is claimed that '[t]he presence of a valid contract, statutory obligation or other relationship of indebtedness, such as a judgment debt, has the effect of blocking restitution' includes reference inter alia to 'the seminal decision' in *Barclays Bank Ltd v WJ Simms Son and Cooke (Southern) Ltd,*[15] as well as the more recent decision of the Court of Appeal in *Test Claimants in the Franked Investment Income Litigation v Revenue and Customs Commissioners.*[16] It had at one stage[17] been uncontroversial to confine the issue of 'enrichment owed' to the context of the defence of good consideration first recognised by Robert Goff J in the *Simms* case, a separate, general defence dealt with in a single chapter of *Goff & Jones* alongside other straightforward defences such as change of

[14] H Scott, *Unjust Enrichment in South African Law: Rethinking Enrichment by Transfer* (Oxford, Hart Publishing, 2013) 13 (footnotes omitted).

[15] *Barclays Bank Ltd v WJ Simms Son and Cooke (Southern) Ltd* [1980] 1 QB 677 (QBD) 695.

[16] *Test Claimants in the Franked Investment Income Litigation v HMRC (No 1)* [2010] EWCA Civ 103; [2010] STC 1251 [175]–[184].

[17] And certainly when I began work on my DPhil in 2002.

position.[18] But the fact that the last two sentences of the passage—in which it is claimed that '[a valid contract, statutory obligation or other relationship of indebtedness] is simply a defence ... by means of which the recipient can defeat this prima facie claim' and 'enjoys no analytical significance in itself'—are heavily qualified by authorities cited in a further footnote[19] shows that at the time of publication, these claims were becoming increasingly difficult to describe as orthodox. Indeed, as Andrew Burrows has shown, the status of the defence of good consideration in English law is extremely unclear.[20]

In my view, the contemporary debate regarding the basis of liability in the modern English law of unjust enrichment can be neatly summarised as a debate about whether 'enrichment owed' constitutes a defence or a denial according to Goudkamp's definitions: is it extrinsic to the claimant's action or does it speak to one of the elements of the claim? These are, of course, that the defendant has been enriched, that this enrichment was gained at the claimant's expense and that the defendant's enrichment is unjust.[21] Burrows himself reaches the conclusion that 'enrichment owed' is an 'upfront' matter which relates to prima facie liability—in other words, that it is a denial[22]—and in particular that it relates to the third element of the claim, that the enrichment is unjust.[23] He bases this conclusion in the first instance on several important judicial dicta. According to Lord Hope in *Kleinwort Benson Ltd v Lincoln CC*, 'the payee cannot be said to have been unjustly enriched if he was entitled to receive the sum paid to him'.[24] This clearly

[18] G Jones, *Goff & Jones: The Law of Restitution*, 7th edn (London, Sweet & Maxwell, 2006) ch 41. See also, eg, G Virgo, *The Principles of the Law of Restitution* (Oxford, Oxford University Press, 2006) 172–76, where good consideration is treated as a defence specific to mistake claims. For a general account of the treatment of the defence of good consideration by academic commentators, see A Burrows, 'Is There a Defence of Good Consideration?' in Mitchell and Swadling (n 6) ch 7, 166–68.

[19] A Burrows, *The Law of Restitution*, 3rd edn (Oxford, Oxford University Press, 2011) 88–91; R Stevens, 'Is There a Law of Unjust Enrichment?' in S Degeling and J Edelman (eds), *Unjust Enrichment in Commercial Law* (Sydney, Thomson Reuters, 2008); G Virgo, 'Demolishing the Pyramid: The Presence of Basis and Risk-Taking in the Law of Unjust Enrichment' in A Robertson and T Hang Wu (eds), *The Goals of Private Law* (Oxford, Hart Publishing, 2009); C Mitchell, P Mitchell and S Watterson, *Goff & Jones: The Law of Unjust Enrichment*, 8th edn (London, Sweet & Maxwell, 2011) [1-09] and the discussion of justification grounds in chs 2 and 3.

[20] Burrows (n 18) 168–73.

[21] eg, Mitchell, Mitchell and Watterson (n 19) [1-09], as well as the authorities cited in fn 24, including, eg, *Portman Building Society v Hamlyn Taylor Neck (A Firm)* [1998] 4 All ER 202 (CA) 206. The fourth 'question' identified in, eg, *Banque Financière de la Cité v Parc (Battersea Ltd)* [1999] 1 AC 221 (HL) 227, namely the existence of defences, is of course irrelevant to the *elements* of the claim.

[22] Burrows (n 18) 179 fn 49.

[23] ibid 174, 184.

[24] *Kleinwort Benson Ltd v Lincoln* CC [1999] 2 AC 349 (HL) 407–08, referred to with approval by Arden LJ giving the judgment of the Court of Appeal in *Test Claimants* (n 16) [181].

suggests that the payee's entitlement to the sum paid goes to the 'unjust' element of the claim. Also compelling is the dissent of Lord Scott in *Deutsche Morgan Grenfell plc v IRC*.[25] In cases where both mistake and entitlement are present, according to Burrows, 'the injustice by reason of the mistake is overridden by the fact that the money was owed anyway'.[26] More fully: 'There is a fundamental interplay between unjust factors and enrichment owed by the claimant. This interplay normally results in the unjust factor being overridden by the enrichment being owed.'[27] These points are also made by Burrows in his *Restatement of the English Law of Unjust Enrichment*. According to section 3(6):[28]

> In general, an enrichment is not unjust if the benefit was owed to the defendant by the claimant under a valid contractual, statutory or other legal obligation.

The notes on section 3(6) specify that:[29]

> [A]n unjust factor does not normally override a legal obligation of the claimant to confer the benefit on the defendant. The existence of the legal obligation means that the unjust factor is nullified so that the enrichment at the claimant's expense is not unjust.

In the context of section 10 ('Mistake') section 10(6) sets out this principle at a lower level of generality.[30]

Sections 11, 12, 13, 14 and 19, dealing with duress, undue influence, exploitation of weakness, incapacity of the individual, and necessity, contain similar provisions.

Burrows' approach is to be contrasted with the way in which 'enrichment owed' is dealt with, for example, in the introductory chapter of the eighth edition of *Goff & Jones* (under the heading 'Justifying Grounds'):[31]

> Under English law, a claimant will be entitled to restitution if he can show that a defendant was enriched at his expense, and that the circumstances are such that the law regards this enrichment as unjust. For example, a claimant will have a prima facie right to restitution where he has transferred a benefit to a defendant by mistake, under duress, or on a basis that fails. Nevertheless, the defendant can escape liability if another legal rule entitles him to keep the benefit, and this rule overrides the rule generated by the law of unjust enrichment which entitles the claimant to restitution ... Although the claimant would otherwise have a

[25] *Deutsche Morgan Grenfell plc v IRC* [2006] UKHL 49; [2007] 1 AC 558 [84]–[85].

[26] Burrows (n 18) 174.

[27] ibid 184. See also Burrows (n 19) 88–89: 'the prima facie injustice established by the unjust factor is normally outweighed by the fact that the defendant is legally entitled to the enrichment. Overall, therefore, the enrichment is not unjust'.

[28] A Burrows, *A Restatement of the English Law of Unjust Enrichment* (Oxford, Oxford University Press, 2012) 31.

[29] ibid 32.

[30] ibid 63.

[31] Mitchell, Mitchell and Watterson (n 19) [1-12]. This passage is substantially repeated at the beginning of ch 2, [2-01].

claim in unjust enrichment, the defendant's enrichment is justified by the statute or contract.

In this passage the authors appear to take the view that the existence of a justifying ground such as a statute or contract is extrinsic to the claimant's prima facie right to restitution; in other words, that 'enrichment owed' is a defence rather than a denial according to Goudkamp's typology.[32] Graham Virgo takes a similar approach:[33]

> [O]nce the elements of the unjust enrichment claim have been established by the claimant, restitution will follow save where a basis for the defendant's retention of the enrichment can be identified by the defendant.

Thus, it seems that several other commentators who continue to attach primary analytical significance to unjust factors treat 'enrichment owed' as a defence. This is also the view that appears to have been taken by the American Law Institute in the *Restatement Third: Restitution and Unjust Enrichment*.[34]

Burrows admits that it is 'arguably more elegant' to hive off the fundamental issue of the interplay between the unjust factors scheme and 'enrichment owed' to be solved by one or more defences.[35] Nevertheless, such 'hiving off' 'gives the mistaken impression that where, for example, a contract has been entered into by a unilateral ("but for") mistake of the claimant, it is sufficient for the claimant who seeks restitution of money paid under the contract to show that the mistake it made was a unilateral mistake in entering into the contract and paying the money'.[36] In other words, it accords insufficient weight to the distinction between transaction mistakes—mistakes in forming the intention to enter into a transaction—and execution mistakes—mistakes in carrying out such transactions.[37] Furthermore, while

[32] See also C Mitchell, 'Unjust Enrichment' in A Burrows (ed), *English Private Law*, 3rd edn (Oxford, Oxford University Press, 2013) 18.16—18.17. Having said that, the prominence of the treatment of justifying grounds in *Goff & Jones* as a whole (in chs 2 and 3, immediately following the introduction) is perhaps difficult to reconcile with this view. *cf* pp 63–64 below, where I consider the alternative possibility that both the presence of an unjust factor and the absence of a justifying ground constitute elements in the claimant's cause of action in English law.

[33] Virgo (n 19) 477, 489. But note that elsewhere in this article (479 fn 16), he labels the presence of a legal ground a 'bar' rather than a defence, and in his *Principles* (n 18) 665, he states that 'a bar relates to the establishment of a cause of action [whereas] a defence only arise once the defendant has established the cause of action'. For further discussion of this apparent conflict, see Goudkamp and Mitchell (n 6) 152 fn 72.

[34] American Law Institute, *Restatement Third: Restitution and Unjust Enrichment* (St Paul, MN, American Law Institute Publishers, 2011) § 62, discussed by Goudkamp and Mitchell (n 6) 151–53; Burrows (n 18) 179–82.

[35] Burrows (n 18) 182.

[36] ibid. *cf Portman Building Society v Hamlyn Taylor Neck* [1998] 4 All ER 202 (CA).

[37] S Meier, Unjust Factors and Legal Grounds' in D Johnston and R Zimmermann (eds), *Unjustified Enrichment: Key Issues in Comparative Perspective* (Cambridge, Cambridge University Press, 2002) 37, 37–54.

in principle the legal burden of proving a defence should be on the defendant, 'it is surely clear that the legal burden of proving the invalidity of an apparent legal obligation, under which enrichment was owed by the claimant to the defendant, is most appropriately placed on the claimant'.[38] Thus, for Burrows, 'the fact that the enrichment was owed by the claimant should be treated as an "upfront" matter relating to prima facie liability, with the legal burden being on the claimant, and not as a defence'.[39]

These points are compelling. However, there is at least one counter-argument: it is unclear whether injustice by reason of an unjust factor such as mistake—the element of 'unjust'—can really be 'overridden' or 'nullified' by the existence of a valid contractual, statutory or other obligation, or vice versa.[40] In order for the defendant's entitlement to the benefit to override or 'outweigh'[41] the claimant's mistake, these two considerations would have to be commensurable. Yet it is not clear that this is the case. Mistake is a primary fact[42] which is morally and legally relevant because it shows that the transfer of the benefit was in some sense involuntary: the impairment or vitiation of the claimant's consent or intent in making the transfer is the reason why it must be returned.[43] Indeed, underlying this unjust factor is a more fundamental commitment to the value of personal autonomy: where the claimant has conferred a benefit under the influence of a mistake, his autonomy is only imperfectly expressed—his plans for the distribution of his property have misfired—and it is this impairment of the claimant's autonomy which provides the moral justification for restitution.[44] Entitlement, however, is a purely legal institution which draws on bodies of rules extraneous to the law of unjust enrichment, principally contract.[45] Unlike in the case of mistake, the normative force of the defendant's tentitlement to the benefit is not transparent: the reasons why entitlement blocks restitution are doctrinal rather than moral. On the one hand, implicit in the rule that

[38] Burrows (n 18) 183.

[39] ibid 184. Burrows makes also a third argument (183) regarding the potentially confusing relationship between 'enrichment legally owed' (if understood as a defence) and change of position.

[40] For discussion of exceptional cases where the claimant's legal obligation seems to have been outweighed by the unjust factor of mistake, as in, eg, *Deutsche Morgan* (n 25), see Burrows (n 18) 176–78.

[41] See, eg, Burrows (n 18) 177 for the use of 'outweigh' in this context.

[42] *cf* L Smith, 'Unjust Enrichment: Big or Small?' in Degeling and Edelman (n 19) 35, 38.

[43] P Birks, *An Introduction to the Law of Restitution*, revised edn (Oxford, Clarendon Press, 1989) 146–73. For more recent authority, see, eg, Burrows (n 28) s 3(2) and (3).

[44] *cf* Scott (n 14) 208–11.

[45] *cf* L Smith, 'Demystifying Juristic Reasons' (2007) 45 *Canadian Business Law Journal* 281, 291. This is not to deny, of course, that contract can itself be construed as an expression of individual autonomy. But in the operation of a plea of entitlement or 'enrichment owed', the expression of this value is mediated through the existence of an objectively constitute legal obligation, rather than directly expressed, as in the case of mistake. *cf* Scott (n 14) 210–11.

restitution is excluded where enrichment is owed is some version of the principle of the subsidiarity of unjust enrichment to contract.[46] This principle is important, indeed fundamental, but it is founded in the need for coherence within the law of obligations rather than in a direct appeal to values. On the other hand, the circularity problem raised by Burrows himself is a serious one: 'there is an upfront problem of inconsistency in saying that C owed D the enrichment and yet that D must make restitution to C'.[47] But, once again, arguments concerning circularity or inconsistency within the law of obligations are purely doctrinal ones, of a different order from those underpinning the unjust factor of mistake. Of course, it remains possible to redefine 'unjust' in such a way that it comprises both kinds of arguments: Danie Visser has proposed this with respect to the term 'unjustified' in South African law.[48] But such an approach threatens to rob the concept of 'unjust' of meaningful content. If it is to express anything more than the conclusion that restitution ought to be permitted, it does not seem that 'unjust' can be made to comprise such disparate considerations.

This point can be illustrated with reference to *Deutsche Morgan Grenfell plc v IRC* itself. The claimant in this case had paid advance corporation tax (ACT) under a statutory scheme that was ultra vires the Revenue (the defendant) because, contrary to EU law, the scheme did not give Deutsche Morgan Grenfell (DMG) an option to avoid paying the tax by making a group income election. The House of Lords held that DMG was entitled to restitution from the Revenue for mistake even though it had a statutory duty to pay the tax unless and until it validly exercised a group income election which—because this had not been provided—it had not done.[49] In one sense, of course, the Revenue was legally entitled to the tax.[50] On the other hand, as the exaction of the ACT was unlawful in relation to companies in DMG's position because it did not allow them to make a group income election, and because it was clear that DMG would have made such an election if that had been permitted, it was arguably 'over-analytical'[51] to say that the tax was due unless and until that group income election was made.

[46] On the slipperiness of this principle, see Mitchell, Mitchell and Watterson (n 19) [2-02]–[2-06]. What is meant here is simply that certain outcomes in the law of unjust enrichment are dictated by conclusions reached elsewhere.

[47] Burrows (n 18) 176 fn 42.

[48] Thus, he has proposed that in a case involving, for example, a mistaken payment, the descriptor 'unjustified' should incorporate both the element of mistake and the absence any obligation to make the payment: D Visser, *Unjustified Enrichment* (Cape Town, Juta, 2008) 171–93, especially 181, and 229–53, especially 251–53. See also my summary of Visser's 'third way' in Scott (n 14) 201–02.

[49] This summary is based on that of Burrows (n 18) 176–78. See also, eg, R Chambers, '*Deutsche Morgan Grenfell Group plc v IRC* [2006] UKHL' (2006) 6 *Oxford University Commonwealth Law Journal* 227, 232–34; Stevens (n 19) 17–19; Burrows (n 19) 91.

[50] Burrows (n 28) 34.

[51] *Deutsche Morgan* (n 25) [143] (Lord Walker).

According to Burrows: 'The force of the unjust factor [mistake] clearly outweighed the force of the tax being due.'[52] Thus, he argues, the normal rule—that the unjust factor is overridden by the enrichment's being owed[53]—did not apply. Yet it is unclear how it was that the claimant's mistake—which, incidentally, was said by Lord Hoffmann to be only a 'deemed mistake'[54]—came to 'outweigh' the defendant's entitlement to the money in this way. There is little sign of any such balancing exercise in the decision itself. The only question asked or answered was as follows: was the defendant entitled to the money or not? The strength (or otherwise) of the claimant's mistake appears to have been irrelevant to the outcome of this inquiry.

This argument raises in turn a series of more fundamental issues: the competing claims of the unjust factor and absence of basis approaches on the English law of unjust enrichment, the relationship between these approaches, and in particular the possibility of a 'mixed approach' to enrichment liability in English law. According to Burrows himself: 'At a deeper level, this [ie, recognising that 'the fact that the enrichment was owed by the claimant should be treated as an "upfront" matter relating to prima facie liability'] involves recognising that the unjust factors and the civilian "absence of basis" approaches are closer than has traditionally been thought.'[55] But at the same time:[56]

> [T]here is no need, as appears to be suggested by Goudkamp and Mitchell in their chapter in the present volume ... to see this approach as involving both unjust factors and the absence of legal basis. The idea of an enrichment owed to the claimant by the defendant [should read, 'by the claimant to the defendant'] is only one aspect of the absence of basis scheme ... nothing is said here, for example, about the unjust factors scheme being qualified by the law on gifts.

The claim by Goudkamp and Mitchell to which Burrows refers is that 'it may be conceptually possible for a legal system to roll the two approaches into one by requiring claimants to show both the presence of an unjust factor and the absence of any legal ground for the transfer'.[57] Burrows may well be correct when he says that treating 'enrichment owed' as an 'upfront matter' relevant to prima facie liability does not mean committing fully to the absence of basis scheme. The reasons he gives for treating 'enrichment owed' in this way—that it is 'the best interpretation of English law', as well

[52] Burrows (n 18) 177.
[53] ibid 184.
[54] *Deutsche Morgan* (n 25) [23].
[55] Burrows (n 18) 184. See also 168 and 176.
[56] ibid 176 fn 42.
[57] Goudkamp and Mitchell (n 6) 153.

as the circularity problem set out above—are relatively specific. Moreover, his conception of 'enrichment owed' or (more fully) 'valid contractual, statutory or other legal obligation' appears to be much narrower than the standard understanding of 'basis' or 'legal ground' in civilian legal systems.[58] Nevertheless, his claim that 'an enrichment is not unjust if the benefit was owed to the defendant'—his account of what he calls the 'fundamental interplay between unjust factors and enrichment owed'—does appear to require him to confront the relationship between unjust factors and the absence of a legal ground, and the possibility of a mixed approach to enrichment liability in English law.

Since the publication of the first edition of Peters Birks' *Unjust Enrichment* in 2003, this debate has tended to centre on the 'pyramid' metaphor used by Birks to describe the continuing relevance of unjust factors within his new absence of basis scheme.[59] According to Birks: 'A pyramid can be constructed in which, at the base, the particular unjust factors such as mistake, pressure, and undue influence become reasons why, higher up, there is no basis for the defendant's acquisition, which is then the master reason why, higher up still, the enrichment is unjust and must be surrendered.'[60] As Birks made clear, according to this scheme, intent-based unjust factors such as mistake are 'subservient' to absence of basis, 'which itself then becomes an intermediate generalization between unjust factors and unjust'.[61] In other words, a 'limited reconciliation' between unjust factors and absence of basis is possible if the relationship between these two analyses is understood as an explicitly hierarchical one. Beyond this, however, he was implacable: 'It would be absurd to suggest, as would be suggested by including absence of basis in the list of unjust factors, that by demonstrating two approaches applicable to that case … we have revealed the presence of two different causes of action.'[62] Further: 'They [absence of basis and unjust factors] are incompatibly alternative methods for deciding which enrichments are unjust.'[63]

In my book, I attempt to refute this claim, arguing that Birks' pyramid gives insufficient weight to impairments to intent which are not also reasons for invalidity.[64] Indeed, I argue—in the words of Lionel Smith—that 'every

[58] *cf* Scott (n 14) 7–9 (on the meaning of 'legal ground' in South African law) and 170–72 (on the meaning of 'legal ground' in German law), as well as J du Plessis, 'Towards a Rational Structure of Liability for Unjustified Enrichment: Thoughts from Two Mixed Jurisdictions' (2005) 122 *South African Law Journal* 142.

[59] P Birks, *Unjust Enrichment*, 2nd edn (Oxford, Clarendon Press, 2006) 116–17, as well as, eg, T Baloch, 'The Unjust Enrichment Pyramid' (2007) 123 *LQR* 636; Virgo (n 19).

[60] Birks (n 59) 116.

[61] ibid.

[62] ibid 114.

[63] ibid 115.

[64] Scott (n 14) 192–94.

legal system can and does mix the two approaches',[65] since the unjust factors and absence of legal ground analyses each incorporate elements of the other.[66] I still believe that this is true. However, it appears that in another sense, Birks was entirely right. Admittedly, in this subsection of *Unjust Enrichment* he had in his sights a rather specific proposition, namely the possibility of including absence of basis in the list of unjust factors alongside mistake, pressure etc.[67] This possibility seemed to have been raised by certain of the swaps case, or at least by certain commentators on those cases, and Birks was concerned to exclude it in particular. Nevertheless, his central claim has much wider application. It is indeed impossible to mix these two approaches at the same level, for the reasons set out above.[68] The reasons for restitution represented by unjust factors and the reasons for retention represented by grounds or bases are incommensurable; they are indeed 'incompatibly alternative'. Thus, the orthodox unjust factors approach relegates the defendant's entitlement to the defences stage, just as the German absence of legal ground analysis deals with the unjust factor of mistake through the defence of knowledge set out in section 814 of the BGB.[69]

In fact, the only mixing or combining at the same level which is possible is that according to which both approaches (unjust factors and absence of basis) are applied in parallel or side by side: this may be what Goudkamp and Mitchell have in mind when they speak of a legal system rolling 'the two approaches into one by requiring claimants to show both the presence of an unjust factor and the absence of any legal ground'.[70] This appears to

[65] Smith (n 45) 304.
[66] These conclusions are summarised in Scott (n 14) 201–03.
[67] In Birks, *Unjust Enrichment* (n 59) 114–16 the subsection is bluntly entitled 'Absence of basis is not another unjust factor'.
[68] See pp 59–60 above.
[69] See, eg, Scott (n 14) 172.
[70] *cf* p 61 above. In support of this claim, see in particular their cross-reference (153 fn 76) to J du Plessis' account of the South African approach (ie, the 'traditional civilian approach') in 'Duress and Related Forms of Pressure: A Comparative Perspective' in Mitchell and Swadling (n 6) 102, as well as their remarks with respect to § 62 of the third American *Restatement* at 152: 'One way to explain it [ie, the denial of restitution where a claimant who owes separate contractual debts to two creditors pays one while intending to pay the other] might be to say that the payee's enrichment is 'unjust' only if the payor's mistake is an 'invalidating mistake' of the kind identified in paragraph 5 *and* there is no basis for the payee's enrichment deriving from the contract. On this view, the absence of a contract between the parties is an element of the payor's action in unjust enrichment, and so the argument that the payee is contractually entitled to the money is a denial. Alternatively, if the making of an "invalidating mistake" is sufficient in itself to render the payee's enrichment "unjust", then the payee's appeal to his contractual rights is not a denial, because the "unjustness" of the payee's enrichment deriving from the mistake cannot be "nullified" by these rights. Instead, they provide a reason why restitution should not be awarded that is external to the definition of the action. On this view, para 62 describes a defence.' It seems to me that the first alternative canvassed comes rather close to the South African 'mixed approach', in that it appears to treat the absence of basis for the payee's enrichment as a separate element in the payor's claim.

be what South African law does.[71] According to the seminal decision in *Willis Faber Enthoven (Pty) Ltd v Receiver of Revenue*, in the paradigm case involving the mistaken payment of tax, the plaintiff must demonstrate both the absence of any liability to make the transfer and the existence of a specific reason for restitution in the form of a (reasonable or excusable) mistake.[72] Such a belt-and-braces approach leads to very conservative outcomes: indeed, South African law may embody that mythical system, hypothesised by Goudkamp and Mitchell, in which all liability rules have been assimilated to the elements of the action, rendering defences (or at least defences specific to the law of enrichment) superfluous.[73] Nevertheless, although arguably over-determined, it is analytically coherent. There is no possibility of 'interplay' between the claimant's mistake and the defendant's entitlement: these considerations are wholly sealed off from one another, in that they are independent, equally weighted elements of the plaintiff's claim.[74]

3. THE CLAIMANT'S CAUSE OF ACTION: 'ENRICHMENT OWED' AND THE ABSENCE OF A LEGAL GROUND

To summarise, it seems that there is at least one objection to be made to Burrows' argument that 'enrichment owed' constitutes a denial rather than a defence in English law, in the sense that it serves to override the injustice generated by unjust factors such as mistake, namely what I have called the problem of incommensurability. However, even if it does constitute a denial, it is important to note that there are nevertheless crucial differences between the way in which 'enrichment owed' functions in English law and the way in which it functions in the context of the absence of legal ground approach, as for example in South African law.[75] These differences relate to the allocation of the burden of pleading and proof as between claimant and defendant.

[71] See generally Scott (n 14), especially ch 6, as well as H Scott, 'Rationalising the South African Law of Enrichment' (2014) 18 *Edinburgh Law Review* 433, especially 448–50.

[72] *Willis Faber Enthoven (Pty) Ltd v Receiver of Revenue* 1992 (4) SA 202 (A).

[73] Goudkamp and Mitchell (n 6) 143. For a sense of the paucity of defences in South African law, see J du Plessis, *The South African Law of Unjustified Enrichment* (Cape Town, Juta, 2012), at 161 ff, 193 ff, 204 ff, 250 ff, 306 ff, 329 ff, 341 ff, where a number of denials (with the exception of estoppel) are discussed under the heading 'defences' in the context of specific causes of action. Visser (n 48) does devote a chapter (ch 12) to defences, but several of these are discussed in theoretical terms only; of those currently recognised in South African law, only one, loss of enrichment, is specific to the law of enrichment. And, in fact, it is likely that loss of enrichment too constitutes a denial rather than a defence: see ch 13 in du Plessis ('The Measure or *Quantum* of Enrichment Liability'), but *cf* Visser (n 48) ch 12, especially 703 ff.

[74] See, eg, Scott (n 14) 203; see also Scott (n 71). Regarding the nature of the claimant's cause of action in the South African law of enrichment, see further s 3 below.

[75] Indeed, Burrows himself makes this point explicitly, ie, that treating 'enrichment owed' as an 'upfront matter' relevant to prima facie liability does not mean committing fully to the absence of basis scheme. See Burrows (n 18) 176 fn 42 and *cf* p 61 above.

Taking as a starting point Burrows' claim that 'the legal burden of proving the invalidity of an apparent legal obligation, under which enrichment was owed by the claimant to the defendant, is most appropriately placed on the claimant',[76] the following scheme might be tentatively proposed for the operation of 'enrichment owed' as a denial in the paradigm case of the mistaken payment in English law:

a) the claimant begins by pleading (and proving) that he made the payment by mistake;
b) the defendant pleads that the payment was in fact due under a valid contractual, statutory or other obligation;
c) it then falls to the claimant to prove that no such valid contact or other obligation exists.

It follows that in the case discussed by Burrows, in which a claimant who owes separate contractual debts to two creditors pays creditor A while intending to pay creditor B, provided that the defendant, creditor A, puts the existence of such an obligation in issue, the burden of proving the non-existence of the obligation falls on the claimant. On the other hand, if the claimant succeeds in proving the existence of a 'but for' mistake and creditor A wholly fails to raise the fact that the payment was due to him in terms of a valid contractual obligation, the claimant will succeed solely by virtue of his causative mistake. In other words, the claimant is under no obligation to plead the absence of such a valid obligation in the first instance. The existence of such an obligation is relevant to the 'unjust' element of the claimant's claim or action, in that it serves to rebut it, but its absence is not an element of his claim; it is not an ingredient in his *cause of* action.

This is to be contrasted with the absence of legal ground element applied, for example, in South African law. As discussed in the previous section, and as cases such as *Willis Faber Enthoven* and the more recent decision of the Supreme Court of Appeal in *Affirmative Portfolios CC v Transnet Ltd t/a Metrorail*[77] show, the South African *condictio indebiti* arises from the absence of any liability on the part of the plaintiff to make the transfer, in combination with the existence of a specific reason for restitution such as mistake.[78] The plaintiff cannot make out even a prima facie case without pleading the absence of liability—that the transfer was *indebitum* in the sense required—and, at least in cases involving an apparent contractual or other obligation, without proving the non-existence or invalidity of that obligation.[79] The non-liability of the plaintiff (in combination with his

[76] Burrows (n 18) 183.
[77] *Affirmative Portfolios CC v Transnet Ltd t/a Metrorail* 2009 (1) SA 196 (SCA).
[78] See generally Scott (n 14) and (for a more succinct account) Scott (n 71).
[79] See, eg, the explicit dictum regarding onus in *Willis Faber* (n 72) 224. On the distribution of the burden of proof with respect to the absence of a legal ground in German law, see, eg, S Meier, 'No Basis: A Comparative View' in A Burrows and Lord Rodger of Earlsferry (eds),

mistake) constitutes part of the gist of his claim: an ingredient in his cause of action. Thus, the degree of uncertainty surrounding the existence of a continuing statutory obligation to pay the tax in question in the *Deutsche Morgan Grenfell* case is inconceivable in South African law. Indeed, the contrast with English law is obvious simply from the use of negative formulations such as 'absence of legal ground', 'non-liability' and *indebitum*, as opposed to the positive formulations 'entitlement' and 'owed': the English rule is 'the payee cannot be said to have been unjustly enriched if he was entitled to receive the sum paid to him',[80] not 'an *indebitum* paid as a result of a mistake ... may be recovered'.[81] This point is linked to the wider significance of the absence of legal ground concept as the 'golden thread' running through this entire body of South African law.[82] While non-liability constitutes the gist of the plaintiff's *condictio indebiti*, in combination with other factors such as mistake, it also constitutes a necessary condition for restitution throughout the law of enrichment.[83]

Of course, in the very common case in which the claimant's mistake concerns his liability to pay, proof of that mistake will necessarily involve pleading and proving the absence or invalidity of an apparent contractual or other obligation to make the payment. In cases such as these, there is no difference in practice between the absence of a legal ground as an ingredient in the claimant's cause of action and 'enrichment owed' as a denial. Nevertheless, it seems important not to neglect the distinction between causes of action (what the claimant must plead and prove in order to make out a prima facie claim) and denials (a plea by the defendant which serves to rebut one of the elements of that claim). Although in the case of a denial the defendant's plea is not extrinsic to or independent of the claimant's action, as in the case of a defence, but rather goes to one of its elements, it is nevertheless analytically significant that the matter is for the defendant to plead rather than the claimant. To draw a parallel with the law of defamation, it is undoubtedly meaningful that the falsehood of the defendant's allegation is not part of the claimant's cause of action, the gist of his claim in defamation, even if, as Goudkamp argues, the truth of that allegation is not a matter extrinsic to the elements of the claim, but rather goes to the element of damage.[84]

Mapping the Law: Essays in Memory of Peter Birks (Oxford, Oxford University Press, 2006) 343, 350–51.

[80] *Kleinwort Benson v Lincoln* (n 24) 407–08 (Lord Hope).
[81] *Willis Faber* (n 72) 224.
[82] *cf* Stevens (n 19) especially 16, 33–34.
[83] *cf* Scott (n 71) 435–37.
[84] *cf* Goudkamp (n 1) 62–65.

4. CONCLUSION

James Goudkamp's analysis of defences is a valuable new analytical tool in the hands of obligations lawyers. Formulated in the context of tort, it is equally useful in the context of unjust enrichment, as his and Charles Mitchell's analysis in *The Restatement Third: Restitution and Unjust Enrichment* shows.[85] If a particular rule—say, change of position or good consideration—is found to be a defence rather than a denial, this implies an important judgement about the nature of the claimant's action itself, namely that it arises independently of that rule. Thus, the question addressed by Andrew Burrows in his contribution to the same volume,[86] that is, whether good consideration—or rather 'enrichment owed'— is a defence or a denial, raises issues of central analytical importance in the English law of unjust enrichment, issues regarding the basis of liability itself.

Burrows takes the view that 'enrichment owed' is a denial; in other words, an 'upfront' matter relating to prima facie liability, specifically to the element of 'unjust': 'the prima facie injustice established by the unjust factor is normally outweighed by the fact that the defendant is legally entitled to the enrichment. Overall, therefore, the enrichment is not unjust'.[87] Burrows' arguments in support of his view are compelling. However, I have argued in response that an unjust factor such as mistake and the defendant's entitlement to the benefit are after all not commensurable considerations capable of overriding or outweighing one another. Whereas mistake is a primary fact, morally and legally relevant because it shows that the transfer of the benefit was in some sense involuntary, entitlement is a legal institution which draws on bodies of rules extraneous to the law of unjust enrichment, principally contract; the reasons why 'enrichment owed' blocks restitution are doctrinal rather than moral.

This point raises in turn a more fundamental issue, namely the competing claims of the unjust factor and absence of basis approaches on the English law of unjust enrichment, and in particular the possibility of a 'mixed approach' to enrichment liability. Since the publication of Peter Birks' *Unjust Enrichment*, this debate has tended to centre on the pyramid metaphor used by Birks to describe the continuing relevance of unjust factors within his new absence of basis scheme. Although Birks believed that a 'limited reconciliation' between the unjust factors and absence of basis approaches was possible, this was the case only if the relationship between these two analyses was understood as an explicitly hierarchical one: beyond that, he took the view that 'they are incompatibly alternative methods for

[85] Once again, the full citation is James Goudkamp and Charles Mitchell, 'Denials and Defences in the Law of Unjust Enrichment' in Mitchell and Swadling (n 6) ch 6.

[86] See, again, Burrows (n 18).

[87] Burrows (n 19) 88–89.

deciding which enrichments are unjust'.[88] On reflection, this turns out to be correct: it is indeed impossible to mix these two approaches at the same level, because these two sets of considerations—the reasons for restitution represented by unjust factors and the reasons for retention represented by grounds or bases—are incommensurable. The only mixing or combining at the same level which is possible is that according to which both approaches (unjust factors and absence of basis) are applied in parallel, the claimant's mistake and the defendant's entitlement treated as independent, equally weighted elements of the claim. This, it seems, is what South African law has elected to do.

Finally, even if Burrows is correct and 'enrichment owed' does constitute a denial rather than a defence, it is important to note that there are nevertheless crucial differences between the way in which the issue of entitlement is treated in English law and the way in which it is treated in the context of an absence of legal ground approach, as for example in South African law. Working with the paradigm case of the mistaken payment, even if the legal burden of proving the invalidity of an apparent legal obligation were placed on the claimant rather than the defendant, as Burrows suggests it should be, it would generally be for the defendant to put the existence of such an obligation in issue in the first instance; if he failed to do so, the claimant would succeed merely by virtue of his mistake. In South African law, on the other hand, the plaintiff cannot make out even a prima facie case without pleading the absence of any liability on his part to make the transfer in question. The non-liability of the plaintiff (in combination with his mistake) constitutes the gist of his claim: his cause of action. This shows that however important the distinction between denials and defences, it is equally important not to neglect the distinction between causes of action and denials. Although in the case of a denial the defendant's plea is not extrinsic to the claimant's action, as in the case of a defence, but rather goes to one of its elements, it is nevertheless analytically significant that the matter in question is for the defendant rather than the claimant to plead.

[88] Birks (n 59) 115.

4

What Kind of Defence is Change of Position?

DENNIS KLIMCHUK*

SUPPOSE THAT P pays D £5,000 mistakenly believing that he was under a legal obligation to do so: contrary to his recollection, her debt had in fact already been repaid, say, or her insurance policy had lapsed,[1] or the terms of the will had been misinterpreted and D was not in fact a beneficiary.[2] Suppose now that, in good faith—believing herself to be entitled to the full sum—D spends £1,000 of the money on a holiday she would otherwise not have taken. D will have, in law, changed her position, and under the defence that bears that name would be able to reduce her liability to P in unjust enrichment to £4,000.

My question is: what kind of defence is this? In asking it, I mean at first to use 'defence' in a broad sense, to name any doctrine under which a defendant can answer a claim against her so as to reduce or defeat liability. So understood, the question disaggregates into two. We can ask, first, whether change of position works to deny that an element of the cause of action in unjust enrichment has been made out or whether instead it serves to reduce the defendant's liability notwithstanding that the elements of the cause of action have been made out. Following James Goudkamp and Charles Mitchell,[3] I will say that in the first case change of position would be a

* I gave an earlier version of this chapter as a talk to my colleagues at Western Law School. Thanks to the participants for their many helpful comments, in particular Andrew Botterell, Jason Neyers, Stephen Pitel and Zoe Sinel. A second version was discussed at the workshop for this volume, at which I learned a great deal. I am particularly indebted to Elise Bant, James Goudkamp, Sonja Meier, Charles Mitchell, Robert Stevens, Graham Virgo and Frederick Wilmot-Smith for their excellent questions, and to James and Frederick as well, for very insightful and detailed written comments and discussion.

[1] As in the classic case of *Kelly v Solari* (1841) 9 M&W 54; 152 ER 24.

[2] Simplifying the facts of *Re Gareau Estate* [1995] 9 ETR (2d) 25; 56 ACWS (3d) 779 (Ontario Gen Div).

[3] J Goudkamp and C Mitchell, 'Denials and Defences in the Law of Unjust Enrichment' in C Mitchell and W Swadling (eds), *The Restatement Third, Restitution and Unjust Enrichment: Critical and Comparative Essays* (Oxford, Hart Publishing, 2013).

denial and, in the second, a *defence* in a narrower sense of the term, one that I will henceforth adopt. So the first question is: is change a position a denial or a defence? The second question is: supposing, as I will argue, that it is a defence (again, in this narrower sense), what kind of defence is it?

I will frame this second question against the background of an account of the kinds of defences in criminal law. One broad issue addressed in this chapter is whether the framework supplied by the structure of defences in criminal law—and, more generally, by criminal law theory—can illuminate private law. However much that is settled here, the questions I will raise are worth asking in any case because getting clear on the conceptual structure of the defence of change of position serves as an illuminating way to engage some basic issues concerning the theoretical foundations of the law of unjust enrichment.[4]

I will begin with some preliminary remarks concerning the scope and core doctrinal elements of the law of unjust enrichment in general and of change of position in particular. Next I will briefly outline an account of the varieties of defences in criminal law and then, against this background, I will turn to answer the questions into which my title question disaggregates.

1. UNJUST ENRICHMENT

To begin, here are three short points about the law of unjust enrichment to frame my discussion in this chapter.

1. By 'unjust enrichment', I mean to refer only to the law concerning recovery under the action in unjust enrichment and to thereby exclude the law concerning gain-based remedies for wrongs articulated in other areas of private law. I think this reflects the best way to organise private law, but in any case, it is dictated by my topic: change of position, at least on the received view, is only available as a defence to unjust enrichment thus narrowly construed.

2. Some readers may take issue with my unqualified reference to '*the* action in unjust enrichment', preferring to distinguish, for example, between mistake and failure of consideration as distinct grounds of recovery. I think that the common structure across these and other particular claims collected in the law of unjust enrichment justifies the definite article, but nothing in my argument here is invested in that. Throughout, I will stick with one example: recovery of a payment made under a liability mistake. If in your

[4] And see Goudkamp and Mitchell, 'Denials' in Mitchell and Swadling (eds), ibid 146–49, for a very helpful list of reasons why we ought to attend to the distinction, in particular, between denials and defences.

view that merits designation as a cause of action itself, then please read 'the cause of action and unjust enrichment' as a placeholder for that.

3. Finally, a few words about that example. One might worry that emphasis on the liability mistaken payment—particularly strong in Peter Birks' influential later work, where he defined the law of unjust enrichment as 'the law of all events materially identical to the mistaken payment of a non-existent debt'[5]—has had or threatens to have a distorting effect on our understanding of this area of law. At the risk of contributing to this distortion, I will stick with the example, for two reasons. First, it is a particularly sharp one because it describes a category of case where, at least on the received view, without the action in unjust enrichment, recovery would be unavailable. It is worth emphasising that it matters that the mistake in the example is about one's legal obligations, because other mistakes, for example, those concerning the payee's identity, will prevent title from passing.[6] If title does not pass, the claimant has an independent claim in, for example, conversion. Second, as we will see, mistaken payments illustrate particularly vividly some of the main puzzles of the law of unjust enrichment, among which are those brought into relief by asking the question given in this chapter's title.

2. CHANGE OF POSITION

The defence of change of position will not allow the defendant to discount every post-transactional expenditure from her liability. Recall the example from my introduction: P pays D £5,000 mistakenly believing that he was under a legal obligation to do so and, believing herself to be entitled to the full sum, D spends £1,000 of the money on a holiday she would otherwise not have taken. It is crucial that D believed herself to be entitled to the full sum. So one necessary condition is that the expenditure has been made in good faith. But it is not sufficient. The defence permits discounting only a subset of expenditures made in good faith.

What is it about the holiday that D would otherwise not have taken that marks it out as an expenditure she is permitted to discount from her liability? There are, by my reckoning, three main candidate answers:

1. It was extraordinary.[7] This answer reminds us that change of position is a conceptual neighbour of estoppel. The expenditure having been extraordinary, we infer that it was made in reliance (detrimental, as it turns out) on D's belief that she was entitled to the full amount of the payment. On this

[5] P Birks, *Unjust Enrichment*, 2nd edn (Oxford, Oxford University Press, 2005) 3.

[6] See D Fox, 'The Transfer of Legal Title to Money' [1996] *Restitution Law Review* 60.

[7] That is the view of the Supreme Court of Canada—see *Storthoaks v Mobil Oil Canada Ltd* [1976] 2 SCR 147 (SCC), 164—though the doctrinal facts of the matter are a bit more complicated than that. See M McInnes, *The Canadian Law of Unjust Enrichment and Restitution* (Markham, ON, LexisNexis Canada, 2014) 1503–14.

view, we might say that change of position protects payees from a kind of vulnerability into which receipt of the payment places them.

2. Were D to repay the full sum she had received from P, she would be worse off relative to the position she would have found herself in had she never received the payment.[8] This answer finds in the defence of change of position an instance of the general principle that restitution for unjust enrichment should never make defendants worse off. This, in turn, is sometimes represented as a kind of compensation for the strictness of liability in unjust enrichment, or in any case as respecting the innocence of the payee.

3. The enrichment is irreversible.[9] The holiday having been taken, the experience having been had, there is nothing in which the value of the enrichment can now be found. This rationale respects a kind of subsidiary principle of the law of unjust enrichment that sometimes, owing to the nature of things, enrichment cannot be undone: 'One cleans another's shoes; what can the other do but put them on?'[10]

While they express distinct ideas, these are complementary, as the fact that each picks out my example suggests. The expense of the holiday was both extraordinary and irreversible, and thus repaying its cost would make D worse off relative to the relevant status quo ante. Perhaps they come apart in some cases. But I will stick in this chapter with my example, in which the three candidate conditions line up and support one another.

3. DEFENCES IN CRIMINAL LAW

The principal conceptual distinction in the classification of defences in criminal law is that between justifications and non-justifications. In raising a justification, one claims that one had a right, or was permitted, to do as one did. The paradigmatic example is self-defence. All other defences begin (conceptually speaking) by granting that one did not have a right to do as one did. These can be sorted into two main groups: exculpatory and non-exculpatory. There is a broad but serviceable sense of 'excuse' by which all exculpatory non-justifications are excuses,[11] but here I will follow an influential current of thinking[12] and reserve 'excuse' for a subset

[8] This is how Andrew Burrows formulates the English law in *A Restatement of the English Law of Unjust Enrichment* (Oxford, Oxford University Press, 2012) 16.

[9] Elise Bant argues that this is the best way to understand Anglo-Australian law in *The Change of Position Defence* (Oxford, Hart Publishing, 2009) 126–42 and in her contribution of this volume (see ch 7).

[10] *Taylor v Laird* (1856) 25 LJ Ex 329, 332; 156 ER 1203 (Pollock CB).

[11] This is so, for example, on JL Austin's classic formulations of the justification/excuse distinction in 'A Plea for Excuses', *Philosophical Papers* (Oxford, Clarendon Press, 1961) 175–204.

[12] For which, see, for example, J Gardner, 'In Defence of Defences' and 'The Gist of Excuses' in his *Offences and Defences* (Oxford, Oxford University Press, 2007).

of this category, one of two. So there are, in my view, three kinds of non-justificatory defences: two exculpatory and one non-exculpatory. It is helpful to think of these as aligned on an ascending scale. At each step, one grants what one denies at the step below.

At the bottom are what are often called failure of proof defences. With these the accused denies that, in a sense, she committed a crime at all. Suppose A has taken from B something of B's without B's permission and exercises control over it as though it is hers. This looks like theft. But it may not be, if, for example, A was sleepwalking (and so would raise the defence of automatism) or thought that the disputed item was hers (and so would raise the defence of mistake of fact). Next on the scale are excuses, such as duress and, on some accounts, necessity, both of which grant that the defendant committed the offence in the sense that its elements have been proven. It is of course a matter of controversy what grounds excuses. One idea is that a person who, for example, commits a wrong under duress merits an excuse because she did not have a realistic choice but to do as she did.[13] Alternatively, we might think she acted freely, but that her choice was in some sense tragic, and we can understand why she chose to do as she did.[14] Though divided on the action-theoretic status of the accused's actions, we can think of these two approaches as expressing in different ways one thought, namely that while she was not entitled to have done what she did, we could not reasonably have expected the accused to have done otherwise. Both failure of proof defences and excuses, then, are exculpatory: each show that the accused, if not always quite or simply blameless, then at least cannot be said to be blameworthy in the sense requisite for conviction for a crime.

At the next and final step, the accused concedes that she is blameworthy in this sense—the elements of the offence with which she has been charged are proven or provable, and she has no excuse (or justification) for what she has done—but argues that she should nonetheless be let off the hook. She thus does not seek exculpation. The non-exculpatory defences are a conceptually heterogeneous class. Examples include the passage of limitation periods, diplomatic immunity and entrapment.

The distinction between denials and defences as I drew it above appears here at the point between failures of proof and excuses. Excuses and justifications are at the same level on this scale. Arguably they are, in turn, organised in a hierarchy, but it is a tricky question as to what the ordering is. One could argue that in offering a justification, one accepts what one denies with an excuse, namely that one stands behind what one has done; on the other

[13] George Fletcher puts the thought by suggesting that the accused's actions were morally or normatively involuntary. See GP Fletcher, *Rethinking Criminal Law* (Oxford, Oxford University Press, 2000) 802–07.

[14] See Gardner, 'Gist' (n 12). A broadly similar view is defended by Jeremy Horder in *Excusing Crime* (Oxford, Oxford University Press, 2007).

hand, one could just as easily say that one would need an excuse only if one's actions were not justified. What is clear, however, is that justifications have a certain moral priority over excuses, or at any case that one would prefer being justified to being excused.[15] It is better to be able to say that one had a right to act as one did than it would be to grant that one did not, but that one should nonetheless not be held accountable for one's actions.

That's the last bit of background. I will turn now to consider the first of the questions into which my title question disaggregates.

4. IS CHANGE OF POSITION A DENIAL OR A DEFENCE?

There are two ways to approach the question whether change of position is a denial or a defence. On both, in my view, the arguments favour reckoning it a defence.

1. We might ask, first, whether one or another element of the cause of action in unjust enrichment is, to the extent of the portion of the enrichment at issue, negated upon proof of the defendant's change of position. The cause of action in unjust enrichment comprises three steps:[16] the claimant must prove: (1) that the defendant has been enriched; (2) that this enrichment was gained at the claimant's expense;[17] and (3) that the defendant's enrichment was unjust, in the technical legal sense of entitling the claimant to its reversal. The third step is satisfied in either of two ways, reflecting a significant point of jurisdictional (and theoretical) difference. On the first (common law) approach, the claimant must show the presence of an 'unjust factor', a positive reason that the enrichment should be undone. In our example, the unjust factor is mistake: having been mistaken as to her legal obligations, the claimant is entitled to the value by which the defendant became enriched by the impugned transfer. On the second (civilian)[18] approach, the

[15] As Doug Husak argues in 'The Serial View of Criminal Law Defences' (1992) 3 *Criminal Law Forum* 369.

[16] C Mitchell, P Mitchell and S Watterson, *Goff & Jones: The Law of Unjust Enrichment*, 8th edn (London, Sweet and Maxwell, 2011) [1–09]. I take this to be the canonical formulation; it is also about as neutral as one can be as among various theoretical and jurisdictional differences. I note the most important of these as they come up.

[17] The formulation of the second step in the leading Canadian cases is narrower, requiring that the claimant show 'a corresponding deprivation' on her part. But in practice, the courts seem to be working with the more inclusive formulation (see McInnes (n 7) ch 3) and sometimes do adopt it explicitly (see, eg, *Garland v Consumers' Gas Co* [2001] 208 DLR (4th) 494 (Ontario CA) 524).

[18] And Canadian—reflecting, it seems, that Canada is a mixed jurisdiction. Though the language of the doctrine reflects the civilian approach, in practice courts sometimes interpret it along common law unjust factors lines, and for years, commentators urged the explicit adoption of the English formulation. In *Garland v Consumers' Gas Co* [2004] 1 SCR 629, the Supreme Court considered these arguments and kept the original judicial formulation according to which at this stage claimant must the 'the absence of any juristic reason' for the enrichment. See *Garland* at [38]–[47] for the Court's survey and argument.

claimant must show that the defendant lacked a legal ground or legal basis for retaining the disputed enrichment. In our example, the possible but, it turned out, illusory legal grounds were the debt, the insurance contract and the will. The payment not having been due, the defendant lacks a basis to retain the enrichment.[19]

Which of these steps could conceivably be negated by change of position? The defendant's divesting herself of some or all of the disputed enrichment could not possibly affect the amount that her gain was at the claimant's expense, so it cannot be the second step. That the defendant spent part of the disputed enrichment in good faith on an extraordinary expenditure (to cast it in terms of that version of the defence) shows neither that the claimant was not mistaken about her legal obligations, nor that in fact the debt had not been paid, or the insurance policy had not lapsed, or the will had been properly interpreted. So change of position cannot negate the third element of the cause of action in unjust enrichment. By contrast, at first glance, the idea that what change of position does is show that the defendant has been disenriched in the amount by which her position has changed post-transaction seems very plausible. But things get less clear as we turn to the details.

To begin, note that what the defendant is claiming depends on the standard we adopt to determine which among her good faith expenditures will count for the defence. For example, if what matters is that the enrichment is irreversible, then the defendant will not necessarily be disenriched by the change of position. Elise Bant argues that this is how we ought to understand, for example, *RBC Dominion Securities Inc v Dawson*.[20] There the defendant spent a mistaken payment on refurbishing some furniture. The court allowed the defence notwithstanding that it held that she had been enriched at least by the amount that her furniture had increased in value.

[19] In *The Law of Restitution*, 3rd edn (Oxford, Oxford University Press, 2011) 27, Andrew Burrows formulates the cause of action in unjust enrichment in terms of a series of four questions. The first three correspond to my three steps; the fourth asks: 'Are there any *defences?*' One might worry that if the absence of a defence is part of the cause of action in unjust enrichment, then the difference between denials and defences disappears, because every possible answer to the action is now a denial. But the worry is, I think, misplaced. Rather than erasing the category of 'defences', Burrows' formulation explicitly relies on it. This might seem a bit quick. On the conceptual issues raised by what Luís Duarte d'Almeida calls the 'incorporationist' view of defences—according to which the absence of relevant defences is an element of every private law cause of action—and more generally the question how 'defence' ought to be understood, see J Goudkamp, *Tort Law Defences* (Oxford, Hart Publishing, 2013) 1–7 and, in reply, Duarte d'Almeida, 'Defining Defences' in A Dyson, J Goudkamp and F Wilmot-Smith (eds), *Defences in Tort* (Oxford, Hart Publishing, 2015) 35–52.

[20] *RBC Dominion Securities Inc v Dawson* (1994) 111 DLR (4th) 230 (Newfoundland CA). See also Bant, *Change of Position* (n 9) 135. Bant collects several judicial statements and judgments in favour of the irreversibility standard at 130–38. See too her contribution in ch 7 of this volume.

Perhaps not too much should be made of this, however. It is a controversial claim that irreversibility bears this weight on its own.[21] But there are difficulties for the idea that change of position goes to the enrichment-to-the-defendant step of the cause of action in unjust enrichment, even if we stick with elements of the defence that are uncontroversial and with widely accepted versions of those elements about which there is controversy. I have two things in mind. The first is the requirement of good faith. The second is the requirement that the good faith expenditure have been either extraordinary or have been such as to leave the defendant in the position that full restitution would make her worse off relative to the status quo ante. I would suggest that the imposition of these conditions show that change of position does not simply correlate to the first element of the cause of action in unjust enrichment just because the latter has no parallel elements. One might reply by saying that this in itself does not show that the disenrichment does not do the normative work. But this misses the moralised nature of these elements of the defence. The requirement that the expenditure has been made in good faith and either was extraordinary or has left the defendant in the position that full restitution would make her worse off relative to the status quo ante collectively serve to protect the defendant from bearing the cost of her detrimental reliance (and *only* her detrimental reliance). In other words, they protect her from a kind of vulnerability into which the circumstances of the claimant's error placed her when set in the context of a regime of liability that in effect requires her to insure the claimant against the self-imposed costs of her (the claimant's) mistakes. This, it seems to me, is more aptly summed by saying that rather than show that she was not enriched by the extent to which she changed her position—that not really being what is at issue—what change of position does is provide her a defence notwithstanding that she was enriched.[22]

2. A second way to answer the question whether change of position is a denial or defence is to ask when the cause of action in unjust enrichment is complete. I will continue to frame this in terms of the example of

[21] See Burrows (n 19) 531–32.

[22] The parallel with failure of proof defences and criminal law might be thought to invite a counter-argument. In some contexts, notably that involving mistaken belief in consent as a defence to sexual assault, the law imposes upon the defence of mistake an objective standard, at least in a qualified way. In Canadian law, for example, one must have taken reasonable steps to ascertain consent to qualify for the defence (Canadian *Criminal Code*, s 273(2)(b)). This too, it might be said, imparts a moralised element into the defence that does not correlate to the positive requirement in the mens rea of the offence. But, in fact, this reply makes my point. It is on this very basis that subjectivists argue that objective standards have no place in the defence of mistake. In other words, the presence of the moralised standard seems to take the defence outside of the category of failure of proof and move it up into excuse. My suggestion is that for the same reason, the moralised elements of change of position have analogous conceptual consequences.

the liability mistaken payment. Is it complete at the point at which the defendant is in receipt of the disputed enrichment or only either when she has become aware of both being in its receipt and of its disputed status, or when having become so aware, she then refuses to return it?

Doctrine suggests the first answer. The claimant need not prove anything beyond the moment of receipt. On the plausible understanding of 'cause of action' as naming just that which a claimant must prove to make out her case,[23] this would seem dispositive.

But perhaps that's too quick. While there is a presumption in favour of the answer that fits doctrine most easily, namely that the cause of action is complete upon the receipt of the mistaken payment, one might argue that liability in unjust enrichment can be reconciled with relatively well-settled principles of legality only if we understand the claimant's case to rest on more than she is required to show. My suggestion, however, is that the strongest arguments against the view that the cause of action is complete upon receipt of the mistaken payment are flawed. And that, in turn, supports the idea that the cause of action is best reckoned a defence, because it follows that it is raised, conceptually speaking, after the cause of action in unjust enrichment will have been made out.

There are two different claims we might consider here. The first is that the cause of action in our example is not complete until the defendant has become aware of being in receipt of the disputed payment and of its disputed status. The second is that the cause of action is not complete until the defendant, becoming so aware, has chosen to nonetheless retain the payment. The strongest argument in favour of the first is that there is something suspicious—indeed, perhaps incoherent—in the idea that the defendant could, properly speaking, be subject to a legal duty in circumstances in which the recipient of a liability-mistaken payment might find herself.[24] She might not only be unaware of being in receipt of the payment, but it might be quite unreasonable and perhaps impossible for her to be aware of it when it occurs (think of electronic transfers across time zones). The point is even more stark when it comes to her awareness of the disputed status of the payment. Think, for example, of a variation of our example in which the defendant is the putative beneficiary of a will, the terms of which turn out to have been misinterpreted. She may well have no practical or, indeed, legal means to access information to determine this and, even if she did, it would

[23] I understand this to be consistent with the view that Lionel Smith defends in his contribution to this volume (see ch 2) that a cause of action is 'a set of facts that are individually necessary and collectively sufficient to generate a legal recourse', if we take these facts to be what the claimant must prove.

[24] See S Smith, 'A Duty to Make Restitution' (2013) 26 *Canadian Journal of Law and Jurisprudence* 157.

be unreasonable to suppose that she were under a legal obligation to do so. So it follows, as an application of the maxim 'ought implies can', that the defendant's duty to repay cannot possibly arise prior to her awareness of both the receipt of the payment and at least the possibility of its insecurity.

This is an initially compelling argument. But it rests, I believe, on a mistake. It relies on a false principle according to which subjection to a duty is conditional on the possibility of compliance with it in a way that cannot be true. It does not always follow from the fact that one is unable to discharge a duty that one is not subject to it. Insanity does not undo the duty to respect others' property, but it may provide a defence to theft. In other words, all the considerations adduced in the last paragraph could just as well go to show that the claimant merits an excuse for not immediately making restitution rather than showing she could not yet have been under a duty to do so. This of course does not show that the cause of action is complete at the moment of receipt of the payment, but it shows that this argument does not rebut the presumption that doctrine as it exists puts in favour of that view.

The strongest argument in favour of the view that the cause of action is not complete until the defendant has shown that she intends to retain the disputed enrichment is that only at that point could we find in her conduct a wrong to which her liability, otherwise surprisingly difficult to explain, could be attached. This, however, simply and straightforwardly begs the question. The defendant's refusal to make repayment is a wrong only if she is already under a duty to make it. Rather than show that the liability upon receipt (or, in any case, prior to refusal) view is wrong, this argument supposes that it is right.

Thus, change of position is a defence rather than a denial. What kind of defence is it? I will approach the question in two stages.

5. IS CHANGE OF POSITION AN EXCULPATORY OR A NON-EXCULPATORY DEFENCE?

First, let's consider whether change of position is a non-exculpatory defence. The question is difficult to settle determinatively because, as I suggested above in the criminal law context, the category of non-exculpatory defences is justificatorily heterogeneous. Diplomatic immunity, the passage of limitation periods and entrapment, for example, rest on irreducibly distinct bases. Each defence, though, exhibits the feature that it depends, in one way or another, on the defendant's showing that a condition of state's entitlement to seek her prosecution does not obtain (or no longer obtains). This basic structure is particularly vivid in cases of non-exculpatory defences in which we might say that the state has disentitled itself from seeking the conviction of the accused, for example, entrapment and officially induced error of law. It is telling of the point that these are sometimes modelled on private law doctrines whose effect is expressly to deny the claimant standing to proceed, namely unclean hands and estoppel. There is thus an important sense in which the non-exculpatory defences are, if I can put it this way, 'about' the state—to generalise, about the party bringing the legal action. Change of position, it seems to me, cannot easily be modelled this way. It seems, instead, to be 'about' the defendant.

Carrying through the analogy, we may conclude that it must be exculpatory, either a justification or an excuse. But one might object that putting it this way, in the language of 'exculpation', shows that something has gone wrong. In the main, and especially clearly in the example with which we are working, defendants to claims in unjust enrichment are utterly faultless. Indeed, not only need the recipient of the liability-mistaken payment not have done anything wrong, she need not have done anything at all. So though she may need a defence, the defendant is, one would say, in no need of *exculpation*. Having done nothing, she has nothing to justify or excuse.

This is a serious objection.[25] But it can, I think, be answered. The answer consists in summing the weight of two considerations. The first is that, notwithstanding the defendant's innocence, the claimant's claim for restitution is nonetheless a claim in justice. In other words, it is a claim to something owed her as of right rather than, say, a claim to the defendant's discretionary aid or charity. So while not as morally robust—not nearly, granted—as in the context in which one must be able to raise a justification or an excuse or be convicted of a crime, the defendant to an action in unjust enrichment must account for something. And here is the second point: while in the paradigmatic cases of the liability-mistaken payment, the defendant need not have done anything for liability to arise, in the paradigmatic cases of change of position[26] she will have done something. She will have spent some of the enrichment in a way that, owing to the operation of the principle that restitution cannot leave the defendant worse off, will leave the claimant worse off even after his claim is settled. Her doing was not a wrong. But it was a doing and was inconsistent with a claim in justice. That's enough, I would suggest, to say that the moralised language of justification and excuse is not out of place.

6. IS CHANGE OF POSITION A JUSTIFICATION OR AN EXCUSE?

It is consistent with the conclusion of the last section to accept that the defendant in my running examples may well be said to have behaved reasonably in taking the security of the disputed enrichment at face value. When

[25] For which I thank Robert Stevens.
[26] I will consider an important exception to this in the section following the next.

that is conjoined with the fact that, after all, the defendant does have legal title to the asset in which the disputed enrichment consists, we seem led to view that D was perfectly well justified in spending the £1,000 on a holiday she would otherwise not have felt herself in a position to take. And so, on this line of reasoning, change of position is a justification.

But wait. Note that the same sort of things may be said on behalf of someone who raises a defence of duress. Imagine you are stopped at a red light and a bank robber jumps into your car and, pointing a gun at your head, orders you to drive. We may well say that it was perfectly reasonable of you to decide to comply. (Indeed, we wouldn't have to add much detail to conclude that it might, in a sense, have been wrong of you not to; suppose, for example, that many people depend on you.) It does not follow from this that you had a right to abet the crime. The structure of the defence bars that inference. The point is more easily made if the victim of the wrong is a particular person rather than, diffusely, society as a whole. However understandable, in the circumstances, B's decision to comply with A's order to harm C on pain of being harmed herself might seem, that the fact that A threatens B with harm unless she harms C does not (cannot!) make it permissible for B to harm C. (Consider: C would surely be acting within her rights to defend herself, whereas my attacker assaults me when he defends himself against my self-defending actions.)

This does not yet show that change of position is not a justification; it just shows that neither the reasonableness of the defendant's actions nor the fact that she holds legal title to the asset in which the disputed enrichment consists, nor even the conjunction of the two, supports the view that it is a justification. What, in my view, weighs decisively against classifying change of position as a justification is that doing so would run afoul of what has come to be known as the *Dadson* principle.[27] I will make the case for that claim and then show that it falls out of the best argument in support of the *Dadson* principle that the same conclusion about the classification of change of position follows even if we reject that principle.

George Dadson was a police constable. He was hired to guard a copse. He shot William Waters as he was making off with some wood. Waters had been twice before convicted of the same offence. This meant he was committing a felony rather than a misdemeanor. But Dadson didn't know this. It mattered because under English law at the time, it was lawful to use the force he did against an escaping felon, but not against someone fleeing having been caught committing a misdemeanor. The court held that: 'The prisoner was not justified in firing at Waters, because the fact that Waters was committing a felony was not known to the prisoner at the time.'[28] *Dadson* thus stands

[27] *R v George Dadson* (1850) 2 Den 35; 169 ER 407.
[28] ibid.

for the proposition that one must be aware of the features of the circumstances in which one acted that justify one's actions to avail oneself of that justification.

Consider now the defendant raising change of position. There is no feature or set of features of the circumstances in which she spent some of the disputed enrichment, awareness of which could be said to confer a right to act as she did. What could those be? The only candidate, it seems, is that she enjoyed legal title to the disputed asset. But that, of course, is consistent with the claimant having a right to restitution for its value.[29] Thus, change of position cannot be squared with the *Dadson* principle and so if that principle is sound, change of position cannot be a justification.

This is a significant qualification: the *Dadson* principle is controversial.[30] What weighs decisively in its favour, on my view, is that it gives doctrinal expression to a view about justification on which the idea that justifications occupy an irreducible space in the taxonomy of defences rests. Let's return to the court's opinion in *Dadson*. While almost certainly Pollock CB et al did not have a framework like the one I sketched above in mind, I think it is reasonable to put some interpretive weight on the language with which they chose to answer the question put to them, which was whether Dadson's conviction 'was right'. They found that it was because, as I quoted just above, he 'was not *justified* in firing at Waters' (emphasis added). Because he did not know that Waters was committing a felony, they continued: 'He was therefore liable to be convicted, though the amount of punishment might deserve great consideration.'[31] I will take this all at face value. What the court found was that Dadson was not justified, and from that concluded that he does not merit acquittal, on the implicit premise that only if he were justified could he be acquitted. But that is not the end of the story: the amount of punishment, they added, might deserve *great* consideration. What is the untold part of the story?

The court does not say. But here's a thought we might supply on its behalf: if Dadson was in fact shooting at a felon, what wrong did he commit? We might think he merited a straight acquittal, for the simple reason that, at least on one construction, he did not perform the actus reus of any offence. It was lawful for a police officer to fire at an escaping felon. That is was Dadson did—no more and no less.

[29] This points to a second consideration that weighs against reckoning change of a position to be a justification: it is difficult to see how one could make a case for it without at the same time making it difficult to understand how a claimant could have a right to restitution for *any* of the disputed enrichment.

[30] There is a large literature, well surveyed by Russell L Christopher in the first section of 'Unknowing Justification and the Logical Necessity of the *Dadson* Principle in Self-Defence' (1995) 15 *OJLS* 229, 230.

[31] *Dadson* (n 27).

Well, *something* less, the reply might go. He was just lucky and innocence requires more. That is the thought underlying the court's view that Dadson's right to an acquittal rested on his showing that he was justified. This expresses in legal doctrine the moral idea that there is a distinction between actions that are permitted *simpliciter* and those calling for and enjoying justification. On this view, justified actions occupy a different deontic space from actions against which there is no prohibition to begin with. One needs to justify assaulting another in a way that one need not justify simply walking down the street;[32] there is, as George Fletcher puts it, 'an important moral difference between events that are innocuous and harm inflicted for good reasons'.[33]

Against this is the view that 'justification' really just names a step in sorting actions into permissible (*simpliciter*) and forbidden. While technically an offence, in the sense that one who commits it has performed the actus reus of an criminal offence with the requisite mens rea, on this view an assault in self-defence, for example, occupies the same space in the deontic catalogue as an action that at no level of description corresponds to the definition of an offence. On this view, in short, justifications show that what one did was permissible, full stop.

For what it's worth, I think this view is wrong about justifications. But I do not need to invest my argument in that here. All I need you to accept is that if this view were right, then 'justification' would no longer name a distinct category of defence. That is because on this view, justifications resolve to failures of proof or, to put the point in non-legal terms, to simple denials of wrongdoing morally on a par with actions performed under non-culpable mistakes of fact.

So *if* there is a distinct question asked in asking whether a defence is a justification, that can only be in the sense that I claim is implicit in the court in *Dadson* finding that he was unjustified. He required a justification because shooting someone is the sort of thing that calls for an accounting. More precisely, it calls for the defendant to provide an accounting. It asks her for a reason, under which she acted, that discloses a licence to do what she did. This is something that D in our examples cannot provide. In raising the defence of change of position, she claims to have spent the portion of the impugned enrichment at issue in good faith, believing it was hers to spend. But that belief was mistaken, and so her having acted under it generates no licence to have done so. If, on the other hand, there isn't a distinct question asked in asking whether a defence is a justification—if justifications resolve

[32] Or, as Fletcher puts it in 'The Right Deed for the Wrong Reason: A Reply to Mr Robinson' (1975) 23 *UCLA Law Review* 293, 310: 'It is the difference between punching a ball and punching someone in the face.'

[33] ibid 318.

to failures of proof—then in asking whether change of position is justification, we are really asking whether it is a denial. And I take myself to have shown above that it is not.

Thus, change of position is not a justification. Nor is it a non-exculpatory defence or, again, a denial. Therefore, it is an excuse. So, I think, we are compelled to find, by elimination. But a bit more can be said on behalf of this conclusion. D's situation in my examples conforms to what I suggested above is the basic idea variously expressed in different accounts of excuses: while she was not entitled to have done what she did, we could not reasonably have expected her to have done otherwise.

7. AN IMPORTANT COUNTER-EXAMPLE[34]

My argument—particularly the brief against classifying change of position as a denial—has rested on it being a common ground among different reconstructions of the elements of the defence that it requires that the defendant has acted in the bone fide belief that she was entitled to the impugned enrichment. This defence, I suggested, protects the defendant against the cost of her detrimental reliance on the false but reasonable belief that the benefit she received was unburdened by the claimant's claim to it. There are, however, cases that many commentators collect under 'change of position' that do not bear this feature.[35] The category of non-reliance cases divides, I suggest, into two, exemplified by the following two cases.

1. *Waitaki*. D receives a payment from a bank knowing that it was conferred by mistake. He informs the bank, but it insists that he is entitled to the money. D invests the money without security in a company that becomes insolvent.[36]
2. *Theft*. P gives a £20 note to D seeking to discharge a debt that he (P) had forgotten had already been repaid. D puts the note in his otherwise empty wallet, which is stolen later that day.

In neither case does the defendant rely on the belief that he is entitled to the impugned enrichment. Does she raise the same kind of defence as the defendant in the examples that have carried my analysis so far?

I think the answer is different in the two kinds of non-reliance cases exemplified by *Waitaki* and *Theft*. We can think of the payee in cases like *Waitaki* as, in effect, an involuntary bailee, with the corresponding (accordingly

[34] I am especially indebted to Mitchell McInnes, Lionel Smith and Fred Wilmot-Smith for discussion of the issues raised in this section.

[35] See, for example, *Goff & Jones* (n 16) [27.27]–[27.28]; Burrows (n 19) 528–30; McInnes (n 7) 1512–14; and Bant, *Change of Position* (n 9).

[36] *National Bank of New Zealand Ltd v Waitaki International Processing (NI) Ltd* [1999] 2 NZLR 211 (CA).

modest) duties to the payor. Her defence, then, rests on her claiming that in seeking to protect the payor's interests as she did—for example, by informing the payor of the mistake and investing the money in a way that did not entangle it with the rest of her assets, as did the defendant in *Waitaki*—the defendant did no less than we could reasonably ask of her. Here, then, change of position is moralised in a way parallel to the paradigmatic reliance cases and shares with those cases the characteristics that I argued mark out the defence as an excuse.

Theft, however, resists this assimilation. In that case the defendant does nothing, and so has nothing to justify or excuse. We might conclude, then, that in such a case, change of position operates as a denial, defeating in part the claimant's claim at the first step of the cause of action. But that is arguably not quite right. It depends on how we understand the defence in cases such as *Theft*. The issue is how it should be structured to respect the fact that, as Birks put it: 'An unrelated supervening disaster is not a relevant change of position.'[37] On what basis do we determine whether the supervening disaster is related in the relevant way?

There is no answer currently in law. Some courts have recognised non-reliance cases—though on this point there are jurisdictional differences[38]—but there are, so far as I know, no reported decisions that turn on the theft of the disputed enrichment. Two views can be found in academic commentary. On the first,[39] more inclusive, approach, the question whether the loss constitutes an appropriately related supervening disaster is settled by asking whether the defendant would have suffered the loss had she not been enriched: if so, then she has no defence. The second[40] adds the requirement that what has been stolen must be either, in our example, the particular £20 note or a substitute assent into which that value of the note

[37] P Birks, 'Change of Position: The Nature of the Defence and its Relationship to Other Restitutionary Defences' in M McInnes (ed), *Restitution: Developments in Unjust Enrichment* (North Ryde, LBC Information Services, 1996) 61; see too McInnes (n 7) 1513.

[38] *Waitaki* is a New Zealand case; in England, the Court of Appeal endorsed the inclusive view of change of position in *Scottish Equitable v Derby* [2001] EWCA Civ 369; [2001] 3 All ER 818, though the case did not turn on it. For a survey of more recent developments in England and the current state of law in Australia, see Bant, ch 7 in this volume. In Canada, the last and highest judicial pronouncement on the issue seems to say that reliance is a necessary element of change of position (*Storthoaks* (n 7) 164). Looking beyond the Commonwealth, the matter is similarly unsettled. The formulation of change of position in the American *Restatement Third: Restitution and Unjust Enrichment* (St Paul, MN, American Law Institute Publishers, 2011) § 65 requires that the receipt of the disputed benefit 'has led a recipient without notice to change position' and so would not include *Theft*. On the other hand, German law would: see BGB, § 818(3).

[39] Implicit, I believe, in Bant's treatment of non-reliance cases in her contribution to this volume and in Burrows' treatment of the same in *Restitution* (n 19) 528–31.

[40] Suggested by Lionel Smith in *The Law of Tracing* (Oxford, Oxford University Press, 1999) 34–37.

can be traced; otherwise the defendant is liable. D has a defence in *Theft* on either approach, but in some cases they come apart.[41]

Either way, in cases like *Theft* the defendant does not raise an excuse. If, as we might reasonably enough hold, two claims that occupy different places in the taxonomy of defences cannot properly speaking be the same defence,[42] I think the conclusion to draw is that 'change of position' collects two defences.[43] There is possibly a second, even more surprising conclusion. On the first approach to the theft cases, change of position is reasonably reckoned a denial, but not so clearly on the second. On that account, the defendant's claim, strictly speaking, is not merely that she has been disenriched. It is rather than she has been dispossessed—that either the particular £20 note, the material bearer or embodiment of the impugned enrichment, or a substitute asset into which its value can be traced, has been taken from her. This is akin to but not quite a denial. We might call it a 'defeat': a claim that undercuts a cause of action without precisely denying any of its elements. Whether cases like *Thief* are *sui generis* in this way and whether 'defeats' mark out a third division of defences in the broad sense of 'defence' deployed in my title[44] are questions I will leave for another occasion.

[41] Suppose that, having received the £20, D puts it in his front pocket and heads to an ATM to deposit it, going down a street he would not otherwise have found himself on. The wallet, which is empty but for a different £20 note, is taken from his back pocket by the pickpocket. If all we ask is whether D would have suffered the loss had he not be enriched, he has the defence available to him. If we impose the further identity condition, as we may call it, he would be liable. I owe this example to Lionel Smith.

[42] A principle that, when one bears in mind that what the taxonomy of defences sorts is justifications for relieving defendants of liability, is complementary to the one advanced by Lionel Smith in his contribution to this volume (see ch 2) that a cause of action can be counted in terms of 'juridically distinct justifications for legal recourses'.

[43] This is at odds with Bant's argument in her contribution to this volume (see ch 7) that there is a simple common ground shared by reliance and non-reliance cases. For both, on her account, what matters is the causal connection between the enrichment and the expenditure. That is the role played by reliance in reliance cases; in non-reliance cases, receipt does the work. This is an intriguing argument, but I am unconvinced. I am unconvinced because it is not clear why receipt wouldn't do the causal work in reliance cases as well, and this suggests that reliance plays a different and independent role—one that bears taxonomically significant moral weight. So, in any case, I have reckoned it in my argument against the classification of change of position as a denial.

[44] Occupied, perhaps, by frustration of contract.

5

The Unity of Pre-receipt and Post-receipt Detriment

AJAY RATAN*

1. INTRODUCTION

1.1. The Underlying Issue: Baseline Selection

Consider the following stripped-down extract from the *Restatement of the English Law of Unjust Enrichment*:[1]

> 23 *Change of position*
>
> (1) The defendant has a defence to the extent that—
> (a) the defendant's position has changed as a consequence of [X], and
> (b) the change is such that the defendant would be worse off by making restitution than if [X had not occurred].

As this skeletal statement makes clear, a counterfactual comparison is embedded at the core of the change of position doctrine.[2] We are directed to compare: (1) how the defendant fares in the real world if she is ordered to

* I would like to thank Charles Mitchell, Graham Virgo and Fred Wilmot-Smith for their helpful comments on earlier drafts. All errors remain my own.

[1] AS Burrows, *Restatement of the English Law of Unjust Enrichment* (Oxford, Oxford University Press, 2012) 117. In order to isolate the issue of baseline selection for scrutiny, I omit the qualifications in para 23(2).

[2] For an alternative view based on a historical baseline, see E Bant, *The Change of Position Defence* (Oxford, Hart Publishing, 2009) 217. The historical and counterfactual views each have their attractions and problem cases: contrast S Perry, 'Harm, History, and Counterfactuals' (2003) 40 *San Diego Law Review* 1283 and V Tadros, 'What Might Have Been' in J Oberdiek (ed), *Philosophical Foundations of the Law of Torts* (Oxford, Oxford University Press, 2014). Two short points in favour of the counterfactual view are as follows. First, the fundamental compensatory principle in the law of tort and contract is based on a counterfactual baseline: see *Livingstone v The Rawyards Coal Company* (1879–80) LR 5 App Cas 25 (HL) 39 and *Robinson v Harman* (1848) 1 Ex 850, 855–56; 154 ER 363, 365. It would be anomalous if unjust enrichment stood alone in the law of obligations by eschewing counterfactual reasoning. Second, a historical baseline is not easily able to catch lost opportunities as a form of detriment. By its nature, an opportunity identifies a benefit which the defendant did not possess prior to the relevant transaction, but *might have* obtained in future.

make restitution; and (2) how she fares in some counterfactual comparator world. The comparator world serves as a baseline against which we assess whether ordering the defendant to make restitution leaves her 'worse off'. This chapter addresses a simple question: what is the appropriate baseline against which to assess whether an order to make restitution would leave the defendant worse off?[3]

A number of leading scholars consider that the appropriate baseline is set with reference to the point of receipt. Thus, a typical formulation is that the change of position defence operates to ensure that restitution does not leave the defendant worse off than she would have been *if she had not received the relevant enrichment*.[4] The appropriateness of this baseline tends to be assumed without argument.[5] This is curious. If it is important that the defendant is not left worse off as against *some* baseline, surely it is also important to explain *which* baseline is relevant and why this is so.

1.2. Why Do Baselines Matter?

The specification of the baseline for assessment of whether restitution leaves the defendant 'worse off' is not a trivial issue. The doctrine of anticipatory change of position is apt to illustrate why this is so. So long as the baseline for assessment is set at the point of receipt, bringing detriment suffered prior to receipt into account within the change of position analysis is bound to seem anomalous. This observation has led some close to rejecting the defence of anticipatory change of position altogether.[6] Others, seeking to reconcile the doctrine of the anticipatory change of position with a baseline set at the point of receipt, slip in a further and distinct principle to account for pre-receipt detriment.[7] The effect of bolting on an additional principle in this way is to bifurcate the change of position defence on two levels. First, on a doctrinal level, the relevance of pre-receipt and post-receipt detriment is ascertained with reference to two different legal tests. Second, on a moral level, the reasons that justify bringing detriment into account to defeat the claimant's prima facie right restitution appear to differ depending on whether the detriment is suffered before or after receipt.[8]

[3] Methodologically, the inquiry is not into which baseline fits best with the case law; rather, the question addressed is which baseline figures in the morally soundest account of the change of position defence.

[4] In this vein see, eg, GJ Virgo, 'Causation and Remoteness within the Law of Unjust Enrichment' in S Degeling and J Edelman (eds), *Unjust Enrichment in Commercial Law* (Sydney, Thomson Reuters Australia, 2008) 164; AS Burrows, *The Law of Restitution*, 3rd edn (Oxford, Oxford University Press, 2011) 528–31.

[5] The assumption has been acknowledged: see Burrows (n 4) 533.

[6] *South Tyneside Metropolitan Borough Council v Svenska International plc* [1995] 1 All ER 545 (QBD) 566.

[7] For examples, see nn 1 and 4 above.

[8] See text to nn 33–37 below.

This chapter proposes a different baseline for the change of position analysis. In essence, on this alternative view, the defendant must not be worse off by making restitution than if the claimant's decision making had not been defective. As we shall see, this alteration allows a single legal test, underpinned by a unified principled rationale, to catch both pre-receipt and post-receipt detriment. If this alternative baseline is adopted, the distinction between pre-receipt and post-receipt detriment bears neither doctrinal nor moral salience for the purposes of the change of position defence. In short, therefore, the baseline advocated in the following pages reveals the unity of pre-receipt and post-receipt detriment.

1.3. Structure of Analysis

The argument proceeds in three stages. First, the competing baselines are defined and their areas of overlap and distinctive coverage identified. The two prevalent baselines in orthodox thinking are labelled the 'no receipt' and 'no anticipatory reliance' counterfactuals. These orthodox baselines are contrasted with their unified challenger, the 'no defect' counterfactual. Second, a number of objections to the orthodox baselines are identified. The 'no receipt' counterfactual is problematic because: (1) it conjures up a miraculous counterfactual world which gratuitously departs from this world's laws of physics; and (2) it fails to vindicate the conviction that it is arbitrary to distinguish between certain instances of pre-receipt and post-receipt detriment. The 'no anticipatory reliance' counterfactual, for its part, is a false competitor in the baseline contest. If the 'no anticipatory reliance' counterfactual has any proper role to play in the law of unjust enrichment, it is as part of the defence of estoppel and not the defence of change of position. Third, a positive case is mounted in favour of the 'no defect' counterfactual. In essence, the claimant should not be allowed to cherry-pick among the consequences of the defect in her decision making by setting up her primary claim based on one of its consequences (viz the defendant's enrichment) and then denying the legal relevance of its other consequences (viz the defendant's detriment) to the change of position defence.

2. CONTESTANT BASELINES

2.1. The 'No Receipt' Counterfactual

According to this familiar baseline, the basic principle is that an order to make restitution must not leave the defendant worse off as a result of her receipt of the relevant enrichment.[9] To apply this principle, a simple

[9] See n 4 above.

counterfactual comparison is required. Let us say that the 'no receipt' counterfactual is the hypothetical world in which the defendant did not receive the relevant enrichment. The orthodox principle asks us to ascertain how the defendant would fare in the 'no receipt' counterfactual and then to ensure she is no worse off than this in the real world after she is required to make restitution.

This principle based on the 'no receipt' counterfactual is on its face unable to catch pre-receipt detriment.[10] Admittedly, it has been suggested that where the defendant incurs detriment in reliance on an expectation that she will receive an enrichment, and she later receives the expected enrichment, she has 'relied' on the receipt which has therefore 'caused' her detriment.[11] This is a deeply misleading use of language. In such a case, the defendant has not relied on the receipt, but rather on the prior acts or events which gave rise to her expectation of receipt.[12] So too, it is these prior acts or events, and not the subsequent receipt of the enrichment, that truly cause the defendant's detriment.[13] Once we reject the spurious assimilation of pre-receipt detriment and post-receipt detriment on the basis that both involve 'reliance on receipt', the need arises to articulate clearly which pre-receipt detriment (if any) is relevant to the change of position defence and why this is so. In this way, the adoption of the 'no receipt' counterfactual as the baseline for the change of position analysis necessitates a further and distinct principle to account for pre-receipt detriment if such detriment is to be relevant to the change of position defence at all.

2.2. The 'No Anticipatory Reliance' Counterfactual

The most influential principle that has been suggested to stand alongside the 'no receipt' counterfactual in order to account for the doctrine of anticipatory change of position is as follows: the defendant must not be 'worse off by making restitution than if the defendant had not … relied in anticipation on obtaining … the benefit'.[14] Let us say that the 'no anticipatory reliance' counterfactual is the hypothetical world in which the defendant did not rely in anticipation on receiving the enrichment which she later received. According to this additional principle, we must ascertain how the defendant

[10] R Nolan, 'Change of Position' in P Birks (ed), *Laundering and Tracing* (Oxford, Clarendon Press, 1995) 163; Bant (n 2) 156; J Edelman, 'Change of Position: A Defence of Unjust Disenrichment' (2012) 92 *Boston University Law Review* 1009, 1015–16; C Webb and T Akkouh, 'Mistake, Misprediction and Change of Position' (2002) 10 *Restitution Law Review* 107, 111.

[11] P Birks, *Unjust Enrichment,* 2nd edn (Oxford, Oxford University Press, 2005) 39: 'Effect can precede cause when the medium is reliance.'

[12] Bant (n 2) 156.

[13] ibid.

[14] Burrows (n 1) 117; Virgo (n 4) 166.

would fare in the 'no anticipatory reliance' counterfactual and ensure that she is no worse off than this in the real world after liability in unjust enrichment is imposed.

For the reasons set out in section 3.2 below, there is good reason to consider that the 'no anticipatory reliance' counterfactual is not properly part of the change of position defence at all. Rather, if this counterfactual has any role to play in the law of unjust enrichment, it is within the defence of estoppel. However, the 'no anticipatory reliance' counterfactual has typically been housed in the change of position section of the leading texts on the law of unjust enrichment. Consequently, at this introductory stage, it merits inclusion on the menu of change of position baselines.

2.3. The 'No Defect' Counterfactual

The unified challenger to the 'no receipt' and 'no anticipatory reliance' counterfactuals adopts a different basic principle: an order to make restitution must not leave the defendant worse off as a result of the relevant defect in the claimant's decision making.[15] The 'relevant defect' is the one on which the claimant grounds her unjust enrichment claim. For example, in a case of mistaken payment, the relevant defect is the mistaken belief of the claimant that causes her to make the payment. Let us say that the 'no defect' counterfactual is the hypothetical world in which the relevant defect in the claimant's decision making does not exist. If this counterfactual baseline is adopted, the change of position defence requires us to ascertain how the defendant would have fared in the 'no defect' counterfactual and ensure that she is no worse off than this in the real world after she is required to make restitution. Thus, in a case of mistaken payment, the 'no defect' counterfactual asks 'How would the defendant have fared if the claimant had not been mistaken?', whereas the 'no receipt' counterfactual asks: 'How would the defendant have fared if she had not received the enrichment?'

The 'no defect' counterfactual is deliberately limited in its scope to the well-known family of unjust factors based on the defective decision making of the claimant.[16] Where the operative unjust factor has a different rationale, it cannot be assumed that the change of position defence will be based on the same counterfactual, if indeed the defence is applicable at all. The present task is to identify the appropriate baseline for the change of position defence as it applies to unjust factors grounded on defective decision

[15] For a short but powerful prior statement of this position, see Webb and Akkouh (n 10) 110–11.

[16] See, eg, P Birks, *An Introduction to the Law of Restitution*, revised edn (Oxford, Clarendon Press, 1989) 100–01.

making. We must leave to another occasion the distinct and logically subsequent investigation into whether this baseline can and should properly be transposed to cases in which other reasons for restitution operate.

It might seem at first glance that the difference between the 'no receipt' counterfactual and the 'no defect' counterfactual is innocuous and perhaps even trivial. What is the impact of rejecting the former and adopting the latter as the basis for the change of position defence? There are two points to make. First, the 'no defect' counterfactual catches certain pre-receipt detriment, whereas the 'no receipt' counterfactual does not. Second, the two counterfactuals produce exactly the same results in relation to post-receipt detriment (subject to two minor wrinkles). Each point is considered in turn. The broad upshot is that the 'no defect' counterfactual does everything that the 'no receipt' counterfactual is able to do (viz account for post-receipt detriment) and more besides (viz account for pre-receipt detriment).

2.3.1. *Distinctive Coverage of the 'No Defect' Counterfactual: Pre-receipt Detriment*

In order to see how the 'no defect' counterfactual is able to catch certain pre-receipt detriment, the crucial point to appreciate is that a defect in the claimant's decision making may persist over a period of time. Consequently, the very same defect in the claimant's decision making may cause the claimant to perform a number of actions, *some of which may precede the transfer of the enrichment*. Consider a case in which Alice is labouring under a mistaken belief that causes her first to tell Brian that she will pay him £100 and later to actually pay him £100. The very same mistaken belief causes Alice first to tell Brian of the payment and later to actually make the payment. This creates the possibility that the defect in the claimant's decision making will cause detriment to the defendant *even before the defective transfer is made*. For example, if Brian detrimentally relies on what he is told by Alice, Brian's detriment is caused by Alice's mistaken belief: Alice's mistaken belief causes her to tell Brian about the payment, and what Alice tells Brian causes him to suffer detriment.

As this example illustrates, the 'no defect' and 'no receipt' counterfactuals come apart in relation to pre-receipt detriment because detriment may be caused by the relevant defect in the claimant's decision making even prior to receipt. Of course, the fact that the 'no defect' counterfactual generates *an* account of anticipatory change of position is one thing; whether this is a *sound* account is quite another. The task of justifying the account of the change of position defence generated by the 'no defect' counterfactual is taken up in section 4 below. For now, the important point is simply to note that the 'no receipt' and 'no defect' counterfactuals do indeed come apart in relation to certain instances of pre-receipt detriment.

2.3.2. *A Substantial Area of Overlap: Detriment Caused by Receipt*

The 'no defect' counterfactual does not require us to reject the well-settled understanding that detriment caused by receipt is relevant to the change of position defence. This is because 'detriment caused by receipt' is essentially a subset of 'detriment caused by the defect in the claimant's decision making'. To elaborate, if: (1) the defect in the claimant's decision making is a 'but for' cause of the defendant's receipt, and (2) the defendant's receipt is a 'but for' cause of certain detriment, then it follows that (3) the defect in the claimant's decision making is also a 'but for' cause of that detriment. Where an unbroken chain of 'but for' links runs from defect through receipt to detriment, the 'no defect' and 'no receipt' counterfactuals are not truly in competition: both counterfactual inquiries produce the same results because they simply direct us to start at different points in the same causal chain. To put the point more intuitively, in every case in which the defect in the claimant's decision making is a 'but for' cause of the defendant's receipt, the 'no defect' counterfactual *includes* the 'no receipt' counterfactual.

Consequently, so long as the defect in the claimant's decision making is a 'but for' cause of the defendant's receipt, the 'no defect' counterfactual does not challenge the significance of the inquiry into whether detriment is caused by receipt. Rather, the 'no defect' counterfactual vindicates that inquiry by showing it to be of vital, albeit derivative, significance. As we shall see in section 4 below, the *complete* picture is that detriment is relevant to the change of position defence whenever it is caused by the defect in the claimant's decision making. But detriment caused by receipt is essentially a subset of detriment caused by the defect in the claimant's decision making and consequently the relevance of detriment caused by receipt is common ground.

The caveat in the preceding analysis creates two small wrinkles. There are two instances in which prima facie unjust enrichment liability may arise even in the absence of a 'but for' causal link between the defect in the claimant's decision making and the defendant's enrichment. In those two instances, the 'no defect' and 'no receipt' counterfactuals may come apart even in relation to post-receipt detriment. There is, however, good reason to bracket those two instances for discussion on another occasion. First, a less stringent 'a reason' test of causation applies, inter alia, in cases of fraudulent misrepresentation and physical duress.[17] But the very reasons that justify the adoption of the 'a reason' test of causation as part of the 'unjustness' inquiry' may also justify a different approach to the change of position defence (or even the disapplication of the defence entirely).[18]

[17] The range of claims to which this test is and ought to be applicable is not entirely settled: see, eg, E Bant 'Causation and Scope of Liability in Unjust Enrichment' [2009] *Restitution Law Review* 60; Virgo (n 4) 154–66; Burrows (n 4).

[18] *cf* Bant (n 2) 177–84 (discussing innocent inducers).

Consequently, it is best to leave until a later occasion the inquiry into which, if any, of the change of position baselines mooted in this chapter is appropriately transposed to cases such as those of fraudulent misrepresentation and physical duress.

Second, if the law of unjust enrichment provides the proper doctrinal foundation for the decision in *Foskett v McKeown*,[19] this is an example of unjust enrichment liability that arises on the basis of transactional links alone despite the absence of any relevant 'but for' causal link. The controversy surrounding almost every aspect of the decision in *Foskett*—including whether the change of position defence ought to be available in respect of claims to unauthorised substitutes—is well known. Consequently, the appropriate course is again to postpone the investigation into which, if any, of the change of position baselines discussed in this chapter is applicable in cases of 'purely transactional' liability.[20]

Wrinkles aside, the basic point remains: the 'no defect' and 'no receipt' counterfactuals produce the same conclusions in relation to post-receipt detriment. This helps us to pin down what is at issue in the contest between the orthodox baselines and their unified challenger: both generate the same treatment of post-receipt detriment, but the 'no defect' counterfactual also encompasses certain pre-receipt detriment without the need to bolt on any further principle. With these similarities and differences between the two accounts in mind, we are now in a position to scrutinise the orthodox baselines before putting the case for the 'no defect' counterfactual.

3. OBJECTIONS TO THE ORTHODOX BASELINES

3.1. 'No Receipt' Counterfactual

3.1.1. Miracles

Let us pause to consider a familiar puzzle about counterfactuals. The counterfactual baselines that we are considering direct us to the hypothetical world in which some X did not occur. But there are many possible worlds in which any given X does not occur. To use the 'no defect' counterfactual as an example to begin with, there are a great many hypothetical worlds in which the claimant's decision making is free from the relevant defect. If the claimant had been hit by an asteroid the instant before she formed

[19] *Foskett v McKeown* [2001] 1 AC 102 (HL).

[20] The label 'purely transactional' is borrowed from B McFarlane, 'Rights and Value; Means and Ends' in C Mitchell and W Swadling (eds), *The Restatement Third: Restitution and Unjust Enrichment* (Oxford, Hart Publishing, 2013) 19 (though McFarlane uses the label to refer to the distinctive character of tracing, whereas the text uses it to describe liability that arises on the basis of transactional links even in the absence of any relevant causal link).

her mistaken belief, her decision making would not have been defective: she would have been thoroughly flattened and so there would be no possibility of her decision making being defective. But clearly such extravagant hypothetical worlds are not what 'but for' counterfactual statements are meant to capture. Rather, we seek to hold constant as much of the real world as possible and alter only as much as is necessary in order to ensure that the 'specified factor' (in our example, the defect in the claimant's decision making) is removed.[21] Thus, the relevant 'no defect' counterfactual is the hypothetical world that perfectly resembles the real world, subject to one change: where the claimant formed a mistaken belief, we imagine that she formed a true belief instead.[22] In this way the defect in the claimant's decision making is 'completely and cleanly excised from history'.[23]

The 'no receipt' counterfactual is problematic in this regard. What does the hypothetical world look like in which we hold the real world constant, except that we excise the receipt from the world's history? Consider a simple case where I take a £50 note from my pocket and hand it to you by mistake. Visualise, frame by frame, a counterfactual world which tracks those events perfectly right up until the moment of receipt. Then try to imagine the receipt not occurring. What does that counterfactual world look like? It seems to be a world in which I take the £50 note out of my pocket, extend my hand out towards you with the note in it, but then, at the instant when you close your hand to grasp the note, it evaporates into thin air. That hypothetical world involves a spooky and miraculous departure from the laws of physics. The difficulty stems from the fact that receipt is by its nature an instantaneous event at the culmination of a transfer. To construct a hypothetical world in which every stage of the transfer occurs apart from the receipt inevitably requires a stark departure from the laws of physics; otherwise the prior stages of the transfer would naturally roll on through to receipt. It is doubtful whether this miraculous world is what proponents of the 'no receipt' counterfactual have in mind. The simple problem with such a stark miracle is that it violates our common-sense understanding of how counterfactuals

[21] J Stapleton, 'Causation in the Law' in H Beebee, C Hitchcock and P Menzies (eds), *The Oxford Handbook of Causation* (Oxford, Oxford University Press, 2009) 747: 'the law is often interested to identify … the hypothetical world notionally constructed by simply removing the specified factor from the actual world'.

[22] Questions may arise as to the precise belief which is to be substituted for the claimant's mistaken belief. For example, we might substitute the mistake for ignorance rather than a true belief. The key to answering these questions is that the 'no defect' counterfactual is already embedded in the primary elements of the claim, as part of the 'unjustness' inquiry: see text to n 57 below. Whichever substitute belief is used for the purpose of the 'unjustness' inquiry will serve equally for the purposes of the change of position analysis.

[23] D Lewis, 'Causation as Influence' in J Collins, N Hall and LA Paul (eds), *Causation and Counterfactuals* (Cambridge, MA, MIT Press, 2004) 90. While Lewis ultimately did not adopt a view based on simple excision, his phrase appears to accurately sum up the typical starting point in many legal causal counterfactual inquiries: see, eg, Stapleton (n 21) 747.

work.[24] Counterfactual reasoning is embedded in many aspects of everyday thinking and the counterfactuals entertained by ordinary people are not of the miraculous variety. Rather, the counterfactuals conjured up by ordinary people are informed by, and consistent with, their 'intuitive understanding of physics'.[25]

What, if not this starkly miraculous world, do proponents of the 'no receipt' counterfactual have in mind? To remove the stark miracle, the 'no receipt' counterfactual needs to be smoothed out. The 'no receipt' counterfactual must be imagined to diverge from the real world *at some point prior to receipt* so as to allow for a more plausible transition from the real world to the imagined state in which receipt does not occur.[26] In other words, what proponents of the 'no receipt' counterfactual need to imagine is a *transition period* in the run-up to the point of receipt rather than an instantaneous evaporation of the enrichment. Let us return to the simple case in which I mistakenly hand you a £50 note. When asked to imagine the world in which I do not receive the note, we might plausibly think of the world in which I simply keep the note in my pocket. Or perhaps the world in which I take the note from my pocket, begin to hand it to you, but then change my mind at the last moment and take it back. Indeed, the ways in which we might envisage the transition period are many and varied, perhaps even infinitely so.

The immediate response may be: 'Yes, some hypothetical transition period must be imagined prior to receipt, but so what?' The answer is as follows: different accounts of the relevant transition period produce different conclusions in concrete cases. In such cases, the choice among different transition periods is decisive of the legal outcome. The problem is that the 'no receipt' counterfactual provides no rational basis for selecting between different transition periods. Consequently, it gives rise to arbitrariness. Two simple examples illustrate the point. First:

> Alice is walking home with her flatmate Brian. Alice mistakenly takes a £50 note out of her pocket and hands it to Brian. A thief sees the mistaken payment take place and as a result follows the flatmates back to their house and, once they go to sleep, steals the television from the flat. The television belonged to Brian and was worth £200.

[24] It is philosophically contentious whether it is proper to introduce miracles into causal counterfactual worlds at all. For the classic debate, contrast D Lewis, 'Counterfactual Dependence and Time's Arrow' (1979) 13 *Noûs* 455 and J Bennett, 'Counterfactuals and Temporal Direction' (1984) 93 *Philosophical Review* 57 (recanted in J Bennett, *A Philosophical Guide to Conditionals* (Oxford, Oxford University Press, 2003) 211–14). The debate is not strictly in point because, in the legal context, the legal inquiry within which the counterfactual is embedded must ultimately determine the permissibility of miracles: *cf* Stapleton (n 21) 749–53.

[25] See generally T Gerstenberg, 'Making a Difference: Responsibility, Causality and Counterfactuals' (PhD thesis, University College London, 2013) ch 6.1.

[26] Lewis (n 24) 463. On the difference between smooth 'ramps' and sudden 'bumps', see generally Bennett, *A Philosophical Guide to Conditionals* (n 24) 209–11.

In this example, Brian gains £50 from Alice and later loses a television worth £200. The 'no receipt' counterfactual directs us to the following inquiry: would restitution leave Brian worse off than if he had not received the £50 note from Alice? Surely we cannot be required to imagine the world in which the £50 note evaporates in Brian's hand and then ask whether the thief would have been drawn in or scared off by such a miraculous turn of events. However, if we reject that miraculous world, how are we to specify the alternative? If Alice had never taken the note from her pocket, the thief's attention would never have been drawn, and thus Brian's television would not have been stolen. By contrast, if Alice had taken the note out of her pocket, begun to hand it to Brian and then changed her mind, the thief would have seen the £50 note, his attention would have been drawn and so he would still have followed the flatmates home and stolen the television. It follows that if Brian were ordered to make restitution of £50 to Alice, he would be left worse off as against the 'keeps note in pocket' baseline but not against the 'last-minute withdrawal' baseline.

As for the second example:

> Alice mistakenly takes a £50 note out of her pocket and begins to hand it to Brian. Brian sees this and as a result excitedly places a losing online bet on his smartphone. Brian then grasps the £50 note.

If Brian were ordered to make restitution, would he be worse off than if he had not received the £50 note? Restitution leaves Brian no worse off than he would be in the starkly miraculous version of the 'no receipt' counterfactual: in that counterfactual world, he would have placed the bet before the note evaporated. But what happens if we build a period of transition into the 'no receipt' counterfactual to avoid the stark miracle? If Alice had simply kept the note in her pocket, Brian would not have seen the note and therefore would not have made the bet. By contrast, if Alice had begun to hand the note to Brian and then changed her mind at the last moment, Brian would have seen the note and made the bet before Alice changed my mind. Thus, these two imagined periods of transition produce different conclusions: as against the 'keeps note in pocket' baseline, restitution leaves Brian worse off; as against the 'last-minute withdrawal' baseline, it does not.

One notable feature of the second example is that it concerns pre-receipt detriment. Quite simply, once it is accepted that any plausible version of the 'no receipt' counterfactual must diverge from the real world *prior to receipt*, the possibility arises that *pre-receipt* detriment will be caught. Of course, it could be stipulated that any pre-receipt detriment caught by the 'no receipt' counterfactual should be disregarded. That would give effect to the intentions of the proponents of the 'no receipt' counterfactual, who almost certainly did not intend the test to catch pre-receipt detriment. But such a stipulation must be rejected. The 'no receipt' counterfactual bears not only a doctrinal but also a moral significance in leading accounts of the law of unjust enrichment. As Burrows puts it, the change of position defence provides the 'normative balance to the strict liability imposed by unjust enrichment: the defendant can have no objection to the reversal of the enrichment provided it is left no worse off than if it had not been enriched in the first place'.[27] In our second example, it surely rings hollow to justify the imposition of liability by telling Brian that restitution leaves him no worse off than if the £50 note had evaporated in his hand. At the least, Brian is entitled to demand that restitution leaves him no worse off than he would be in a *plausible* counterfactual in which he does not receive the enrichment. In our second example, Brian can rightly point out that one plausible world in which he does not receive the £50 note is the world in which Alice never takes the note out of her pocket. Restitution leaves Brian worse off than he would be in *that* version of the 'no receipt' counterfactual. If the imposition of unjust enrichment liability on Brian is to be justified with reference to the 'no receipt' counterfactual, some reason must be found as to why Brian's proposed formulation of that counterfactual is the wrong one. Consequently, the pre-receipt detriment caught by some versions of the 'no receipt' counterfactual cannot be so readily dismissed. What the second example illustrates is that the same basic problem for the 'no receipt' counterfactual also arises in relation to pre-receipt detriment: the possible specifications of the necessary transition period prior to the point of receipt are many, varied and conflicting.

If proponents of the 'no receipt' counterfactual are unwilling to accept its starkly miraculous incarnation, they must find some non-arbitrary means for resolving between different and conflicting accounts of the transition period from the real world to the imagined state in which receipt does not occur. It is doubtful for two reasons whether such a non-arbitrary means of selection exists. First, the 'no receipt' counterfactual starts in the middle of the story: we are directed to imagine a state in which receipt does not occur, but once we rule out the implausible possibility of the enrichment simply evaporating, we are then required to reason backwards, asking what the real world 'would have to have been like' prior to receipt if receipt was plausibly not to occur. This awkward backtracking inquiry produces no single answer: it is equally true that receipt would not have occurred if the transferor had left the note in her pocket, changed her mind at the last minute, or if any number of other hypothetical periods of transition had occurred.[28] The second reason for indeterminacy follows on from the first: among the myriad possible transition periods, a great number are *equally factually plausible* even though they produce different results. It is no more or less factually plausible to suppose, in the example of a mistaken

[27] AS Burrows, 'Good Consideration in the Law of Unjust Enrichment' (2013) 129 *LQR* 329, 330.

[28] Contrast Lewis (n 24) 463 and Bennett, 'Counterfactuals' (n 24) 79–80.

payment by hand, that your non-receipt stems from me keeping the note in my pocket rather than me changing my mind (and the possible transitions could readily be multiplied).[29] The existence of such equally plausible and yet conflicting transition periods gives rise to a two-horned dilemma for the 'no receipt' counterfactual. The 'no receipt' counterfactual gives rise to either: (1) a stark miracle; or (2) indeterminacy due to the many equally plausible accounts of the transition period prior to receipt which is required to avoid a stark miracle.

There is a way out of these difficulties. It is wrongheaded to begin by imagining a state in which receipt does not occur and then try to reason backwards to what the world would have to have looked like if receipt was plausibly not to occur. Instead, what is required is a counterfactual baseline which does not require such a stark miracle in the first place. The 'no defect' counterfactual is markedly more promising in this regard. By definition, when applying the 'no defect' counterfactual, the only change from the real world that must be imagined to get the counterfactual going is a subtle alteration to the claimant's decision making. In the case of mistaken belief, for example, we need only imagine that the claimant does not form the belief in question.[30] Similarly, in relation to other defects in decision making, the necessary alteration by definition takes place solely within the claimant's mind. This is on a par with the counterfactual variations that are familiar in other areas of the law of obligations. For example, in a negligent road traffic accident, the 'but for' test of causation might require us to imagine that the tortfeasor had braked when he ought to have done. We have no difficulty in imagining a subtle alteration to the neurons firing in the tortfeasor's brain which results in him braking rather than careening on. The 'no defect' counterfactual is similarly free from sudden and implausible leaps. Consequently, the problems of stark miracles and indeterminate transition periods lie squarely at the door of the 'no receipt' counterfactual; the same difficulties are not faced by the 'no defect' counterfactual.

3.1.2. *Taking Arbitrariness Seriously*

This section begins with a simple example which has already been set out in section 2 above. Alice is labouring under a mistaken belief which causes her first to tell Brian that she will pay him £100 and later to actually pay him £100. Brian may incur detriment either (1) prior to receipt as a result

[29] *cf* S Steel, 'Defining Causal Counterfactuals in Negligence' (2014) 130 *LQR* 564, 566.

[30] Strictly, we could 'remove' a mistaken belief in two ways. Take a case where Alice mistakenly believes that Brian likes paella. We could imagine a world in which Alice forms the belief that Brian does not like paella. Alternatively, we could imagine a world in which Alice's belief is unaltered, but Brian actually likes paella. The 'no defect' counterfactual uses the former method of removal; that is, the counterfactual is formed by altering the claimant's decision making rather than the outside world. See also n 22 above.

of what Alice tells him or (2) after he receives the money as a result of his receipt. Courts and commentators alike have expressed the conviction that it is *arbitrary* to distinguish between these instances of pre-receipt and post-receipt detriment. On this view, there is 'no significant distinction' between the two cases, and consequently if Brian ought to have a defence based on the detriment he has suffered, he ought to do so irrespective of the timing of his receipt.[31]

It is important to unpack this sense of arbitrariness. What it means to say that it is arbitrary to distinguish between these cases is that, whatever reason it is that supports a defence of change of position in the case of post-receipt detriment, *that reason* applies equally in certain cases of pre-receipt detriment. The sense is not that distinct but equally strong reasons apply in respect of pre-receipt and post-receipt detriment; rather, the sense is that the *same reason* applies equally in both cases and the timing of receipt is immaterial to that reason. In this way, the sense that it is arbitrary to distinguish between certain instances of pre-receipt and post-receipt detriment, if sound, is indicative of an underlying unity: at some meaningful level of abstraction, there exists a unified rationale which supports bringing both pre-receipt and post-receipt detriment into account in the change of position analysis.[32]

As we have seen, orthodoxy applies different counterfactual tests in relation to pre-receipt and post-receipt detriment. This in itself is not inconsistent with the intuitive sense of arbitrariness; it is sometimes possible to identify a unitary principled rationale to support two legal tests that are distinct as a matter of surface-level doctrine.[33] The problem, however, is that it is difficult if not impossible to state a unitary rationale that underpins the tests based on the 'no receipt' and 'no anticipatory reliance' counterfactuals.[34] This is because the very same baselines which are embedded in the change of position doctrine appear also to be embedded in the moral rationale for the doctrine. For example, if the adoption of the 'no receipt' counterfactual as a matter of doctrine is to be justified, it appears that an important part of the justification is that it is morally important that the defendant not be

[31] *Dextra Bank & Trust Company Ltd v Bank of Jamaica* [2002] 1 All ER (Comm) 193 (PC (Jam)) [38] ('it is difficult to see what relevant distinction can be drawn'); Burrows (n 4) 533 ('no significant distinction'). *cf* Nolan (n 10) 165.

[32] By way of analogy, the timing of the formation of contract appears similarly immaterial to the shared reasons that support the doctrines of both common mistake and frustration: see, eg, J Edelman, 'Liability in Unjust Enrichment Where a Contract Fails to Materialise' in A Burrows and E Peel (eds), *Contract Formation and Parties* (Oxford, Oxford University Press, 2010) 173; and F Wilmot-Smith, 'Failure of Condition' (DPhil thesis, University of Oxford, 2013) ch 7.

[33] See n 32 above.

[34] To rest simply on the proposition that it is inequitable to require the defendant to make restitution in both cases would amount to an unsatisfactory abandonment of the search for determinate principles to ground the defence.

left worse off than if she had not received the enrichment.[35] Thus, at least in relation to the 'no receipt' counterfactual, it appears that the doctrinal and moral baselines are aligned.[36] If this is true, then just as the doctrinal test based on the 'no receipt' counterfactual fails to catch pre-receipt detriment, so too the moral rationale for that test is inapplicable to pre-receipt detriment. Consequently, so long as the change of position doctrine and its attendant rationale are focused on the point of receipt, some novel and different reason is required if the defence of anticipatory change of position is to be justified.[37] Thus, the 'no receipt' counterfactual and its attendant rationale fail to vindicate the sense that it is arbitrary to leave certain instances of pre-receipt detriment out of account.

There are two conclusions that could be drawn from this. First, it could be that the sense of arbitrariness ought to be abandoned as unsound. If no unified principle can be found to justify the relevance of both pre-receipt and post-receipt detriment, then the distinction between the two is far from arbitrary; in fact, it is rationally necessary to distinguish the two in order to identify the different reasons that apply in each case. This direction of travel—from the endorsement of a basal principle focused on receipt to the abandonment of the sense of arbitrariness—has distinguished supporters.[38] However, it may be that the appropriate move is actually in the opposite direction. That is, the sense that the timing of receipt is immaterial to the rationale of the change of position defence could call into question the soundness of an account that fixes the basal principle of the defence at the moment of receipt. At the very least, all else being equal, we ought to prefer an account of the change of position defence that vindicates rather than debunks that intuitive conviction.

If the 'no receipt' counterfactual is replaced with the 'no defect' counterfactual, it is readily explicable why the timing of receipt seems immaterial to the reasons for affording the defendant a change of position defence. On this alternative view, detriment is relevant to the change of position defence whenever it is caused by the defect in the claimant's decision making on which she grounds her claim. This is true irrespective of whether detriment occurs before or after receipt. Applying the 'no defect' counterfactual to the example at the start of this section, there is a simple reason why it is arbitrary to distinguish between the detriment Brian suffers as a result of

[35] See, eg, Burrows (n 4) 526.

[36] The 'no anticipatory reliance' counterfactual may be different in this regard: its justification may comprise an appeal to the moral significance of the 'no receipt' counterfactual plus a concern with practical evidential difficulties: see n 37 below.

[37] For example, Bant finds the relevant additional reason in a practical concern to avoid difficult evidential issues in cases involving a series of payments: Bant (n 2) 156–57.

[38] See eg, ibid 156 (drawing distinction between pre-receipt and post-receipt detriment 'as a matter of principle').

what he is told by Alice and the detriment he suffers as a result of receipt: both are instances of detriment caused by Alice's mistaken belief. Further, as the argument of section 4 below will show, a unitary principled rationale supports bringing into account all of the defendant's detriment which the claimant causes by the defect in her decision making on which she grounds her claim.

3.2. 'No Anticipatory Reliance' Counterfactual

This section argues that it is an error to view the 'no anticipatory reliance' counterfactual as part of the change of position defence. If the 'no anticipatory reliance' counterfactual has any proper role to play in the law of unjust enrichment, it is as part of the defence of estoppel. The argument proceeds in three stages. First, it is argued that the 'no anticipatory reliance' counterfactual catches detriment in which the claimant is not causally involved and is therefore over-inclusive. Second, a simple solution to this over-inclusivity is proposed. The 'no anticipatory reliance' counterfactual must be pared down by adding a requirement that the defendant's expectation of enrichment must be caused by the claimant if it is to ground a defence. Third, it is shown how, once the 'no anticipatory reliance' counterfactual is pared down in this way, it is most plausibly analysed as part of the estoppel defence rather than the change of position defence.

The over-inclusivity of the 'no anticipatory reliance' counterfactual is most easily explained with reference to a concrete example:

> On Monday, Brian reads in his horoscope that he will receive £500 from his next-door neighbour. On Tuesday, buoyed up by the good news, Brian treats himself to luxury spa treatments costing £500. On Wednesday, Brian's next door neighbour Alice pays him £500 by mistake.

In this example, but for Brian's reliance on his expectation of receipt from Alice, he would not have spent £500 at the spa. In other words, Brian's anticipatory reliance on the expectation of Alice's payment has made him worse off. The test based on the 'no anticipatory reliance' counterfactual would therefore give Brian a complete defence of change of position to a claim brought by Alice. This cannot be correct. Alice is in no meaningful way involved in Brian's detriment at the spa. It is nothing more than a brute coincidence that Brian was expecting a payment from Alice. The success of the change of position defence cannot properly be contingent on whether Albert's horoscope happened to talk about his next-door neighbour or a tall dark stranger.

The source of the problem is that the 'no anticipatory reliance' counterfactual is preoccupied with the question of how to link pre-receipt detriment to the *subject matter of the unjust enrichment claim*, and therefore neglects the more fundamental need to link pre-receipt detriment to the *unjust enrichment claimant.* The point needs elaborating. The change of position defence operates, on the orthodox understanding, to defeat the claimant's prima facie right to restitution. The claimant is owed a justification if detriment is to be brought into account to defeat her prima facie right.[39] One question the claimant can legitimately ask is why the detriment in question is being brought into account against her *to defeat her prima facie right* (as distinct from being brought into account against her in in other ways, such as in a counterclaim against her). In answer to that question, it is, of course, necessary to point to some link between the subject matter of the unjust enrichment claim and the detriment which is brought into account to defeat the claim. Otherwise, the detriment suffered by the defendant would be irrelevant to the claim at hand. But the claimant is entitled to ask a more fundamental question: why is this detriment being brought into account against *her* at all? In answer to this question, what must be identified is some reason for picking out the claimant as a person against whom the detriment is appropriately brought into account in the first place.

The 'no anticipatory reliance' counterfactual neglects the fundamental need to justify bringing the detriment in question into account against the claimant. It is all very well to point out that the defendant has incurred detriment in the expectation of the very same benefit that she later received. But if the claimant was in no way involved in bringing about the defendant's expectation or the detriment that followed, there is no justification for bringing the defendant's detriment into account against *her* at all. In the absence of a link between the detriment and the unjust enrichment claimant, to point to a link between the detriment and the subject matter of the claim rings hollow. The horoscope example illustrates the point. Alice was in no meaningful way involved in either Brian's horoscope reading or the resulting detriment. Consequently, to point out that Brian's detriment was incurred in the expectation of Alice's payment is to identify a merely coincidental connection between Brian's detriment and the subject matter of Alice's claim. The coincidental connection does nothing to answer the fundamental question as to why Brian's detriment should be brought into account against Alice at all. The lesson to be drawn from the horoscope example is that a sound account of the change of position defence must identify some significant link between the claimant and the defendant's detriment in order to justify bringing that detriment into account against the claimant. What is the nature of that link? The answer proposed here is a simple one: *the claimant must have been causally involved in the defendant's detriment.* The moral grounding for this proposition is provided by Honoré's account of outcome responsibility, to which we now turn.

[39] Webb and Akkouh (n 10) 111.

Honoré has influentially shown how outcome responsibility—that is, the idea that the outcomes which a person causes by her acts and omissions are morally attributable to her—is embedded in our thinking in two basic ways.[40] First, this notion of responsibility for outcomes makes an important contribution to each person's understanding of his or her own personhood.[41] Second, society allocates credit and discredit to each of its members for the outcomes that they cause. In short, the outcomes that we cause are 'ours' in a way that other happenings are not.[42] The most familiar discussions of outcome responsibility focus on its relevance to the justification of legal liability. However, it is important to keep in mind that outcome responsibility is distinct from, and more fundamental than, legal liability.[43] Outcome responsibility figures in the *moral grounds for* legal liability and cannot therefore be *equated with* legal liability. The true position is that outcome responsibility operates to morally attribute outcomes to agents.[44] This moral attribution may then serve as a stepping stone on the way to justifying a great many different responses: praise, blame, criminal sanctions, civil liability and more besides.[45]

The proposal made here is that where a claimant bears outcome responsibility for the defendant's detriment, one of the responses which may be justified is the defeat of her prima facie right to restitution by the change of position defence. By morally attributing outcomes to the agency of certain actors, outcome responsibility provides exactly what a normative account of the change of position defence requires; that is, a morally significant connection between the claimant and the detriment that is brought into account against her. The unjust enrichment claimant may indeed ask: 'Why is this detriment being brought into account against *me*?' The question should be met with the simple response: 'You brought this detriment about and therefore bear responsibility for it.' This answer is not available where the claimant is not causally involved in the defendant's detriment: in such cases, the claimant is not responsible for the defendant's detriment and consequently it is unjustifiable for the detriment to be brought into account against her.

[40] The classic essays are collected in T Honoré, *Responsibility and Fault* (Oxford, Hart Publishing, 1999). Certain details are honed and clarified in T Honoré, 'Appreciations and Responses' in P Cane and J Gardner (eds), *Relating to Responsibility* (Oxford, Hart Publishing, 2001) 223–32.

[41] Honoré, 'Appreciations' (n 40) 226.

[42] ibid.

[43] ibid 223.

[44] ibid 225 (outcome responsibility comprises a set of 'objective and interpersonal principles of attribution').

[45] See Honoré, *Responsibility and Fault* (n 40) 89–90 (overtly recognising that outcome responsibility can morally ground legal consequences other than the imposition of liability and giving the doctrine of contributory negligence as an example: there, a tort claimant's outcome responsibility for her own detriment is an important part of the justification for reducing the remedy recoverable by her).

On this view, a necessary condition for the justification of detriment being brought into account against the claimant by the change of position defence is that the claimant bears outcome responsibility for that detriment. However, outcome responsibility is not sufficient. Once it is established that the claimant bears outcome responsibility for the defendant's detriment, a further question arises: why should this detriment be brought into account against the claimant *to defeat her prima facie right to restitution*? If on the same day Alice sets fire to Brian's car and happens also to mistakenly pay £100 to Brian, Alice's outcome responsibility for the fire damage does not in itself justify affording Brian a change of position defence. A reasoned account is required of which subset of the detriment for which the claimant is responsible is *relevant* to the change of position defence, and why this is so. The 'no defect' and 'no receipt' counterfactuals can fruitfully be regarded as offering competing accounts of the relevant subset. The 'no defect' counterfactual says that detriment is relevant if the claimant causes it by the very defect in her decision making on which she grounds her claim. The 'no receipt' counterfactual, by contrast, fastens onto detriment caused by receipt, and, as we have seen, 'detriment caused by receipt' is a subset of 'detriment caused by the claimant' in cases in which the change of position defence is at issue.[46] In order to argue in favour of either of these counterfactuals, reasons must be offered why that particular subset of the detriment caused by the claimant is the relevant one. By contrast, the 'no anticipatory reliance' counterfactual breaks the pattern in an unjustifiable manner by including within its scope detriment for which the claimant bears no causal responsibility at all. It is for this reason that the 'no anticipatory reliance' counterfactual is over-inclusive.

In sum, detriment for which the claimant bears no outcome responsibility cannot properly be brought into account against her to defeat her prima facie right to restitution. Consequently, the 'no anticipatory reliance' counterfactual needs cutting down to size. The solution is a relatively simple one. On a suitably constrained account of the 'no anticipatory reliance' counterfactual, detriment is relevant to the change of position defence if: (1) the detriment is suffered as a result of the defendant's expectation that she will receive a certain benefit; (2) the defendant later receives the benefit that she was expecting; and (3) the claimant caused the defendant's expectation to arise. The addition of the third condition ensures that detriment in which the claimant was not causally involved is taken outside the scope of the 'no anticipatory reliance' counterfactual. In this way, we can ensure that the 'no anticipatory reliance' counterfactual does not bring into account against the claimant detriment for which she is not responsible.

Once the 'no anticipatory reliance' counterfactual is appropriately pared down, an interesting and difficult question comes to the foreground. Is the

[46] See section 2.3.2 above.

'no anticipatory reliance' counterfactual better analysed as part of the estoppel defence? The similarities between the pared-down 'no anticipatory reliance' counterfactual and the estoppel defence are readily apparent. Both doctrines catch detriment which the defendant suffers due to an assumption brought about by the claimant. The estoppel defence bites on the defendant's assumption that she is entitled to keep the benefit which she has received. The 'no anticipatory reliance' counterfactual bites on the defendant's assumption that she will receive a benefit and then be entitled to keep it. Admittedly, the former assumption concerns the present and the latter concerns the future. However, this temporal distinction is no barrier to the argument that the pared-down 'no anticipatory reliance' counterfactual should be assimilated into the estoppel defence. As Bant and Bryan have recently and persuasively argued, the distinction between assumptions as to the present and future is not fundamental to the estoppel rationale.[47] At base, the core principled question raised in estoppel cases is whether a person takes an undue risk by acting on the relevant assumption.[48] This is true whether the estoppel in question is founded on an assumption concerning the present or the future. The significance of the present/future distinction is a derivative one: namely, that in many contexts, a person will take an undue risk by acting on an assumption as to the future. Of course, there is ample room for argument over whether an unjust enrichment defendant who incurs detriment in the expectation that she will later receive enrichment is taking an undue risk. If so, she should not be able to set up an estoppel defence where she incurs detriment on the assumption that she will later receive an enrichment. But that is a debate which can readily be conducted within the confines of estoppel defence.

Thus, the distinction between present and future assumptions does not impede the argument that the 'no anticipatory reliance' counterfactual should be assimilated into the estoppel defence. But is there a positive case for such assimilation? Yes: there are important differences between the rationales of the estoppel and change of position defences, and the pared-down 'no anticipatory reliance' counterfactual is most plausibly justified by an estoppel rationale.

As to the distinctive rationales of the estoppel and change of position defences, the following brief remarks may well amount to a polarised simplification. They should, however, suffice.[49] The rationale of the estoppel defence attaches intrinsic moral significance to the claimant causing the defendant to form some assumption (for example, that she is entitled to the

[47] E Bant and M Bryan, 'Fact, Future and Fiction: Risk and Reasonable Reliance in Estoppel' (2015) 35 *OJLS* 1.

[48] ibid.

[49] For a more thorough discussion, see section 5.2 of Elise Bant's contribution to this volume (see ch 7).

enrichment she has received). The estoppel defence is then concerned with protecting the defendant from the harm she would suffer if her assumption were undercut by the imposition of liability. The change of position defence, by contrast, is justified by the principle that restitution must not leave the defendant worse off as against some specified baseline. This rationale does not attach any intrinsic significance to the claimant bringing about any assumption on the part of the defendant. Insofar as the defendant's reliance on assumption is morally relevant to the change of position defence, it is simply because it is one way of establishing causation. For example, consider the generic case of a defendant who detrimentally relies on the assumption that she is entitled to keep the enrichment that she has received. Such a defendant will be left worse off as a result of receipt if she is required to make restitution of the enrichment. In such a case, from a change of position standpoint, it is the fact that restitution will leave the defendant worse off, and not the fact that the defendant has relied on an assumption induced by the claimant, which is of basic moral significance.[50]

There is a central feature of the 'no anticipatory reliance' counterfactual which can only be rendered morally intelligible by an estoppel rationale. The 'no anticipatory reliance' counterfactual requires that the defendant incurs detriment in the expectation of *the very benefit* which she later receives.[51] If a change of position rationale is adopted, this requirement of exact correspondence between actual and expected benefit is rather puzzling. Consider a case in which Alice mistakenly tells Brian she will give him a bag of apples worth £5. Brian then spends £5 in reliance on his expectation of receipt. Alice might later mistakenly give Brian a bag of apples worth £5. Or, she might mistakenly give Brian a bag of pears worth £5. The 'no anticipatory reliance' counterfactual would give Brian a defence if he receives apples; not so if he receives pears. In both cases, Brian receives an abstract enrichment of £5. Is it not a matter of fortuity whether this abstract enrichment is brought about by the receipt of apples or pears? Why should exact correspondence between actual and expected benefit make all the difference? The tendency in change of position scholarship is simply to assert that pre-receipt detriment is only 'relevant' if incurred in the expectation of the very enrichment later received.[52] But this provides no reason *why* pre-receipt detriment is relevant only in cases of exact correspondence between actual

[50] A related distinction between the estoppel and change of position defences is drawn by Elise Bant in ch 7 of this volume. Bant distinguishes between the temporal baseline of the change of position defence and the counterfactual baseline of the estoppel defence. In my view, both defences use counterfactual baselines. The difference is in how those counterfactual baselines are defined. The change of position baseline is the counterfactual world in which some defined X (receipt, defect etc) did not occur. The estoppel baseline is the counterfactual world in which the defendant's assumption is made good.

[51] See n 4 above.

[52] *cf* Burrows (n 1) 120.

and expected benefit. So long as the 'no anticipatory reliance' counterfactual is treated as part of the change of position defence, the exact correspondence requirement appears to be an ad hoc stipulation aimed to keep the defence within practically manageable, if not rationally justifiable, bounds. Insofar as post-receipt detriment is concerned, it is now tolerably clear that post-receipt change of position is not limited to cases of detrimental reliance. Other causally relevant post-receipt detriment may also be taken into account. The exact correspondence requirement gives rise to a rather different position in relation to pre-receipt detriment: there, the defendant's reliance on the precise expectation later fulfilled is elevated to a position of paramount importance. This difference in the treatment of pre-receipt and post-receipt detriment seems anomalous.

An estoppel rationale, by contrast, provides an attractive explanation for why correspondence between actual and expected benefit makes all the difference. In short, restitution cannot undercut an assumption which was never fulfilled in the first place. For example, imagine that Brian is expecting apples and in fact receives pears. Requiring Brian to make restitution of the pears does not undercut his assumption that he would receive apples. That assumption was doomed to be frustrated because he never received any apples at all. In this way, the requirement of exact correspondence between actual and expected benefit is built into the bricks of the estoppel rationale. The function of the requirement is, in essence, to ensure that only expectations which have in fact been fulfilled are able to ground a defence. In this way the estoppel rationale naturally explains the requirement of exact correspondence between actual and anticipated benefit, which serves to police the boundary between fulfilled and unfulfilled expectations.

Given that the 'no anticipatory reliance' counterfactual is most plausibly justified by an estoppel rationale, it ought to be categorised as part of the estoppel defence. The list of competitors in our baseline contest therefore shrinks from three to two. It is the 'no receipt' and 'no defect' counterfactuals which compete with one another as the potential baselines for the change of position defence.

4. THE CASE FOR THE 'NO DEFECT' COUNTERFACTUAL

It is time for a change of tack. The analysis thus far has been concerned with objections to the orthodox baselines. We move now to a more constructive project: building a positive argument in support of the 'no defect' counterfactual. The tendency in existing accounts of the change of position defence is to assume without argument the specification of the relevant baseline for analysis.[53] As a result, there is a dearth of positive arguments in favour of any particular baseline. What might such a positive argument look like?

[53] See n 5 above.

One attractive way to proceed would be to exploit the link between the change of position defence and certain foundational questions about the justification of unjust enrichment liability.[54] This chapter has so far considered the principle that restitution must not leave the defendant 'worse off' specifically in relation to the change of position defence. However, as Wilmot-Smith has identified, there is an underdeveloped but widespread line of thinking according to which the same principle plays an important part in the justification for the imposition of unjust enrichment liability in the first place.[55] Consequently, there is an impulse at this point to delve into the normative theory of unjust enrichment. The pertinent question would be: which counterfactual baseline figures in the most compelling moral justification for the imposition of unjust enrichment liability? The baseline adopted in that fundamental debate could then be doctrinally implemented by the change of position defence. Unfortunately, this line of attack must be left aside for the moment. It seems that the normative theory of unjust enrichment is yet to produce a convincing justification for unjust enrichment liability based on the principle that restitution leaves the defendant 'no worse off', let alone an argument sufficiently developed to resolve between the competing baselines currently under consideration.[56] Moreover, even if a successful justification based on this principle is eventually found, the possibility remains that it will be partially indeterminate and thus unable to tell between the competing baselines.

Does this mean that we have reached an impasse in our inquiry? Fortunately not: an alternative line of attack is available. This section advances an argument in support of the 'no defect' counterfactual which consists of two steps. First, it is shown how the unjust enrichment claimant sets up her primary claim by identifying one consequence of the defect in her decision making (viz the defendant's enrichment). Second, it is argued that the claimant must not be allowed to cherry-pick among the consequences of the defect in her decision making by denying the legal relevance of its other consequences (viz the defendant's detriment) to the change of position defence. If these two steps are accepted, it follows that the proper baseline for the change of position analysis must catch all of the detriment which the claimant causes to the defendant by the defect in decision making on which she grounds her claim. The baseline which achieves this is the 'no defect' counterfactual.

Turning to the first step, leaving to one side claims contingent on tracing, at the core of the claimant's doctrinal case in favour of restitution is the proposition that the defect in her decision making caused the defendant

[54] On the relative neglect of this issue, see R Grantham and C Rickett, 'A Normative Account of Defences to Restitutionary Liability' (2008) 67 *CLJ* 92, 94.

[55] Wilmot-Smith (n 32) 110–12.

[56] The fundamental difficulty is in justifying the adoption of any baseline other than the status quo in which the enrichment lies where it falls: ibid 112–21.

to be enriched. This proposition is established by the joint operation of the 'unjustness' and 'at the expense of' inquiries. First, the 'unjustness' inquiry requires the claimant to establish that the defect in her decision making is a 'but for' cause of her initial loss.[57] Second, the 'at the expense of' inquiry requires the claimant to establish a counterfactual link between her initial loss and the defendant's enrichment. Of course, the need to establish a counterfactual link between initial loss and enrichment does not exhaust the 'at the expense of' inquiry: the scope of unjust enrichment liability may then be curtailed by a privity principle or remoteness constraint. But the important point for present purposes is that, claims contingent on tracing aside, a counterfactual link between the claimant's initial loss and the defendant's enrichment is necessary, even if not sufficient, to satisfy the 'at the expense of' inquiry. The combined effect of the counterfactual links established by the 'unjustness' and 'at the expense of' inquiries is as follows: (1) the defect in the claimant's decision making is a 'but for' cause of her initial loss; (2) 'but for' the claimant's initial loss, the defendant would not have been enriched; and therefore (3) the defect in the claimant's decision making is a 'but for' cause of the defendant's enrichment. In this way, the primary claim in unjust enrichment is grounded on the identification of a particular consequence of the defect in the claimant's decision making: the defendant's enrichment.

Step two requires us to show that it is morally objectionable for the claimant to cherry-pick among the consequences of the defect in her decision making by setting up her primary claim based on one of its consequences (viz the defendant's enrichment) and then denying the legal relevance of its other consequences (viz the defendant's detriment) to the change of position defence. One potential argument is that the cherry-picking claimant is guilty of logical contradiction. This thin argument based on alleged contradiction is likely to fail for the reasons set out below. However, its failure lays the ground for a second and more promising reason to object to cherry-picking. This more promising reason is based on a richer moral principle, namely that the claimant must take the rough with the smooth.

It might be argued that the cherry-picking claimant logically contradicts herself. The argument would run that cherry-picking involves asserting both X and not-X, where X is 'the consequences of the defect in my decision making are relevant to the unjust enrichment analysis'. The difficulty

[57] Burrows (n 4) 91. A different test of causation is applicable, for example, in cases of fraudulent misrepresentation and physical duress. But the very same reasons which justify the adoption of a different test of causation in the 'unjustness' inquiry might also justify a different approach to the change of position defence (or even the disapplication of the defence): see n 17 above. Consequently, we must leave to a later occasion the inquiry into whether the change of position baseline advocated in the text can be generalised to cases such as those of fraudulent misrepresentation and physical duress.

with this argument is obvious: the contradiction is created only by stating the proposition asserted by the claimant at an unacceptably high level of generality. For a start, the claimant's assertion concerns only the relevance of the consequences of the defect in her decision making to the *primary unjust enrichment claim*. Such an assertion cannot be logically contradicted by a later assertion which is focused specifically on the *change of position defence*. Furthermore, there is no purely logical objection to the claimant drawing a distinction between the beneficial and detrimental consequences of the defect in her decision making; the claimant can argue without logical incoherence that only the beneficial consequences ought to be allocated to her by the law of unjust enrichment. For these reasons, logic alone is insufficient to show why it is objectionable to allow the claimant to cherry-pick among the consequences of the defect in her decision making.

Fortunately, a second and richer argument is available. This argument is based on the principle that the claimant must take the rough with the smooth. The consequences of a defect in a claimant's decision making may be many and varied. On the one hand, the defect may cause others to be enriched. On the other hand, the defect may cause others detriment. If the defect turns out to cause another to be enriched, the law of unjust enrichment confers on the claimant a prima facie right to restitution. In this way, should the defect in the claimant's decision making turn out to enrich another, the law of unjust enrichment confers a significant upside on the claimant: although the enrichment lies with the defendant in the status quo, the law of unjust enrichment disturbs the status quo by insisting that the enrichment is properly allocated to the claimant. If the same defect in the claimant's decision making turns out also to cause detriment to the defendant, who then is to bear the cost of that detriment? The change of position defence cannot avoid allocating this cost. To the extent that the defendant is afforded a change of position defence based on such detriment, it is the claimant who bears the cost (by having her prima facie right to restitution defeated). Conversely, if the defendant has no defence based on such detriment, the detriment is left to lie with her and it is she who bears the cost. Of course, there are limits to the extent to which the change of position defence is able to allocate costs: the change of position defence can go no further than defeating the claimant's prima facie right to restitution in its entirety. The change of position defence cannot stretch as far as to impose liability on the unjust enrichment claimant for the detriment which she has caused to the defendant. Nonetheless, within the limited scope of its operation, the change of position defence raises a serious question as to who ought properly to bear the cost of the detriment the claimant has caused to the defendant by the defect in her decision making on which she grounds her claim. The proposal here is that the claimant must take the rough with the smooth: the claimant accepts the upside when the law of unjust enrichment allocates the beneficial consequences of the defect in her decision making to her (for this is the basis of her primary claim); she cannot then object to the corresponding downside when the costs of the detrimental consequences of the same defect are also allocated to her (by the operation of the change of position defence).

The intuitive appeal of the 'rough with the smooth' principle has been noted. For example, in the eyes of Honoré, 'its moral force can hardly be denied'.[58] No doubt it would be desirable to support the 'rough with the smooth' principle with more than a direct appeal to intuition. But that task presents a significant dilemma. On the one hand, a deeper argument in support of the 'rough with the smooth' principle would help to stave off any criticism that it is an empty catchphrase. On the other hand, previous attempts to offer a deeper argument of this kind appear to have succeeded only in paraphrasing the principle rather than providing a foundation for it.[59] The possibility must therefore be acknowledged that the 'rough with the smooth' principle is morally irreducible. However, at risk of lapsing once more into paraphrase, the 'rough with the smooth' principle might be more fully articulated in the following way. In essence, the principle is concerned to avoid self-serving distinctions. The unjust enrichment claimant positively asserts that one consequence of the defect in her decision making should be allocated to her by the law of unjust enrichment (viz the defendant's enrichment). Our previous consideration and rejection of the argument from non-contradiction has shown that there are logically tenable distinctions that might be drawn between the defendant's enrichment and the other consequences of the defect in the claimant's decision making. But the more interesting question is whether these distinctions are morally material. Why should the claimant be able to have the consequences of the defect in her decision making allocated to her by the law of unjust enrichment when it works to her advantage but not otherwise? The claimant will no doubt be better off if the law of unjust enrichment coercively reallocates enrichment to her while leaving the detrimental consequences of the defect in her decision making to lie with the defendant. But here lies the gist of the 'rough with the smooth' principle: the unjust enrichment claimant cannot justify distinguishing between the consequences of the defect in her decision making simply on the basis that this distinction furthers her own interests. Such self-serving distinctions are precisely what the 'rough with the smooth' principle rules out.

[58] Honoré, *Responsibility and Fault* (n 40) 134.

[59] See, eg, Honoré's argument that the 'rough with the smooth' principle embodies a fair distribution of risk: ibid 9, 134. Honoré's argument prompts the following question: why is *this* distribution of risk fair rather than any other? To answer this question, it would seem that we are thrown back onto the 'rough with the smooth' principle itself: *cf* J Steele, *Risks and Legal Theory* (Oxford, Hart Publishing, 2004) 94 fn 18.

The argument of this section so far has sought to establish that it is morally objectionable for the claimant to cherry-pick among the consequences of the defect in her decision making by setting up a primary claim based on one of its consequences and then denying the legal relevance of its detrimental consequences to the change of position defence. If this is accepted, the final point to make is a short and simple one. In order to prevent cherry-picking, the baseline for the change of position defence must be formulated to catch all of the detriment which the claimant causes to the defendant by the defect in her decision making on which she grounds her claim. The baseline which catches all of this detriment is none other than the 'no defect' counterfactual.

5. CONCLUSION

It is no inexorable truth that the baseline for the change of position analysis must be set at the point of receipt. At least one serious challenger is available: the 'no defect' counterfactual. The selection of a particular baseline must be justified and, in particular, justified against competitors that might alternatively be adopted. The prevailing favourite in the baseline contest, the 'no receipt' counterfactual, is on its face starkly miraculous. Attempts to avoid such startling miracles create more difficulties for the 'no receipt' counterfactual than are often appreciated. The 'no defect' counterfactual avoids such difficulties and is also independently morally attractive. Cherry-picking by the unjust enrichment claimant among the beneficial and detrimental consequences of the defect in her decision making is morally objectionable and should not be permitted.

6

Proprietary Restitution and Change of Position

ROBERT CHAMBERS

THE ISSUE ADDRESSED in this chapter is the application of the defence of change of position to claims for proprietary restitution. It is difficult because of uncertainties over both the defence and those claims. While it is generally agreed that the defence of change of position applies only to claims for restitution of unjust enrichment, it is not clear which of these claims are subject to the defence and which are not. Also, it is not clear whether and to what extent claims for proprietary restitution are based on unjust enrichment.

This issue is also difficult because there are no cases directly on point. Perhaps this means that there is no problem in need of a solution and that any speculation on the subject is therefore pointless or at least premature. However, as many law teachers know, it is surprising how often hypothetical problems find their way into real courtrooms. Professors Birks and Burrows both worried about the possibility that proprietary claims might not be subject to the defence in cases where both personal and proprietary claims were available. Burrows said:[1]

> [T]o ignore the defendant's change of position in relation to proprietary restitution would be to ignore a fundamental aspect of the explanation and justification of proprietary restitution. ... It would also produce the oddity that a claimant would be presented with the opportunity to outflank the change of position defence by invoking proprietary, rather than personal, restitution.

And Birks said:[2]

> [T]he defence must apply not only to personal claims but also to proprietary claims arising from unjust enrichment. If this were not so, there would be a stampede towards proprietary claims. That must not happen.

[1] A Burrows, *The Law of Restitution*, 3rd edn (Oxford, Oxford University Press, 2011) 547.
[2] P Birks, *Unjust Enrichment*, 2nd edn (Oxford, Oxford University Press, 2005) 209–10.

In any event, a consideration of these issues may lead to a better understanding of the defence and of proprietary restitution, and, for that reason alone, is worth pursuing.

This chapter is divided into five main sections: (a) change of position and its limits; (b) personal and proprietary restitution; (c) kinds of enrichment; (d) successors in title; (e) unjustly enriched defendants and others. An opinion is expressed in each section as to what the law is or ought to be.

The main conclusions are that the defence of change of position should in principle be available to both personal and proprietary claims for restitution of unjust enrichment. However, in most cases of proprietary restitution, the defendant is unlikely to be in a position to satisfy the defence. Also, the original defendant who is unjustly enriched should be treated differently from successors in title. While the property right is created by unjust enrichment, its enforcement against successors is not based on their unjust enrichment and therefore it should not be subject to the defence of change of position at that stage. This leads finally to the problem of drawing fine distinctions between defendants who are similarly situated, with some being entitled to the defence, but not others. The solution to that particular problem would require a reconsideration of the views expressed in *Foskett v McKeown*,[3] concerning the relationship between unjust and enrichment and proprietary claims based on tracing.

1. CHANGE OF POSITION AND ITS LIMITS

Change of position was recognised by the House of Lords as a defence to a claim for restitution of unjust enrichment in *Lipkin Gorman v Karpnale Ltd*, where Lord Goff said:[4]

> At present I do not wish to state the principle any less broadly than this: that the defence is available to a person whose position has so changed that it would be inequitable in all the circumstances to require him to make restitution, or alternatively to make restitution in full.

By stating the defence in general terms, Lord Goff left it to others to work out its exact limits. Professor Bant identified four areas of uncertainty, which she called reliance, fault, ambit of operation and rationale.[5] First, is it necessary that defendants have relied on their apparent entitlement to the enrichment? Second, will defendants be unable to invoke the defence if they have been at fault in some way, for example, by inducing the enrichment or committing a wrong? Third, to which claims is the defence available? Finally, what is the underlying rationale for the defence?

[3] *Foskett v McKeown* [2000] UKHL 29; [2001] 1 AC 102.
[4] *Lipkin Gorman v Karpnale Ltd* [1991] 2 AC 548 (HL) 580.
[5] E Bant, *The Change of Position Defence* (Oxford, Hart Publishing, 2009) 3–9.

The third and fourth of these questions are most relevant to the issue discussed in this chapter. Should the defence apply to claims for proprietary restitution? This depends primarily on why it exists.

1.1. Rationale

There is strong support for the view that the defence is concerned with the question of enrichment. Burrows said that 'the essential justification for the change of position defence is that the defendant has lost the enrichment, ie, disenrichment'.[6]

Although Lord Goff stated the defence in broad terms in *Lipkin Gorman*, it applied in that case precisely because of the defendant's disenrichment. Money had been misappropriated from the plaintiffs by one of their partners, who lost it gambling in the defendant's casino. The defendant had changed its position by paying some of that money back to the partner when he won his bets. In other words, the defence of change of position was used to reduce the defendant's liability from the value it initially received at the plaintiffs' expense to the net value it had retained.

Bant has argued that primary purpose of the defence is to protect defendants from harm when their changes of position are irreversible, regardless of whether they remain enriched in terms of value. She wrote:[7]

> Disenrichment is a common feature of change of position cases and its presence is a strong indicator of when the defence may apply. However ... it is a too restrictive concept to explain the sorts of cases which may, and arguably should, attract the change of position defence. For example, the defence should be capable of applying in cases where the defendant's change of position is irreversible but defies a balance-sheet analysis, as where a defendant decides to conceive a child in reliance on his receipt, or remains enriched on a balance-sheet approach but has re-ordered his life radically and irreversibly in reliance on his receipt.

Some support for this approach can be found in *Commerzbank Ag v Price-Jones*.[8] The defence failed in that case because the defendant remained enriched by the mistaken payment, but Mummery LJ suggested that other kinds of changes of position would suffice if proven:[9]

> The second point is whether there was ... any relevant disenrichment or change of position on the part of Mr Price-Jones. It was for him to establish that, in all the circumstances, it would be inequitable to require him to make restitution. The obvious cases occur where there has been a reduction in the assets of the recipient of the overpayment. In those cases he must prove that there has been a

[6] Burrows (n 1) 526; also see Birks (n 2) 208–09.
[7] Bant (n 5) 211.
[8] *Commerzbank Ag v Price-Jones* [2003] EWCA Civ 1663.
[9] ibid [39].

> reduction of assets, although it is unnecessary for him to produce precise financial calculations quantifying the amount of the reduction. Lord Goff did not, however, restrict the scope of the defence to cases in which there has been a reduction of assets. The defence would also be available, in my view, in various employment situations in which the recipient has made a relevant change of position as a result of the mistaken payment to him: for example, by giving up his current job to lead a life of leisure in circumstances where it would be difficult to find another job, or by turning down a firm offer of a better paid job.

The High Court of Australia recently provided strong support for Bant's approach in *Australian Financial Services and Leasing Pty Ltd v Hills Industries Ltd*.[10] The judges all agreed that change of position should not be confined to disenrichment. French CJ said:[11]

> It may be that disenrichment is a criterion which, applied at the time of demand for repayment, defines a sufficient condition for the application of the change of position defence. It suffices to say, for present purposes, that irreversible detriment is a more useful and flexible guiding criterion to the examination of a change of position defence than disenrichment and is certainly more appropriate to the circumstances of this case.

In the *Australian Financial Services* case, the plaintiff had been fraudulently misled to make payments to the defendants, who believed they were paid to discharge debts owed to them by companies controlled by the fraudster. In reliance on those payments, the defendants continued to deal with those companies and refrained from taking action to enforce the debts. This change of position provided a complete defence even though the defendants could not quantify the exact amount of financial detriment they had suffered.

This was similar to *Philip Collins Ltd v Davis*,[12] where the defendant musicians had been overpaid royalties for six years and spent the money as it came in. They could not quantify the exact amount of the expenditures made in reliance on their apparent entitlement to the mistaken payments, but this operated as a defence for half the value received. Parker J said that 'the court should adopt a broad approach to this question' and decided that one-half was 'on the evidence, a conservative assessment of the extent to which the overpayments led to a change of position on the part of the defendants'.[13]

In both cases, the defence of change of position was successful because the defendants would be left in a worse financial position if they were required to make restitution in full than they would have been in if the mistaken payments had never occurred. The focus was on the overall effect on their

[10] *Australian Financial Services and Leasing Pty Ltd v Hills Industries Ltd* [2014] HCA 14; (2014) 253 CLR 560.

[11] ibid [24].

[12] *Philip Collins Ltd v Davis* [2000] 3 All ER 808 (Ch D).

[13] ibid 830.

wealth, with more or less generous approaches taken with respect to the burden of proof placed upon them.

A generous approach to the defence is essential in cases like these where an innocent defendant is being asked to save a claimant from the consequences of her or his own folly or misfortune. The liability to return a mistaken payment has been compared with a duty to rescue.[14] While repayment is generally regarded as the right thing to do, what justifies turning this 'imperfect moral duty' into a 'perfect legal duty' to make restitution?[15] Unlike the witnesses to an emergency, the recipient of a mistaken payment is the only person in the world who can save the payer from loss without bearing the cost of doing so. However, this is only true to the extent that restitution would leave the recipient in no worse position than if the mistake had never occurred. Where there is any doubt about this issue, it should be resolved in the defendant's favour.

1.2. Ambit

If the defence of change of position is required to ensure that innocent defendants do not bear the cost of rescuing misfortunate claimants, then in principle it should apply as necessary to every kind of unjust enrichment. However, there are serious questions over the ambit of its application in relation to the various unjust factors recognised in English law. It is clear that it can apply to payments made by mistake or with misappropriated funds, so long as the defendant is innocent.[16] In cases where the mistake was caused by the defendant, it may be appropriate to place the burden of rescue on the defendant, even if the misrepresentation was innocent.[17] The defendant's fault is also a complicating factor in most cases of duress and undue influence. The defence normally does not apply to claims based on failure of consideration,[18] but in those cases, the defendant is aware of the basis on which payment was made and so normally does not rely on a false belief of absolute entitlement.

[14] J Penner, 'We All Make Mistakes: A "Duty of Virtue" Theory of Restitutionary Liability for Mistaken Payments' (2014) unpublished.

[15] ibid.

[16] Bant (n 5) 193–94; Burrows (n 1) 544. See, eg, *Storthoaks (RM) v Mobil Oil Canada Ltd* [1976] 2 SCR 147; *Lipkin Gorman v Karpnale Ltd* [1991] 2 AC 548 (HL); *Scottish Equitable plc v Derby* [2001] EWCA Civ 369; [2001] 3 All ER 818; *Dextra Bank v Bank of Jamaica* [2001] UKPC 50; [2002] 1 All ER (Comm) 193; *Australian Financial Services and Leasing Pty Ltd v Hills Industries Ltd* [2014] HCA 14; (2014) 253 CLR 560.

[17] Bant (n 5) 177–84.

[18] R Stevens, 'Is There a Law of Unjust Enrichment?' in S Degeling and J Edelman (eds), *Unjust Enrichment in Commercial Law* (Sydney, Lawbook Co, 2008) 11, 32. See, eg *Goss v Chilcott* [1996] AC 788 (PC (NZ)); [1996] 3 NZLR 385. *cf* Bant (n 5) 197–98; Burrows (n 1) 545–47.

Since our concern is not with the various unjust factors, but with the various kinds of enrichment and methods of restitution, we can sidestep these issues by focusing on claims to proprietary restitution from an innocent defendant on the basis of the claimant's mistake. These are cases where the defence of change of position would potentially be available to a personal claim for the value of the enrichment. We can thereby hope to identify the differences between personal and proprietary claims in relation to the defence, as well as differences among different kinds of enrichment and different forms of proprietary restitution.

2. PERSONAL AND PROPRIETARY RESTITUTION

In 2009, I argued that there are two different kinds of enrichment: monetary value and assignable rights.[19] Since most cases of unjust enrichment concern money paid to the defendant, the enrichment is usually a valuable right. However, defendants can receive value without receiving rights, such as debts discharged or services performed for their benefit. The enrichment can also be the use value of a right rather than the right itself.[20] This does not pose a problem, since a personal claim to restitution of unjust enrichment is always a claim to the monetary value of that enrichment. The essential question is whether and to what extent the defendant is financially better off because of it.

It is easy to understand why the defence of change of position is focused on disenrichment in those cases. The claim is not to any particular asset, but for a sum of money equal to the value of the enrichment. Whether this would impose the cost of rescue on the defendant by putting her or him in a worse financial position than if the enrichment had never occurred is measured by the combined effect on the defendant's overall wealth of the receipt and retransfer of value. The relevant change of position will almost always be a reduction in wealth, which might be caused by a loss of the asset received or a decrease in its value, but can also be caused by expenditures made or other actions taken by the defendant in reliance on the enrichment. Therefore, change of position is commonly understood as a form of disenrichment, even in cases where the defendant still retains the valuable asset which produced the original enrichment.

[19] R Chambers, 'Two Kinds of Enrichment' in R Chambers, C Mitchell and J Penner (eds), *The Philosophical Foundations of the Law of Unjust Enrichment* (Oxford, Oxford University Press, 2009) 242.

[20] *Ministry of Defence v Ashman*; (1993) 25 HLR 513 (CA); *Sempra Metals Ltd v Inland Revenue Commissioners* [2007] UKHL 34; [2008] 1 AC 561.

Cases of proprietary restitution raise different concerns. The claim is for the transfer of a specific asset and, as discussed below, its value may be wholly irrelevant to the claim. Any loss of that asset or reduction in its value will be borne by the claimant who recovers it and so would not count as a relevant change of position. However, if the defendant has incurred expenses or taken other actions in reliance on the apparent entitlement to that asset, the defendant could suffer a financial detriment if required to give it up.

Claims for restitution from an innocent defendant should not impose the cost of rescue on that defendant regardless of whether the claim is for value or rights. A loss of value in reliance on an enrichment should count as a relevant change of position and a potential defence to both personal and property claims. However, if value is irrelevant to the claim for restitution, then a loss of value cannot be understood as a form of disenrichment. Perhaps this is merely a quibble about terminology, but the question in those cases is not whether the defendant is still enriched, but whether the defendant would suffer a detriment.

3. KINDS OF ENRICHMENT

There are several different ways to obtain proprietary restitution. In some cases, the claimant can recover an asset transferred to the defendant by rescinding or rectifying the transfer.[21] Pending rescission or rectification, the claimant has a power to obtain title which can be enforced not just against the defendant, but also against successors in title, subject to defences protecting good faith purchasers. The exercise of that power may cause legal title to return to the claimant,[22] but more often leads to a trust of the asset for the claimant. In other cases, there is no transaction to rescind or rectify and it appears that a trust arises at the outset. This can occur when money is misappropriated or paid by mistake.[23] The registration of a forged transfer of land will cause title to pass even though there is no underlying transaction to rescind, but an application for rectification of the register is required in order to recover title.[24] There are also cases in which the claimant is entitled to an equitable lien or mortgage to secure a personal claim to restitution.[25]

The defence of change of position should in principle be available regardless of the method of proprietary restitution. How the defence might apply

[21] *Blacklocks v JB Developments (Godalming) Ltd* [1982] Ch 183 (Ch D).

[22] *Car & Universal Finance Co Ltd v Caldwell* [1963] EWCA Civ 4; [1965] 1 QB 525.

[23] *Evans v European Bank Ltd* [2004] NSWCA 82; (2004) 61 NSWLR 75; *Chase Manhattan Bank NA v Israel-British Bank (London) Ltd* [1981] Ch 105.

[24] *Malory Enterprises Ltd v Cheshire Homes (UK) Ltd* [2002] EWCA Civ 151; [2002] Ch 216.

[25] *Boscawen v Bajwa* [1996] 1 WLR 328 (CA).

and why it should apply may differ depending on the method of restitution, but a more important distinction can be made on the basis of the kind of enrichment, primarily because the reasons for seeking proprietary restitution can be very different.

Three different kinds of enrichment are considered here: transfers, payments and purchases. The first category consists of those transactions in which an asset other than money is transferred from the claimant to the defendant, and the claimant seeks recovery of that specific asset. In the second category are payments made to or on behalf of the defendant and where the claimant seeks a trust or lien. In the third category are assets other than money purchased for the defendant at the claimant's expense.

3.1. Transfers

Where an asset is transferred by mistake from the claimant to the defendant, the claim to recover it is often made without regard to its value.[26] For example, in *Blacklocks v JB Developments (Godalming) Ltd*,[27] the plaintiff and his uncle transferred land by mistake. They had intended to keep a small portion of the land they were selling, but the plaintiff incorrectly marked the plan which was attached to the contract of sale and the title registered in the purchaser's name. After the uncle died and the land had been sold on to the defendant, the plaintiff was able to recover the mistakenly transferred portion. Judge Mervyn Davies declared that the defendant held it 'on trust absolutely for the plaintiff' and ordered rectification of the registered title.[28]

At no point in the reported judgment in *Blacklocks* was any mention made of the value of the recoverable land; it was irrelevant to the claim. No doubt the land had market value, but the claim was not based on the unjust addition to the purchaser's wealth. The plaintiff wanted to recover the land and not its value because he continued to occupy and use it. The payment of money would not have been an adequate substitute.

There was no possibility of a change of position defence in *Blacklocks* (nor would it have been considered as a possibility a decade before *Lipkin Gorman*). The initial purchaser was unaware that the land had been transferred by mistake and therefore never relied on any apparent entitlement to it. If the purchaser had honestly believed that the land was included in the purchase, then a claim for restitution would have been impossible because the transaction could not have been rectified or rescinded on the basis of the plaintiff's unilateral mistake.

[26] Chambers (n 19) 258–67.
[27] *Blacklocks* (n 21).
[28] ibid 196.

This helps demonstrate why there are no cases directly on point. Even if the defence of change of position should be available in principle, the conditions for invoking it will rarely be satisfied. The mutual mistake required for rectification negates reliance. Rescission of a transfer for value is not possible unless the defendant caused or was at least aware of the claimant's mistake.[29] This either negates reliance or means that the defendant was at fault. In any event, most claims for rescission are brought by the purchaser who is not seeking proprietary restitution, but wants personal restitution of the purchase price. The seller successfully rescinded a sale of company shares in *Spence v Crawford*,[30] but that was on the basis of the buyer's fraudulent misrepresentation. However, Lord Thankerton did say that the defendant's change of position might have been raised as 'a bar to restitution' if his misrepresentation had been innocent.[31]

Today, if a claimant seeks rescission of a transfer made either as a gift or as a transfer for value induced by an innocent misrepresentation, then in principle the defendant's change of position in reliance could operate as a defence to the claim. It might be a total defence and thus a bar to restitution if it is not possible to quantify the value of the detriment suffered. However, there is no reason why compensation for that detriment might not be imposed as a condition for recovery in cases where it can be quantified. A generous approach is needed only to ensure that the cost of rescue is not imposed on an innocent defendant, and no further.

3.2. Payments

When the enrichment consists of the payment of money rather than the transfer of land, shares or some other special asset, the motivation for proprietary restitution is usually different. When money is paid by mistake, repayment of an equivalent sum will provide perfect restitution, regardless of its source. In other words, the claimant is normally concerned only with the value of the enrichment. The main reason for seeking proprietary restitution is to avoid the adverse consequences of the defendant's insolvency.[32] There are exceptions. For example, in *Pitt v Holt*,[33] the claimant sought rescission of a trust settlement in order to avoid its adverse tax consequences. In *Westdeutsche Landesbank Girozentrale v Islington LBC*,[34] the

[29] See *Daventry District Council v Daventry & District Housing Ltd* [2011] EWCA Civ 1153; [2012] 1 WLR 1333; Burrows (n 1) 244–45.

[30] *Spence v Crawford* [1939] 3 All ER 271 (HL).

[31] ibid 281; see Bant (n 5) 110–11.

[32] *Re Berry* 147 F 208 (CA 1906); *Chase Manhattan Bank* (n 23).

[33] *Pitt v Holt* [2013] UKSC 26; [2013] 2 AC 108.

[34] *Westdeutsche Landesbank Girozentrale v Islington LBC* [1996] AC 669 (HL).

claim that money paid under a void contract was held in trust was motivated by a desire for compound interest and based on the false assumptions that the personal claim included only simple interest[35] and that a trust claim would attract compound interest.[36]

The worry expressed by Birks and Burrows (quoted above) is that a desire to avoid the defence of change of position would provide an additional incentive to seek proprietary restitution. Of course, this is only a problem if that defence is unavailable or less effective in response to the property claim.

There would be no practical difficulty providing for a defence of change of position in cases where a mistaken payment is held in trust for the claimant. If the change was the expenditure of the money held in trust, the fund would diminish with no additional personal liability being imposed on the defendant trustee for its loss.[37] If the change consisted of expenses incurred or other actions taken in reliance on the defendant's apparent beneficial ownership of the trust fund, then the defendant trustee should be entitled to reimbursement from the fund for the financial detriment suffered as a result. So long as trustees are not in breach of trust, they are entitled to reimbursement from the trust assets for expenses and liabilities incurred because they are trustees, even if those payments are not normally authorised by the terms of the trust.[38] Any financial detriment suffered which could count as a relevant change of position would be a detriment only because the defendant was unexpectedly a trustee.

In *Westdeutsche Landesbank Girozentrale v Islington LBC*, Lord Browne-Wilkinson said that a person could not be a trustee until he was aware of the trust or the reason for its existence:[39]

> Since the equitable jurisdiction to enforce trusts depends upon the conscience of the holder of the legal interest being affected, he cannot be a trustee of the property if and so long as he is ignorant of the facts alleged to affect his conscience, i.e. until he is aware that he is intended to hold the property for the benefit of others in the case of an express or implied trust, or, in the case of a constructive trust, of the factors which are alleged to affect his conscience.

If this is correct (and with great respect, I do not believe it is),[40] a change of position defence would never be possible once the trust comes into existence.

[35] *cf Sempra Metals Ltd v Inland Revenue Commissioners* [2007] UKHL 34; [2008] 1 AC 561.

[36] A trustee is liable to account for the interest actually earned or the interest that should have been earned. An innocent recipient of money paid by mistake owes no duty to invest and earn compound interest.

[37] See C Mitchell and S Watterson, 'Remedies for Knowing Receipt' in C Mitchell (ed), *Constructive and Resulting Trusts* (Oxford, Hart Publishing, 2010) 115.

[38] *Benett v Wyndham* (1862) 4 De GF&J 259; 45 ER 1183.

[39] *Westdeutsche Landesbank Girozentrale* (n 34) 705.

[40] R Chambers, *Resulting Trusts* (Oxford, Clarendon Press, 1997) 203–09; R Chambers, 'Distrust: Our Fear of Trusts in the Commercial World' (2010) 63 *Current Legal Problems* 631, 645–49.

This raises the problem of how best to deal with reliance expenditures that take place before the trust arises. If the defendant has received the mistaken payment and relied on her or his apparent entitlement to it, this should count as a relevant change of position that can operate with respect to the trust fund which arises later when the defendant is informed of the claimant's mistake. This creates no practical problem, but poses a conceptual puzzle. This sort of change of position is a defence because the defendant relied on an honest but false belief that she or he was entitled to the enrichment. If there is no trust when the change of position occurs, then the belief was not false. The defendant was the beneficial owner of the money at that time. Perhaps the false belief is the defendant's ignorance of the liability that a trust might arise.

If a trust of a mistaken payment is subject to the defence of change of position, it begins to look less like a trust and more like a security interest. The sum owing to the claimant is not the entire fund, but an amount equal to the personal claim for restitution, which is the value of the enrichment received less the value of any changes of position that occur from time to time. The claimant would be perfectly satisfied if paid an equivalent sum, and so the actual source of the payment is irrelevant. The real purpose of the property right is protection from the defendant's insolvency. In substance, it is no different from a lien on the fund to secure performance of the defendant's obligation to make personal restitution to the claimant.

There remains one significant difference. The trust would capture increases in the value of the fund, while the lien might not. This depends on how the obligation secured by the lien is measured. If the increase in the value of the fund is regarded as part of the enrichment of the defendant at the claimant's expense, then the secured debt would increase along with it. If not, then the trust would be preferable from the claimant's point of view. However, if the increase in value was not at the claimant's expense, but was due to the defendant's effort and expertise, and would have been earned with other funds had the defendant been aware of the claimant's mistake,[41] then perhaps a lien is the proper response. Another possible approach in that situation would be to treat all or part of the increase in value as a detrimental loss of opportunity suffered by the defendant, which should count as a relevant change of position.

3.3. Purchases

Purchases are different from transfers because the asset purchased for the defendant was not previously owned by the claimant. This means that the

[41] *cf Re Tilley's Will Trusts* [1967] Ch 1179 (Ch D).

claimant is not seeking to rescind or rectify a transaction and thereby restore an old right, but wants to claim a new right to a new asset by way of a trust or equitable lien.

A payment of any significant amount is usually not accomplished by transfer, but takes the form of a purchase in which the balance of the defendant's bank account is increased at the claimant's expense. This is not true where the payment reduces the defendant's indebtedness (such as a payment into the defendant's overdrawn account or to another creditor) or where cash is paid directly from the claimant to the defendant. Purchases are discussed separately because they are different from payments in cases where the asset purchased has special significance to the claimant, and therefore even if the claimant paid for or contributed money towards the cost of purchase, the payment of the value of the asset purchased might not provide an adequate substitute for that asset.

Claims to purchased assets are most commonly placed in one of two categories: purchase money resulting trusts or tracing. In the former category, the claimant usually pays or contributes intending to acquire a proportionate share of the asset purchased in the defendant's name or at least not intending to make a gift to the defendant.[42] In the latter category, the traceable proceeds are typically acquired with assets that have been misappropriated from the claimant. However, it appears that these are not wholly separate categories. The trust of the traceable proceeds of misappropriated assets is probably best described as 'an old-fashioned institutional resulting trust'.[43]

There are no cases in which a resulting trust was subject to the defence of change of position. However, the defendant is normally aware of the claimant's contribution and therefore is not entitled to raise the defence in any event. In the few cases in which the defendants were unaware of the contribution, they were also unaware that the assets in question had been purchased in their names[44] and so there was no possibility of reliance on their apparent entitlement to those assets. In principle, the defence of change of position should be available if resulting trustees honestly believe they are entitled to the assets free of the trust. This is most likely to occur in the misappropriation cases.

[42] *Brown v Brown* (1993) 31 NSWLR 582 (CA); *Tinsley v Milligan* [1994] 1 AC 340 (HL).

[43] *El Ajou v Dollar Land Holdings plc* [1993] 3 All ER 717 (Ch D) 734, per Millett J; reversed on other grounds [1994] 2 All ER 685(CA). See also *Evans v European Bank Ltd* [2004] NSWCA 82; (2004) 61 NSWLR 75, [112]–[113]; R Chambers, 'Trust and Theft' in E Bant and M Harding (eds), *Exploring Private Law* (Cambridge, Cambridge University Press, 2010) 223, 237–40.

[44] *Birch v Blagrave* (1755) Amb 265; 27 ER 176; *Childers v Childers* (1857) 1 De G&J 482; 44 ER 810; *Re Vinogradoff* [1935] WN 68 (Ch D); *Re Muller* [1953] NZLR 879 (SC).

The main impediment to the application of the defence of change of position in the tracing cases is the view expressed by Lord Millett in *Foskett v McKeown* that claims based on tracing are not based on unjust enrichment:[45]

> The transmission of a claimant's property rights from one asset to its traceable proceeds is part of our law of property, not of the law of unjust enrichment. There is no 'unjust factor' to justify restitution (unless 'want of title' be one, which makes the point). The claimant succeeds if at all by virtue of his own title, not to reverse unjust enrichment.

Perhaps this does not apply to all tracing cases, but only to those which begin with assets misappropriated from a trust, on the basis that the 'beneficiary of a trust is entitled to a continuing beneficial interest not merely in the trust property but in its traceable proceeds also'.[46] This leaves open the possibility that the traceable proceeds of fraud or theft can be recovered on the basis of unjust enrichment and that property rights to those proceeds might be subject to the defence of change of position in the appropriate case.

4. SUCCESSORS IN TITLE

The two main reasons for seeking proprietary restitution discussed above are recovery of a specific asset, regardless of its value, and protection from the consequences of the defendant's insolvency. There is a third important reason, which is the enforcement of the right to restitution against successors in title. This was demonstrated in *Blacklocks v JB Developments (Godalming) Ltd*,[47] discussed above. The defendant was not the original purchaser from the plaintiff, but a subsequent purchaser. To succeed, the plaintiff had to establish not only that he had a proprietary interest in the recoverable land but also that his interest was binding on the defendant. The resolution of this second issue turned on the priority rules under the land registration system.[48] Because the plaintiff had remained in actual occupation of the land, his right to recover it was an overriding interest 'binding on the land in the hands of the defendant'.[49] Judge Davies also said: 'I add that my finding would be the same were the land unregistered.'[50] In that case, the defendant would not have been protected by the defence of bona fide purchase because it had constructive notice of the plaintiff's equitable interest.

45 *Foskett v McKeown* (n 3) 127.
46 ibid.
47 *Blacklocks* (n 21).
48 Land Registration Act 1925 (UK), s 70(1)(g).
49 *Blacklocks* (n 21) 196.
50 ibid.

An important point to note is that the first issue (whether the plaintiff had a proprietary interest) was a question of unjust enrichment, but the second issue (the enforcement of that interest against successors in title) was not. The resolution of the second issue was not affected by the fact that the plaintiff's proprietary interest was created by unjust enrichment. This should mean that change of position, even if relevant at one stage, would be irrelevant to the claim against the successor in title.

Generally speaking, the source of a property right is not relevant when it is enforced against successors in title or other members of society. A property right is deserving of the same protection whether it was acquired for value or as a gift, or even if acquired by finding or theft.[51] This is also true of property rights arising by operation of law. For example, the creation of a constructive trust through proprietary estoppel will depend on the owner's role in creating the claimant's reasonable expectation of acquiring that interest, but when that interest is enforced against others, such as successors in title or mortgagees, we do not ask whether they were responsible in any way for those expectations; it is not relevant.

Property rights to restitution arise when the defendant acquires an asset as an unjust enrichment at the claimant's expense. The factors that brought it into existence (ie, enrichment, expense and an unjust factor) no longer matter when the right is being enforced against successors in title or others. In other words, it is enforced against others because it is a property right and not because they are unjustly enriched.

The creation of property rights and their priority are two separate issues. Professor McFarlane refers to these issues as 'the acquisition question' and 'the defences question'.[52] This is probably just a difference in terminology, but the reference to defences raises an important question: where does the defence of change of position belong in this scheme? The defences of bona fide purchase and indefeasible title and the exceptions to *nemo dat* are general property rules which apply regardless of the source of the property right. The defence of change of position is different, applying only to claims based on unjust enrichment.

The defence of change of position should only be relevant when a right to restitution is enforced against a defendant because that defendant is unjustly enriched. Someone standing in the defendant's shoes, such as a trustee in bankruptcy or executor, should also be able to invoke the defence based on changes of position incurred by the defendant. However, when a property right created by unjust enrichment is enforced against any another person, its enforcement does not depend on the unjust enrichment of that other

[51] *Armory v Delamirie* (1722) 1 Strange 505; 93 ER 664; *Costello v Derbyshire Constabulary* [2001] EWCA Civ 381; [2001] 1 WLR 1437.

[52] B McFarlane, *The Structure of Property Law* (Oxford, Hart Publishing, 2008).

person. Unjust enrichment becomes irrelevant at that stage and so too does the defence of change of position.

The enforcement of the property right against subsequent purchasers or mortgagees might cause them hardship if, for example, they paid full market price and found themselves unexpectedly subject to the claimant's right to restitution because of constructive notice or the priority rules of a land registration system. However, that is the nature of a typical priority dispute. The law of property provides a detailed set of rules to determine who should bear the loss when things go wrong, and often it must choose between two innocent people who are involved in the problem through no fault of their own.

It is at this point that the distinction drawn by Professor Lionel Smith between tracing and following becomes especially important.[53] If the property right arises in response to the defendant's unjust enrichment, and the defendant exchanges the asset received for another asset, the claimant can assert that right to the new asset as the traceable proceeds of the original. The defence of change of position should continue to be relevant. In other words, if the defendant was unjustly enriched by receipt of an asset at the claimant's expense, then the defendant continues to be unjustly enriched because the proceeds were also acquired at the claimant's expense. Changes of position which occur after the exchange should also count.

However, if the defendant transfers the asset to another person, the claimant can follow that asset and assert the restitutionary property right against that other person. At that point, unjust enrichment and change of position cease to be relevant. The claimant's property right is enforceable because it is a property right and not because the successor in title was unjustly enriched.

It might be argued that the source of the property right can be relevant even when that right is being enforced against successors in title. That is because an equitable right to rescind or rectify a transaction is commonly regarded as a 'mere equity', following the obiter dictum of Lord Westbury LC in *Phillips v Phillips*.[54] As such, it is weaker than other equitable property rights and subject not just to the defence of bona fide purchase but also to competing equitable interests acquired in good faith for value without notice of the mere equity.[55] However, even in those situations, its enforcement depends on the application of a particular priority rule and not on whether successors in title or others are unjustly enriched. In a similar way, legal options to rescind a sale of goods are also less durable than other legal property rights,[56] and a legal right to possession of money is lost when it

[53] L Smith, *The Law of Tracing* (Oxford, Clarendon Press, 1997) 6–14.

[54] *Phillips v Phillips* (1862) 4 De GF&J 208, 218; 45 ER 1164, 1167.

[55] *Latec Investments Ltd v Hotel Terrigal Pty Ltd* (in liquidation) (1965) 113 CLR 265 (HCA).

[56] Sale of Goods Act 1979 (UK), s 23.

is paid as currency to a bona fide purchaser.[57] Although special priority rules are used to resolve these disputes, it is still a simple question of priority which is not resolved by reference to unjust enrichment or change of position.

5. UNJUSTLY ENRICHED DEFENDANTS AND OTHERS

If change of position is a defence to property rights to restitution of unjust enrichment, but only when they are enforced against defendants on the basis of their unjust enrichment, this raises the difficult problem of drawing fine distinctions between those property rights which are subject to the defence and those which are not. Similarly situated defendants may be treated differently and that would require justification.

Imagine, for example, that I paid £300,000 to my daughter who honestly believed that the money was a gift from me which she was entitled to spend as she saw fit. In reliance on this, she sold her flat, bought a house, quit her job and went back to university for graduate studies. The £300,000 was used to purchase the house and the proceeds from selling the flat financed her studies. House prices soared over the next few years and the house and the flat both doubled in value. She then discovered that the money I paid to her had been misappropriated from a trust.

From *Foskett v McKeown*,[58] we know that the beneficiaries of the trust are entitled to her house (and possibly also its use value over the intervening years) and that their right is not based on unjust enrichment. Her irreversible change of position does not count. Though better educated, she is homeless and unable to get back on the property ladder. Should it make a difference if the money was not misappropriated from a trust, but was obtained by fraud or theft, or was simply paid to me by mistake? If paid by mistake, should it matter whether I was aware of the mistake when I paid her?

With all these variations, the problem is still the same: my daughter mistakenly believed that she was entitled to the £300,000 and rearranged her life accordingly. It was her honest but mistaken decision to use that money to purchase the house which left her impoverished. If free to argue the point, I would say that regardless of the source of the claimants' property right to the £300,000, their property right to the house was based on unjust enrichment and therefore subject to the defence of change of position.[59] Without

[57] *Miller v Race* (1758) 1 Burr 452; 97 ER 398; *Ilich v The Queen*; (1987) 162 CLR 110, 128.

[58] *Foskett v McKeown* (n 3) 129.

[59] Burrows (n 1) 118–19; R Chambers, 'Tracing and Unjust Enrichment' in J Neyers, M McInnes and S Pitel (eds), *Understanding Unjust Enrichment* (Oxford, Hart Publishing, 2004) 263.

that option, it will become necessary to find some other solution or at least a justification for the problem.

What if instead of paying the money to my daughter, I purchased the house in my name and then transferred it to her? The claim to the house in my name can be understood as restitution of my unjust enrichment, but the claim against her, as a successor in title, is not based on her unjust enrichment. Yet she honestly finds herself in the exact same predicament. Would we be comfortable allowing the defence of change of position to operate in the previous examples, but not in this one?

Perhaps the simplest and best solution is to leave things as they are. Change of position remains a defence of disenrichment which is available only to claims for restitution of unjust enrichment. It applies to claims for proprietary restitution, but only to the extent that the enrichment itself (that is, the right acquired by the defendant at the claimant's expense) is lost or diminished. Since the enrichment is that right and not its value, other reliance losses and harms would not count as disenrichment and are therefore not relevant changes of position. They might, however, operate as bars to rescission or rectification, or as reasons for courts to impose conditions on the exercise of those powers.

If the defence of change of position is allowed to expand beyond disenrichment to include other forms of detriment, this could create two serious problems. First, it would be difficult to explain why the defence should apply only to claims for restitution of unjust enrichment. For example, honest, well-meaning defendants can be guilty of trespass or conversion. The protection provided by English law for rights to possession would be substantially weakened if those tortfeasors could plead hardship as a defence.[60] Second, a general hardship defence would expand the scope of relevant issues in claims for restitution of unjust enrichment (and any other claims for which the defence of change of position becomes available). This would increase the uncertainty, complexity and expense of litigation. So, while in principle the defence should apply to both personal and proprietary claims for restitution of unjust enrichment from innocent defendants, care must be taken to avoid causing greater harm in the pursuit of a solution to a relatively minor problem.

[60] See Bant (n 5) 169–72.

7

Change of Position: Outstanding Issues

ELISE BANT

1. INTRODUCTION

SINCE ITS RECOGNITION a little over two decades ago,[1] a series of important state Supreme Court and High Court decisions have fleshed out key features of the defence of change of position under Australian law. We now know that the recipient's change of position 'must be legally or practically irreversible or there must be significant difficulties in reversing the change'.[2] We know that it is not only positive expenditure or active changes of position that count for the purposes of the defence; forgoing valuable opportunities[3] and decisions *not* to act[4] also clearly fall within its scope of operation. It has now been clarified that the defendant must have 'a foundation of information obtained in connection with the receipt to justify acting on the basis of the receipt.'[5] That is, the defendant's good faith is assessed objectively, having regard to the 'state of mind reasonably engendered'[6] in the recipient by the broader context of the receipt.

[1] *David Securities Pty Ltd v Commonwealth Bank of Australia* (1992) 175 CLR 353 (HCA). In England, see *Lipkin Gorman (A Firm) v Karpnale Ltd* [1991] 2 AC 548 (HL).

[2] *Alpha Wealth Financial Services Pty Ltd v Frankland River Olive Company Ltd* [2008] WASCA 119 [202], discussed below at 3.2.

[3] eg, *TRA Global Pty Ltd v Kebakoska* [2011] VSC 480, discussed below at 161–162.

[4] eg, *Gilsan (International) Ltd v Optus Networks Pty Ltd* [2004] NSWSC 1077 [260] (McDougall J), approved on this point on appeal in *Optus Networks Pty Ltd v Gilsan (International) Ltd* [2006] NSWCA 171 [79] (Hodgson JA, Beasley and McColl JA concurring).

[5] *Perpetual Trustees Australia Ltd v Heperu Pty Ltd* [2009] NSWCA 84; (2009) 76 NSWLR 195 [139] (Allsop P and Campbell JA, Handley AJA separately concurring) (emphasis added), explaining and endorsing *State Bank of New South Wales Ltd v Swiss Bank Corporation* (1995) 39 NSWLR 350 (CA). A similar analysis was pressed, in obiter, in *Hills Industries Ltd v Australian Financial Services and Leasing Pty Ltd* [2014] HCA 14; (2014) 253 CLR 560 [204]–[205] (Meagher JA).

[6] *Citigroup Pty Ltd v National Australia Bank Ltd* [2012] NSWCA 381; (2012) 82 NSWLR 391 [81]; see also [70]–[83], [95]–[102] (Barrett JA) and concurring analysis [4]–[6] (Bathurst CJ, Allsop P and Meagher JA), [17] (Macfarlan JA).

Moreover, the defendant must change her position in a manner that is objectively consistent with the understood basis of her receipt. Thus, a defendant who knows that a benefit is conferred on a conditional basis but, before the condition is fulfilled, acts as if her interest were absolute will not be entitled to the defence. The change of position is inconsistent with the defendant's knowledge of the circumstances of the receipt. This has led to the refusal of the defence in a number of 'failure of basis' cases.[7] This objective approach to good faith has now only further been strengthened by the High Court's recent approval of estoppel as a relevant source of analogy for change of position.[8] The requirement that a defendant's reliance must be reasonable is a very well-established element of all reliance-based estoppels.[9]

In terms of the ambit of operation of change of position, it is also fairly clear following the High Court decisions in *Miller v Miller*[10] and *Equuscorp Pty Ltd v Haxton*[11] that the defence will not be permitted where its application would undermine or stultify some overriding policy or prohibition of the law. Thus, the defence was denied to a landlord in a case of overpaid rent, where allowing the defence would have undermined the protection afforded to tenants under the applicable housing statute.[12] The same principle underpins the growing recognition in England that the defence does not apply to claims pursuant to the principle in *Woolwich Equitable Building Society v Inland Revenue Commissioners*[13] for restitution of unlawfully exacted tax.[14] Similarly, 'wrongdoers' who breach some common law or

[7] *State Bank of New South Wales Ltd* (n 5); *Sanwa Australia Finance Ltd v Finchill Pty Ltd* [2001] NSWCA 466 [29]–[30] (Davie AJA, Beazley and Heydon JJA concurring); *Gilsan (International) Ltd v Optus Networks Pty Ltd* [2004] NSWSC 1077 [358]–[381] (McDougall J); *cf* on appeal *Optus Networks* (n 4) [79] (Hodgson JA, Beasley and McColl JA concurring); *Saba Yachts Ltd v Fish Pacific Ltd* [2006] NZHC 1452 [59]–[62] (Winklemann J).

[8] Discussed below at 148, 150, 154, 5.2.

[9] eg, *Freeman v Cooke* (1848) 2 Ex 654, 681; 154 ER 652, 663; *Standard Chartered Bank Australia v Bank of China* (1991) 23 NSWLR 164 (SC) 180, discussed further in E Bant, *The Change of Position Defence* (Oxford, Hart Publishing, 2009) 43–48.

[10] *Miller v Miller* [2011] HCA 9; (2011) 242 CLR 446.

[11] *Equuscorp Pty Ltd v Haxton* [2012] HCA 7; (2012) 246 CLR 498 [29]–[30].

[12] *Jeffrey v Fitzroy Collingwood Rental Housing Association Ltd* [1999] VSC 335 [44] (Harper J).

[13] *Woolwich Equitable Building Society v Inland Revenue Commissioners* [1993] AC 70 (HL).

[14] *Test Claimants in the FII Group Litigation v HMRC (No 1)* [2008] EWHC 2893 (Ch); [2009] STC 254 [339] (*FII* 2008), approved on appeal [2010] EWCA Civ 103 [109] (Arden LJ giving the judgment of the Court); *Bloomsbury International Ltd v Sea Fish Industry Authority* [2009] EWHC 1721 (QB) [134] (Hamblen J); *Prudential Assurance Co Ltd v Revenue and Customs Commissioners* [2013] EWHC 3249 (Ch) [188] (Henderson J); *Test Claimants in the FII Group Litigation v HMRC (No 2)* [2014] EWHC 4302 (Ch); [2015] STC 1471 [309]–[315] (Henderson J) (*FII* 2014). See further E Bant, 'Change of Position as a Defence to Restitution of Unlawfully Exacted Tax' [2012] *Lloyd's Maritime and Commercial Law Quarterly* 122. The same principle underlies why mistake claims brought in the alternative to *Woolwich* claims cannot be subject to the defence: for discussion of the relevant considerations, see *FII* 2014 [309]–[338] (Henderson J), who, however, declined to express a final view.

equitable duty will not be allowed to avail themselves of the defence where to do so would stultify the law's prohibition.[15]

There have also been active steps taken to locate the defence within its broader legal context. For example, there is increasing support for the view that the agent's defence of payment over[16] is better understood as an early (and limited) manifestation of the change of position defence.[17] In most cases, as the courts have repeatedly acknowledged, a defence of payment over will replicate change of position.[18] This is because its core elements of an irreversible payment over made by the defendant in reliance on the receipt and without notice of the claimant's restitutionary right largely mirror the application of a change of position defence. The only point of distinction between the two lies in the putative[19] requirement for the payment over defence that the principal must be disclosed. But where an agent knows that the principal has not been disclosed, the agent must be aware that the payment is proceeding under a mistake, cannot establish the requirement of objective good faith (as defined previously) and cannot thereby satisfy the change of position defence in any event. It follows that there will be little if any independent work for the agent's defence of payment over that cannot be accommodated through change of position.

Some other matters are yet to be directly addressed by the courts, yet seem inevitably to be resolved in a principled manner, so as to promote consistency in related bodies of rules and doctrines across the wider body of private law. For example, it is yet to be expressly recognised that the defence applies to equitable unjust factors such as undue influence. However, the requirement of *restitutio in integrum* in equitable rescission has arguably

[15] *Lipkin Gorman* (n 1) 580; endorsed in *FII* 2008 (n 14) [320] (Henderson J); *Western Areas Exploration Pty Ltd v Streeter (No 3)* [2009] WASC 213; (2009) 234 FLR 265 [40] (Heenan J). This approach leaves open the possibility that in some cases, allowing the defence to (for example) an innocent wrongdoer will not undermine the law's prohibition: see, eg, *Cavenagh Investment Pte Ltd v Rajiv* [2013] SGHC 45 [60]–[65] (Chan Seng Onn J), a case of innocent trespass. Similar sentiments were expressed by Lord Nicholls in obiter dictum with respect to innocent converters in *Kuwait Airways Corp v Iraqi Airways Co (Nos 4 and 5)* [2002] UKHL 19; [2002] 2 AC 883 [79].

[16] As opposed to the stronger defence of ministerial receipt, which undoubtedly retains an independent existence as a complete defence: see discussion in E Bant, 'Payment Over and Change of Position: Lessons from Agency Law' [2007] *Lloyd's Maritime and Commercial Law Quarterly* 225, 225–27. On this stronger defence, the claimant's cause of action is against, and only against, the principal; it is irrelevant whether or not the agent has paid the benefit over to the principal.

[17] First raised curially in *Lipkin Gorman* (n 1) 578 (Lord Goff), but see, eg, *Hills Industries Ltd* (n 5) [198] (Meagher JA), discussed with apparent approval on appeal in *AFSL v Hills Industries* [2014] HCA 14; (2014) 253 CLR 560 [9] (French CJ).

[18] *Jones v Churcher* [2009] EWHC 722 (QB); [2009] 2 Lloyd's Rep 94 [78] (HHJ Havelock-Allan QC); *Citigroup Pty Ltd* (n 6) [12] (Bathurst CJ, Allsop P and Meagher JA) [16]–[17] (Macfarlan JA) [109]–[113] (Barrett JA).

[19] Compare *Portman Building Society v Hamlyn Taylor Neck* [1998] 4 All ER 202 (CA) 207 (Millett LJ) and *Transvaal and Delagoa Bay Investment Co Ltd v Atkinson* [1944] 1 All ER 579 (KB).

long operated as a functional equivalent to change of position.[20] It therefore comes as no surprise to see that the rules limiting defendant liability in undue influence cases involving rescission closely approximate the application of a change of position defence.[21] The High Court's recent adumbration of the equitable foundations of the defence,[22] taken together with its reiteration of an overriding principle of coherence in the law,[23] surely makes the rationalisation of the two concepts inevitable.[24]

Notwithstanding the significant ground that has been won by courts in developing a coherent law of change of position, key issues remain outstanding.[25] These include the rationale of the defence, whether the defence applies to non-reliance-based changes of position and the uncertain interplay between change of position and other defences such as good consideration and estoppel. This chapter seeks to explore these three issues, to identify the key factors that must be addressed if they are to be resolved and examine some of the broader implications of the analysis. It does so through the prism of the recent High Court of Australia decision in *Australian Financial Services & Leasing Pty Ltd v Hills Industries Ltd* (*AFSL v Hills Industries*),[26] in which each outstanding issue arose either directly or indirectly for consideration.

2. *AFSL v HILLS INDUSTRIES*

The fact pattern of this case is unfortunately only too familiar.[27] The appellant, AFSL (a financier), was induced by a fraudster (S) to make payments to a number of businesses, including Hills and Bosch, for the purchase of what transpired to be non-existent equipment. S advised Hills and Bosch that the payments were for the discharge of debts owed to them by his companies (the 'company debts'). In reliance on their receipts, Hills and Bosch applied the payments in discharge of the company debts,[28] continued to trade with

[20] Bant (n 9) ch 4; and E Bant, 'Rights and Value in Rescission: Some Implications for Unjust Enrichment' in D Nolan and A Robertson (eds), *Rights and Private Law* (Oxford, Hart Publishing, 2011) ch 21.

[21] eg, *Quek v Beggs* (1990) 5 BPR 11,761; *Hartigan v International Society for Krishna Consciousness Inc* [2002] NSWSC 810 [98] (Bryson J).

[22] *AFSL* (n 17) [68]; see also [69]–[76] (Crennan, Kiefel, Bell and Keane JJ).

[23] See also ibid [156] (Gageler J): 'the coherence of the law is enhanced if commonality of concepts results, so far as possible, in commonality of principle'.

[24] Discussed further below at 146, 149, 154.

[25] As many other chapters in this collection demonstrate, these are not the only outstanding issues.

[26] *AFSL* (n 17).

[27] For further scenarios involving third party fraudsters, see, eg, *Dextra Bank & Trust Co Ltd v Bank of Jamaica* [2002] 1 All ER (Comm) 193 (PC); *State Bank of New South Wales Ltd* (n 5); *Port of Brisbane Corp v ANZ Securities* [2002] QCA 158; (2003) 2 Qd R 661; *Orix Australia Corp Ltd v Moody Kiddell & Partners Pty Ltd* [2005] NSWSC 1209; *Bank of Tejarat v Hong Kong and Shanghai Banking Corp Ltd* [1995] 1 Lloyd's Rep 239 (QBD).

[28] Whether the purported discharge was successful is surprisingly unclear from the judgments of the High Court; see below at 148 and 158–160.

the companies and gave up the opportunity to pursue remedies in enforcement proceedings against them or their directors. Both recipients also gave up the opportunity of taking other steps to better their position, such as by seeking security from third parties.

The question of the extent to which a defendant must prove the value of any pleaded change of position, especially where the pleaded change consists of a foregone opportunity, or loss or rights or property (such as the discharged company debts), lay at the heart of the appeal before the High Court.[29] The appellant argued that it was necessary for the respondents to have demonstrated that, at the time of the respondents' change of position, the company debts were valuable as a matter of practical reality (beyond their face value) and thus the extent to which their discharge disenriched the defendants.[30] Second, and more broadly, the respondents' abandonment of various potential actions to seek recovery of the debts or (in the case of Bosch) to consent to set aside judgment in their favour in relation to the debts also required proof of value.[31] This should be done in the same manner and to the same standard as is required, for example, in cases of professional negligence.[32] On the appellant's case, the prospects of recovery elsewhere were extremely limited because of the impecuniosity and in some cases insolvency of the fraudster's companies and the bankruptcy of their directors. Moreover, the appellants denied that the fraudster's wife, who had given security to AFSL for debts owed to it, would have been prepared to do the same for the respondents.[33]

In response, the respondents argued that they had indeed proven that their losses were substantial.[34] They discharged debts owed by the fraudster's companies in reliance on their receipt and, in so doing, gave up opportunities to recover the debts elsewhere. At the time of discharging the debts, the debts were valuable and might well have been fully recovered, potentially from the company debtors but also through the fraudster's wife, who subsequently was prepared to give security to AFSL over the family home. In that sense, the respondents argued that AFSL took the benefit of the opportunity given up by them. These broader changes were not capable of precise valuation because of the passage of time that followed the discharge of the debts. Moreover, the appellant's approach to valuation involved 'a complex unravelling of completely hypothetical dealings between the parties'.[35] In essence,

29 Appellant's Submissions [6] www.hcourt.gov.au/cases/case_s163-2013.
30 ibid [42].
31 ibid [67].
32 ibid [70]–[74].
33 ibid [75]–[76]; Appellant's Reply to the First and Second Respondent's Submissions [2]–[4] www.hcourt.gov.au/cases/case_s163-2013.
34 First Respondent's Submissions [38]–[40] www.hcourt.gov.au/cases/case_s163-2013; Second Respondent's Submissions [34]–[35] www.hcourt.gov.au/cases/case_s163-2013.
35 First Respondent's Submissions (n 34) [38], expanded upon in the Second Respondent's Submissions (n 34) [36].

this submission accepted that detriment must be proven and that although a precise amount could not be placed on the pleaded changes, they roughly equated to the value of the payments received.

More controversially, however, the respondents alleged that, in any event, it is not always necessary to value detrimental changes of position for the purposes of the defence.[36] Denying the analogy with assessing damages in tort, they argued that a better analogy was with estoppel, where it is well accepted that detriment can consist of non-pecuniary changes of position, provided that this is substantial.[37] Similarly, they said, in the case of change of position, provided that the detriment is substantial, where valuation is very uncertain or impossible, the defence should be permitted in full.

Finally, the respondents argued that they gave 'good consideration' for the payments, or were akin to bona fide purchasers, when they bona fide discharged the debts owed to them by the fraudster's companies.[38] The balance of this chapter considers each of these matters in the context of their relationship to the outstanding core issues identified earlier.

3. FINDING THE RATIONALE OF THE DEFENCE: THE ROLE AND MEANING OF 'DETRIMENT'

3.1. Detriment as 'Disenrichment'

In *David Securities Pty Ltd v Commonwealth Bank of Australia*, the High Court of Australia identified as the core requirement of the defence the fact that 'the defendant has acted to his or her detriment on the faith of the receipt'.[39] The importance of detriment or disadvantage as a guiding criterion of the defence was affirmed by the plurality in *AFSL v Hills*,[40] who considered that the defence would apply where 'the recipient has so far altered its position in relation to the receipt that it would be a detriment to it if it were now required to repay'. This emphasis lends support to the view that one[41] rationale of the defence lies in the prevention of detriment or harm

[36] First Respondent's Submissions (n 34) [41]–[59]; Second Respondent's Submissions (n 34) [41]–[44].

[37] First Respondent's Submissions (n 34) [43]–[45]; Second Respondent's Submissions (n 34) [32] and [45]–[47].

[38] First Respondent's Submissions (n 34) [61]–[70]; Second Respondent's Submissions (n 34) [58]–[70].

[39] *David Securities* (n 1) 385 (Mason CJ, Deane, Toohey, Gaudron and McHugh JJ) (emphasis in original omitted); see also *Australia and New Zealand Banking Group Ltd v Westpac Banking Corp* (1988) 164 CLR 662 (HCA) 673 (Mason CJ, Wilson, Deane, Toohey and Gaudron JJ) on the need to establish an 'adverse' change of position.

[40] *AFSL* (n 17) [77] (Hayne, Crennan, Kiefel, Bell and Keane JJ).

[41] This is not the only aim of the defence: as argued in Bant (n 9) ch 9, the defence has a mixed rationale of both protection from harm (detriment) and prophylaxis. The second strand accepts that the defendant's right to protection is not absolute: the defence may be denied

to the defendant.[42] The key question for courts and commentators in that context has been to flesh out this underpinning conception of 'detriment'.

In *AFLS v Hills Industries*, the appellant argued that the rationale of the defence is 'disenrichment'.[43] On this model of the defence, only changes of position that lead to the loss of all or part of the value of the benefit received are taken into account. The disenrichment analysis has been strongly favoured by English courts and commentators.[44] At least one of its perceived attractions is that it tends to exclude the influence of more malleable conceptions of 'unconscionability'[45] or fault[46] in the award of the defence, favouring bright line certainty over an open-textured judicial discretion.[47] But it also seems to tie in nicely with the nature of the claim in unjust enrichment: if a defendant must make restitution where she is unjustly enriched, surely she should be relieved of that liability to the extent that she has become disenriched as a result of her receipt, provided that she has acted in good faith and no bars apply? Otherwise, she will be left unjustifiably in a worse position than she occupied prior to her receipt (the 'no worse off' rationale).[48]

because of the defendant's fault (implicit in the objective requirement of good faith and in other features of the defence) and is more overtly instrumentalist in nature, discussed in ibid 217–18.

[42] The harm-based rationale is powerfully developed in H Dagan, *The Law and Ethics of Restitution* (Cambridge, Cambridge University Press, 2004) 46–47 and nuanced in Bant (n 9) 215–20.

[43] Appellant's Submissions (n 29) [51]–[54].

[44] eg, *Dextra Bank* (n 27); *FII* 2014 (n 14) [309]–[354] (Henderson J). See P Birks, *Unjust Enrichment*, 2nd edn (Oxford, Oxford University Press, 2005) 208–12; A Burrows, *The Law of Restitution*, 3rd edn (Oxford, Oxford University Press, 2011) 526.

[45] See, eg, the judgment of Munby J in *Commerzbank Ag v Price-Jones* [2003] EWCA Civ 1663, criticised in A Burrows, 'Clouding the Issues on Change of Position' (2004) 63 *CLJ* 276, 279.

[46] As applied in such cases as *National Bank of New Zealand Ltd v Waitaki International Processing (NI) Ltd* [1999] 2 NZLR 211; and *Foai v Air New Zealand Ltd* [2012] NZEmpC 57, upheld on appeal in *Air New Zealand Ltd v Foai* [2012] NZCA 341 [14] (Glazebrook, White and Simon France JJ).

[47] *Dextra Bank* (n 27) [45], adopting the arguments of P Birks, 'Change of Position and Surviving Enrichment' in W Swadling (ed), *The Limits of Restitutionary Claims: A Comparative Analysis* (London, United Kingdom Committee of Comparative Law, 1997) 36, 41. See also Burrows (n 44) 526–27; and, in Canada, Mitchell McInnes, *The Canadian Law of Unjust Enrichment and Restitution* (Markham, ON, LexisNexis, 2014) 1495–502.

[48] I do not adopt the counterfactual formulation of this rationale as expressed, for example, by A Burrows, *A Restatement of the English Law of Unjust Enrichment* (Oxford, Oxford University Press, 2012) 117 (and analysed in detail by Ajay Ratan in ch 5 of this volume) for two main reasons. The first is that the formulation preferred here, which looks to the parties' respective historical positions, in my view most closely tracks the approach taken in equitable rescission with which the defence is, and should in my view remain, closely aligned: see below at section 3.2. The second is the inherently ad hoc and entirely speculative nature of the hypothetical worlds often called up for the purposes of contrast on the counterfactual formulation, which are in my view an unprincipled basis on which to determine liability arising from the facts as they actually occurred, a view apparently shared by French CJ in *AFSL* (n 17) [30], below at 151, and a strong focus of the Respondents' submissions, above at 137. See also the analysis

As we will see, this rationale has strong support from the Australian authorities. But the role of disenrichment in establishing or reflecting that rationale is not without its difficulties. It was originally conceived by Peter Birks as going to and negating the core requirement of 'enrichment' in the primary claim.[49] This 'absent element' approach results in the claimant's prima facie right to restitution being determined by reference to the net benefit abstractly surviving at the date of hearing. There are two initial concerns about this approach. The first is the danger—realised in some cases—that by focusing on the extent to which a defendant's assets remain swollen by her receipt, the defence will come to be treated simply as an aspect of the general enrichment enquiry.[50] This is contrary to the vast preponderance of authority that conceives of and treats the defence as having a role independent of the elements of the primary claim.[51]

The second and related issue is that any shift in focus when identifying the actionable enrichment, from the benefit received to the benefit retained, may encourage confusion of the distinct remedies of restitution and disgorgement. As the House of Lords and, subsequently, the UK Supreme Court have now affirmed, personal restitution involves giving back the (generally objective) value of a benefit received by a defendant from a claimant.[52] Disgorgement, by contrast, is a remedy that reaches to profits that have come from third parties and not from the claimant, such as a bribe received by a fiduciary. In this aspect, disgorgement does not obviously overlap with the field of operation of claims for restitution. However, the remedy of disgorgement also extends to the actual or subjective profit obtained by a defendant from, for example, the use of the claimant's property.[53] These profits are (in part)

of Ajay Ratan in ch 5 this volume. The same concern has been expressed repeatedly in relation to estoppel: see, eg, *Brikom Investments v Carr* [1979] QB 467 (CA) 482 (Lord Denning); *Greasely v Cooke* [1980] 1 WLR 1306 (CA) (Lord Denning); *cf Sidhu v Van Dyke* [2014] HCA 19; (2014) 251 CLR 505 [67]–[78] (French CJ, Kiefel, Bell and Keane JJ). The concern is less acute where there are clear patterns of behaviour by the defendant (weekly expenses, regular mortgage repayments) that provide some sound basis for testing the proposed counterfactual.

[49] P Birks, *Restitution—The Future* (Leichhardt, Federation Press, 1992) 128–42; P Birks, 'Overview: Tracing, Claiming and Defences' in P Birks (ed), *Laundering and Tracing* (Oxford, Clarendon Press, 1995) 331; Birks (n 44) 207–09. See also R Chambers, 'Two Kinds of Enrichment' in R Chambers, C Mitchell and J Penner (eds), *Philosophical Foundations of the Law of Unjust Enrichment* (Oxford, Oxford University Press, 2009) 247–49, 268.

[50] The inexorable tendency of this reasoning is demonstrated in the line of cases employing 'unjust retention of benefit' reasoning: see *Ford v Perpetual Trustees Victoria Ltd* [2009] NSWCA 186; (2009) 75 NSWLR 42; *Heperu Pty Ltd v Belle* [2009] NSWCA 252; (2009) 76 NSWLR 230; [150]–[158] (Allsop P, Campbell JA and Handley AJA concurring); *Break Fast Investments Pty Ltd v Giannopoulos (No 5)* [2011] NSWSC 1508 [75]–[84] (Black J), favouring the language of Lord Templeman over Lord Goff in *Lipkin Gorman* (n 1); see also Gummow J in *Roxborough v Rothmans of Pall Mall Australia Ltd* (2001) 208 CLR 516 (HCA) [83]–[89].

[51] Most obviously, in Australia, *David Securities* (n 1) and now *AFSL* (n 17).

[52] *Sempra Metals Ltd v Inland Revenue Commissioners* [2007] UKHL 34; [2008] 1 AC 561; *Benedetti v Sawiris* [2013] UKSC 50; [2013] 3 WLR 351.

[53] *Sempra Metals* (n 52) [32] (Lord Hope), [117] (Lord Nicholls), [180] (Lord Walker).

attributable to the defendant's labours and so do not come wholly 'from' the claimant. This actual or subjective benefit is a different measure of benefit from the market or objective value of what was received from the claimant and which is the subject of the order for restitution. Disgorgement requires 'giving up' benefits that may not have come from the claimant: restitution requires 'giving back' enrichments that have from the claimant's assets or labour.

The remedy of disgorgement also requires quite different justifications for its award. It is very difficult if not impossible to justify a disgorgement remedy (as defined above) on the basis of unjust enrichment. Unjust enrichment is a strict liability claim, which is not dependent on proof of any fault or wrongdoing on the part of the defendant.[54] For this reason, an unjust enrichment defendant should only be liable to return (make restitution of) the benefit received from the claimant. This 'weak' form of liability is justified because it does no harm to the defendant; rather, it simply returns the parties to their respective former positions.[55] By contrast, where a claimant seeks an order with respect to profits generated from the defendant's use of the claimant's asset, the relevant remedy is disgorgement, not restitution. And to support that form of relief, the claimant must point to some form of claim other than unjust enrichment, such as wrongdoing on the part of the defendant or an applicable statutory claim. The lack of fit between disgorgement and unjust enrichment is underscored by the fact that the usual remedial purposes identified for disgorgement remedies—deterrence and prophylaxis of wrongdoing[56]—have no application to innocent recipients.

Pertinently for the 'disenrichment' analysis, this necessary and important distinction between the remedies of disgorgement and restitution not only applies to circumstances where the defendant has made a subjective profit from her use of the benefit received from the claimant, but also applies where the defendant has suffered a *loss* from its actual use. In those circumstances, a disgorgement measure reaches to the actual (subjective) benefit obtained by the defendant from the impugned transaction. Where the defendant's use has diminished the value of the benefit originally received, that amount will be less than and distinct from what would be the applicable restitutionary award measured at the point of receipt of the enrichment from the claimant. By looking at the benefit retained as the primary measure of relief rather than identifying the actionable enrichment as the benefit received, subject to

[54] Affirmed in *AFSL* (n 17) [83] (Crennan, Kiefel, Bell and Keane JJ).

[55] Birks (n 44) 7–8.

[56] eg, J Edelman, *Gain-Based Damages: Contract, Tort, Equity and Intellectual Property* (Oxford, Hart Publishing, 2002) 83–86; S Worthington, 'Reconsidering Disgorgement for Wrongs' (1999) 62 *MLR* 218; M Conaglen, *Fiduciary Loyalty: Protecting the Due Performance of Non-fiduciary Duties* (Oxford, Hart Publishing, 2002); *cf* L Smith, 'Deterrence, Prophylaxis and Punishment in Fiduciary Obligations' (2013) 7 *Journal of Equity* 87.

defences such as change of position, there is a clear danger that what should be a restitutionary claim will transform into a claim for disgorgement.

To avoid this elision of remedies, the point must be kept clearly in view that claims for restitution of unjust enrichment are not established by reference to the actual (subjective) benefit derived by the defendant from the claimant's asset; this wrongly equates the remedy of restitution with that of disgorgement. Rather, as recognised by Henderson J in *Test Claimants in the FII Group Litigation v HMRC*,[57] a failure to use a received benefit profitably (such as where a defendant places money under her bed rather than placing it in an interest-bearing account)[58] in a case of unjust enrichment should be characterised as a plea of change of position in diminution of the defendant's restitutionary liability. Importantly, whether the defendant is entitled to protection in those circumstances depends on a number of factors going beyond mere loss of value—it includes, for example, whether she has acted in good faith. This approach also leaves open the possibility that the defence may operate beyond 'disenriching' changes of position, a point to which we will return below.

Even putting aside these preliminary concerns, it remains the case that critical to the 'disenrichment' model of the defence is that the change of position enquiry must mirror the enrichment element of the cause of action. However, the concepts of 'enrichment' for the purposes of the primary claim and 'disenrichment' for the purposes of the defence do not readily align. It is noticeable that the answers to the question of what kinds of changes of position are relevantly 'disenriching' have evolved over time. Initially, reliance expenditure was seen as occupying centre stage.[59] The apparent requirement for an outflow of wealth caused there to be some doubt over whether decisions not to act, or to forego a benefit, fell within the scope of the defence.[60] Over time, it was gradually accepted that the defence should extend to such changes.[61] This development was largely consistent with the growing realisation for the purposes of the primary claim that a defendant may be enriched by so-called 'negative' benefits, such as by being saved necessary expenditure.[62] To this extent, the concept of 'disenrichment' evolved alongside and consistently with a better understanding of the core element of 'enrichment'.

[57] *FII* 2014 (n 14).

[58] *Sempra Metals* (n 52) [119] (Lord Nicholls); [233] (Lord Mance).

[59] Birks, 'Overview' (n 49) 328. The same focus is apparent in *David Securities* (n 1) 385.

[60] *National Westminster Bank Plc v Somer International (UK) Ltd* [2001] EWCA Civ 970; [2002] QB 1286 [47] (Potter LJ).

[61] Above, nn 3 and 4.

[62] eg, *Brasher v O'Hehir* [2005] NSWSC 1194 [36] (Brereton J); *Young v ACN 081 162 512* [2005] NSWCA 139; (2005) 218 ALR 449; *Anaconda Nickel Ltd v Tarmoola Australia Pty Ltd* (2000) WAR 101 (CA); *Monks v Poynice Pty Ltd* (1987) 8 NSWLR 662 (SC). See also J Edelman and E Bant, *Unjust Enrichment in Australia* (Melbourne, Oxford University Press, 2002) 110–12.

But it is now said that changes of position that do not appear to be inherently pecuniary in nature, such as the decision to have a child, also have their 'foundations in disenrichment'.[63] No doubt children do have pecuniary consequences. But as Peter Birks himself noted, the concept of a relevant 'enrichment' *excludes* things like children, who cannot and should not be regarded as relevant material gains for the purposes of unjust enrichment law.[64] To label the conception and delivery of a child as relevantly 'disenriching' for the purposes of change of position therefore seems to stretch the concept well beyond its natural domain. In one sense, this extension of the concept of disenrichment is very welcome, because it rightly ensures that defendants who have made 'life-changing decision[s] with irreversible consequences of a profoundly personal nature'[65] can be and are brought within the protection of the defence. We consider in the next section whether there is another (and better) way of conceptualising the detriment which the defence is concerned to avoid, which incorporates such cases but does not meet similar difficulties.

There are further issues of 'fit' between the concepts of enrichment and disenrichment. For the purposes of the primary claim, enrichment is most clearly established where the defendant has chosen the benefit that was in fact received from the claimant.[66] This finding is not affected by the fact that the chosen enrichment was a service that produced no lasting end product or perishable goods. Applying the same test to the defence, the fact that the defendant has chosen to purchase such a benefit (for example, a holiday or a fine meal) in reliance on her receipt should mean that she was enriched by her purchase and, on the 'disenrichment' version of the defence, does not qualify for the defence. However, this result is not consistent with the authorities[67] and is starkly contrary to the outcome sought by those who adopt a 'disenrichment' analysis.[68]

Birks recognised the problem and sought to save the disenrichment analysis by relying on the concept of 'subjective devaluation':[69] on this approach,

[63] P Birks, 'Change of Position: The Two Central Questions' (2004) 120 *LQR* 373, 375. See also Birks (n 44) 260; Burrows (n 44) 526.

[64] Birks (n 44) 51. This point is explored in detail and with particular regard to lessons from the law of torts in Bant (n 9) 132–34.

[65] *Donis v Donis* [2007] VSCA 89 [34] (Nettle JA, Maxwell ACJ and Ashley JA concurring), in which the pleaded detriment in a case of proprietary estoppel included marrying and conceiving a child.

[66] *Lumbers v W Cook Builders Pty Ltd (in liquidation)* [2008] HCA 27; (2008) 232 CLR 635 [79] (Gummow, Hayne, Crennan and Kiefel JJ); *Benedetti* (n 52) [112]–[117] (Lord Reed).

[67] Clear from cases such as *Philip Collins Ltd v Davis* [2000] 3 All ER 808 (Ch D), where the defendants simply spent the value of the overpayments on an increased standard of living which left no residual benefit in their hands.

[68] eg, Birks, *Restitution—The Future* (n 49) 138; and McInnes (n 47) 1494, citing the example of a defendant who takes a holiday in reliance on his receipt as a prime example of the disenrichment defence.

[69] P Birks, *An Introduction to the Law of Restitution*, revised edn (Oxford, Clarendon Press, 1995) 413–15; Birks, *Restitution—The Future* (n 49) 137–39; Birks, 'Overview' (n 49)

a defendant is entitled to subjectively devalue (or, perhaps more accurately, revalue)[70] the choice she made once she becomes aware of the claimant's demand for restitution. It has to be said that the concept of subjective devaluation is ambiguous and accordingly remains contentious, even when employed in the context of establishing enrichment for the purposes of the primary claim.[71] However, accepting for the moment a role for the concept in the context of the primary claim, its application in relation to the defence is problematic. This is because the critical role proposed for subjective devaluation by disenrichment proponents suggests that the unpinning rationale of the change of position defence is not in truth disenrichment (which becomes instead a mere element of the defence), but that the defendant's decision to change her position (in a way that was relevantly disenriching) was *vitiated* (usually by her mistaken belief in the security of her receipt). It is the defendant's vitiated consent that underpins her right to reassess, or subjectively devalue, her choice to change her position and it is this that underpins the 'disenrichment' analysis. This more nuanced analysis proposes that, just as the claimant's autonomy must be protected by allowing restitution in cases where her consent was impaired or conditional, so too must the defendant's autonomy be protected where her decision to change her position was similarly vitiated or qualified. On this closer analysis of the mechanics of the disenrichment model, the rationale of the change of position defence becomes equal protection for the defendant's autonomy, a model known as 'unjust disenrichment'.[72]

However, this emphasis on the importance of the defendant's autonomy to this model of the defence reveals the very reason why unjust disenrichment cannot be accepted as reflecting the rationale of the change of position defence, at least as the defence appears in the authorities. On the authorities, the very fact of impairment that underpins the unjust disenrichment analysis

331–32. *cf* J Edelman, 'Change of Position: A Defence of Unjust Disenrichment' (2012) 92 *Boston University Law Review* 1009, 1020, who argues that just as a claimant's choice of enrichment must be characterised and valued by reference to any conditions she placed on that choice, so too a defendant who changes his position on the condition that he is not subject to any restitutionary obligation must be treated as disenriched. This analysis avoids any role for 'subjective devaluation' while aligning the enrichment and disenrichment enquiries. However, it must be said that the condition seems to be one that is identified *ex post facto* and only highlights the critical importance of the defendant's vitiated consent to any disenrichment analysis, discussed immediately below.

[70] The 'fit' between change of position and subjective devaluation is carefully examined by R Nolan, 'Change of Position' in Birks, *Laundering* (n 49) 139–43, who concludes that there remains room for a non-enrichment-related defence of change of position.

[71] Compare the differing analyses of the concept in *Benedetti* (n 52) [12]–[26] (Lord Scott), [110]–[118] (Lord Reed) and the extended analysis in *Littlewoods Retail Ltd v HM Revenue and Customs* [2014] EWHC 868 (Ch); [2014] STC 1761 [363]–[374] (Henderson J), preferring Lord Reed's analysis.

[72] Powerfully argued in Edelman (n 69). See also the similar but distinct analysis of Ajay Ratan in ch 5 of this volume.

also means that, in some cases, the defendant will be able to reverse her change of position by bringing an action in unjust enrichment arising from the defendant's mistaken transfer of benefit to a third party. Where that is so, the defence will be denied, not applied. Thus, in a long line of cases, the change of position defence failed where defendants paid tax on the received benefit in reliance on their receipt and simple procedures existed to reclaim that amount from the third party taxing authorities.[73] These cases and others discussed further below clearly indicate that the reversibility of a defendant's change of position (on the grounds of the defendant's impaired consent) will exclude the defence. These authorities accordingly demonstrate that 'disenriching' changes of position founded on a defendant's vitiated consent will not suffice to qualify for the defence; the change of position must be irreversible. The conclusion must be that the concept of 'disenrichment', whether considered independently or as part of a more subtle 'unjust disenrichment' enquiry, ultimately fails satisfactorily to align with the concept of 'enrichment' for the purposes of the primary claim and is inconsistent with the established operation of the defence. Taken together, these considerations suggest that 'disenrichment' remains an incomplete and problematic explanation of the concept of detriment at the heart of change of position.

The final concern regarding the disenrichment concept of the defence is that, unless (as discussed earlier) it adopts a broader (and strained) definition of 'disenrichment' than applies to the concept of enrichment for the purposes of the primary claim, it threatens artificially to restrict the kinds of changes of position that may attract the defence. As Allsop P observed in the New South Wales Court of Appeal decision in *Hills Industries Ltd v Australian Financial Services and Leasing Pty Ltd*:[74]

> There are difficulties ... in using purely monetary and expenditure based considerations to decide upon change of position. Given the broad range of acts and omissions that may legitimately be done or not done on the faith of a receipt, to require the measurement of the payee's position in terms only of the currency of the payer's mistake may unfairly or mechanically restrict the just reconciliation of the competing rights.

In *AFSL v Hills Industries*, the High Court endorsed and emphasised this point in emphatically rejecting the disenrichment analysis.[75] While generally accepting (without analysing the question) that disenriching changes

[73] *K & S Corp Ltd v Sportingbet Australia Pty Ltd* [2003] SASC 96; (2003) 86 SASR 312, 348 (Besanko J); *Fazzolari v Couchouron* [2003] VCAT 503; *Hinckley and Bosworth BC v Shaw* (1999) 1 LGLR 385 (QBD) 425 (Bell J); *Hillsdown Holdings plc v Pensions Ombudsman* [1997] 1 All ER 862 (QBD) 904 (Knox J).

[74] *Hills Industries Ltd* (n 5) [153], Bathurst CJ concurring on this point.

[75] *AFSL* (n 17) [22]–[25] (French CJ), [78]–[84] (Crennan, Kiefel, Bell and Keane JJ), [147]–[148] (Gageler J).

of position might well attract the defence, the disenrichment enquiry was seen wrongly to exclude relevant changes of position that are difficult or impossible to value. Moreover, it artificially restricts the considerations that inform the defence, contrary to what the High Court identified as the equitable foundations of both the unjust enrichment concept and the defence of change of position. In that context, the concept of 'irreversibility' was seen to be a far better guide to the role and nature of detriment in the change of position defence, to which we now turn.

3.2. 'Irreversible' Change and the Rationale of the Defence

A developing, alternative formulation to 'disenrichment' of the requirement for a 'detrimental' change of position, which has been articulated most forcefully by the Australian supreme courts, is that a relevant change of position must be irreversible.[76] As expressed by the Western Australian Supreme Court of Appeal in *Alpha Wealth Financial Services Pty Ltd v Frankland River Olive Company Ltd*,[77] this conception of the defence requires that 'the recipient must have changed his or her position, and the change must be legally or practically irreversible or there must be significant difficulties in reversing the change'. Similarly to the process regularly undertaken in rescission,[78] the court's aim is to to make an order that reverses the original transfer while ensuring that the defendant is (to the extent the defence applies) not placed in a worse position than the one she occupied prior to her receipt. The object is to restore both parties in substance to the status quo ante, so far as is possible in light of any irreversible change of position.[79] To this end, the court undertakes a valuation of the irreversible changes to the defendant's position (changes that are readily reversible by

[76] The requirement is pervasive in the authorities. Outside the taxation context, see, eg, *Scottish Equitable plc v Derby* [2001] EWCA Civ 369; [2001] 3 All ER 818 [34] (Robert Walker LJ); *Jaffer v Commonwealth Bank of Australia Ltd* [2001] SASC 191 [61]–[67] (Perry J); *Eden Productions Pty Ltd v Southern Star Group Ltd* [2002] NSWSC 1166 [226] (Gzell J); *Day v Day* [2005] EWHC 1455 (Ch) [49] (Henderson J). Similar requirements are found in estoppel, the agent's defence of payment over and the requirement of *restitutio in integrum* found in rescission: see Bant (n 9) chs 2–4. For recent payment over cases that expressly endorsed the reversibility requirement, see *Jones* (n 18) [69] (HHJ Havelock-Allan QC); *Citigroup Pty Ltd* (n 6) [109] (Barrett JA) (Bathurst CJ, Allsop P, Meagher JA and Macfarlan JA agreeing on this point).

[77] *Alpha Wealth* (n 2) [202]; see also *Fitzsimons v Minister for Liquor Gaming and Racing for the State of New South Wales* [2008] NSWSC 782 [128]–[129] (McDougall J); *Glad Cleaning Service Pty Ltd v Vukelic* [2010] NSWSC 422 [51] (Slattery J). However, for a recent authority expressly rejecting the irreversibility requirement, see *FII* 2014 (n 14) [353]–[355].

[78] For a good example with clear change of position insights, see *Hartigan* (n 21).

[79] In the context of rescission, see *Erlanger v The New Sombrero Phosphate Company* (1878) 3 App Cas 1218 (HL) 1278 (Lord Blackburn); *Alati v Kruger* (1955) 94 CLR 216 (HCA) 224 (Dixon CJ, Webb, Kitto and Taylor JJ).

the defendant, such as by sale of an asset, are left out of the account) and offsets that amount against what would otherwise be the full measure of the defendant's restitutionary liability. Courts are, in general, eminently capable of engaging in such nice questions of valuation. In rare cases where the irreversible change of position is very significant viewed against the receipt and very difficult or impossible to value, the defence will operate to defeat entirely the claimant's prima facie right to restitution.[80]

Unlike the 'disenrichment' model of the defence, the irreversibility requirement emphasises that the concept of a 'detrimental' change of position properly extends well beyond inherently pecuniary changes to changes such as the decision to marry, divorce[81] or bear a child.[82] But it also emphasises that the value of a defendant's apparently pecuniary change of position is not really the critical question in this enquiry. A decision (for example)[83] by a company director made in reliance on her receipt of a benefit to give up that directorship and let the company take a new direction is not relevant because it is 'disenriching': it might or might not involve some alteration in the defendant's overall fiscal position. What is relevant is that, notwithstanding that the defendant may remain 'net enriched' on a balance-sheet approach, she has effected a radical and irreversible change to her life in reliance on her receipt. The defence similarly succeeded where a defendant gave up her employment to take up full-time university studies in reliance on her receipt of a mistaken payment.[84] Unless we take the unpalatable view that the university studies she received were not beneficial or valuable, she remained net enriched by her receipt. Indeed, in the longer term, her change of position might well have led to substantial increased wealth through realising her higher earning potential as a university graduate. But that was not really the point. In such cases, it is not possible to reverse, unwind or restore the transaction through some *pro tanto* order for restitution so as to restore the defendant substantially to the status quo ante. *Restitutio in integrum* is impossible. Rather, to require the defendant to make restitution in those circumstances would be to place her in an entirely different position from the one she occupied prior to his receipt. This is contrary to the aims of restitution for unjust enrichment (discussed earlier) and is unjustified in the absence of some bad faith, wrongdoing or other barring conduct or circumstance applying to the defendant.

[80] As in *Kinlan v Crimmin* [2006] EWHC 779 (Ch) (discussed immediately below).

[81] An example suggested by Munby J in *Commerzbank Ag* (n 45) [68] as a change of position that would come within the defence.

[82] As in *Donis* (n 65) [34] (Nettle JA, Maxwell ACJ and Ashley JA concurring), in which marrying and conceiving a child were found to be sufficiently detrimental changes of position to establish a claim of a proprietary estoppel. The requirement is examined in detail in Bant (n 9) ch 5.

[83] *Kinlan* (n 80).

[84] *Gertsch v Atsas* [1999] NSWSC 898; (1999) 10 BPR 18 431.

In *AFSL v Hills Industries*, the requirement of irreversibility was adopted expressly by French CJ[85] and underpinned the critical reasoning of the plurality[86] on the application of the defence to the particular facts of that case. For French CJ, the practical exercise of applying the defence in accordance with the criterion of 'irreversible detriment' requires courts to consider the 'detriment suffered by the defendant at the point of demand for recovery'.[87] As his Honour explained, in the present case, at the point at which the appellant demanded repayment, the respondents had irreversibly lost any prospect of recovering some or all of the monies owed to them. Justices Crennan, Kiefel, Bell and Keane applied the same criterion. In particular, they rejected the appellant's claim that the appropriations by the defendants of the payments to satisfy the companies' debts were 'mere book entries' that could be reversed without affecting the substance of the transactions or relationships.[88] Rather, the payments were genuinely applied by the defendants to discharge the company debts. Importantly, their Honours noted that even if those discharges themselves were somehow reversible as a matter of law (for example, due to the fraud of the companies against the appellant), by the time the appellant's error came to light, these changes, together with others such as the decision to keep trading with the companies, were irreversible as a practical matter of business.[89]

It must be concluded that the High Court's emphasis on irreversibility as a key criterion of the defence strongly supports a 'no worse off' rationale of the defence. However, there is also express support for this conclusion to be found in the judgments. Thus, in the course of their joint reasons, Crennan, Kiefel, Bell and Keane JJ explained that the law of estoppel is concerned with avoiding the detriment that would be suffered by the defendant if the claimant were to resile from the assumption on which he changed his position. So too, they said, change of position serves to protect a defendant from 'the detriment which would flow from a party's change of position … if the [claimant] were to be permitted to recover payments as mistakenly made where they have been applied by the [defendant]'.[90] Also drawing strongly from the equitable doctrine of estoppel, Gageler J similarly identified as an important condition attracting the defence that 'by reason of having so acted or refrained from acting, the defendant would be placed in a worse position if ordered to make restitution of the payment than if the defendant had not received the payment at all'.[91]

[85] *AFSL* (n 17) [23]–[25].
[86] ibid [95].
[87] ibid [23].
[88] ibid [95].
[89] ibid.
[90] ibid [84]–[85].
[91] ibid [157]. On the counterfactual formulation, see comment above at n 48.

Both these characterisations of the aim of the defence strongly echo the principle of *restitutio in integrum* found in rescission.[92] They also emphasise the close relationship noted earlier between the defence and the remedies of restitution and rescission. It is uncontentious under Australian law that these remedies aim to reverse, unwind or restore any transaction from claimant to defendant by which the defendant was enriched. They do not aim to compensate the claimant or to punish the defendant. As the plurality noted in *AFSL v Hills Industries*,[93] such claims are not founded upon a wrong done to the payer, and so any analogy with or reference to compensation is inapt. It follows that restitution can only be permitted where it will not cause harm to innocent defendants, otherwise the remedy operates (contrary to its purpose) to impose harm on the defendant.

In conclusion, acceptance in Australia of the core requirement of irreversibility, as well as insights drawn from estoppel and rescission, strongly support the harm-based rationale of the defence adumbrated in *AFSL v Hills Industries*. This rationale is that the defendant should not be placed as a result of her receipt (and hence restitutionary liability) in an unjustifiably[94] worse (including wholly different) position from the one she occupied prior to her receipt.

3.3. The Standard of Proof of Detriment

We have seen that a defendant must demonstrate that she faces significant legal or practical difficulties in reversing the change in order for it to count as 'detrimental' for the purposes of the defence.[95] Thus, where a defendant purchases an asset in reliance on her receipt, courts generally regard any detriment as limited because the asset can be sold and thus the change reversed.[96] The value of the defence will be limited to any proven depreciation of the asset.[97] The defence is only available if the defendant can show that there are significant legal or practical difficulties in reversing the change, as, for example, where the market for an asset is negligible or has disappeared since its purchase, or extensive modifications have been

[92] See also D O'Sullivan, S Elliott and R Zakrzewski, *The Law of Rescission*, 2nd edn (Oxford, Oxford University Press, 2014) [18.07]–[18.08].

[93] AFSL (n 17) [83].

[94] As discussed above at 133–134, fault plays a role in the defence through an objective requirement of good faith.

[95] *Alpha Wealth* (n 2) [202].

[96] *Lipkin Gorman* (n 1) 560 (Lord Templeman); *Credit-Suisse (Monaco) SA v Attar* [2004] EWHC 374 (Comm) [98] (Gross J); *Campden Hill Ltd v Chakrani* [2005] EWHC 911 (Ch); [2005] NPC 65 [87] (Hart J). McInnes cites *RBC Dominion Securities Inc v Dawson* (1994) 111 DLR (4th) 230 (NFSC) as authority to the contrary.

[97] *Lipkin Gorman* (n 1) 560 (Lord Templeman).

made to the asset which have personal value to the defendant, but render it less likely to be sold, or where there are other, consequential difficulties in returning the defendant to his former position.[98] We have seen that in *AFSL v Hills Industries*, the respondents established that their changes of position were practically irreversible by the time they became aware of the appellant's claim.

Once a defendant has established an irreversible change of position, the court undertakes the process of valuing the change. As noted earlier, in *AFSL v Hills Industries*, the appellant had argued that the respondents must prove the value of their detrimental changes of position to the same standard as required for proving loss in the context of a claim in tort. But well prior to that case, it was increasingly well established in the authorities that the defendant is not held to an exacting standard in proving the value of her proven changes of position. And the analogy with proving damages in tort has generally not found favour. As the Newfoundland Supreme Court explained in *RBC Dominion Securities Inc v Dawson*:[99]

> [T]o require that a private individual, who believed she was spending her own money, prove her expenditures as if she were claiming damages in an action for negligence would be most unfair. It was the plaintiff's error that put her in the funds in the first place and led her to believe that the funds were hers to spend without having to account to anyone for her expenditures.

In such circumstances, the court could be 'satisfied with reasonable approximations'.[100]

In *AFSL v Hills Industries*, the High Court firmly rejected any analogy with tort in preference for insights drawn from estoppel, emphasising that in some cases (of which this was one), proof of a substantial and irreversible change of position will suffice to constitute a complete defence. Justices Crennan, Kiefel, Bell and Keane emphasised that 'restitutionary claims are not founded upon a wrong done to the payer'.[101] Analogising from 'the equitable doctrine concerning detriment'[102] which they identified as underpinning estoppel, their Honours explained that the concept of detriment is more broad than purely compensable losses and is not to be understood in a narrow or technical way. Therefore, far from requiring that courts undertake

[98] eg, *Gertsch* (n 84) (uninsured car purchased in reliance on the receipt later stolen); *Corporate Management Services (Australia) Pty Ltd v Abi-Arraj* [2000] NSWSC 361 (renovations commenced and left incomplete subsequently deteriorated and abandoned). See also *Saunders & Co v Hague* [2004] 2 NZLR 475 (HC) 495–96 (Chisolm J); C Mitchell, 'Change of Position: The Developing Law' [2005] *Lloyd's Maritime and Commercial Law Quarterly* 168, 173–74.

[99] *RBC Dominion Securities* (n 96) 240.

[100] ibid. See also *Philip Collins* (n 67) 827 (Jonathan Parker J); *Scottish Equitable* (n 76) [33] (Robert Walker LJ).

[101] *AFSL* (n 17) [83].

[102] ibid [84].

a 'mathematical assessment of enduring economic benefit', it is clear that: 'So long as [the detriment] is substantial, it need not consist of expenditure of money or other quantifiable financial detriment.'[103] Chief Justice French came to a similar view.[104] In particular, his Honour noted that it was impossible and unhelpfully speculative (due to the passage of time) to determine what might have been recovered had the defendants not treated the debts as paid and given up their various avenues of recovery. His Honour considered that elaborate and potentially expensive enquiries into the exact quantum of loss might be appropriate in the context of certain torts, but are wholly inapt in the very different context of change of position.

4. INDEPENDENT CHANGES OF POSITION

The second major, outstanding issue to be considered is whether the defence applies to non-reliance-based changes of position ('independent' changes of position), such as where a thief steals a benefit received by the defendant or where it independently devalues or is destroyed. In England, this question appears to have been resolved strongly in the affirmative, with the courts repeatedly endorsing a 'broad' version of the defence that reaches to such changes, over a 'narrow,' reliance-based version.[105] In Australia, the position has been far more complex.

New South Wales[106] recently saw the development of an alternative unjust enrichment jurisprudence, which re-aligns the unjust enrichment enquiry to focus on whether there has been an 'unconscionable retention of benefit'. Under this approach, the claimant is limited to restitution of the enrichment traceably surviving in the hands of the defendant.[107] It is possible that this model developed (at least initially)[108] to deal with cases concerning independent changes of position.[109] To date, the defence of change of position in Australia has been formulated in the context of cases where the defendant has pleaded that she has changed her position by doing or refraining from certain acts. Its recognised elements have accordingly and properly reflected a causal requirement that the pleaded changes must have been made in reliance on the receipt. The leading example of this analysis is found in

[103] ibid [88].

[104] ibid [29]–[30].

[105] See, eg, *Scottish Equitable* (n 76) [31] (Robert Walker LJ, Keene and Simon Brown LJJ concurring), discussed and adopted in *FII* 2014 (n 14) [343]–[347] (Henderson J).

[106] *Ford* (n 50); *Heperu* (n 50) [150]–[158] (Allsop P, Campbell JA and Handley AJA concurring); *Break Fast Investments* (n 50) [75]–[84] (Black J).

[107] A shift expressly rejected by Henderson J in *FII* 2014 (n 14) [348].

[108] The desire to retain a distinctive equitable jurisprudence may also have been a factor.

[109] In *Ford* (n 50), the defendant's son had siphoned the received money from the defendant's account and the change of position defence was not pleaded.

David Securities Pty Ltd v Commonwealth Bank of Australia, where the High Court of Australia identified as the core requirement of the defence the fact that 'the defendant has acted to his or her detriment *on the faith of* the receipt'.[110] The question that has been left unresolved in the case law is whether independent changes of position are also caught by the defence.

The development of a concept of 'unconscionable retention of benefit' met the issue of non-reliance based changes of position by restricting the claimant's prima facie right to restitution to the value of what was traceably retained rather than received. However, as Henderson J noted in *Test Claimants in the FII Group Litigation v Revenue and Customs Commissioners*,[111] this step wrongly applies proprietary tracing principles to a non-proprietary claim for personal restitution. Moreover, the analysis will not always extend the degree of protection offered to the defendant beyond that granted by the change of position defence. Suppose I received a cheque from the lottery commission, representing my winnings from the weekly 'powerball'.[112] I put it on my mantelpiece. In reliance on my receipt, I donate money to charity. I am then told there was a mistake. On the 'retention of benefit' analysis, I still have the cheque and arguably must return it. It is only if a broader approach is taken to what constitutes a 'retained' benefit that the defence will apply. It is far from clear on the current authorities that anything beyond the original benefit or its traceable substitutes will count. What is clear is that, on this approach, non-pecuniary changes of position (such as a decision to marry or have a child) certainly will not count. Therefore, far from broadening the protection offered to good faith defendants beyond that offered by a reliance-based change of position defence, the concept of 'unconscionable retention of benefit' significantly restricts it. For this reason, perhaps, courts have tended to use unconscionable retention of benefit and unjust enrichment reasoning in the alternative, so that the change of position defence can be called into play if need be.[113] But this leads to the position that we have two overlapping and inconsistent regimes, triggered by the same facts and leading to different results. This can hardly be a positive outcome for the law.

Rather than developing a whole new parallel jurisprudence to meet the issue of how to deal with independent changes of position, the problem is better resolved by recognising the causal role played by reliance in cases where a defendant has instigated the change of position. When I decide to change my position in reliance on my receipt, my reliance signifies that the receipt is playing a causal role in my decision; that is, reliance signifies causation in

[110] *David Securities* (n 1) 385 (Mason CJ, Deane, Toohey, Gaudron and McHugh JJ).
[111] *FII* 2014 (n 14) [348].
[112] This example is taken from Bant (n 20) 621.
[113] eg, *Heperu* (n 50); *Break Fast Investments* (n 50).

the context of defendant-instigated changes of position. Consistently with the role of reliance in areas such as estoppel and payment over,[114] in cases of change of position, reliance breaks down into two stages of enquiry: (1) the receipt must have caused the defendant's assumption regarding the receipt; and (2) the defendant must have acted on that assumption. Although courts have tended to assume that the 'but for' test will apply to the defence,[115] the better view is that the relevant test of causation at each of the two stages of reliance—common with other areas involving 'decision causation' in the private law[116]—is the 'a factor' test.

By contrast with defendant-instigated changes of position, reliance is not the required causal concept where the change of position has occurred independently of the defendant. In this category of case, receipt is the sine qua non for the change of position to have occurred. Causation is simply resolved either through the application of the 'but for' test (but for my receipt of the benefit, the thief would not have stolen it) or the 'a factor' test (the receipt of the benefit was a factor in its subsequent theft).

Once the causal role of reliance is understood, there is no reason for excluding independent changes of position from the operation of the defence. On the contrary, its application to such circumstances will prevent an otherwise qualified defendant (ie, one in good faith and to whom no bars apply) from being placed in a worse position *as a result of the receipt* than she occupied prior to her receipt through the order for restitution. This protective purpose or rationale of the defence cannot rationally be restricted to cases of reliance by a defendant, but must equally extend to situations where the benefit received is independently destroyed or diminished in value.

Until recently, it was possible to state with confidence that no obstacle existed as a matter of precedent to Australian courts adopting this approach, so as to extend the protection of the defence to independent changes of position. *David Securities* did not involve an independent change of position, so there was no need for the High Court in that case to consider the

114 Discussed in detail in Bant (n 9) 28–41, 73–78.

115 eg, *FII* 2014 (n 14) [343] (Henderson J); *Scottish Equitable* (n 76) [31] (Robert Walker LJ).

116 *Amalgamated Investment and Property Co Ltd (in liquidation) v Texas Commerce International Bank Ltd* [1982] QB 84 (CA) 104–05 (Robert Goff J) (estoppel); *Sidhu* (n 48) [73] (French CJ, Kiefel, Bell and Keane JJ); *Gould v Vaggelas* (1985) 157 CLR 215 (HCA) 236 (Wilson J); 250–51 (Brennan J); *San Sebastian Pty Ltd v Minister Administering the Environmental Planning & Assessment Act 1979 (NSW)* (1986) 162 CLR 340 (HCA) 366–67 (Brennan J) (misrepresentation); *Salib v Gakas* [2010] NSWSC 505 [328]; *Lahoud v Lahoud* [2010] NSWSC 1297 [176] (mistake); *Henville v Walker* [2001] HCA 52; (2001) 206 CLR 459, 493 (McHugh J) (misleading or deceptive conduct under s 52 Trade Practices Act 1974 (Cth), now s 18 of sch 2 ('Australian Consumer Law') to the Competition and Consumer Act 2010 (Cth)); *Barton v Armstrong* [1976] AC 104 (PC) (duress); and cases of undue influence, discussed in detail in E Bant, 'Causation and Scope of Liability in Unjust Enrichment' (2009) 17 *Restitution Law Review* 60.

application of the defence in that context. The test formulated by the High Court arguably reflected that fact. However, in the recent case of *Citigroup Pty Ltd v National Australia Bank Ltd*,[117] Barrett JA considered that it was not open to the Australian supreme courts to adopt a wider version of the defence that took into account non-reliance changes, in light of the High Court's pronouncement. Of greater concern is that, in *AFSL v Hills Industries*, and taking estoppel as the primary (or sole) analogy for the purposes of developing the Australian law of change of position, Gageler J[118] suggested that only reliance-based changes counted for the purposes of the defence, with the result that independent changes of position must be excluded from its ambit of operation. This view seems to have been shared by the plurality.[119]

However, quite apart from the fact that, as explained above, the causal role of reliance does not require this outcome, there are good grounds for resisting their Honours' obiter views as premature. First, where estoppel is used as a defence, the nub of the defendant's plea is that she has changed her position in reliance on some assumption induced by the claimant, usually as a result of some representation or equivalent conduct.[120] There is no requirement that the defendant has received a benefit and often will not have done. The doctrine does not therefore have to address what occurs when a benefit received by the defendant is independently damaged or destroyed. And given (as we have seen) that the causal requirement in estoppel solely relates to the role played by the claimant's conduct in inducing an assumption on which the defendant acts, it makes complete sense that reliance is the sole causal concept in that context. However, the situations to which change of position may apply go beyond those considered by estoppel to cases where the received benefit independently devalues or is independently damaged or destroyed.

Further, as a matter of precedent and looking beyond estoppel as the sole source of analogical reasoning, the equitable doctrine of rescission offers many examples of non-reliance-based changes (such as deterioration of land following receipt) that traditionally have been taken into account by courts in making orders for restitution and counter-restitution following rescission in applying the equitable requirement of *restitutio in integrum*.[121]

[117] *Citigroup Pty Ltd v National Australia Bank Ltd* (n 6) [64] (but *cf* [6] Bathurst CJ, Allsop P and Meagher JA, seemingly leaving the question open).

[118] *AFSL* (n 17) [142].

[119] ibid [81].

[120] *Grundt v Great Boulder Pty Gold Mines Ltd* (1937) 59 CLR 641 (HCA) 674–77 (Dixon J), cited with approval in *AFSL* (n 17) [85]–[87] (Crennan, Kiefel, Bell and Keane JJ) [149] (Gageler J); *Sidhu* (n 48) [80] (French CJ, Kiefel, Bell and Keane JJ), [89] (Gageler J agreeing on this point).

[121] Explored in Bant (n 20) 628–33.

In sum, therefore, there seems little reason why independent changes of position should be left out of the equation in the context of the change of position defence. Indeed, the consequence of so doing is to limit artificially the scope of the defence in circumstances where both its rationale and broader equitable principle (as seen in the light of both estoppel and the doctrine of rescission) demands its application.

In concluding this discussion, it is worthwhile emphasising that the so-called 'narrow' and 'broad' versions of the defence present a false dichotomy. 'Detrimental reliance' does not stand opposed to a 'but for' test, as was recently suggested by Henderson J in *Test Claimants in the FII Group Litigation v HMRC*.[122] Reliance denotes the causal links between receipt, assumption by the defendant and action on that assumption. It is a separate (and not conflicting) step to ask what test should be applied to satisfy each part of this two-stage causal enquiry. As noted above, there is considerable authority favouring the view that this should be the 'a factor' test. In any event, however, the point remains that otherwise qualified defendants should be protected from the consequences of irreversible changes of position caused by their receipt, however those changes come about.

5. THE RELATIONSHIP BETWEEN CHANGE OF POSITION AND OTHER DEFENCES

5.1. Good Consideration and Bona Fide Discharge

The final, major issue before the High Court in *AFSL v Hills Industries* arose out of the argument concerning the respondents' pleaded discharge of the company debts. These facts were variously submitted (and found by the Court of Appeal) to support a finding of change of position, a defence of 'good consideration' and a novel defence of 'bona fide discharge'. The relationship between these three defensive factors merits further consideration.

The nature of the defence of 'good consideration' has been debated ever since it was first enunciated in *Barclays Bank Ltd v WJ Simms, Son and Cooke (Southern) Ltd*.[123] There, Robert Goff J said that a claim to recover a mistaken payment may fail where:[124]

> [T]he payment is made for good consideration, in particular if the money is paid to discharge, and does discharge, a debt owed to the payee (or a principal on

[122] *FII* 2014 (n 14) [347].

[123] *Barclays Bank Ltd v WJ Simms, Son and Cooke (Southern) Ltd* [1980] QB 677 (Comm). For a recent account of the doubts surrounding the defence, see A Burrows, 'Is There a Defence of Good Consideration?' in C Mitchell and W Swadling (eds), *The Restatement Third: Restitution and Unjust Enrichment* (Oxford, Hart Publishing, 2013) ch 7.

[124] *Barclays Bank Ltd* (n 123) 695.

> whose behalf he is authorised to receive the payment) by the payor or by a third party by whom he is authorised to discharge the debt.

The difficulty is that analysis of the authorities reveals that there are at least two, and perhaps three, different principles harboured under the umbrella label of 'good consideration'. The first is a concept of 'receipt in satisfaction of a right', whereby the defendant's receipt of a benefit from the claimant simultaneously satisfies a right held against the claimant. An example of the defence is where the payment discharges a debt owed by the claimant to the defendant. Thus, in *David Securities Pty Ltd v Commonwealth Bank of Australia*, the plurality stated that restitution of a payment made under a mistake of law:[125]

> [W]ould not, for example, extend to a case where the moneys were paid under a mistaken belief that they were legally due and owing under a particular clause of a particular contract when in fact they were legally due and owing under another clause or contract.

Provided that the debt is due and owing at the time of receipt,[126] the received benefit simultaneously extinguishes the debt, affecting the value of the actionable enrichment. Another way of reaching the same conclusion is to recognise that in such cases, retention of the receipt is justified and therefore cannot be impugned.

Although seemingly similar to change of position,[127] the defence of receipt in satisfaction of right differs in key respects. For example, there is no requirement that the debt must have been discharged in good faith. Provided that the debt itself was properly incurred and untainted, its discharge should be effective even if the payment was the result, for example, of duress or misrepresentation by the defendant.[128] This is either because the defendant was not enriched by the receipt or because the defendant was entitled to the receipt. Further, it seems likely that no enquiry will be made as to the adequacy of a sum received in satisfaction of right relative to the size of the debt.[129] This is unlike change of position, where the value of irreversible changes of position will normally be a relevant consideration.

[125] *David Securities Pty Ltd v Commonwealth Bank of Australia* (n 1) 376 (Mason CJ, Deane, Toohey, Gaudron and McHugh JJ).

[126] *Queensland University of Technology v Project Constructions (Aust) Pty Ltd (in liquidation)* [2002] QCA 224; [2003] 1 Qd R 259 [9] (Holmes J; Davies JA and Mullins J agreeing); *Orix Australia Corp Ltd* (n 27) [102]–[103] (White J).

[127] *Lloyds Bank plc v Independent Insurance Co Ltd* [1999] 2 WLR 986 (CA) 999; *K & S Corp* (n 73) 348 (Besanko J).

[128] *Equiticorp Finance Ltd (In Liquidation) v Bank of New Zealand* (1993) 32 NSWLR 50 (CA) 151 (Clarke and Cripps JJA); see, however, the contrary comments by the plurality in *AFSL* (n 17) considered below at 160.

[129] *Hills Industries Ltd* (n 5) [83] (Allsop P), applying a different conception of good consideration (see below at 158–159); however, there seems no principled reason for a different treatment of discharge of debt in this context.

The second defence one can see in the case law harbouring under the label of 'good consideration' is a counterclaim by way of set-off for failure of consideration. On this model of defence, the defendant's restitutionary liability for her receipt is offset against benefits transferred by her to the claimant with respect to, and on the basis of, the same transaction. Examples of this concept in action are commonly found in the mutual accounting processes that take place as part of the requirement of *restitutio in integrum* in cases of equitable rescission.[130] Where a claimant rescinds a transaction to recover the benefit transferred to the defendant, the basis on which the defendant transferred any benefits to the claimant (that is, enjoyment of the claimant's counter-performance) fails. The claimant must accordingly make counter-restitution to the defendant as part of the process of mutual restitution and counter-restitution.[131] The defence also arises outside the rescission context. In *Ovidio Carrideo Nominees Pty Ltd v The Dog Depot Pty Ltd*,[132] for example, the Victorian Court of Appeal held that a landlord had a defence of 'good consideration' to a claim by its tenant for restitution of monies paid to it by mistake. The landlord had a good counterclaim against the tenant for the use and occupation of its premises for the disputed period, in an amount 'broadly equivalent'[133] to the amount mistakenly paid by the tenant.[134] The landlord's claim for counter-restitution[135] was a complete defence to the tenant's claim. This analysis has subsequently been approved and applied on numerous occasions.[136]

It follows from this second characterisation of the defence of good consideration that it is in the nature of a counterclaim by way of set-off against the claimant's demand. As that classification also makes clear, it is open to a

[130] Bant (n 9) ch 4. The requirement is often couched in terms of 'doing equity' (eg, in *Maguire v Makaronis* (1997) 188 CLR 449 (HCA), discussed in E Bant and M Bryan, 'Defences, Bars and Discretionary Factors' in E Bant and M Bryan (eds), *Principles of Proprietary Remedies* (Sydney, Thomson Reuters, 2013) ch 11). Whether characterised as an equitable condition on recovery or as a common law counterclaim in unjust enrichment, the defensive principle arguably remains the same: *Plan B Trustees Ltd v Parker (No 2)* [2013] WASC 216 [89]–[91] (Edelman J).

[131] A conflicting analysis suggested by Hobhouse J in *Kleinwort Benson Ltd v Sandwell Borough Council* [1994] 1 WLR 938 (CA) 941, whereby the process of restitution and counter-restitution is seen solely in terms of determining the net enrichment of the defendant, is contrary to the preponderance of rescission authority and the very structure of the claim in unjust enrichment: see Bant (n 9) 96–101; Bant (n 20) 615–19.

[132] *Ovidio Carrideo Nominees Pty Ltd v The Dog Depot Pty Ltd* [2006] VSCA 6.

[133] ibid [22] (Chernov JA).

[134] ibid [34]–[50] (Nettle JA and Ashley JA agreeing).

[135] ibid [49] (Nettle JA).

[136] *R & Z Mazzei Nominees Pty Ltd v Aegean Food Import Export Pty Ltd* [2006] VSC 210 [45] (Osborn J); *Kiwi Munchies Pty Ltd v Nikolitsis* [2006] VCAT 929 [23]; *Fensford Pty Ltd v Nour Pty Ltd* [2006] VSCA 118 [40] (Nettle JA, Chernov and Ashley JJA concurring); *Ragi Pty Ltd v Kiwi Munchies Pty Ltd* [2007] NSWADT 108 [145]–[146] (the Tribunal); *Cook's Construction Pty Ltd v SFS 007.298.633 Pty Ltd* [2009] QCA 75; (2009) 254 ALR 661 [139]–[140] (Fraser JA, Daubney JA concurring with Fraser JA and Keane JA).

claimant to rely on defences such as the change of position defence in relation to the defendant's set-off for failure of consideration.[137]

In *AFSL v Hills Industries*, Allsop P in the Court of Appeal proposed a novel third model of defence, also adopting the language of 'good consideration', the elements of which are considered below. For ease of reference, it is labelled here a defence of 'bona fide discharge of debt'. Which of the three 'good consideration' principles was in play in *AFSL v Hills Industries*?

The second category can be put to one side for present purposes: *AFSL v Hills Industries* did not raise the sort of fact pattern relevant to a counterclaim of failure of basis. Hills and Bosch conferred no benefits on AFSL on the basis of their receipt of AFSL's payments. By contrast, the defence of receipt in satisfaction of right seems fairly apposite at first blush. However, it generally applies where a payment discharges rights the defendant had *against the claimant* (or the claimant's *principal*) under a contract or statute.[138] AFSL neither owed money to the respondents nor was acting as agent for the companies which did. It had been tricked into paying money to the respondents on its own account, thinking that it was thereby purchasing goods. Therefore, there is no sense in which Hill and Bosch discharged debts owed by AFSL or its principal.

The defence was rejected by Meagher JA in the Court of Appeal[139] and the plurality in the High Court[140] on the further ground that the appellant had no relevant intention to discharge the debts owed to the respondents. The appellant had only intended to purchase goods from the respondents (ie, to discharge its own debts), not to enable discharge of debts owed by a third party (the fraudster's companies) to the respondents, particularly given the absence of any agency relationship between the appellant and the third parties. In rejecting the application of this defence, the characterisation of this defence of good consideration as independent of change of position must be considered as confirmed by the High Court.

It was in view of the difficulties identified with aligning the independent defence of receipt in satisfaction of right with the facts of *AFSL v Hills Industries* that a third manifestation of the defence of good consideration was proposed[141] by Allsop P in the Court of Appeal.[142] In a detailed review of the authorities, his Honour analogised the defence to that of bona fide

[137] See generally Bant (n 9) ch 4; Bant (n 20) 609. There is a tension between the claimant's right to rely on the change of position defence and the defendant's right to counter-restitution, which generally should be settled in favour of allowing the defence of change of position. Contrast Burrows (n 44) 569–71.

[138] eg, *Lloyds Bank* (n 127).

[139] *Hills Industries Ltd* (n 5) [186].

[140] *AFSL* (n 17) [101].

[141] Justice Meagher dissented from this analysis, discussed immediately below. Chief Justice Bathurst declined to comment on the disagreement, given the accord reached by all three judges on change of position: [2].

[142] *Hills Industries Ltd* (n 5) [76]–[145], see particularly [83].

purchase and, in a similar fashion to that defence, found that it was rooted in the need for security and certainty in certain business transactions.[143] In particular, his Honour approved certain US decisions on the defence of 'discharge for value', which had held that it would introduce intolerable risk and uncertainty into commercial transactions if discharges of debts for value were liable to be undone.[144] In that context, it did not matter that the appellant had not actually intended its payments to discharge debts owed by the third party companies to the respondents. Nor did it matter that the debts were not owed to the respondents by the appellant or some principal of the appellant (had they done, the defence of receipt in satisfaction of right would have clearly applied). What counted was that the respondents had discharged the company debts in good faith and, in the interests of commercial certainty, those discharges must be final.

Justice Meagher disagreed with this analysis. As we saw above, his Honour considered that the case did not fall within the defence of good consideration in the first sense (that is, a defence of receipt in satisfaction of right).[145] Nor did he consider that the scope of the defence should be broadened in the manner suggested by Allsop P. Again reviewing the American authorities, Meagher JA considered that the illustrations of the discharge of debt cases that fell outside receipt in satisfaction of right could be better characterised in Anglo-Australian law as instances of the defence of payment over by an agent to her principal[146] and, in that aspect, a particular manifestation of the change of position defence.[147] In the High Court, we have seen that the plurality agreed with Meagher JA's analysis of the operation of the defence of good consideration. Their Honours did not, however, squarely address the novel defence of discharge of debt proposed by Allsop P.

Whether such a defence should develop in the future in large part depends on whether it addresses a need currently not met either by change of position or good consideration in the sense of receipt in satisfaction of right. Justice Allsop clearly conceived the proposed defence of discharge of debt as being a broader manifestation of the defence of receipt in satisfaction of right.[148] As formulated in his judgment, it is certainly broader in that it does not require that the debt have been immediately due at the time of receipt and discharge[149] or that the debt be owed to the claimant or his principal. However (and this is not something addressed by Allsop P), the defence of

143 ibid [83].
144 ibid [107]–[112].
145 ibid [186].
146 ibid [195].
147 ibid [198]–[199].
148 ibid [114], [116]–[117].
149 *Sarkis v Watfa* [2006] EWHC 374 (QB) (HHJ Seymour QC) is probably on this account best understood as applying a defence of discharge of debt.

discharge of debt also appears to be narrower, to the extent that it appears to require that the debt was discharged by the defendant in good faith.[150]

These features suggest that any defence of bona fide discharge of debt is not enrichment-related or founded on an existing entitlement to the receipt (unlike receipt in satisfaction of right); rather, it is founded on the public policy grounds of protecting the security of certain business transactions. In this aspect, it has more in common with the doctrine of bona fide purchase than the defence of receipt in satisfaction of right. The defence as expounded by Allsop P also suggests a line of demarcation with change of position: provided that the payment is effective to discharge the debt, there is no need to enter into an enquiry as to the value of the amount paid by way of discharge.[151]

In conclusion, it seems that there is room for the development of a defence of bona fide discharge of debt, provided that the policy reasons justifying it are accepted by the courts. It is noteworthy in this regard that the *Restatement (Third) Restitution and Unjust Enrichment* recognises all three models of the defence of good consideration identified in this chapter and categorises them by reference to their distinct elements and rationales in a manner that closely approximates the taxonomy suggested here.[152] On the other hand, the plurality's obiter suggestion in *AFSL v Hills Industries* that discharges brought about as a result of a third party's fraud may be liable to be reversed in some circumstances[153] may suggest an unwillingness to give preference to any public interest in commercial certainty over victims' rights to recovery.[154] It therefore remains an open question as to whether a defence of bona fide discharge will be recognised under Australian law.

5.2. Change of Position and Estoppel

The final question that continues to looms large after *AFSL v Hills Industries* is the relationship between estoppel and change of position. The plurality and Gageler J clearly found it a potent source of analogical reasoning, a view with which most would likely concur. More problematic, however, is

[150] *Hills Industries Ltd* (n 5) [103]–[104].

[151] ibid [83] (Allsop P). The positions can, however, be elided by saying that once the debt is discharged, the face value of the debt constitutes the relevant change of position: ibid [142]–[143] (Allsop P); [211], [214] (Meagher JA).

[152] American Law Institute, *Restatement Third, Restitution and Unjust Enrichment* (St Paul, MN, American Law Institute, 2011) § 62, approximating our defence of receipt in satisfaction of right, § 67, incorporating discharge of debt, and § 27 and § 63(d), which together address counterclaims for failure of consideration.

[153] *AFSL* (n 17).

[154] The plurality's decision in this space is not entirely easy to reconcile: compare comments ibid [95] and [101].

the proposed merger of the two defences by Gageler J. While stopping short of taking a final position on the question, Gageler J stated his preference for the view that change of position is but a particular instance of estoppel. In articulating the required conditions for the defence, his Honour expressed his purpose to identify the 'commonality of principle'[155] found in change of position and estoppel. On this approach, the defence of change of position is established[156] where (1) the defendant has acted or refrained from acting 'in good faith on the assumption that the defendant was entitled to deal with the payment' and (2) as a result, 'the defendant would be placed in a worse position if ordered to make restitution ... than if the defendant had not received the payment at all'.

This conception of the defence as operating consistently with estoppel underpinned his view (discussed previously) that change of position is likely limited to reliance-based changes of position. However, it also had other consequences. Thus, his Honour stated:[157]

> [W]here the defence [of change of position] is so established, the prima facie entitlement of the defendant is *to maintain the assumption on which the defendant acted and, on that basis, to retain the whole of the payment.* That entitlement is qualified to the extent that retention of the whole of the payment can be shown to be disproportionate to the degree of the detriment. Where the detriment is financial or pecuniary, can be quantified, and is less than the amount received, the entitlement of the defendant to retain the payment is reduced pro tanto.

While this model would certainly reconcile the practical effect of change of position and estoppel,[158] it reverses the usual *pro tanto* operation of change of position. On Gageler J's approach, the defence operates completely unless shown to be disproportionate. This is quite a novel step and one that was made without consideration of the scholarly debates on the issue or, more importantly, the recent Australian authorities in which the relationship between change of position and estoppel have been explored. In particular, prior to *AFSL*, the position appeared to have been significantly clarified by the Victorian Supreme Court decision of *TRA Global Pty Ltd v Kebakoska*.[159] An employee was mistakenly advised by her employer that she was entitled to a redundancy payment, which was subsequently paid to her in accordance with the advice. In reliance on both the representation and her receipt, she disclosed the fact of her redundancy payments to the relevant social security authority and was accordingly denied unemployment benefits. Since she had no other source of income, she spent a large

[155] ibid [156].
[156] ibid [157].
[157] ibid [158] (emphasis added).
[158] Meeting the concerns of courts in cases such as *Scottish Equitable* (n 76); *National Westminster Bank* (n 60) and *RBC Dominion Securities* (n 96).
[159] *TRA Global Pty Ltd* (n 3) [41]–[83] (Osborn J).

proportion of the redundancy payments on living expenses before eventually finding re-employment. Justice Osborn of the Victorian Supreme Court upheld the magistrate's findings that she was entitled to a partial defence of change of position. However, in a careful and full review of the arguments raised in the authorities and scholarly commentary, his Honour rejected the submission made by the employer that the defence of estoppel by representation has been displaced by change of position or must operate *pro tanto*, and held that estoppel by representation operated in the circumstances to defeat the employer's claim completely.

The clarity of this position was then slightly, but not irretrievably, muddied by the subsequent New South Wales Court of Appeal decision of *Citigroup Pty Ltd v National Australia Bank Ltd*.[160] Justice Barrett considered in *obiter dictum* that the defence of estoppel 'may have been subsumed'[161] in the defence of change of position. However, *TRA Global* was not cited to the Court and his Honour was therefore without the benefit of Osborn J's considered reasoning on the point. Justice Macfarlan disagreed with Barrett JA, holding that an estoppel properly and independently arose on the facts, although it produced on the facts of the case the same result as application of the change of position defence.[162] Chief Justice Bathurst, Allsop P and Meagher JA noted the continuing distinction between the two defences, but considered that the issue did not need to be resolved in this case.[163] Given the division of opinion and the fact that the Victorian decision was very fully reasoned, it was open to conclude that estoppel continues to operate as an independent defence to claims in unjust enrichment in Australia.

There is insufficient space in this chapter to examine the interaction between estoppel and change of position in full detail.[164] What can be said, however, is that the merger proposed by Gageler J should not be undertaken without consideration of the full arguments considered by Osborn J and any other relevant considerations. In this respect, two points relevant to this question have not yet been considered by the courts and are worthy of brief mention. The first is that, notwithstanding the undoubted similarities between the concepts of irreversible detriment found in estoppel and change of position, the two arguably remain distinct. Change of position is concerned to prevent the harm that would come from requiring a defendant to make restitution in full, where that order would return her to a worse (including entirely different) position than she occupied prior to her receipt. The focus is on where the defendant used to be and the harm that she would suffer relative to that point, as a result of her receipt, if required to make restitution or restitution in full. Again, the concept of *restitutio in*

[160] *Citigroup Pty Ltd* (n 6).
[161] ibid [64].
[162] ibid [18]–[19].
[163] ibid [5], [13]–[14].
[164] For detailed discussion, see Bant (n 9) 224–30.

integrum is a helpful comparator concept in this context. Estoppel is arguably subtly different: it arises to protect the defendant from the harm she would suffer if the claimant was allowed to resile from his representation and so deny the assumption on which the defendant acted. The focus is on where the defendant would be if the assumption were maintained and the harm the defendant will suffer if that assumption is rendered false. The foci of the detriment elements of the defence are different: one looks to the former (historical) position of the defendant; the other to where (contrary to the true facts) she assumed she would be. Although the measures of the defences may frequently overlap in practice, it is too early to state that they always will do so, given this subtle but real distinction.

Further, it is true that in successful change of position cases, the defendant normally assumes that she is entitled to the payment and the operation of the defence shields her from the harm she would suffer arising from changes made in that belief. These cases are covered by Gageler J's formulation of the defence. However, the defence should also apply where, for example, the defendant knew (or thought she knew) she was not entitled to the received benefit and changed her position in good faith consistently with that belief. An example is where a defendant receives a payment knowing it was conferred by mistake and, pending its return to the payer, places the money for safekeeping with a bank that subsequently fails.[165] Another relatively common example from the cases is where a defendant pays the value of the benefit to a third party in the reasonable belief that the third party is entitled to the sum.[166] These cases should continue to be caught by the defence of change of position, but would not do so on the model of defence advanced by Gageler J. Indeed, on Gageler J's approach, the sorts of cases the subject of the agent's defence of payment over would no longer be encompassed by the defence of change of position, contrary to the clear trend of authority discussed earlier.[167] These matters, along with others, are the sorts of issues that need to be worked through before taking any further steps towards the merger of these two defences.

6. CONCLUSION

The aim of this chapter has been to identify and explore three key outstanding issues that remain following the important decision of *AFSL v Hill Securities*. Much progress has been made. The decision provides significant

[165] *cf National Bank of New Zealand* (n 46).
[166] As in *Thomas v Houston Corbett* [1969] NZLR 151 (CA); *Dextra Bank* (n 27); *Orix Australia Corp Ltd v M Wright Hotel Refrigeration Pty Ltd* [2000] SASC 57; (2000) 155 FLR 267.
[167] Above at 135.

support for the view that one[168] rationale of the defence is to prevent defendants from being placed as a result of their receipt (and thus restitutionary liability) in unjustifiably worse (including wholly different) positions than they occupied prior to their receipt. Consistently with this rationale, defendants must show that changes of position caused by their receipt are legally or practically irreversible, or there must be significant difficulties in reversing the change. The changes may be pecuniary or non-pecuniary. Normally, where they can be valued, any irreversible changes will be brought into account *pro tanto* against the defendant's initial receipt. However, in those comparatively rare cases where the change of position is significant and very difficult to value, the defence will operate completely. The analysis also showed that the rationale of the defence extends to protect defendants both in respect of irreversible changes of position made in reliance on their receipt and in respect of independent changes of position, such as where a benefit received by a defendant is stolen by a thief or destroyed. Finally, the role of change of position as an independent defence has been confirmed, including in relation to the separate 'good consideration' defence of receipt in satisfaction of right.

What cannot at this stage be settled is the relationship between change of position and estoppel. In part, this reflects the continued uncertainty over the rationale and remedial purpose of estoppel(s),[169] a matter far too large to address here. It is, however, possible to say that this question cannot addressed without full consideration of the issues and authorities that bear upon it, some of which are considered in this chapter. This required and considered review was something that (quite understandably) was not attempted in *AFSL v Hills Industries*. In those circumstances, it is to be hoped that other Australian courts will not be too quick to adopt and follow its dicta[170] favouring merger of these important defences.

[168] On the other rationale, see above n 41.

[169] The references to estoppel by members of the High Court in *AFSL* (n 17) are notably in the singular. For a recent argument favouring unification of reliance-based estoppels, see E Bant and M Bryan, 'Fact, Future and Fiction: Risk and Reasonable Reliance in Estoppel' (2015) 35 *OJLS* 1.

[170] In Australia, a serious issue following the direction of the High Court in *Farah Constructions Pty Ltd v Say-Dee Pty Ltd* [2007] HCA 22; (2007) 230 CLR 89 [134] that lower courts are bound by its 'seriously considered dicta'.

8

The Defence of Illegality in Unjust Enrichment

GRAHAM VIRGO

1. INTRODUCTION

MOST OF THE defences to claims in unjust enrichment focus on the relationship between the claimant and the defendant, and are normatively related to the principle of corrective justice.[1] That is not the case with the defence of illegality,[2] which is influenced by external considerations of public policy rather than securing justice between the parties.[3] It is for this reason that the illegality defence has such a bad reputation, being perceived as complex, capricious and unjust.[4] Fundamental questions relating to the defence's role are under-examined and under-theorised. It is difficult even to identify an acceptable definition of illegality; to determine whether it should defeat unjust enrichment claims in all, some or any cases, and, if it applies, what might be the basis for determining its application. Further, where the defendant has been unjustly enriched at the expense of the claimant in circumstances where the transfer of the enrichment to the defendant has been tainted by illegality, there is no a priori reason why restitution should necessarily follow or be denied. As Wade recognised:[5]

> [O]n one side the view that a court should not help a man who has engaged in an illegal transaction out of the predicament in which he has placed himself, and on the other the view that a court should not permit unjust enrichment of one person

[1] R Grantham and C Rickett, 'A Normative Account of Defences to Restitutionary Liability' (2008) 67 *CLJ* 92.

[2] But see EJ Weinrib, *The Idea of Private Law* (Oxford, Oxford University Press, 1995) ch 5; B McLachlin, 'Weaving the Law's Seamless Web: Reflections on the Illegality Defence in Tort Law' in A Dyson, J Goudkamp and F Wilmot-Smith (eds), *Defences in Tort* (Oxford, Hart Publishing, 2015) 221.

[3] *Hounga v Allen* [2014] UKSC 47; [2014] ICR 847 [42] (Lord Wilson), [55] (Lord Hughes); *Les Laboratoires Servier v Apotex Inc* [2014] UKSC 55; [2015] AC 430 [13] (Lord Sumption).

[4] Lord Sumption, 'Reflections on the Law of Illegality' [2012] *Restitution Law Review* 1, 12.

[5] JW Wade, 'Benefits Obtained Under Illegal Transactions—Reasons for and against Allowing Restitution' (1946) 25 *Texas Law Review* 31, 60.

> at the expense of another. Of these two arguments, each of which seems most nearly determinative upon its side of the question, neither takes precedence upon logical analysis.

Confusion about the role of the illegality defence runs throughout the law of obligations.[6] This confusion has been compounded by two decisions of the Supreme Court which, although not concerned with the law of unjust enrichment, betray a significant difference of approach about the role of illegality generally in private law which is of relevance to the analysis of the defence in unjust enrichment.

In *Les Laboratoires Servier v Apotex Inc*,[7] the Supreme Court considered whether damages were recoverable for lost sales in Europe after the vendor had been prevented from selling drugs exported from Canada, the sale of which would have infringed a valid Canadian patent, which constitutes a strict liability statutory wrong in that jurisdiction. Although the Justices in the Supreme Court unanimously held that the claim for damages should succeed on the ground that the illegality defence was not engaged on the facts, their judgments reflected a different approach to its proper role. The Court of Appeal had approached the defence on the basis that 'it required in each case … an intense analysis of the particular facts and of the proper application of the various policy considerations underlying the illegality principle so as to produce a just and proportionate response to the illegality'.[8] This approach was specifically rejected by Lord Sumption, with whom Lords Neuberger and Clarke agreed. Lord Sumption emphasised that the defence was grounded on general rules of law and was not a mere discretionary power, involving fact-based evaluations of the effect of the rules in individual cases.[9] He considered the only key issues to be whether the relevant conduct involved sufficient turpitude and whether this was sufficiently related to the claim.[10]

This strict approach to illegality can be contrasted with that of Lord Toulson in the same case, who refused to criticise the approach of the Court of Appeal and who considered that, when determining whether the illegality defence should apply, 'it is right to proceed carefully on a case by case basis, considering the policies which underlie the broad principle'.[11] This is also

[6] For tort, see G Virgo, 'Illegality's Role in the Law of Tort' in M Dyson (ed), *Unravelling Tort and Crime* (Cambridge, Cambridge University Press, 2014) ch 7.

[7] *Apotex* (n 3).

[8] *Les Laboratoires Servier v Apotex Inc* [2012] EWCA Civ 593; [2013] Bus LR 80 [75] (Etherton LJ).

[9] *Apotex* (n 3) [13] and [22]. See also the judgment of Lord Mance.

[10] ibid [22].

[11] ibid [57], relying on the judgment of Lord Wright in *Vita Food Products Inc v Unus Shipping Co Ltd* [1939] AC 277 (PC (Can)) 293. See also *Gray v Thames Trains Ltd* [2009] UKHL 33; [2009] 1 AC 1339 [30] (Lord Hoffmann); *Stone and Rolls Ltd v Moore Stephens* [2009] UKHL 39; [2009] 1 AC 1391 [25] (Lord Phillips).

the approach which was adopted by a differently constituted Supreme Court in the earlier decision of *Hounga v Allen*.[12] That Court held that a claim in tort for race discrimination,[13] following wrongful dismissal from employment, succeeded, even though the claimant was an illegal immigrant who knew that it was illegal to work in the UK.[14] This had been sufficient for the Court of Appeal to dismiss her claim. But the Supreme Court considered that the illegality defence was not engaged, explicitly for policy reasons. Crucially, Lord Wilson said, in the judgment of the majority, that it was necessary, first, to ask 'What is the aspect of public policy which founds the defence?' and, second, to ask: 'But is there another aspect of public policy to which application of the defence would run counter?'[15] Lord Hughes, with whose judgment Lord Carnwath agreed, emphasised that in assessing what public policy requires, it is necessary to have regard to various factors, including the gravity of the illegality and the claimant's knowledge of it.[16] This is consistent with Lord Hoffmann's oft-quoted dictum in the seminal case of *Gray v Thames Train Ltd*, who said that the illegality defence 'expresses not so much a principle as a policy. Furthermore, that policy is not based on a single justification but on a group of reasons, which vary in different situations'.[17]

To the extent that there is division amongst the Justices of the Supreme Court,[18] the strict approach of Lord Sumption would appear to prevail, being a judgment in the more recent case which had the explicit support

[12] *Hounga* (n 3). See also *Parkingeye Ltd v Somerfield Stores Ltd* [2012] EWCA Civ 1338; [2013] QB 840 [40] (Sir Robin Jacob). The decision of the majority in *Hounga* was considered to provide 'the best guidance on the relevant analytical framework' by Sales LJ in *Best v The Chief Land Registrar* [2015] EWCA Civ 17 [51]. See also *McCracken v Smith* [2015] EWCA Civ 380 [43], (Richards LJ) and *Quinn v Irish Bank Resolution Corporation Ltd* (2015) 150/2012 (Irish Supreme Court) [8.2] (Clarke J).

[13] Contrary to the Race Relations Act 1976 (UK), s 4(2)(c). See now the Equality Act 2010 (UK), s 39(2)(c).

[14] A claim for unlawful dismissal was rejected by the Employment Appeal Tribunal on the basis that this would have required the enforcement of an illegal contract. Similarly, a claim for unpaid wages was unenforceable for illegality. Neither conclusion was challenged before the Supreme Court, although Lord Wilson acknowledged that a different conclusion might have been reached had the issue been raised.

[15] *Hounga* (n 3) [42], with whom Baroness Hale and Lord Kerr agreed.

[16] ibid [55].

[17] *Gray* (n 11) [30]. See also *Stone* (n 11) [25] (Lord Phillips); *Best* (n 12) [52] (Sales LJ). Lord Hoffmann in *Gray* did, however, focus on the causal connection between the illegality and the tort, which was criticised in *Hounga*: ibid [36] (Lord Wilson).

[18] In *Best* (n 12) [61], Sales LJ considered the approach of the Supreme Court in both cases to be compatible, although his approach was more consistent with that adopted in *Hounga*. In *Jetivia SA v Bilta (UK) Ltd* [2015] UKSC 23; [2015] 2 WLR 1168, the disagreement between the Justices in the Supreme Court was reinforced, with Lord Sumption again emphasising the rule-based interpretation and Lords Toulson and Hodge the policy-based, context-dependent interpretation of the illegality defence. Lord Neuberger (at [14]), with whom Lords Clarke, Carnwath and Mance agreed, identified the disagreement, but refused to resolve it, preferring the matter to be resolved as soon as appropriately possible and preferably by a panel of

of two Justices and the implicit support of another. But more Justices support the more flexible and fact-sensitive approach of Lord Toulson, with all the Justices in *Hounga* having adopted it.[19] It follows that a fundamental difference of approach to dealing with illegality has emerged. We are at a crossroads. Which route should the law of unjust enrichment follow?

2. PUBLIC POLICY AND JUSTICE

2.1. The *Ex Turpi Causa* Principle

The illegality defence has tended to be formulated as a rule, in the form of the maxim *ex turpi causa non oritur actio* ('No action can arise from a base cause'),[20] meaning that the courts will not assist a claimant to obtain a remedy where the action is founded on illegal conduct. This rule was recognised by Lord Mansfield in *Holman v Johnson*:[21]

> The objection, that a contract is immoral or illegal as between the plaintiff and defendant, sounds at all times very ill in the mouth of the defendant. It is not for his sake, however, that the objection is ever allowed; but it is founded in general principles of policy, which the defendant has the advantage of, contrary to the real justice, as between him and the plaintiff, by accident, if I may so say. The principle of public policy is this; ex dolo malo non oritur actio. No Court will lend its aid to a man who founds his cause of action upon an immoral or illegal act. If, from the plaintiff's own stating or otherwise, the cause of action appears to arise ex turpi causa, or the transgression of a positive law of this country, there the Court says he has no right to be assisted.

This rule negating liability is explicitly founded on policy rather than justice. As Lord Goff said in *Tinsley v Milligan*:[22]

> [I]t is a principle of policy, whose application is indiscriminate and so can lead to unfair consequences as between the parties to litigation. Moreover the principle

nine Justices. Lord Neuberger summarised the spectrum of views (at [13]) as 'epitomising the familiar tension between the need for principle, clarity and certainty in the law with the equally important desire to achieve a fair and appropriate result in each case'.

19 The fact that *Apotex* arose in a commercial context and *Hounga* in an employment context was not identified as a reason for distinction and would, in any case, be difficult to defend on that basis. Further, the reasoning in *Hounga* was not addressed in *Apotex* (*Jetivia* (n 18) [17] (Lord Neuberger)), although Lord Sumption in *Jetivia* did consider the reasoning in *Hounga* and concluded that it did not involve any statement of principle of general application: ibid [102]. Lords Toulson and Hodge explicitly disagreed: ibid [173].

20 Windeyer J in *Smith v Jenkins* (1969) 119 CLR 397 (HCA) 410 considered that 'causa' did not refer to 'cause of action', but referred to illegal or immoral consideration, so the doctrine was only relevant to contractual claims. This was rejected by Dillon LJ in *Pitts v Hunt* [1991] 1 QB 24 (CA) 56.

21 *Holman v Johnson* (1775) 1 Cowp 341, 343; 98 ER 1120, 1121. In *Hewison v Meridian Shipping Services Pte Ltd* [2002] EWCA Civ 1821; [2003] ICR 766 [57] Ward LJ described Lord Mansfield's judgment as the source of the illegality principle.

22 *Tinsley v Milligan* [1994] 1 AC 340 (HL) 355. See also *Gray* (n 11) [30] (Lord Hoffmann).

> allows no room for the exercise of any discretion by the court in favour of one party or the other.

In *Les Laboratoires Servier v Apotex Inc*, Lord Sumption emphasised that the defence was not based 'on the perceived balance of merits between the parties to any particular dispute',[23] thus squarely placing it within the external relationship between the court and the claimant[24] rather than the internal relationship between the claimant and the defendant.

The significance of public policy has often been repeated, but rarely do the courts or commentators consider exactly what policy is sought to be achieved and why, and even how a 'policy' should be identified. There is, indeed, a danger in relying on public policy, as recognised by Burroughs J in *Richardson v Mellish*:[25]

> [I]t is a very unruly horse, and when once you get astride it you never know where it will carry you. It may lead you from the sound law. It is never argued at all but when other points fail.

What is needed is the identification of clear principles, which provide 'the rails within which the unruliest horse may safely run'[26] and to enable it to jump over the obstacles in its path.[27]

2.2. Qualifying *Ex Turpi Causa*

The strict application of the *ex turpi causa* rule in denying a remedy to the claimant might produce unjust results where, for example, the illegality is minor or the defendant is more responsible than the claimant for participation in illegal conduct. The judiciary consequently sought to temper the strict rule to secure justice. For a few years in the 1980s in England, this was achieved through the reformulation of the illegality rule by reference to the public conscience test, whereby the defence only applied where the public conscience would be affronted if relief was granted. This test originated in *Thackwell v Barclays Bank plc*,[28] where an action for conversion failed by virtue of the illegality defence, but only after the court had considered all the circumstances of the case, including the nature of the illegality, to determine whether, by granting a remedy to the claimant, it would be seen to be

[23] *Apotex* (n 3) [13].

[24] See *Hounga* (n 3) [56] (Lord Hughes).

[25] *Richardson v Mellish* (1824) 2 Bing 229, 252; 130 ER 294, 303.

[26] *Hunter v Butler* [1996] RTR 396 (CA) 403 (Waite LJ).

[27] *Enderby Town Football Club v Football Association Ltd* [1971] Ch 591 (CA) 606; (Lord Denning MR).

[28] *Thackwell v Barclays Bank plc* [1986] 1 All ER 676 (QBD). See also *Saunders v Edwards* [1987] 1 WLR 1116 (CA); *Howard v Shirlstar Container Transport Ltd* [1990] 1 WLR 1292 (CA); *Euro-Diam Ltd v Bathurst* [1990] 1 QB 1 (CA).

assisting or encouraging his criminal act. A remedy was eventually denied because the claimant had been a knowing party to a fraudulent transaction.

The public conscience test was rejected by the House of Lords in Equity on the ground that it was inconsistent with the authorities and too uncertain.[29] The courts were surely right to do so. The public conscience test resulted in inconsistent decisions,[30] often turning on judicial outrage arising from the facts of the case.[31] Justice is dependent on a high degree of predictability, which is lacking under the public conscience test. But even though subsequent cases have not resurrected the test, there remains a clear judicial desire to temper the rigidity of the *ex turpi causa* rule to avoid unjust results, as reflected especially by *Hounga v Allen*. Yet the *ex turpi causa* rule was never absolute; it has always been qualified. As Lord Wright recognised in *Vita Food Products Inc v Unus Shipping Co Ltd*, in respect of a contract claim, 'public policy understood in a wider sense may at times be better served by refusing to nullify a bargain save on serious and sufficient grounds'.[32] The flexibility of the *ex turpi causa* rule was recognised by Lord Mansfield in *Holman v Johnson*, for his dictum continued as follows:[33]

> It is upon that ground the Court goes; not for the sake of the defendant, but because they will not lend their aid to such a plaintiff. So if the plaintiff and defendant were to change sides, and the defendant was to bring his action against the plaintiff, the latter would then have the advantage of it; for where both are equally in fault, potior est conditio defendentis.

It is the recognition of this other principle, known as the *in pari delicto est conditio defendentis* defence ('in the case of mutual fault, the position of the defendant is the stronger one'—*in pari delicto* for short) that provides an important mechanism for qualifying the *ex turpi causa* defence, and it is of particular relevance to the law of unjust enrichment. This *in pari delicto* principle enables the court to analyse the particular circumstances of the case to determine whether the claimant is less responsible for the illegality than the defendant, for then, as between the claimant and the defendant, the just result is that the claimant should not be denied relief, since the parties are not *in pari delicto*. But where the claimant is more responsible for the illegality or the parties are considered to be equally responsible, the *in pari delicto* principle applies and restitution will be denied.

That the illegality defence was always intended to be applied flexibly is reflected by *Holman v Johnson* itself, which concerned an action to recover

[29] *Tinsley* (n 22). It was subsequently rejected in tort cases: *Stone* (n 11) [97] (Lord Scott).
[30] *Tinsley* (n 22), 363 (Lord Goff).
[31] *Hewison* (n 21) 788–99 (Ward LJ).
[32] *Vita Food Products* (n 11) 293.
[33] *Holman* (n 21).

the price of tea supplied by the claimant to the defendant pursuant to a contract made in Dunkirk, which the defendant intended to smuggle into England. The claimant was aware of the defendant's intention, but was not part of the smuggling scheme. The defendant having failed to pay for the tea, the claimant sued for the price. The claim succeeded, both because mere knowledge of the smuggling was held not to be sufficient to bar the claim and because the claimant had not committed any crime. Although he knew of the smuggling, he was not concerned in the illegal transaction itself. It would have been different if the price would only have become due once the tea had landed in England, but the claimant's interest was considered to be at an end once the tea had been delivered in Dunkirk. In later cases, the seller's claim failed where he both knew of the defendant's illegal purpose and assisted the defendant in that purpose. So, for example, in *Clugas v Penaluna*, the claimant assisted in the smuggling by packing the brandy and gin which was to be smuggled into England from Guernsey.[34] Buller J distinguished *Holman v Johnson* on the ground that 'if he take[s] part in the transaction, it taints the whole of it'.[35]

A test stating that the court's assistance will be denied where the parties are *par delictum* is a test judged by reference to the comparative responsibility of the parties or, perhaps preferably, the comparative taint of the illegality. Consequently, if the claimant is less responsible for the illegality than the defendant, relief should not be denied, because the illegality taints the defendant more than the claimant.

2.3. Public Policy and the Law of Unjust Enrichment

If a claimant seeks restitution for unjust enrichment, the fact that the claim is tainted by illegality will operate as a defence[36] rather than a denial of the claim. This is illustrated by *Parkinson v College of Ambulance*,[37] where the claimant had given a donation to a charity on the understanding that he would receive a knighthood as a result. When no knighthood was forthcoming, he sought restitution of the money on the ground of total failure of basis, but the claim failed because the contract was illegal as being contrary to public policy. Similarly, a defendant whose change of position

[34] *Clugas v Penaluna* (1791) 4 Term Rep 466; 100 ER 1122.

[35] ibid 468; 1123. See also *Bernard v Reed* (1794) 1 Esp 91; 170 ER 290; *Waymell v Reed* (1794) 5 Term Rep 599, 600; 101 ER 335 (Lord Kenyon CJ).

[36] See *Muckleston v Brown* (1801) 6 Ves Jr 52, 69; 31 ER 934 (Lord Eldon LC) and *Gordon v Chief Commissioner of Metropolitan Police* [1910] 2 KB 1080 (CA) 1090 (Vaughan Williams LJ).

[37] *Parkinson v College of Ambulance* [1923] 2 KB 1 (KBD). See also *R v Wacker (Perry)* [2002] EWCA Crim 1944; [2003] QB 1207 [32] (Kay LJ).

has been tainted by illegality will not be able to rely on the defence of change of position.[38]

Although the illegality defence was intended to be applied flexibly, in the nineteenth and twentieth centuries it came to be applied more rigorously, so much so that it was used to bar the claim whenever the claimant had been tainted by illegality. For example, in *Wild v Simpson*,[39] Atkin LJ gave the example of a taxi-driver who was engaged to drive to a particular destination and who was informed by his passenger halfway through the journey that he was going to perpetrate a burglary at the destination. Atkin LJ suggested that if the driver proceeded with the journey, he would not be able to recover his fare or even half of it, since, assuming that the contract was void for illegality, the driver's restitutionary claim would also have been tainted by the illegality. But surely the driver would be much less responsible than the passenger for the illegality, so there is no sufficient reason why his claim for restitution should be defeated.[40] The harshness of the existing law is also illustrated by the facts of *Wild v Simpson* itself, where a solicitor had entered into an illegal agreement with a client, whereby the client agreed to pay a percentage of whatever he recovered to the solicitor. The client having succeeded in his claim, the solicitor sought to recover his costs, but his action failed because the contract of service was illegal. This hardly seems just. The solicitor had done work for the client which had benefited him, but was unable to recover anything because of the illegal nature of the original agreement. It is right that the illegal agreement itself is not enforced, so the solicitor would not be allowed to sue for a percentage of what the client recovered, but why should this affect the restitutionary claim? This suggests that the role of illegality in the law of unjust enrichment is determined solely by public policy, as between the court and the claimant, without regard to the justice of the case, as between the claimant and the defendant.

3. THE POLICIES BEHIND THE ILEGALITY DEFENCE

A number of policy reasons have been recognised for denying the claimant restitutionary remedies where he or she has been tainted by illegality.[41] Some of these policies had been identified by Etherton LJ in *Les Laboratoires Servier v Apotex Inc*, although he emphasised that the defence does not

[38] *Barros Mattos Jr v MacDaniels Ltd* [2004] EWHC 1188 (Ch); [2005] 1 WLR 247.

[39] *Wild v Simpson* [1919] 2 KB 544 (CA) 566.

[40] Alternatively, it might be concluded that the illegality was not sufficiently closely connected to the claim. See p 187, below.

[41] See JK Grodecki, '*In Pari Delicto Potior Est Conditio Defendentis*' (1955) 71 *LQR* 254, 265–73.

necessarily apply simply because one of the policy rationales is relevant, but 'must find its justification firmly in one or more of them'.[42]

3.1. Consistency

Consistency between the criminal law and private law is a legitimate policy aim, which is furthered by the illegality defence.[43] As Lord Hughes said in *Hounga v Allen*, the law 'cannot give with one hand what it takes away with another, nor condone when facing right what it condemns when facing left'.[44] Consequently, where the illegality constitutes the commission of a crime, it is not for the law to stultify the criminal law by providing a remedy.[45]

The operation of this policy within the law of unjust enrichment assumes that there is a necessary inconsistency between criminal law and the law of unjust enrichment if a gain-based remedy is awarded despite the claimant's participation in criminal conduct. But that does not necessarily follow, especially where the claimant is less responsible for the illegality than the defendant and where a literal restitutionary remedy involving a giving back, rather than disgorgement remedy involving a giving up, is awarded to restore to the claimant what had been received by the defendant at the claimant's expense. The inconsistency between the criminal law and the law of unjust enrichment would be clearer if the award of a gain-based remedy enabled the claimant to profit from the commission of a crime, for it is a fundamental principle that a party should not be allowed to profit from his or her illegal conduct;[46] therefore, it would not be appropriate for the law of unjust enrichment to enable the claimant to profit from the commission of a crime. This would apply where the claimant seeks an account of profits from the defendant in circumstances where the profits arose from the commission of a crime. But this will not occur where the claimant seeks a remedy to reverse the defendant's unjust enrichment, since the defendant's gain will necessarily correspond with the claimant's loss.[47] Crucially, this

[42] *Apotex* (n 8) [66]. This was based on Law Commission, *The Illegality Defence* (CP No 189, 2009) [3.142].

[43] See generally *Hall v Hebert* [1993] 2 SCR 159 (SCC) 165 (McLachlan J); G Virgo, 'We Do This in the Criminal Law, and That in the Law of Tort: A New Fusion Debate' in E Chamberlain, JW Neyers and SG Pitel (eds), *Tort Law: Challenging Orthodoxy in Tort Law* (Oxford, Hart Publishing, 2013).

[44] *Hounga* (n 3) [55].

[45] EJ Weinrib, 'Illegality as a Tort Defence' (1976) 26 *University of Toronto Law Journal* 28, 52.

[46] *Beresford v Royal Insurance Co Ltd* [1938] AC 586 (HL). See also *Hall v Hebert* [1993] 2 SCR 159 (SCC) 169 (McLachlan J).

[47] See G Virgo, *The Principles of the Law of Restitution*, 3rd edn (Oxford, Oxford University Press, 2015) ch 5.

does not involve any enforcement of an illegal transaction;[48] there is only a giving back and not a carrying forward.

Usually the principle of consistency will not be applicable where the illegality involves conduct which is not criminal,[49] although there may be circumstances where the principle should operate outside the criminal law where the claimant's conduct is considered only to be civilly unlawful, for the denial of a remedy in such a case might be consistent with the reason why the conduct was rendered unlawful in the first place. This was recognised by the High Court of Australia in *Equuscorp Pty Ltd v Haxton*, where a restitutionary claim was defeated by a defence of statutory illegality, since the court was concerned to prevent the common law from stultifying the statute's purpose.[50]

3.2. Deterrence

The deterrence policy is founded on the principle that the court should not assist or encourage the claimant in his or her illegal conduct or encourage others in similar acts.[51] But it is difficult to see how this policy justifies the denial of restitutionary relief to a claimant who has participated in illegal conduct.[52] Whether the denial of a remedy will actually deter participation in illegal activity depends on a variety of assumptions, particularly that the claimant knows or suspects that the conduct is illegal and is aware of the existence and effect of the illegality defence. In fact, if the defendant, who expects to receive a benefit from the claimant, is aware of the illegality and of the policy denying restitution, he or she is more likely to participate in the transaction, knowing that any benefit which is received may be retained.[53] Consequently, the policy of deterrence is just as likely to be fulfilled by allowing restitution to a claimant who has been tainted by illegality than by denying relief to such a person.[54] But this is a highly artificial argument, since it is unlikely that either party will be aware of the illegality defence and its implications.[55] Even if the parties were so aware, it would be very difficult for them to predict whether or not restitution would be denied, because of the uncertain operation of the defence. Also, in those cases where the illegality is criminal, it is unlikely that the denial of a remedy will be a greater deterrent than that of the criminal law.[56]

[48] See *Aqua Art Pte Ltd v Goodman Development (S) Pte Ltd* [2011] SGCA 7; [2011] 2 SLR 865 [30] (Leong JA).

[49] See section 4 below.

[50] *Equuscorp Pty Ltd v Haxton* [2012] HCA 7; (2012) 246 CLR 498.

[51] *Euro-Diam* (n 28) 35 (Kerr LJ).

[52] *Tinsley* (n 22) 368 (Lord Lowry).

[53] *Nelson v Nelson* (1995) 184 CLR 538 (HCA) 610 (McHugh J).

[54] *Smith v Bromley* (1760) 2 Doug KB 696, 698; 99 ER 441.

[55] See *Tribe v Tribe* [1996] Ch 107 (CA) 134 (Millett LJ).

[56] *Hewison* (n 21) [73] (Ward LJ).

3.3. Punishment

It has been recognised that the denial of a remedy for illegality might be justified on the ground that it punishes the claimant.[57] But that is what the criminal law is for and, since the definition of illegality is not confined to criminal conduct, the punishment rationale cannot explain all cases where the defence has been applied. To the extent that illegality encompasses criminality and operates to bar the claim completely then, if this is justified for reasons of punishment, it is not possible for the court to ensure that the punishment fits the crime, especially since the effect of the 'punishment' will depend on the value of the benefit which has been received by the defendant: the greater the value, the more severe the claimant's punishment.[58] Further, there is a danger of double punishment, because the claimant might be punished through the imposition of a criminal sanction and also be denied a restitutionary remedy, the value of which might be much greater than any penalty which the criminal court may impose,[59] making the denial of relief disproportionate to the claimant's responsibility for the illegality. There may even be particular reasons why the criminal law will not impose liability, such as the age of the offender, which would not be recognised in the law of unjust enrichment. The punishment justification is consequently unconvincing.

3.4. Dignity of the Court

The court may be unwilling to award the claimant a remedy where he or she has been tainted by illegality, for fear of the court itself becoming tainted.[60] This is sometimes justified by a desire to preserve the court's credibility by its not appearing to condone illegal conduct.[61] For example, in *Everet v Williams*, the court refused to take an account between two highwaymen, because the claim was 'scandalous and impertinent'.[62] As a consequence the claimant's solicitor was arrested and fined. Similarly, in *Parkinson v College of Ambulance Ltd*, Lush J considered that no court could award a remedy following breach of an illegal contract 'with any propriety or decency'.[63]

However, protecting the dignity of the court is an unsatisfactory justification for the illegality defence because it suggests that the court is more

[57] *Tinsley v Milligan* [1992] Ch 310 (CA) 334 (Ralph Gibson LJ).
[58] *cf* proceeds of crime legislation which does not depend on punishment, but on confiscation.
[59] *St John Shipping Corp v Joseph Rank Ltd* [1957] 1 QB 267 (QBD) 288 (Devlin J).
[60] *Collins v Blantern* (1767) 2 Wils KB 347, 350; 95 ER 850 (Wilmot CJ).
[61] *Apotex* (n 3) [23] (Lord Sumption).
[62] *Everet v Williams* (1725) (unreported); see (1893) 9 *LQR* 197.
[63] *Parkinson v College of Ambulance Ltd* [1925] 2 KB 1 (KBD) 13.

concerned with its own dignity as a matter of policy without any regard to securing justice between the parties. It appears to stem from a fundamental objection to assisting a person who has participated in criminal behaviour, involving a return to the medieval law of outlawry whereby an outlaw forfeited any rights to assistance from the courts. But, as Judge LJ recognised in *Cross v Kirkby*, 'today there are no outlaws. However abhorrent the crime, whatever the subsequent conviction, the protection of the law extends to the criminal who enjoys rights not only in theory but enforceable in practice'.[64]

Analysis of these different justifications of the illegality defence suggests that there is no completely convincing policy reason in favour of denying restitution to a claimant who is tainted by illegality. Of all the suggested policies, that which seeks to ensure the consistency or integrity of the legal system is the most persuasive, but its operation should not be considered to be absolute. This policy was considered to be significant in *Hounga v Allen* with regard to international obligations, but, after careful consideration of the facts, was held not to require a denial of remedy to the claimant in her tort claim, because allowing the claim would not enable the claimant to profit from her crime and would not encourage people such as the claimant to enter into illegal contracts of employment.[65] On the other hand, it was considered that the denial of a remedy to the claimant by virtue of her illegality would encourage those in the position of the defendant to enter into illegal contracts of employment.

This illustrates an appropriate resolution of the tension between public policy and justice in the operation of the defence. Where the defence is engaged, in principle it will defeat the claim for reasons of public policy, notably the need for consistency in the law, but there will be circumstances where this policy can be considered to be weak, or even non-existent, and so considerations of the demands of justice as between the parties should prevail. But *Hounga v Allen* was a tort case. Can the same balanced approach also apply in the law of unjust enrichment?

4. THE OPERATION OF ILLEGALITY AS A DEFENCE IN THE LAW OF UNJUST ENRICHMENT

It has been assumed so far that illegality operates as a defence within the law of unjust enrichment. It is certainly the case that illegality can be pleaded by the defendant and, since this does not operate to defeat an element of the

[64] *Cross v Kirkby* [2000] EWCA Civ 426; The Times, 5 April 2000 [94]. See also *Olmstead v United States* 277 US 438, 484 (1828) (Brandeis J); *Mills v Baitis* [1968] VR 583 (SC).

[65] *Hounga* (n 3) [44] (Lord Wilson).

cause of action, it is properly analysed as a defence rather than a denial.[66] But, by virtue of its public policy foundations, illegality may defeat a claim even though it has not been pleaded.[67] As Lord Sumption recognised in *Les Laboratoires Servier v Apotex Inc*:[68]

> It is because the public has its own interest in conduct giving rise to the illegality defence that the judge may be bound to take the point of his own motion, contrary to the ordinary principle in adversarial litigation ... But in general, although described as a defence, it is in reality a rule of judicial abstention.

However, since the effect of illegality is to defeat the claim rather than to deny any of its elements, illegality is still properly analysed as a defence, even though it may not have been pleaded by the defendant.

Although the illegality defence in its embodiment of public policy is applied strictly, at least as interpreted by the Supreme Court in *Les Laboratoires Servier v Apotex Inc*, the majority in that case did recognise that there were two questions which needed to be considered before the defence was engaged, namely whether the claimant's conduct or purpose involves sufficient turpitude to engage the defence and whether the turpitude was sufficiently related to the claim.[69] How these two questions are interpreted and answered will have an important effect on the ambit of the defence in the law of unjust enrichment.

5. DEFINING TURPITUDE

There is no accepted definition of what constitutes illegality,[70] although it has been described as anything which is 'morally reprehensible'.[71] The word has often been used not as a term of art, but simply to describe a state of affairs which is contrary to law; however, mere unlawfulness does not necessarily equate with illegality, otherwise it would encompass a simple breach of contract.[72]

A number of categories of illegality can be identified. It clearly encompasses the commission of criminal conduct, because the interest of

[66] A distinction recognised by J Goudkamp and C Mitchell, 'Denials and Defences in the Law of Unjust Enrichment' in C Mitchell and W Swadling (eds), *The Restatement Third, Restitution and Unjust Enrichment: Critical and Comparative Essays* (Oxford, Hart Publishing, 2013) ch 6.

[67] *Selangor United Rubber Estates Ltd v Cradock (No 3)* [1968] 1 WLR 1555 (Ch D) 1653 (Ungoed-Thomas J). For an example of illegality being raised by the judge, see *Patel v Mirza* [2014] EWCA Civ 1047; [2015] 1 All ER 326.

[68] *Apotex* (n 3) [23]. See also *Jetivia* (n 18) [100] (Lord Sumption).

[69] *Apotex* (n 3) [22] (Lord Sumption).

[70] See H Beale (ed), *Chitty on Contracts*, 31st edn (London, Sweet & Maxwell, 2012) [16–03] et seq.

[71] *Safeway Stores Ltd v Twigger* [2010] EWHC 11 (Comm); [2012] 2 Lloyd's Rep 39 [26] (Flaux J).

[72] *Apotex* (n 3) [30] (Lord Sumption).

the state is engaged, save perhaps where the criminality is minor, as will sometimes be the case where the crime involves a strict liability offence,[73] at least where the claimant was unaware that his or her conduct was illegal.[74] It also includes conduct which is subject to civil penalties, such as breach of competition law,[75] involving payment to the claimant rather than the state, but where the relief still operates to punish the defendant rather than compensate the claimant for loss suffered. This has been described as 'quasi-criminal' because the interest of the state is engaged.[76]

Lawful conduct which is considered to be immoral may also be characterised as illegal. This was recognised by Hamblen J in *Nayyar v Denton Wilde Sapte*,[77] in holding that the receipt of a bribe was illegal because it evinced 'serious moral turpitude'.[78] Such immoral conduct has been held to include champertous agreements,[79] conduct relating to prostitution[80] and agreements concerning the sale of offices and honours.[81] Illegality by virtue of immorality is illustrated by *Sutton v Mischon de Reya*, where the claimant entered into what purported to be a cohabitation agreement with a third party.[82] The relationship between the claimant and the third party was one of master and slave, and it was held that this made the contract illegal since it was a contract for sexual services. Although the expansion of the ambit of illegality to such immoral conduct has been justified on the ground that it too can be characterised as quasi-criminal,[83] this treatment of perceived immoral conduct as illegal is controversial.[84] It enables the law of unjust enrichment to be used to supplement the criminal law, through the denial of relief where the claimant's conduct is considered to be unacceptable in some way even though it is lawful, which is difficult to defend convincingly.

Conduct which is characterised as involving wrongdoing under the civil law is generally not considered to constitute illegality. Crucially, in *Les Laboratoires Servier v Apotex Inc*, the Supreme Court held that the infringement of a patent did not constitute a sufficient taint of illegality to engage the defence because, although a patent is granted by the state, the public interest

[73] *Gray* (n 11) [83] (Lord Rodger).

[74] *Stone* (n 11) [24], [27] (Lord Phillips).

[75] *Safeway* (n 71) (price-fixing contrary to the Competition Act 1998 (UK)). However, Flaux J justified the application of the illegality defence with reference to the claimant's immoral conduct rather than because it was unlawful.

[76] *Apotex* (n 3) [25] (Lord Sumption).

[77] *Nayyar v Denton Wilde Sapte* [2009] EWHC 3218 (QBD); [2010] PNLR 15 [92]. See also *Apotex* (n 3) [13] (Lord Sumption).

[78] This may now be a crime: see the Bribery Act 2010 (UK).

[79] *Giles v Thompson* [1994] 1 AC 142 (HL).

[80] *Girardy v Richardson* (1793) 1 Esp 13; 170 ER 265.

[81] *Parkinson* (n 37).

[82] *Sutton v Mischon de Reya* [2003] EWHC 3166 (Ch D); [2004] 1 FLR 837.

[83] *Apotex* (n 3) [25] (Lord Sumption).

[84] See J Goudkamp, '*Ex Turpi Causa* and Immoral Behaviour in the Tort Context' (2011) 127 *LQR* 354.

was not considered to be engaged by a breach of the patentee's rights.[85] The infringement of private rights does not constitute illegality, although conduct which involves the commission of a tort has exceptionally been characterised as illegal where the tort requires proof of dishonesty,[86] presumably because this can also be considered to be quasi-criminal.[87] Apart from this exceptional situation, there is no public interest in denying a remedy to the claimant where private rights are wrongfully interfered with, because, as Lord Sumption recognised: 'The public interest is sufficiently served by the availability of a system of corrective justice to regulate their consequences as between the parties affected.'[88]

In determining the correct definition of illegality, it is important to consider the consequences of concluding that the claimant is tainted by illegality, for if the illegality defence is interpreted as applying strictly without qualification, this will lead to a desire for the defence to be interpreted narrowly. But if the defence is analysed as not being absolute in its application, it is not necessary to restrict the definition of illegality artificially because the effect of the taint of illegality will be assessed separately and, more appropriately, with regard to identified principles. If the defence can be applied flexibly, it follows that it is entirely appropriate to expand the definition of illegality to encompass certain types of civil wrongdoing and even immoral conduct. It is significant that although the Supreme Court in *Les Laboratoires Servier v Apotex Inc* adopted a strict interpretation of the defence of illegality, the Justices were able to avoid this by virtue of their narrow interpretation of what constitutes illegality, whereas in *Hounga v Allen*, although the claimant had clearly been tainted by illegality, this taint was avoided by virtue of the flexible interpretation of the defence and the policies which underpin it.[89] Consequently, if it is acknowledged that it does not follow automatically from the characterisation of conduct as illegal that the unjust enrichment claim must be defeated, there is much less concern about adopting a wide definition of turpitude, although this will depend on whether the principles for avoiding the taint of illegality are sufficiently robust.

6. MECHANISMS FOR EXCLUDING THE ILLEGALITY DEFENCE

In a number of instances, restitutionary remedies may be awarded despite the fact that the claimant has been tainted by illegality. In these cases,

[85] *Apotex* (n 3) [30] (Lord Sumption).

[86] *Parkingeye* (n 12) (tort of deceit). See also *Brown Jenkinson and Co Ltd v Percy Dalton (London) Ltd* [1957] 2 QB 621 (CA).

[87] The tort of deceit will typically, but not always, constitute a crime under the Fraud Act 2006 (UK).

[88] *Apotex* (n 3) [28].

[89] *Hounga* (n 3).

illegality is not a ground of restitution itself,[90] but the claim will be founded on other grounds of restitution where the consequences of the illegality can be excluded on the ground that they are merely collateral to the claim.[91] Various mechanisms have been identified for establishing this. It is a matter of some controversy as to whether these mechanisms are considered to be rule-based, as the Supreme Court in *Les Laboratoires Servier v Apotex Inc* indicated, or discretionary.[92] In the *Apotex* case, Lord Sumption indicated that the mechanisms were not dependent on 'a value judgment about the significance of the illegality or the consequences for the parties of barring the claim',[93] and were not based on achieving proportionality between the claimant's misconduct and his or her loss, a concept which he considered to derive from public law and not to be relevant to the law of obligations. But this supposed dichotomy between a rule-based and a discretionary approach is false. Hart recognised that discretion is fundamentally different from arbitrary choice: discretion by its nature is guided by rational principles, so that a decision which is not susceptible to principled justification is not an exercise of discretion at all, but involves the making of an arbitrary choice.[94] Hart rejected arbitrary choice as a basis for judicial decision making. He was right to do so. Judges must, by virtue of their office, act judicially and not arbitrarily. Similarly, the decision to disapply the illegality defence should not be founded on arbitrary choice; judicial decision making must be founded on recognised principles. Whilst the role of judicial discretion is essential to ensure that justice is achieved, if the resort to justice is to be defensible and predictable, there need to be identifiable principles to guide that discretion and to ensure that like cases are treated alike, for the benefit of the parties, their advisers and, if the case goes to trial, the judge. The question then is whether the mechanisms which have been identified for disapplying the illegality defence can be considered to be sufficiently clear to enable the exercise of judicial discretion in the correct sense.

6.1. No Reliance on Illegality

Since the illegality defence is typically formulated in terms of the claimant being prevented from relying on the illegality to establish the claim,[95]

[90] *cf* A Burrows, *The Law of Restitution*, 3rd edn (Oxford, Oxford University Press, 2011) 488.

[91] *Apotex* (n 3) [18] (Lord Sumption).

[92] Rejected in *Apotex* (ibid), but consistent with the decision of the same court in *Hounga* (n 3). See also *Gray* (n 11) [30] (Lord Hoffmann).

[93] *Apotex* (n 3) [18].

[94] HLA Hart, 'Discretion', written in 1956 and published in (2013) 127 *Harvard Law Review* 652.

[95] See Lord Mansfield in *Holman* (n 21); *Taylor v Chester* (1868–69) LR 4 QB 309 (QBD); *Stone* (n 11) [86] (Lord Phillips).

it follows that a claim might succeed where its elements can be established without needing to rely on the illegality.[96] In *Tinsley v Milligan*, a majority of the House of Lords recognised that the claimant could vindicate proprietary rights even though she had participated in an illegal transaction,[97] since it was not necessary to plead the illegality because the presumption of resulting trust was engaged.[98] But if the claimant needs to refer to illegality to make good the claim, it will be defeated for reasons of public policy.[99] Consequently, where money has been paid to the defendant pursuant to a contract which is void for illegality, the claimant will not be able to recover it if he or she has to rely on the illegality to establish the claim. Since the claimant needs to establish that the contract is no longer operative before a claim in unjust enrichment can be brought,[100] typically it will be necessary to plead the illegality to show that the contract is void and that a failure of basis can be identified,[101] save if another reason for invalidating the contract could be established or another mechanism for avoiding the taint of illegality can be identified.[102] This is a potentially significant expansion of the illegality defence within the law of unjust enrichment. In *Patel v Mirza*,[103] Gloster LJ, rather than considering whether the claimant needed to rely on the illegality, preferred to consider whether illegality necessarily formed an essential element of the claimant's cause of action. But this simply repackages the rule and, anyway, in that case it was essential to the claim that the contract was void and this could only be established by reference to its illegal purpose.

Whether the claimant can establish the claim without relying on illegality turns on chance. The Law Commission concluded that such a principle 'produces complex and arbitrary results, depending on the detailed intricacies of trust law'.[104] For example, the result in *Tinsley v Milligan* would have been different had the presumption of advancement applied, for then the claimant would have needed to plead the illegal agreement to rebut the

[96] See *Bowmakers Ltd v Barnet Instruments Ltd* [1945] KB 65 (CA).

[97] *Tinsley* (n 22) 376 (Lord Browne-Wilkinson). See also *O'Kelly v Davies* [2014] EWCA Civ 1606, applying the same rule to the common intention constructive trust.

[98] This was a proprietary restitutionary claim which was not based on establishing unjust enrichment.

[99] *Patel* (n 67) [20] (Rimer LJ), [102] (Vos LJ). See *Barrett v Barrett* [2008] EWHC 1061 (Ch); [2008] 2 P & CR 17.

[100] *Guinness plc v Saunders* [1990] 2 AC 663 (HL) 697–98 (Lord Goff); *Sandher v Pearson* [2013] EWCA Civ 1822.

[101] *Berg v Sadler and Moore* [1937] 2 KB 158 (CA) 163 (Lord Wright MR); *Patel* (n 67) [21] (Rimer LJ). Rimer LJ's assertion that allowing an unjust enrichment claim would involve the enforcement of the illegal contract is plainly incorrect since it harks back to the discredited thinking of such claims being grounded on implied contracts.

[102] Such as withdrawal from the illegal purpose, which was engaged in *Patel* (n 67). See section 6.2 below.

[103] ibid [79].

[104] Law Commission, *The Illegality Defence* (No 320, 2010) [1.7].

presumption. Also, no satisfactory explanation has been suggested as to why the claimant should not be allowed to rely on his or her illegality. It does not necessarily follow that the claim will be defeated even where the claimant needs to plead the illegality to establish the claim.[105] Further, the illegality defence applies even if illegality has not been pleaded, since it may be raised by the judge.

In *Cross v Kirkby* Beldam LJ said:[106]

> I do not believe that there is any general principle that the claimant must either plead, give evidence of or rely on his own illegality for the principle to apply. Such a technical approach is entirely absent from Lord Mansfield's exposition of the principle.

Lord Phillips recognised in *Stone and Rolls Ltd v Moore Stephens*:[107]

> I do not believe ... that it is right to proceed on the basis that the reliance test can automatically be applied as a rule of thumb. It is necessary to give consideration to the policy underlying ex turpi causa in order to decide whether this defence is bound to defeat [the claimant's] claim.[108]

Since there was no express reference in *Holman v Johnson* to the need to plead the illegality for the defence to be engaged, the preferable view is that this rule should be rejected because it involves artifice and formalism. It follows that it should be possible for the claimant to refer to the illegality to establish that any contract does not provide a lawful basis for the defendant's receipt of an enrichment.

6.2. Withdrawal from an Illegal Transaction

Where the claimant has withdrawn from an illegal transaction before any part of it has been performed, he or she is no longer considered to be tainted by the illegality and restitution will be awarded.[109] In *Patel v Mirza*, it was recognised that withdrawal does not require proof of repentance on the part of the claimant.[110] It is sufficient that the claimant has sought restitution

[105] In *Silverwood v Silverwood* (1997) 74 P & CR 453 (CA) 457, Peter Gibson LJ accepted that the claimant could rely on the illegal purpose of the parties to rebut the defendant's defence that the transferor of the property had intended it to be a gift to the defendant.

[106] *Cross* (n 64) [76].

[107] *Stone* (n 11) [25].

[108] Affirmed by Lord Wilson in *Hounga* (n 3) [29], but inconsistent with the approach adopted in *Apotex* (n 3).

[109] See *Taylor v Bowers* (1876) 1 QBD 291 (CA); *Tribe* (n 55). *cf Kearley v Thomson* (1890) 24 QBD 742 (CA): restitution denied where the illegal agreement was carried out. For the operation of the withdrawal principle in tort, see *Miller v Miller* [2011] HCA 9; (2011) 242 CLR 446.

[110] *Patel* (n 67). This had also been recognised by Millett LJ in *Tribe* (n 55) 135.

before any part of the illegal agreement has been carried into effect to any extent, or the claimant has attempted to carry it into effect,[111] even though the only reason for withdrawal is that it is impossible to carry out the agreement as originally envisaged for reasons outside the control of the claimant. In *Patel v Mirza*, the claimant had paid money to the defendant pursuant to a contract which was illegal because it related to the crime of insider dealing.[112] The claimant was found to have withdrawn from the agreement even though the only reason for the withdrawal was that the illegal purpose was frustrated for reasons outside his control, namely that the expected inside information was not obtained. Consequently, withdrawal does not require any change of mind on the part of the claimant; it is sufficient that the illegal purpose was frustrated.[113]

Where the claimant has effectively withdrawn from an illegal transaction, he or she can bring a claim in unjust enrichment with the ground of restitution preferably analysed as being total failure of basis, since the withdrawal principle will only be engaged if no part of the illegal purpose has been carried into effect.[114] Restitution is justified in such circumstances on the ground that the claimant is no longer tainted by the illegality and from a policy of deterring the performance of illegal contracts. Crucially, following the decision in *Patel v Mirza*, the notion of voluntary withdrawal has been watered down to such an extent that it is now possible to assert that the taint of illegality will be removed if no part of the illegal purpose has been carried out for whatever reason,[115] even if it is the defendant who withdrew, thus frustrating the illegal purpose, save, presumably, where the illegality is so grave that 'withdrawal' can never remove the taint of the illegality.[116] This is consequently a very significant restriction on the operation of the illegality defence, which enables the taint of illegality to be ignored so that the court can focus on correcting the injustice as between the claimant and the defendant.

[111] As occurred in *Alexander v Rayson* [1936] 1 KB 169 (CA); *Berg* (n 101); *Harry Parker Ltd v Mason* [1940] 2 KB 590 (CA); *Collier v Collier* [2002] EWCA Civ 1095.

[112] Contrary to the Criminal Justice Act 1993 (UK), s 52.

[113] *cf Bigos v Bousted* [1951] 1 All ER 92 (KBD), where the withdrawal principle did not apply where the frustration of the illegal purpose resulted from the refusal of the other party to participate. The decision was described as 'dubious' by Millett LJ in *Tribe* (n 55) 135, although Rimer LJ in *Patel* (n 67) [41] considered it to be sound because there had been no 'voluntary withdrawal'. But there was no 'voluntary withdrawal' in *Patel* either, save that, once the agreement was frustrated, the claimant then sought restitution. Distinguishing between *Bigos v Bousted* and *Patel* with reference to the voluntariness of the withdrawal is unconvincing. See *Patel* [96] (Gloster LJ).

[114] See *Tribe* (n 55); *Q v Q* [2008] EWHC 1874 (Fam); [2009] 1 FLR 935.

[115] In Singapore, the test is whether the illegal purpose has been substantially achieved: *Aqua Art* (n 48) [30] (Leong JA).

[116] See section 7 below.

6.3. The Parties are not *In Pari Delicto*

The claimant's restitutionary claim will succeed even though it arises from participation in an illegal transaction where the parties are not *in pari delicto*, which will usually be the case where the defendant is more responsible for participating in the illegal transaction than the claimant. This was recognised as being relevant in *Hounga v Allen*,[117] because the defendants bore much greater responsibility for the illegal employment contract than the claimant. The significance of comparative responsibility of the parties is also relevant to unjust enrichment claims. So, for example, the claimant will be able to bring a restitutionary claim by virtue of compulsion, despite the fact that he or she has been tainted by illegality.[118] Similarly, where the defendant has acted oppressively towards the claimant,[119] or where statute imposes an obligation on the defendant to ensure that the transaction complies with the law.[120] Restitution has also been awarded by the European Court of Justice in the context of a claimant who is less responsible for entering into an anti-competitive agreement which is illegal by EU law.[121] Where the ground of restitution is mistake, it has been recognised that restitution can be awarded despite the taint of illegality.[122] Where the mistake was induced by the defendant, allowing restitution despite the illegality can easily be justified on the ground that the parties are not *in pari delicto*. This has tentatively been recognised as the justification where the claimant alone was mistaken, but not where both parties are mistaken because no party is more responsible for participating in the illegal transaction than the other.[123] Restitution might, however, be justified on the alternative ground that where both parties are mistaken, this negates the taint of illegality because it is not sufficiently connected to the claim.[124]

Although it has been generally recognised that a restitutionary claim grounded on total failure of basis will be defeated if the claimant participated in an illegal transaction, this will not be the case where the claimant is not as blameworthy as the defendant. This is illustrated by *Mohamed v Alaga and Co*, where the claimant sued the defendant firm of solicitors for work done in preparing and presenting asylum claims.[125] A contract between

117 *Hounga* (n 3) [39] (Lord Wilson). *cf* Lord Hughes at [57], who did not consider that the comparative turpitude of the parties was a relevant consideration. It is unclear whether any useful distinction can be drawn between comparative responsibility and turpitude.

118 *Astley v Reynolds* (1731) 2 Stra 915; 93 ER 939.

119 *Smith v Cuff* (1817) 6 M & S 160; 105 ER 1203.

120 *Kiriri Cotton Co Ltd v Dewani* [1960] AC 192 (PC).

121 Case C-453/99 *Courage Ltd v Crehan* [2001] ECR I-6297; [2002] QB 507 (ECJ).

122 *Oom v Bruce* (1810) 12 East 225; 104 ER 87.

123 *Aqua Art* (n 48) [25] (Leong JA).

124 See p 187, below.

125 *Mohamed v Alaga and Co* [2000] 1 WLR 1815 (CA).

the claimant and the defendant concerning payment to the claimant for the introduction of clients to the defendant was illegal, as it was an unlawful fee-sharing agreement, but the claimant's restitutionary claim succeeded as regards the professional work he had legitimately done. This work could be severed from the illegal fee-sharing part of the contract because the claimant was less responsible for the illegality than the defendant firm of solicitors, which was assumed to know the rules of the profession.[126]

The not *in pari delicto* mechanism is very significant in restricting the ambit of the illegality defence as regards claims in unjust enrichment. Despite the taint of illegality, it enables the court to focus on the comparative responsibility of the parties and enables the public policy of the illegality defence to be trumped by the need to secure justice between the parties.

6.4. The Policy behind the Illegality

In Australia, the operation of the illegality defence is determined by reference to the policy of the law by virtue of which the relevant transaction was found to have been illegal.[127] This was recognised by the High Court of Australia in *Nelson v Nelson*,[128] where Deane and Gummow JJ indicated that statutory policy might be less likely to defeat a claim where the claimant sought restitution, in order to restore the claimant to his original position, rather than where the claimant sought to enforce a contract.[129]

This focus on the policy behind the law which renders a transaction illegal was considered further by the High Court in *Equuscorp Pty Ltd v Haxton*.[130] Money had been advanced under loan agreements which were made in furtherance of an illegal purpose to get tax deductions through an investment scheme in blueberry farms. The claimant sought restitution of the money transferred to the defendant, but it was held that the illegality which rendered the loan agreements unenforceable also denied the restitutionary claim, by reference to the scope and purpose of the statute which rendered the transaction illegal, particularly the purpose of protecting a class of persons from whom the claimant sought restitution. But the court also had regard to the responsibility of the claimant and whether it was innocent or was involved in the illegality,[131] which was specifically recognised as indicating that the parties were not *in pari delicto*.

[126] *cf Awwad v Geraghty & Co* [2001] QB 570 (CA), where the claimant was a partner in the firm of solicitors and so was as equally responsible as the defendant.

[127] See also P Birks, 'Recovering Value Transferred under an Illegal Contract' (2000) 1 *Theoretical Inquiries in Law* 155.

[128] *Nelson* (n 53).

[129] ibid 552.

[130] *Equuscorp* (n 50). See also *Miller* (n 109).

[131] *Equuscorp* (n 50) [34] (French CJ, Crennan and Kiefel JJ).

Denying restitution where its award would stultify the purpose of the statute which rendered the relevant transaction illegal in the first place is justified by the need to ensure coherence in the law by avoiding its stultification.[132] This has been recognised by the American Law Institute's *Restatement of the Law, Third: Restitution and Unjust Enrichment*,[133] with reference to the need to ensure that the policy of the statute is not defeated or frustrated. The difficulty, of course, is seeking to divine the policy of the statute, which involves the exercise of arbitrary choice rather than principled discretion.

In England, whether it is possible to recover the value of a loan made pursuant to a void transaction has been held to depend on whether restitution would undermine the policy which rendered to transaction void. So, for example, in *Haugesund Kommune v Depfa ACS Bank*, the value of a loan could be recovered by means of a claim in unjust enrichment, albeit that in that case the loan was unenforceable by virtue of the defendant's incapacity to borrow the money rather than because of illegality.[134] But the Court of Appeal still emphasised that it was necessary to consider whether allowing restitution would be contrary to public policy with reference to the reason why the loan was void.[135] It is likely that, where the loan transaction is illegal, the policy of the statute which renders the transaction void will deny restitution, especially where the policy is founded on the need to protect the defendant. Consequently, it is likely that *Equuscorp Ltd v Haxton* would be decided the same way in England. In *Best v The Chief Land Registrar*,[136] it was held that the registration of title to land acquired by adverse possession was not defeated by the adverse possessor having committed the crime of squatting,[137] since Parliament in creating the crime was not considered to have intended to have any impact on the law of adverse possession, which was identified as fulfilling valuable social and economic objectives.

That legislative policy is relevant to the operation of the illegality defence was acknowledged by the majority in *Hounga v Allen*,[138] where an additional reason for rejecting the illegality defence to the tort claim was that allowing the defence to succeed would run counter to the international public policy against people trafficking and the need to protect victims of trafficking, such as the claimant.[139] It was specifically recognised that the public

[132] *Boissevain v Weil* [1950] AC 327 (HL) 341.

[133] American Law Institute, *Restatement of the Law, Third: Restitution and Unjust Enrichment* (2011) § 32(2), 505–06.

[134] *Haugesund Kommune v Depfa ACS Bank* [2010] EWCA Civ 579; [2012] QB 549.

[135] See also *Boissevain* (n 132); *Dimond v Lovell* [2002] 1 AC 384 (HL); *Wilson v First County Trust (No 2)* [2003] UKHL 40; [2004] 1 AC 816.

[136] *Best* (n 12).

[137] Contrary to the Legal Aid, Sentencing and Punishment of Offenders Act 2012 (UK), s 144.

[138] *Hounga* (n 3). See also *Patel* (n 67) [65] (Gloster LJ) and *Quinn* (n 12).

[139] *Hounga* (n 3) [52] (Lord Wilson).

policy in favour of the illegality defence should give way to the public policy against trafficking; one public policy trumped the other.

6.5. Close Connection or Inextricable Link

A further mechanism to limit the operation of the illegality defence is slowly emerging, namely whether there is a sufficiently close connection or inextricable link between the claim and the illegality that the court cannot permit the claimant to recover without appearing to condone the illegal conduct.[140] This was recognised by the Law Commission,[141] which suggested that it would only be a proportionate response to deny the claimant a remedy where there was such a close connection. This was also recognised by the Supreme Court in *Les Laboratoires Servier v Apotex*,[142] in holding that the turpitude must be sufficiently related to the claim.

This test of close connection has proved to be especially important in the law of tort, where the defence will be engaged if the illegality is a proximate cause of the claimant's loss.[143] It follows that the claimant cannot recover for a loss arising from a punishment imposed for the commission of a crime[144] by virtue of the policy to ensure consistency between the law of tort and the criminal law.[145] Further, the illegality defence prevents the claimant from recovering for loss which was a consequence of his or her own illegal act,[146] which has also been justified by the need to ensure consistency between tort and criminal law.[147] The need to identify a close connection between the illegality and the claim was another reason why the illegality defence was rejected in *Hounga v Allen*,[148] since the fact that the claimant was an illegal immigrant was considered to be collateral to the tort claim, in that it only provided a context for the relationship which gave rise to the claim. It was recognised, however, that a claim to recover for breach

[140] *Cross* (n 64) [76] (Beldam LJ).

[141] Law Commission (n 42) [3.143].

[142] *Apotex* (n 3) [22] (Lord Sumption).

[143] *Gray* (n 11) [32] (Lord Hoffmann). Lord Hoffmann preferred the language of causation to that of inextricable link: ibid [53]. Some cases have focused on the language of remoteness, eg, *21st Century Logistic Solutions Ltd v Madysen Ltd* [2004] EWHC 231 (QB); [2004] 2 Lloyd's Rep 92 [18] (Field J).

[144] *Askey v Golden Wine Co Ltd* [1948] 2 All ER 35 (KBD) 38 (Denning J).

[145] *Gray* (n 11) [37] (Lord Hoffmann); *Delaney v Pickett* [2011] EWCA Civ 1532; [2012] 1 WLR 2149 [35] (Ward LJ).

[146] *Gray* (n 11) [54] (Lord Hoffmann). In *Stone* (n 11) [20], Lord Phillips described the principle as preventing a claimant 'from using the court to obtain benefits from his own illegal conduct'. See *Delaney* (n 145); *Joyce v O'Brien* [2013] EWCA Civ 546; [2014] 1 WLR 70 [29] (Elias LJ).

[147] Lord Sumption (n 4) 9.

[148] *Hounga* (n 3) [55] (Lord Hughes).

of the contract of employment would have failed because, the contract being tainted by illegality, that illegality was closely connected to the claim.[149] This can be contrasted with *Parkingeye Ltd v Somerfield Stores Ltd*, where a claim for breach of contract succeeded despite illegality in the manner of its performance.[150] This was because the taint of illegality only related to one of three letters demanding payment of a parking penalty, which was considered to be too far removed from the basic operation of the contract to taint it, such that failure to enforce the contract was considered to be a disproportionate result.[151]

This principle of close connection between the illegality and the claim could be relevant to restitutionary claims as well. It was recognised by Lords Goff and Keith in *Tinsley v Milligan*, who, as dissentients, rather than focusing on whether the claimant needed to rely on the illegality to establish her claim, favoured a rule which would bar any claim tainted by a sufficiently close factual connection with the illegal purpose and would consequently have dismissed the claim to an equitable proprietary interest for that reason.[152] The absence of a close connection between the illegality and the claim might also, albeit somewhat unconvincingly, explain why a claim grounded on mistake is not defeated by illegality.[153]

The validity of this close connection test is, however, controversial, since it will often be unclear when the test is satisfied. In *Best v The Chief Land Registrar*, Sales LJ considered the test simply to be 'a way of saying that the public policy associated with the particular crime in issue is not centrally engaged and is outweighed by other general public policies inherent in the relevant civil law to be applied'.[154] But this does nothing to dispel the uncertainty, since it is both necessary to identify the relevant public policies and then identify appropriate mechanisms for weighing them up. If the close connection test is to be retained, it is far better to treat it as a generic test for disapplying the illegality defence which will be met if any of the other mechanisms are established. So, for example, if allowing restitution is consistent with the policy of the statute which renders the conduct criminal, it could be concluded that the illegality is then not sufficiently connected to the claim. Similarly, where the claimant has withdrawn from the illegal transaction or where the claimant is less responsible than the defendant for the illegal transaction, the defence should not be engaged.

149 ibid [58].
150 *Parkingeye* (n 12).
151 ibid [38] (Sir Robin Jacob).
152 *Tinsley* (n 22) 357.
153 See p 184, above.
154 *Best* (n 12) [61].

7. SERIOUS CRIMINAL CULPABILITY

7.1. A Limitation on the Qualifications to the Illegality Defence

Where the illegality involves particularly serious turpitude, the policy behind the *ex turpi causa* principle should be absolute.[155] Only in such exceptional circumstances is it appropriate to recognise that the public policy of protecting the dignity of the courts should prevail. Consequently, a court would never order restitution of money paid to the defendant to kill a third party, simply because the agreement involves such turpitude that no court would assist the claimant,[156] even if the victim had died from natural causes so frustrating the conspiracy.[157] Similarly, the court should not allow a claimant to vindicate his or her proprietary rights in respect of property which is held on resulting trust, where the claimant had contributed to the purchase of a house which was vested in the sole name of the defendant, in circumstances in which the house was intended to be used as a base for terrorist activities.[158]

The decision of the Court of Appeal in *Taylor v Bhail* can be justified on similar grounds.[159] In that case, the claimant builder had agreed with the defendant that he would submit an estimate for building work which was £1,000 above the actual cost of the estimated work in order to enable the defendant to defraud his insurance company. The restitutionary claim for the value of the work which he had actually done failed. This can be justified on the ground that the claimant and the defendant had committed the serious crime of conspiracy to defraud.[160] As Millett LJ recognised, such insurance fraud is a serious problem which needs to be deterred.[161] In *Patel v Mirza*,[162] however, restitution was awarded even though money had been paid pursuant to a criminal conspiracy to commit insider dealing, which presumably should be deterred as well. It follows that it will be difficult to determine when the illegality is sufficiently grave to deny restitution.

It has sometimes been suggested that it is not appropriate for the civil courts to grade illegality according to moral turpitude,[163] but that is something which the criminal courts do all the time as part of the sentencing exercise and there is no reason why the civil courts should be unable to

[155] See *Bowmakers* (n 96) 72 (du Parcq LJ).

[156] *Tappenden v Randall* (1801) 2 Bos & Pul 467, 471; 126 ER 1388, 1390 (Heath J); *Kearley v Thomson* (1890) 24 QBD 742 (CA) 747 (Fry LJ).

[157] *Patel* (n 67) [117] (Vos LJ).

[158] See *Tinsley* (n 22) 362 (Lord Goff). See also *Best* (n 12) [67] (Sales LJ) as regards bribery and murder.

[159] *Taylor v Bhail* [1996] CLC 377 (CA).

[160] ibid 381 (Russell LJ).

[161] ibid 384.

[162] *Patel* (n 67).

[163] *Pitts* (n 20) 56 (Dillon LJ). Described by the judge as a 'graph of illegalities'.

do so as well. It has also been suggested that the illegality defence should generally apply to any crime which is punishable with imprisonment,[164] but this has no regard to the circumstances in which the crime was committed. Factors which are relevant to the sentencing exercise in the criminal courts should also be relevant in the civil law, so it is not sufficient just to consider the maximum sentence available for the crime; the circumstances in which the offence was committed and by whom should be examined to determine whether the offender would have been imprisoned and for how long.[165] This was effectively recognised by Elias LJ in *Joyce v O'Brien*,[166] when he concluded that the illegality defence would not usually apply in tort where the crime involves minor traffic offences, even though they may be punished with imprisonment, but did apply on the facts of that case, since the illegality involved the theft of ladders, an offence which carries a maximum prison sentence of seven years.

7.2. Confiscation by the State

A further significant restriction on the ability of a claimant to obtain restitution from the defendant arises where the defendant has profited from the commission of a crime against the claimant. In such circumstances the state has a power to confiscate the proceeds of crime, primarily under the Proceeds of Crime Act 2002 (UK).[167] Where the defendant has been convicted of a crime, the state can ensure that he or she is deprived of the value of any benefit arising from the commission of that crime. This is significant as regards the operation of the illegality defence, since one of the concerns about its operation relates to the perceived unfairness of the defendant retaining the benefit received, even though the defendant is tainted with the illegality as much as the claimant. This concern disappears once it is recognised that the value of the defendant's enrichment might be seized by the state.

The essence of the statutory confiscation scheme is that once the defendant has been convicted of a crime, the Crown Court can make a confiscation order as part of the sentencing process.[168] The essence of such orders is to remove from criminals the proceeds of their crimes[169] by valuing the proceeds and imposing a personal liability on the defendant to pay this amount to the

[164] *Vellino v Chief Constable of Greater Manchester Police* [2001] EWCA Civ 1249; [2002] 1 WLR 218 [70] (Sir Murray Stuart-Smith).

[165] *Hewison* (n 21) [85] (Ward LJ).

[166] *Joyce* (n 146) [51]. See also *McCracken* (n 12) [86] (Christopher Clarke LJ).

[167] See generally G Virgo, 'Crime and Restitution Revisited' [2009] *Restitution Law Review* 29.

[168] *R (Virgin Media Ltd) v Zinga (Munaf Ahmed)* [2014] EWCA Crim 52; [2014] 1 WLR 2228.

[169] *R v Waya (Terry)* [2012] UKSC 51; [2013] 1 AC 294 [20] (Lord Walker and Hughes LJ).

state. The operation of this confiscation scheme is unnecessarily complex, and its interpretation has regularly been considered by the House of Lords and Supreme Court. When determining whether a confiscation order can be made against the defendant, three separate issues need to be considered:[170] first, whether the defendant had benefited from general criminal conduct if he or she has a criminal lifestyle or, if he or she does not have such a lifestyle, whether he or she had benefited from particular criminal conduct;[171] second, the objective market value of the benefit is assessed;[172] third, the recoverable amount is identified, which may be less than the objective value of the benefit obtained if the amount available to the defendant is less.[173]

The operation of the confiscation regime is notoriously draconian. The statutory regime trumps the private law claim of the claimant such that if the defendant's assets have been confiscated, there may be little point in the claimant bringing a claim in unjust enrichment, even if the illegality defence was inapplicable. In *May*,[174] the House of Lords held that the relevant benefit for the confiscation regime is the total value of the property or advantage obtained and is not limited to the defendant's net profits after deduction of expenses. So, for example, where the defendant sells drugs, the relevant benefit is not the defendant's profit, but the sale price.[175] Determining the value of the benefit is, however, moderated by the need to ensure that the confiscation order is not disproportionate.[176] Thus, for example, if the defendant has already restored the proceeds of crime to the victim, a confiscation order should not be made.[177]

Part V of the Proceeds of Crime Act 2002 (UK) also enables certain state officials to apply to the High Court for a civil recovery order to recover property obtained through the commission of criminal conduct even though the defendant may not have been convicted of a crime in respect of that property and may simply be the recipient of property which is the product of a crime.[178] It is not necessary for anybody to have been convicted of a crime for this civil process to apply.[179] This provides another route for the state to trump a private law claim of the victim of a crime, even if the defence of illegality is not engaged. Since the state may have recovered the

[170] *R v May (Raymond George)* [2008] UKHL 28; [2008] 1 AC 1028 [8].

[171] Proceeds of Crime Act 2002 (UK), s 6(4)(b) and (c).

[172] ibid ss 76(7) and 79(2).

[173] ibid s 7(2).

[174] *May* (n 170) [48(1)].

[175] *R v Simons (Leslie Lionel)* (1994) 98 Cr App R 100 (CA); *R v Green* [2008] UKHL 30; [2008] 1 AC 1053.

[176] A test which, paradoxically, the Supreme Court considered not to be relevant to the operation of the defence of illegality: *Apotex* (n 3) [18] (Lord Sumption).

[177] *Terry* (n 169) [28] (Lord Walker and Hughes LJ).

[178] See *Serious Organised Crime Agency v Perry* [2012] UKSC 35; [2013] 1 AC 182 [39].

[179] A criminal court does, however, have the power to make a restitution order to the victim on conviction: Powers of Criminal Courts (Sentencing) Act 2000 (UK), s 148.

property taken from the victim, any restitutionary claim brought by the victim might be met with a defence of change of position, although the defendant's criminality will presumably negate this defence since he or she will be a wrongdoer.

The most significant consequence of the statutory confiscation powers is that the defendant criminal is much less likely to be worth suing, even if the claimant is not tainted by the illegality so that any claim for restitution is not defeated by the illegality defence.

8. SYNTHESIS

The law on the defence of illegality in private law generally is at a crossroads. Rather than returning back to an unprincipled and confused body of law, there are three possible routes forward. The first is the purely public policy route, where illegality is treated as an absolute defence and is constrained only by the adoption of a restricted definition of illegality and by the need to consider whether the illegality is sufficiently connected with the claim.[180] Such an approach has no regard to the justice of the case as between the parties. The second route focuses on the public policies which underpin the illegality defence, but seeks to ascertain whether the operation of the defence can be justified by virtue of those policies.[181] The legitimacy of this approach turns on the validity and acceptance of the underlying policies. There is a danger that this collapses from being a principled exercise of judicial discretion into the exercise of an arbitrary choice, potentially even returning to the old public conscience test. The third route adopts a middle way between the other two. It recognises the public policy dimension of the illegality defence as a starting point for its application, but then moderates this by reference both to how illegality is defined and to various recognised mechanisms which can be analysed as involving both countervailing policy considerations and the need to consider the justice of the case as between the parties. This involves the exercise of judicial discretion in a principled way.

This middle way is preferable and should be adopted generally for the defence of illegality in private law. But even if this is not accepted for claims in tort or breach of contract, there is no reason why this route should not be followed for claims in unjust enrichment, where the illegality defence can be considered to have a much weaker role. As Gloster LJ recognised in

[180] *Apotex* (n 3).

[181] This was the approach adopted in *Stone* (n 11) [25] (Lord Phillips); *Hounga* (n 3); *Parkingeye* (n 12) and *Patel* (n 67) [62] (Gloster LJ). It was also adopted by the Court of Appeal in *Apotex*, which was rejected by the Supreme Court, and also by the Singapore Court of Appeal: *Ting Siew May v Boon Lay Choo* [2014] SGCA 28; [2014] 5 LRC 474.

Patel v Mirza,[182] recognising a restitutionary remedy to reverse the defendant's unjust enrichment does not involve the enforcement of an illegal agreement and does not enable the claimant to benefit from wrongdoing, but simply restores the claimant to his or her original position without any net benefit arising from the illegality. Consequently, where the claimant is no longer tainted by the illegality or can be considered to be less responsible for participation in the illegal transaction than the defendant, it is appropriate for a restitutionary remedy to be awarded, save where the turpitude is especially serious.

In *Tinsley v Milligan*,[183] Lord Goff said: 'I would be more than happy if a new system could be evolved which was both satisfactory in its effect and capable of avoiding the kind of result which flows from the established rules of law.'

Subsequently, there have been demands for a statutory reform of the rule-based illegality defence,[184] along the lines of the law in New Zealand[185] and Israel,[186] in order to allow restitution despite the taint of illegality through the exercise of a structured judicial discretion. But there is no need for such statutory reform; the existing law can be rationalised in such a way as to avoid the perceived injustices identified by Lord Goff. The Law Commission has rejected statutory reform,[187] save where a trust has been created to conceal the beneficiary's interest in connection with a criminal purpose. It was right to do so.[188] The right approach was identified by Toulson LJ in *Parkingeye Ltd v Somerfield Stores Ltd*:[189]

> [I]n the area of illegality, experience has shown that it is better to recognise that there may be conflicting considerations and that the rules need to be developed and applied in a way which enables the court to balance them fairly.

The law can be summarised as follows: illegality should be recognised as a defence to unjust enrichment claims by virtue of public policy, primarily founded on the need for consistency between the criminal law and the law of unjust enrichment, but justice demands that the defence should not operate where the claimant is less responsible than the defendant for involvement in the illegal activity or cannot be considered to be tainted by the illegality

[182] *Patel* (n 67) [70].

[183] *Tinsley* (n 22) 364.

[184] Law Commission (n 42). See B Dickson, 'Restitution and Illegal Transactions' in A Burrows (ed), *Essays on the Law of Restitution* (Oxford, Clarendon Press, 1991) 195; Lord Sumption (n 4).

[185] Illegal Contracts Act 1970 (UK), s 7.

[186] Contracts (General Part) Law 1973 (UK), s 31.

[187] Law Commission, *The Illegality Defence* (Law Com No 320, 2010).

[188] *cf* Lord Sumption (n 4); Lord Mance, '*Ex Turpi Causa*—When Latin Avoids Liability' (2014) 18 *Edinburgh Law Review* 175.

[189] *Parkingeye* (n 12) [54].

anymore. Further, there may be countervailing policy reasons which trump the illegality defence, notably that the rule which makes the conduct illegal is not stultified by allowing restitution. The mechanisms for avoiding the illegality defence should not be considered to involve arbitrary judicial choice,[190] but, instead, are founded on clear and defensible principles and should involve the exercise of judicial discretion in the proper sense of that term.

[190] ibid [38] (Sir Robin Jacob), [47] (Toulson LJ).

9

Minority and Unjust Enrichment Defences

BIRKE HÄCKER

1. INTRODUCTION

Infancy ... is a legal disability and an infant, in the absence of evidence to the contrary, is universally considered to be lacking in judgment, since his or her normal condition is that of incompetency. In addition, an infant is deemed to lack the adult's knowledge of the probable consequences of his or her acts or omissions and the capacity to make effective use of such knowledge as he or she has. It is the policy of the law to look after the interests of infants, who are considered incapable of looking after their own affairs, to protect them from their own folly and improvidence, and to prevent adults from taking advantage of them.[1]

[M]iserable must the condition of minors be; excluded from the society and commerce of the world; deprived of necessaries, education, employment, and many advantages; if they could do no binding acts. Great inconvenience must arise to others, if they were bound by no act. The law, therefore, at the same time that it protects their imbecility and indiscretion from injury through their own imprudence, enables them to do binding acts, for their own benefit; and, without prejudice to themselves, for the benefit of others.[2]

IT IS A curious fact about legal education in England that the problems associated with a party's minority are rarely discussed in great detail. Most students leave university with a vague notion that a child or adolescent is able to enter into a valid contract for 'necessaries',[3] and perhaps that the standard of care in the tort of negligence may vary depending on the defendant's age,[4] but little beyond that. However, minority—or 'infancy', as it is still frequently called—potentially impacts all areas of the law. Although the overall number of cases where it becomes relevant may have fallen since

[1] *City of New York v Stringfellow's of New York Ltd* 253 AD 2d 110, 120, 684 NYS 2d 544, 550–51 (1999).

[2] *Zouch v Parsons* (1765) 3 Burr 1794, 1801; 97 ER 1103, 1106–07.

[3] See n 9 and the accompanying text.

[4] *Mullin v Richards* [1998] 1 WLR 1304 (CA), following the approach adopted by the High Court of Australia in *McHale v Watson* (1966) 115 CLR 199 (HCA).

the age of majority was reduced from 21 to 18 years,[5] modern phenomena like online transactions concluded by internet-savvy 12-, 14- or 17-year-olds continue to mark the field out as one of practical significance.[6]

The purpose of this chapter is to review the effect of minority on defences[7] in the law of unjust enrichment. Are there any special defences capable of arising where one of the parties to a transaction is a minor? And when and how ought the operation of ordinary unjust enrichment defences to be modified so as to take account of his being under age? While the treatment is not intended to be wholly exhaustive (the rules on limitation, for example, may also vary depending on age),[8] it does seek to engage with the most pertinent points specific to the law of restitution for unjust enrichment. We will first consider the situation where the minor himself brings a claim in unjust enrichment, and then the scenario where such a claim is brought against him.

Before addressing these issues, it is convenient to remind ourselves of the broader context of the present inquiry. The law of restitution for unjust enrichment, though long emancipated from the realm of 'quasi-contract', often interlinks with contract law. While some of the defences discussed below are free-standing in the sense of potentially applying to any unjust enrichment claim (as in a simple mistaken payment case), others depend on an actual or purported exchange transaction between the parties. Moreover, the contractual rules governing minority mean that there will typically be no question of restitution or correlated defences where a minor and an adult have contracted for necessary goods or have entered into a service contract which is for the minor's benefit.[9] Problems will thus only arise if the minor repudiates a voidable contract[10] or—more usually—where the common law's default regime renders the contract unenforceable against the minor (albeit theoretically subject to his ratification upon reaching adulthood).[11]

[5] By virtue of the Family Law Reform Act 1969 (UK), s 1(1).

[6] The rise of e-commerce in particular has already led some US commentators to question the infancy doctrine as such, eg, JL Daniel, 'Virtually Mature: Examining the Policy of Minors' Incapacity to Contract through the Cyberscope' (2008) 43 *Gonzaga Law Review* 239, drawing on LA DiMatteo, 'Deconstructing the Myth of the "Infancy Law Doctrine": From Incapacity to Accountability' (1995) 21 *Ohio Northern University Law Review* 481.

[7] The term 'defences' is here used in the widest possible sense of everything which the defendant may rely on to ward off liability, including—in the terminology suggested, eg, by J Goudkamp, *Tort Law Defences* (Oxford, Hart Publishing, 2013)—outright 'denials' of the cause of action as well as 'defences' in the narrower sense.

[8] See Limitation Act 1980 (UK), ss 28, 38(2).

[9] For an overview of those contracts which the law treats as valid despite a party's minority, see E Peel, *Treitel: The Law of Contract*, 13th edn (London, Sweet & Maxwell, 2011) [12-003]–[12-016] (hereinafter *Treitel on Contract*).

[10] On the category of contracts which are 'voidable' at the minor's instance, see ibid [12-017]–[12-026].

[11] On the legal effects of such contracts, see ibid [12-027]–[12-032].

The Infants Relief Act 1874 (UK), by virtue of which many such contracts were 'absolutely void',[12] was repealed by the Minors' Contracts Act 1987 (UK).[13]

2. MINOR AS CLAIMANT

When seeking to assess the situation in which an under-age claimant brings an action against a fully competent defendant, eg, to recover property he has 'transferred', it may be asked at the outset what effect minority has on purported conveyances by the minor.[14] The general thrust of the cases is that it is possible for a minor to pass title to a chattel by delivery or otherwise to transfer property. Minors seem to be able to make prima facie operative gifts out of their assets,[15] and it has been explicitly held that where a minor's contract is disclaimed by him, 'the transfers of property made by the [minor] remain effective against him, even if the contract is otherwise revocable'.[16] Although that position is not beyond doubt as a matter of principle, it is rarely questioned,[17] and so the present analysis will proceed on the assumption that it accurately reflects the present state of English law.

[12] Infants Relief Act 1874 (UK), s 1. The problems to which the wording of this statute, its interpretation and application gave rise may be exemplified by the exchange between Professors Treitel and Atiyah: GH Treitel, 'The Infants Relief Act, 1874' (1957) 73 *LQR* 194; PS Atiyah, 'The Infants' Relief Act, 1874—A Reply' (1958) 74 *LQR* 97; GH Treitel, 'The Infants' Relief Act, 1874—A Short Rebutter' (1958) 74 *LQR* 104.

[13] Minors' Contracts Act 1987 (UK), ss 1(a), 4(2).

[14] There is a question (which will not be pursued further here) over whether, in 'transfer' cases, a claim in unjust enrichment to recover the asset transferred or its value presupposes that the transferor-claimant's right to that asset has been validly conveyed to the transferee-defendant.

[15] In *Taylor v Johnston* (1882) 19 Ch D 603 (Ch) 608, Bacon VC said that he was 'not aware of any law which prevents an infant from making a donation of any chattels or personal property in his actual possession'. As Hyde J observed in *Manby v Scott* (1659) 1 Mod Rep 124, 137; 86 ER 781, 789: 'If *an infant* give or sell goods, and deliver them with his own hand, he shall have no action of trespass [or trover] against the donee or vendee, by reason of the delivery'. It is, however, strongly arguable that such gifts should be recoverable on the ground of incapacity (see the end of n 26 below), and a number of cases actually treat them as voidable rather than irrevocably valid. In *Zouch v Parsons* (n 2) Burr 1804; ER 1109, for example, Lord Mansfield expressly endorsed the proposition that 'all such gifts, grants or deeds made by infants, which do not take effect by delivery of his hand, are void: *but all gifts, grants or deeds made by infants, by matter in deed or in writing, which do take effect by delivery of his hand, are voidable*' (emphasis added).

[16] *Chaplin v Leslie Frewin (Publishers) Ltd* [1966] Ch 71 (CA) 94 (Dankwerts LJ; Winn LJ agreeing). Dankwerts LJ continued: 'This, I think, is the true effect of the authorities cited to us.' Two things are worth noting about this statement. First, it was—strictly speaking—obiter, since the majority in the Court of Appeal considered the contract in question to be binding on the minor on account of it being analogous to a contract of service and for his benefit. Second, the judges' assumption that if the contract was not binding on the claimant, it was therefore 'revocable' or 'voidable' by him (a somewhat misleading description in conceptual terms), may have been due to the fact that even the Infants Relief Act 1874 declaring certain contracts 'absolutely void' was predominantly understood to mean 'void only as against the infant' and thus 'voidable at the infant's option': *cf* Treitel (1957) (n 12) 195, 200; Atiyah (n 12) 99–100.

[17] Note, however, that in *Chaplin v Leslie Frewin (Publishers) Ltd* (n 16) 90, Lord Denning MR (dissenting) opined that: 'The law is not so absurd as to hold that a contract to make a

2.1. Estoppel Based on Fraudulent Misrepresentation of Age?

Can a defendant faced with a minor's unjust enrichment claim ever argue that the latter is simply estopped from seeking restitution on account of the fact that he has fraudulently misrepresented his age when the underlying transaction was entered into? This issue, which arises primarily in the contractual sphere, requires a bit of background information by way of explanation.

It was traditionally thought that although most contracts entered into by a minor were not binding upon him or could at any rate be avoided at his option, any performance which the minor had rendered in pursuance of such a contract was nevertheless irrecoverable unless he could establish a total failure of consideration.[18] In *Pearce v Brain*, for example, where a contract by which a minor exchanged his motorcycle for a car (which subsequently broke down) was impugned under the Infants Relief Act 1874 (UK), Swift J noted with some regret that there was 'direct authority that money paid under a void contract cannot be recovered unless there is a total failure of consideration'[19] and said that he could not 'see any difference in principle

disposition is voidable [on this terminology, see second comment in n 16], and that the disposition itself is not. If the infant is to be protected, the law must be able to intervene as well after as before the disposition is made.' In *Fisher v Brooker* [2009] UKHL 41; [2009] 1 WLR 1764, [25], the diverging views in *Chaplin* led Baroness Hale to observe that 'the effect of even a contractual assignment of copyright by a minor is, to say the least, controversial'.

[18] On this approach, the only concession made to the claimant's minority was that, contrary to the principle in *Thomas v Brown* (1876) 1 QBD 714 (QBD), the minor was allowed to claim restitution for failure of consideration even where the defendant was 'ready and willing' to perform his side of the bargain.

[19] *Pearce v Brain* [1929] 2 KB 310 (KB) 314. Swift J was here referring to the case of *Valentini v Canali* (1890) 24 QBD 166 (QBD), where a minor rented the defendant's house and bought the furniture therein. Having paid part of the purchase price and having occupied the premises and used the furniture for some months, he sought to recover the amount paid on the ground that the contract was 'absolutely void' under the Infants Relief Act 1874 (UK). Lord Coleridge CJ said (at 167) that: 'When an infant has paid for something and has consumed or used it, it is contrary to natural justice that he should recover back the money which he has paid.' The minor's claim was dismissed because: 'He could not give back this benefit or replace the defendant in the position in which he was before the contract' (ibid). It has rightly been pointed out that *Valentini v Canali* is thus by no means 'direct authority' for a total failure of consideration requirement (as Swift J thought in *Pearce v Brain*), but is instead concerned with the need for the claimant to make counter-restitution to the defendant (an issue discussed further in section 2.4 below): A Burrows, *The Law of Restitution*, 3rd edn (Oxford, Oxford University Press, 2011) 312–14; C Mitchell, P Mitchell and S Watterson (eds), *Goff & Jones: The Law of Unjust Enrichment*, 8th edn (London, Sweet & Maxwell, 2011) [24-20]–[24-23] (hereinafter *Goff & Jones*); Treitel (1957) (n 12) 202–04; G Virgo, *The Principles of the Law of Restitution*, 3rd edn (Oxford, Oxford University Press, 2015) 386–87. However, authority for a failure of consideration requirement may be found in *Steinberg v Scala (Leeds) Ltd* [1923] 2 Ch 452 (CA) 458, where Lord Sterndale MR, relying inter alia on *Re Burrows, ex p Taylor* (1856) 8 De G M & G 254; 44 ER 388, said that whether a minor can rescind the contract and whether he/she can recover any money paid under it 'are two very different questions' and that 'although the contract may be rescinded the money paid cannot be recovered back unless there has been an entire failure of the consideration for which the money has been paid'. See also *Wilson v Kearse* (1800) Peake Add Cas 196; 170 ER 243; *Holmes v Blogg* (1818) 8 Taunt 508; 129 ER 481; *Corpe v Overton* (1833) 10 Bing 252; 131 ER 901.

between the recovery of a chattel given in exchange and the recovery of money paid as the purchase price of goods'.[20] The minor's claim[21] therefore failed.

However, this line of authority has come under strong attack,[22] and it is unlikely that courts would nowadays maintain it without qualification. It is arguably a remnant from the days when judges disliked disturbing executed transactions more generally.[23] The preferred view today would appear to be that the claimant's minority itself can function as an unjust factor,[24] either on the ground that his consent was impaired by reason of his incapacity[25] or on the policy basis of aligning the restitutionary regime with the relevant contractual principles.[26]

Yet it is worth considering whether the traditional approach can to some extent be rescued on the footing that an estoppel-type defence arises in cases where the minor fraudulently misrepresented his age to the defendant, pretending to be an adult, but where he later relies on his minority in order to seek restitution of his performance.

The counter-argument which immediately comes to mind is, of course, that 'a fraudulent representation of capacity cannot be an equivalent for actual capacity'.[27] Nevertheless, assuming that the unjust factor involved

[20] *Pearce v Brain* (n 19) 314.

[21] He had sought to recover either specifically the motorcycle with its side-car or their monetary value.

[22] See the literature listed in n 19.

[23] *cf* the so-called rule in *Seddon*'s case, deriving from *Seddon v The North Eastern Salt Company Ltd* [1905] 1 Ch 326 (Ch), according to which a contract, once executed, could no longer be rescinded for innocent misrepresentation. The supposed rule was abolished by the Misrepresentation Act 1967 (UK), s 1(b).

[24] Note, however, that if this were openly recognised by the courts, it would create a follow-on conundrum of a theoretical kind. The very notion of 'unenforceability' suggests that a contract, once executed, can provide a valid legal basis for the defendant retaining what he has received. We could overcome this problem by resorting to the terminology used by the Infants Relief Act 1874 (UK) and regarding the contract as 'void'. Restitution would then not be barred by it. Yet such a move would deprive the affected minor of the possibility of ratifying the contract upon reaching adulthood. The only other option is to extend the category of 'voidable' contracts (on which see n 10 and the accompanying text) so as to embrace those contracts which are hitherto considered to be 'unenforceable'.

[25] This may be the view of Burrows (n 19) 311, who writes that 'the closest analogy to incapacity should lie with mistake for the claimant who lacks capacity does not truly intend to benefit the defendant'. But *cf* also the quote set out in n 26 immediately below, indicating a more policy-orientated stance.

[26] The policy justification is supported by S Arrowsmith, 'Ineffective Transactions, Unjust Enrichment and Problems of Policy' (1989) 9 *Legal Studies* 307, 316–17; *Goff & Jones* (n 19) [24-05]; Virgo (n 19) 379–80, 386. Burrows (n 19) 313–14 also invokes it when he writes that: 'The policy justification for allowing minors out of contracts—that a minor's consent should not count because one needs to protect the young against foolishness and poor judgement—should surely be fully carried over to restitution of an unjust enrichment.' At 314, he explicitly calls for the same approach to be applied to gifts, by way of analogy. The editors of *Goff & Jones* (n 19) [24-27] agree that restitution should follow in gift cases 'where that would be consistent with the policy objectives that deprive minors of the legal capacity to contract'.

[27] The quote is from the decision of the US Supreme Court in *Sims v Everhart* 102 US 300, 313 (1880), a case which was followed in *Myers v Hurley Motor Co Inc* 273 US 18 (1927). An English decision making essentially the same point is *Levene v Brougham*, discussed in n 138 below.

is primarily policy-based rather than actually reflecting the claimant's defective consent, it is arguable that the policy ought to be disapplied where the claimant has been deceitful. That, at any rate, was the view taken by the Roman Emperors Diocletian and Maximian[28] when faced with comparable cases, as two passages preserved in the Justinianic Code[29] demonstrate.[30] They read:

> If someone who now alleges that he is a minor deceived you by falsely stating that he is of age, he should not, according to the law, be afforded restitution of rights [*restitutio in integrum*], since public laws only aid those minors who err, not those who mislead.[31]
>
> If, as a minor, you tried to prove by your appearance that you were of age in order to deceive another, then—since malice makes up for the want of age—the aid of restitution must be denied to you both according to imperial constitutions and by the authority of [imperial] rescripts.[32]

In the US, there is a vast body of case law and literature dealing with the problem of fraudulent minors and the effects of their behaviour on the parties' mutual rights and liabilities.[33] It is impossible within the confines of this chapter to give a full account of the different approaches adopted by various states at various times,[34] but it is worth outlining at least the main strands of thinking to set the scene for the discussion of English law which follows. In order to better understand these strands of thinking, the English

[28] Diocletian and Maximian were co-emperors between AD 286 and 305.

[29] The *Codex Iustinianus* forms part of the *Corpus Iuris Civilis*, a huge sixth-century compilation of Roman legal texts initiated by the Emperor Justinian.

[30] Though note that both passages are concerned with the 'extraordinary' remedy of *restitutio in integrum*, a type of equitable relief, not with the regular *condictio*.

[31] Codex 2.42.2 (Diocletian and Maximian to Vitalius on 30 November 287): 'Si is, qui nunc minorem se adseverat, fallaci maioris aetatis mendacio te decepit, iuxta statuta iuris, cum errantibus, non etiam fallentibus minoribus publica iura subvenerunt, in integrum restitui non debet.'

[32] Codex 2.42.3.pr. (Diocletian and Maximian to Theodota on 19 September 293/294): 'Si alterius circumveniendi causa minor aetate maiorem te probare adspectu laboraveris, cum malitia suppleat aetatem, restitutionis auxilium tam sacris constitutionibus quam rescriptorum auctoritate denegari statutum est.' The passage continues by adding various qualifications which are not set out here.

[33] Academic treatment of that question alone spans more than a century. See, eg, HAL Hall, 'The Liability of an Infant Who Represents Himself of Age' (1899) 8 *Yale Law Journal* 235; ALL, 'Infants—Liability for Fraudulent Misrepresentation of Age' (1915) 63 *University of Pennsylvania Law Review* 323; JT Britt, 'May an Infant Disaffirm a Contract Which He Has Induced the Other Party to Enter by Misrepresenting His Age?' (1925) 10 *St Louis Law Review* (now *Washington University Law Review*) 124; C Miller, 'Fraudulent Misrepresentations of Age as Affecting the Infant's Contract—A Comparative Study' (1953) 15 *University of Pittsburgh Law Review* 73; AD Kaufman, 'Infant's Misrepresentation as to His Age as Estopping Him from Disaffirming His Voidable Transaction' (1970) 29 *American Law Reports 3d* 1270; CB Preston and BT Crowther, 'Infancy Doctrine Inquiries' (2012) 52 *Santa Clara Law Review* 47, 59–62.

[34] Detailed overviews with further references may be found in the contributions by Miller (n 33) and Kaufman (n 33).

reader should bear in mind that US lawyers tend to regard all contracts except those for necessaries (which are fully valid) as 'voidable'[35] and usually therefore address the fraud issue at the preliminary level of whether or not the deceitful minor should be allowed to escape the contract at all.

One approach is that, irrespective of his deliberate misrepresentation, the minor can always disaffirm the transaction and will not incur any liability in tort.[36] Another is that although the minor can disaffirm the transaction, he is tortiously liable for fraud/deceit provided he has reached a sufficient 'age of discretion' and is thus capable of forming the relevant intent.[37] According to a third approach, which goes a step further, the fraudulent minor is simply estopped from disaffirming the contract.[38] In *Byers v Lemay Bank & Trust Co*, the Supreme Court of Missouri said:[39]

> Protecting those lacking in experience and of immature mind from designing adults developed in the common law of feudal England.[40] The purpose is to shield minors against their own folly and inexperience and against unscrupulous persons, but not to give minors a sword with which to wreak injury upon unsuspecting adults.

In *Merrick v Stephens*,[41] the particular form of estoppel envisaged by *Byers v Lemay Bank & Trust Co*[42] was described as 'qualified' in that it would only prevent the minor recovering his performance, but would not allow the

[35] S Goodfellow, 'Who Gets the Better Deal? A Comparison of the US and the English Infancy Doctrines' (2005) 29 *Hastings International & Comparative Law Review* 135, 139–41.

[36] See, eg, *Mulholland v Berlinsky* 16 Ohio Dec 183; 3 Ohio Law Rep 350 (1905); *Raymond v General Motor-Cycle Co* 230 Mass 54; 119 NE 359 (1918); *Summit Auto Co v Jenkins* 20 Ohio App 229; 153 NE 153 (1925); *Winter & Hirsch Inc v Redmond* 20 Ill App 2d 600; 156 NE 2d 599 (1959); *Gillis v Whitley's Discount Auto Sales Inc* 70 NC App 270, 278; 319 SE 2d 661, 666 (1984). Cf also *Sternlieb v Normandie National Securities Corp* 263 NY 245; 188 NE 726 (1934), where the Court felt bound to reach this conclusion, but questioned the result in policy terms.

[37] See, eg, *Creer v Active Automobile Exchange Inc* 99 Conn 266; 121 A 888 (1923); *Wisconsin Loan and Finance Corp v Goodnough* 201 Wis 101; 228 NW 484 (1930); *Doenges-Long Motors v Gillen* 138 Colo 31; 328 P 2d 1077 (1958); *Keser v Chagnon* 159 Colo 209, 213; 410 P 2d 637, 639 (1966); *Kiefer v Fred Howe Motors* Inc 39 Wis 2d 20; 158 NW 2d 288 (1968). *cf* also *Royal Finance Co v Schaefer* 330 SW 2d 129 (1959).

[38] See, eg, *County Board of Education v Hensley* 147 Ky 441; 144 SW 63 (1912); *La Rosa v Nichols* 92 NJL 375; 105 A 201 (1922); *Tuck v Payne* 159 Tenn 192; 17 SW 2d 8 (1929); *Pinnacle Motor Co v Daugherty* 231 Ky 626; 21 SW 2d 1001 (1929); *Carney v Southland Loan Co* 92 Ga App 559; 88 SE 2d 805 (1955); *Johnson v McAdory* 228 Miss 453; 88 So 2d 106 (1956).

[39] *Byers v Lemay Bank & Trust Co* 365 Mo 341, 345; 282 SW 2d 512, 514 (1955), presumably alluding to Lord Mansfield's statement in *Zouch v Parsons* (n 2) Burr 1802; ER 1107, that the privilege accorded to infants is 'given as a shield, and not as a sword' and 'that it never shall be turned into an offensive weapon of fraud or injustice'.

[40] The Court here referred to (1292) YB 21 Edw I, p 318.

[41] *Merrick v Stephens* 337 SW 2d 713 (1960).

[42] In that case itself, the Supreme Court of Missouri actually relied primarily on the defendant's claim in tort, while suggesting that, under the given circumstances, '[t]he result may be the same as an estoppel'. See *Byers v Lemay Bank & Trust Co* (n 39) Mo 350; SW 2d 518.

contract partner to enforce any part of the contract not yet performed.[43] By contrast, other decisions frame the doctrine in much more absolute terms, for example through approving the statement that: 'If an infant procures an agreement to be made through false and fraudulent representations that he is of age, a court of equity will enforce his liability as though he were an adult'.[44] A number of states have even enacted specific estoppel provisions to the effect that: 'No contract can be ... disaffirmed in cases where, on account of the minor's own misrepresentations as to his majority ... the other party had good reasons to believe the minor capable of contracting.'[45]

The recent *Restatement Third: Restitution and Unjust Enrichment* seems to subscribe to the 'qualified estoppel' view, as may be deduced from one of the examples given:[46]

> Minor sells Blackacre to Purchaser, fraudulently representing that he is of age. The terms of the sale are otherwise fair and reasonable. Minor thereafter attempts to rescind the transaction, tendering repayment of the price paid plus interest. Minor is not entitled to rescission.

Under English law, where most contracts concluded by minors are treated as 'unenforceable' rather than 'voidable',[47] the estoppel issue is better

[43] *Merrick v Stephens* (n 41) 717–18: 'If the minor has reached "the age of discretion" and has misrepresented his age and in so doing has misled the person with whom he dealt, the equity courts will not permit him to take advantage of his own fraud in order to mulct the opposite party. While it would seem that a pure estoppel would preclude the deceitful party from denying representation in respect to age, and this would have the practical effect of leaving the contract wholly in force, the law of Missouri now seems to be that the estoppel arising from an infant's misrepresentation of his age is a limited one. The fairly recent case of *Byers v Lemay Bank & Trust Co* [(n 39)] has cited and reviewed most of the prior decisions on this subject. That case denied to the infant the right to rescind and recover back payments which had theretofore been applied on mortgaged cars he disposed of (and which consequently could not be delivered in rescission). But it likewise denied the bank its counterclaim on the plaintiff's unpaid notes on the theory that the action for enforcement of the executory portion of the arrangement would not lie' (footnotes omitted).

[44] *Tuck v Payne* (n 38) 9, quoting from JN Pomeroy, *A Treatise on Equity Jurisprudence, as Administered in the United States of America*, 4th edn, vol 2 (San Francisco, Bancroft-Whitney Co and Lawyers Co-operative Publishing Co, 1918) 2009 (§ 945), who in turn cites various old English cases in support of the proposition. See also *Evans v Henry* 230 SW 2d 620, 621 (1950): 'The rule is well settled in this State [Texas] that if an infant induces a seller to enter into a contract of sale by fraudulently representing himself to be a person sui juris, then he is estopped to disaffirm his contract.' However, despite these broad statements, it has been noted that 'the courts have generally stopped short of enforcing against the minor a contractual obligation, entered into while she was a minor, even though by means of fraud': RA Lord, *A Treatise on the Law of Contracts by Samuel Williston*, revised 4th edn, vol 5 (Eagan, MN, Thomson-West, 2009) § 9:22, 240 (hereinafter *Williston on Contracts*).

[45] Such sweeping provisions are contained in Iowa Code Ann § 599.3; Kansas Statutes Ann § 38-103; Utah Code Ann § 15-2-3; Washington Rev Code Ann § 26.28.040.

[46] American Law Institute, *Restatement Third: Restitution and Unjust Enrichment*, vol 1 (St Paul, MN, American Law Institute Publishers, 2011) 225 (illustration 20 to § 16). As the commentary explains (at 230), the illustration is based on *Nichols v English* 223 GA 227; 154 SE 2d 239 (1967). The *Restatement* further invokes *Merrick v Stephens* (n 41); *Brinkman v Dorsey Motors Inc* 121 NJL 115; 1 A 2d 473 (1938); and *Evans v Henry* (n 44).

[47] See nn 10–11 and the accompanying text, but *cf* also the comment at the end of n 24.

considered at the defences stage of the inquiry.[48] Is an estoppel based on a misrepresentation of age conceivable? A side-glance at tort law would suggest that it is not. It was held as long ago as 1665 in *Johnson v Pye* that an action for deceit would not lie against a minor who had defrauded another to contract with him by pretending to be of age, 'for such affirmations are in every contract'.[49] This special immunity from tortious liability[50] has been confirmed on numerous occasions, most prominently in *Stocks v Wilson*[51] and in *R Leslie Ltd v Sheill*,[52] though it should be noted that the courts' primary concern in all of these cases was apparently to protect the minor against effectively having to fulfil an executory contractual promise.[53]

While it could be argued that a qualified estoppel—effectively holding the minor to his executed promise—is a fortiori objectionable where a tort claim is excluded, this need not be the last word on the matter. First, the blanket immunity conferred on fraudulent minors in respect of misrepresentations of age is itself questionable.[54] One would expect at least a reliance measure of damages to be available where an otherwise astute and discerning minor protests his majority in order to defraud the other party. Making the minor bear the other party's resulting losses is not the same as enforcing the contract. Second, it is by no means true that 'such affirmations [as to age] are in every contract', as intimated by *Johnson v Pye*.[55] The act of contracting alone does not invariably imply a representation of age. There is no duty to disclose one's minority. Any deception has to be actively practised in

[48] To the extent that contracts fall into the 'voidable' category, it would be possible for English law, too, to factor the estoppel issue into the disaffirmance stage of the inquiry, but it would then run into the conceptual problem of how to avoid holding the minor to the purely executory part of his bargain while barring rescission with respect to the executed part.

[49] *Johnson v Pye* [or *Johnson v Pie*] (1665) 1 Keb 913, 914; 83 ER 1317. See also the reports of the case in 1 Sid 258; 82 ER 1091, and in 1 Lev 169; 83 ER 353.

[50] Minority as such is not otherwise a defence to claims based on tort. As Lord Kenyon CJ remarked in *Jennings v Rundall* (1799) 8 Term Rep 335, 337; 101 ER 1419, 1420–21, 'if an infant commit an assault, or utter slander, God forbid that he should not be answerable for it in a Court of Justice', while at the same time recognising that: 'If it were in the power of a plaintiff to convert that which arises out of a contract into a tort, there would be an end of that protection which the law affords to infants.'

[51] *Stocks v Wilson* [1913] 2 KB 235 (KB) 242–43.

[52] *R Leslie Ltd v Sheill* [1914] 3 KB 607 (CA) 611–12, 620–21, 625. In this case, the judges' observations on the unavailability of damages for deceit were—strictly speaking—obiter, since the defrauded money-lenders had admitted the point and abandoned their claim on that count.

[53] This is particularly evident in *Stocks v Wilson* (n 51) 242–43, where Lush J was keen to ensure that the minor should not have to 'pay damages or compensation for the loss of the other party's bargain' by being 'compelled to make good his promise or to make satisfaction for its breach'.

[54] In fact, the Law Commission at one point recommended changing the law so as to allow minors who fraudulently misrepresent their age to be held liable in the tort of deceit irrespective of whether this would be an indirect way of enforcing the contract, but it later decided not to pursue the proposal any further: see Law Commission, *Minors' Contracts* (Working Paper No 81, 1982) paras 11.2 and 13.34, as well as Law Commission, *Law of Contract: Minors' Contracts* (Law Com No 134, 1984) para 5.3.

[55] See n 49 and accompanying text.

order to give rise to a tort claim or warrant an estoppel, and inferences from conduct must not be lightly drawn.[56] Finally, like a potential liability in the tort of deceit, an estoppel would depend on the adult defendant honestly believing and detrimentally relying on the claimant's protestations as to age. Hence, the estoppel argument should not ordinarily work where the minor seeks to recover a gift from the defendant, or where there is a contract, but the defendant has not yet performed any part of his obligations under it. In this respect, the qualified estoppel floated here mirrors the 'total failure of consideration' requirement we find in the existing case law.

The preceding discussion was intended to show that there *could* be a defence of estoppel based on a fraudulent misrepresentation of age in English law where a minor seeks to reclaim a contractual performance, not that there *has* to be one. If one accepts that minority itself may function as an unjust factor,[57] then recognising this type of estoppel is a way of rescuing some of the old case law by refining it (particularly by insisting on an express representation of age) and by putting it onto a new conceptual footing. If the traditional approach is not to be so rescued, then the minor will never be held to his bargain. All of the work will then have to be done through fine-tuning the requirement of him making counter-restitution to the defendant,[58] possibly coupled with the imposition of a yet to be established loss-based liability in the tort of deceit.

2.2. Illegality and Operation of the *In Pari Delicto* Principle

The next issue to consider is what impact the claimant's minority has on the operation of the illegality defence.[59] Here the position appears to be relatively straightforward. Our starting point is the principle that a claimant cannot recover a performance rendered to the defendant in circumstances where the parties were jointly engaged in an illegal scheme, usually expressed by the maxim *in pari delicto potior est conditio defendentis*.[60] Two points have to be borne in mind where the claimant is a minor.

[56] See *Stikeman v Dawson* (1847) 1 De G & Sm 90; 63 ER 984; *Maclean v Dummett* (1869) 22 LT 710 (PC) 711–12; *Re Jones, ex p Jones* (1881) 18 Ch D 109 (CA) 120–21, where Jessel MR said that fraud could not be 'invented' from the mere fact that an infant traded in goods.

[57] See the text accompanying nn 22–26.

[58] Discussed in section 2.4 below.

[59] There is currently a great deal of conceptual uncertainty about the illegality defence and its operation in general (see, eg, *Jetivia SA v Bilta (UK) Ltd* [2015] UKSC 23, [2015] 2 WLR 1168; especially [13]–[17]), but a discussion of this complex issue is beyond the scope of this chapter, which will therefore proceed along orthodox lines.

[60] The maxim literally postulates that the defendant's position is stronger than the claimant's where the parties are equally at fault. The *in pari delicto* principle is closely connected with the idea that no action arises from a base cause (*ex turpi causa non oritur actio*). However, while these maxims reflect the current state of English law, it is also possible to argue that there is no absolutely compelling reason for preferring the defendant to the claimant and that allowing restitution would be a better way of 'wiping out' the illegality.

First, the defence can never apply against the minor if the very reason why the transaction is considered illegal is that the law wants to prevent him engaging in it on account of his age. Here the claimant is specifically protected as a member of a vulnerable class, and the illegality involved may actually function as an unjust factor in its own right.[61] For example, if an adult conspired with a 15-year-old to sell alcohol or cigarettes to him,[62] the minor should be able to recover any payments made to the defendant despite the illegality of the transaction.[63]

Second, where we are concerned with some other unjust factor (typically failure of consideration) and the claimant is a minor, it is always necessary to check very carefully whether the parties really are *in pari delicto* before allowing the defendant to escape liability. One aspect of this is that if the minor could not be held criminally responsible for his conduct,[64] then—for the sake of the unity of the legal system—this may indicate that the illegality defence ought not to operate against him.[65] What of the claimant's capacity to commit a tort? The difficulty here is that there is no fixed age of civil responsibility for wrongdoing and some uncertainty about the exact principles governing the tortious liability of minors. While minority as such is not ordinarily a defence,[66] it seems that children may in appropriate circumstances be judged 'incapable of forming the state of mind necessary for commission of [a] particular tort'.[67] But even assuming that they have reached a sufficient level of intellectual maturity to form the relevant intent, their moral culpability may still be less than that of the defendant. Thus,

[61] See generally Burrows (n 19) 307–09, 595; *Goff & Jones* (n 19) [25-04]–[25-13] and [35-02]; Virgo (n 19) 286–88, 720–21.

[62] Selling alcohol or cigarettes to a person aged under 18 is an offence: Licensing Act 2003 (UK), s 146; Children and Young Persons Act 1933 (UK), s 7 (as amended).

[63] Where the minor has already consumed a part or all of the goods, there is a problem about making counter-restitution to the seller. If one adopts the view advanced below (in the text accompanying nn 118–20) that the minor need only return what he still retains of the performance, then the prospect of having to repay the full purchase price without receiving back the goods could, in fact, operate as a kind of regulatory tool reinforcing the prohibition on sale through economic disincentives.

[64] The current age of criminal responsibility in England and Wales is 10 years: Children and Young Persons Act 1933 (UK), s 50 (as amended), establishing a 'conclusive presumption' that 'no child under the age of ten years can be guilty of any offence'.

[65] See—albeit in the different context of applying the *ex turpi causa* maxim to claims in the tort of negligence—*Gray v Thames Trains Ltd* [2009] UKHL 33; [2009] 1 AC 1339 [15] (Lord Phillips). But contrast the Australian case of *Hunter Area Health Service v Presland* [2005] NSWCA 33; (2005) 63 NSWLR 22, which suggests that even a claimant's insanity (and hence lack of criminal responsibility) would not prevent the illegality defence from operating.

[66] *cf* n 50 and the accompanying text, also adverting to a possible qualification. This proposition is now challenged by Goudkamp (n 7), who accepts that—as the law stands—infancy occasionally operates as a 'denial' (at 103), but argues that it should also be recognised as a 'defence' capable of releasing under-age defendants from liability (at 184–86). Unfortunately, he does not say anything more specific about the age group to which such an 'infancy' defence might apply, nor does he elaborate further on its conditions or coverage.

[67] R Bagshaw, 'Children through Tort' in J Fionda (ed), *Legal Concepts of Childhood* (Oxford, Hart Publishing, 2001) 127, 128.

if a minor aged 13 pays an adult thug to beat up a romantic rival who is now going out with his ex-girlfriend and the thug fails to perform the promised service (eg, because he mistakes the victim's identity and beats up the wrong person),[68] restitution should arguably be available because the minor's responsibility is not on a par with the adult accomplice's.[69] Things may well look different where the plans of a 17-year-old are frustrated under similar circumstances.

It could, of course, be asked whether the claimant's minority should not rule out the illegality defence *in limine*, even in the latter example of the 17-year-old claimant. That particular question seems never to have been considered in England.[70] However, the German Imperial Court (*Reichsgericht*) addressed it in connection with a 1922 case concerning the equivalent defence in § 817 BGB.[71] The claimant in that case was a person who had been incapacitated on account of his intellectual disability. He wanted to recover the purchase price paid under a contract of sale which contravened a statutory prohibition. At first instance and on appeal, he won because it was thought that the defence could never be invoked against a person lacking full legal capacity. On the defendant's further appeal, the Imperial Court disagreed.[72] Since the illegality defence was not conceptually based on the claimant's voluntary renunciation of a right of action, it did not depend on his being able to give valid contractual consent, the Court held. Instead, the defence was to be understood as a *penalty* for the claimant deliberately disregarding the statutory prohibition in question. Hence, all that was required was that he should have the requisite delictual capacity.[73]

[68] Following the decision in *Patel v Mirza* [2014] EWCA Civ 1047; [2015] 2 WLR 405, it appears that the illegality defence may be inapplicable not only where the *claimant* voluntarily withdraws from the transaction before it has been performed, but whenever the illegal purpose has—for whatever reason—not been carried into effect: see the discussion by Graham Virgo in ch 8 of the present volume at 182–83. This could conceivably also prevent reliance on the defence in cases where the *defendant* thug withdraws from the transaction and refrains from harming anybody, though the incentive structure should dictate otherwise.

[69] *cf* also the discussion by Virgo (n 68) 184–85 of cases where 'the parties are not *in pari delicto*'.

[70] The Law Commission did not raise the problem of minors at all its report on the illegality defence: Law Commission, *The Illegality Defence* (Law Com No 320, 2010).

[71] § 817 BGB provides: 'If the purpose of a performance was so defined that the recipient has, by his acceptance of it, violated a statutory prohibition or good morals, the recipient is obliged to surrender what he has so obtained. *The claim for surrender is excluded if the person making the performance is also guilty of such a violation,* unless the performance consisted in the undertaking of an obligation; a performance rendered in order to discharge such an obligation cannot be reclaimed' (emphasis added).

[72] RG (8.11.1922) RGZ 105, 270. In a similar vein: L Klöhn, 'Die Kondiktionssperre gem. § 817 S. 2 BGB beim beidseitigen Gesetzes- und Sittenverstoß' (2010) 210 *Archiv für die civilistische Praxis* 804, 836 and 847–48.

[73] Under German law, the relevant provisions are §§ 827–828 BGB. § 827 BGB concerns the delictual responsibility of those who lack the ability to exercise free will, eg, on account of a mental illness. § 828 BGB deals with minors. According to § 828(1) and (3) BGB, children aged 7–17 are, as a matter of civil law, not responsible for the loss or damage they caused to others if they lacked the insight and ability to appreciate their responsibility when acting.

2.3. Modifications to Change of Position Defence vis-à-vis the Minor?

Does the claimant's minority in any way affect the defendant's ability to plead change of position? Or, to come at it from another angle, why might it? There are two reasons for thinking that it might.

The first is that the broad change of position defence as recognised in *Lipkin Gorman (a firm) v Karpnale Ltd*[74] has the effect of shifting the risk of the defendant's disenrichment onto the claimant. Yet sometimes it is thought inappropriate for the claimant to bear that risk, as for instance where a private individual seeks restitution from the state under the so-called *Woolwich* principle.[75] Could it not similarly be maintained that it is inappropriate for the risk of the adult defendant's disenrichment to be shifted to an under-age claimant, given that the latter cannot necessarily be held responsible for creating the impression that the defendant is entitled to what he has received? This seems arguable, at any rate, if the 'real function of the defence is to identify those cases where the justice of the defendant not making restitution outweighs the justice of the claimant obtaining restitution'.[76]

The second point to consider is connected with the earlier observation that English law appears to treat transfers of property by minors as fully valid.[77] In legal systems which hold such conveyances invalid on account of the transferor's lack of capacity, as German law does,[78] there is much less scope for pleading change of position vis-à-vis minors. The claimant minor will in most cases be able to recover the object of his purported conveyance by means of a *vindicatio*,[79] and it will simply not avail the defendant to prove that he has disenriched himself in good faith in reliance on his receipt.[80]

[74] *Lipkin Gorman (a firm) v Karpnale Ltd* [1991] 1 AC 548 (HL) (hereinafter '*Lipkin Gorman*').

[75] In *Test Claimants in the FII Group Litigation v HMRC (No 1)* [2008] EWHC 2893 (Ch); [2009] STC 254 [335]–[342], Henderson J suggested that although the change of position defence did not apply to claims brought under the rule established in *Woolwich Equitable Building Society v IRC* [1993] AC 70 (HL), it could in principle operate in respect of mistake-based claims to restitution from the state. Revisiting the issue in the most recent sequel, *Test Claimants in the FII Group Litigation v HMRC (No 2)* [2014] EWHC 4302 (Ch); [2015] STC 1471, Henderson J refined the explanation for why change of position was unavailable as a defence to *Woolwich* claims (at [309]–[315]) and discussed various aspects of the debate about its applicability to mistake-based claims (at [316]–[338]). Yet, having already answered the latter question in the Revenue's favour, he saw himself precluded from deciding it again, while strongly encouraging the matter to be brought before an appellate court at the earliest opportunity (at [339]–[341]).

[76] The quote is from Virgo (n 19) 680–81, who does not—however—himself draw such a conclusion.

[77] See the text accompanying nn 14–17.

[78] Like all legal transactions which are not purely beneficial to the minor, conveyances made by persons aged 7–17 need to be authorised by their parents or guardians (and may even require court approval): see §§ 104–110, 1643, 1821 BGB.

[79] Provided for in § 985 BGB.

[80] The disenrichment defence in § 818(3) BGB applies only to *in personam* claims based on unjustified enrichment (§§ 812 ff BGB) and related provisions, not to *in rem* claims like the *vindicatio*.

However, as regards English law, the better arguments probably point the other way. Changes of position should be taken into account quite irrespective of the claimant's age. For one thing, the fact that some *defendants* (such as the state or other public bodies) may be disqualified from the defence by virtue of certain characteristics peculiar to them[81] does not mean that it is possible to disqualify an ordinary defendant from invoking it by reference to the *claimant's* peculiar characteristics.

Connected is the aspect that change of position—unlike the traditional estoppel defence—is not based on the idea that the claimant-enrichor has somehow expressly or impliedly represented to the defendant-enrichee that the benefit bestowed upon the latter is his to keep.[82] Instead, it is generally rationalised through some version of the postulate that the defendant, being strictly liable, should not be left out-of-pocket by his obligation to make restitution.[83] English judges and commentators have thus rejected the approach adopted by the Court of Appeal of New Zealand in *National Bank of New Zealand Ltd v Waitaki International Processing (NI) Ltd*[84] of identifying and weighing against each other '[t]hose factors which render either restitution, on the one hand, or retention on the other, just or unjust'[85] and for this purpose considering the relative fault of the parties and comparable factors.[86] Under such a flexible regime of 'balancing the equities',[87] it would certainly be much easier to accommodate elements of risk allocation and loss apportionment in assessing the merits of each party's case and thereby to make allowances for the claimant's minority.

[81] As the discussion in n 75 shows, it is not even clear whether the inapplicability of the change of position defence to so-called *Woolwich* claims is actually down to the state's peculiar characteristics as defendant or whether it is a consequence of some other feature of the claim.

[82] On this aspect of the traditional estoppel defence as applicable to restitutionary claims, see, eg, Burrows (n 19) 524, 550–53; *Goff & Jones* (n 19) [30-01]–[30-03]; Virgo (n 19) 667–68.

[83] See Burrows (n 19) 526, tying change of position closely to the concept of disenrichment; similarly P Birks, *Unjust Enrichment*, 2nd edn (Oxford, Oxford University Press, 2005) 208–10; *Goff & Jones* (n 19) [27-03], focusing on the protection of the defendant's reliance. Compare and contrast Virgo (n 19) 680, who writes: 'The defence should be considered to have a dual function in that it exists to protect the defendant's reliance on the security of his or her receipt, so that if the defendant changes his or her position as a result of the receipt of the enrichment it is not appropriate to make restitution, in order to protect the defendant's autonomy. But the defence should also be interpreted as existing to counter-balance the principle of corrective justice which underpins the unjust enrichment principle itself' (footnotes omitted).

[84] *National Bank of New Zealand Ltd v Waitaki International Processing (NI) Ltd* [1999] 2 NZLR 211 (CA) (hereinafter *Waitaki*).

[85] ibid 229.

[86] In *Dextra Bank & Trust Co Ltd v Bank of Jamaica* [2002] 1 All ER (Comm) 193 (PC) [45], for example, Lords Bingham and Goff, delivering the advice of the Privy Council, stated that: 'Their Lordships are ... most reluctant to recognise the propriety of introducing the concept of relative fault into this branch of the common law, and indeed decline to do so.' The availability of the change of position defence was said to depend exclusively on the 'good faith on the part of the recipient', with factors like the claimant's conduct or fault being entirely irrelevant.

[87] *Waitaki* (n 84) 220, 225, 229, 232.

Finally, if in a legal system like the German, good faith changes of position on the part of the defendant (such as spending money in reliance on the security of his receipt) do not avail him when faced with a minor's *vindicatio* claim,[88] this is simply the consequence of an incongruity between the regime governing restitution for unjustified enrichments on the one hand and that governing the relationship between the owner of an object and the person who possesses it on the other.[89] It is not the result of a conscious decision to deny adult enrichees the benefit of the disenrichment defence vis-à-vis under-age enrichors. Moreover, the claimant minor will always bear the risk of the object itself (that which he purported to transfer and which he how seeks to reclaim) being accidentally damaged or destroyed,[90] and his claim will be subject to the ordinary disenrichment defence as soon as the *vindicatio* is converted into a *condictio* by operation of law (eg, where ownership is lost through accession or specification).[91]

2.4. Impossibility of Counter-Restitution by the Minor

The last issue we need to consider with respect to cases where the minor is in the position of claimant pertains to the scenario of a contract which has been (at least partially) executed on both sides. Where the minor has rendered some performance to the other party which he is now seeking to recover, is his unjust enrichment claim barred because counter-restitution is or has become impossible? This question can potentially arise in connection with any unjust factor allowing the contract to be unwound, but it has particular relevance if and to the extent that the claimant's minority is accepted as providing an independent ground for restitution.[92]

The claimant's ability and willingness to make counter-restitution to the defendant—whether specifically or in the form of a monetary substitute—is widely recognised as being either a condition of,[93] or if not given, a defence to an unjust enrichment claim in the contractual context.[94] If the claimant

[88] For a summary of the defendant *bona fide* possessor's position under German law, see B Häcker, *Consequences of Impaired Consent Transfers* (Tübingen, Mohr Siebeck, 2009; Oxford, Hart Publishing, 2013) 79–81.

[89] The various incongruities between §§ 812 ff BGB and §§ 987 ff BGB, of which the problem of the defendant's disenriching expenditure is only one, are described in Häcker (n 88) 83–93, especially 87–91.

[90] Under German law, the *bona fide* possessor is not liable to the owner under these circumstances: see Häcker (n 88) 80–81.

[91] See Häcker (n 88) 81, especially fn 100 on that page.

[92] See the text accompanying nn 18–26 above and especially the discussion in n 19.

[93] Impossibility of *restitutio in integrum* is considered to be one of the traditional 'bars' to rescission of contract.

[94] See Birks (n 83) 225–29; Burrows (n 19) 569–72; *Goff & Jones* (n 19) ch 31, esp [31-01]–[31-02]; Virgo (n 19) 25.

wishes to recover what he has bestowed upon the defendant, he needs to give up what he has received in return. Where precise *restitutio in integrum* is not possible (on account of the nature of the defendant's performance or due to the fact that it has perished in the claimant's hands), so the usual argument runs, we should follow the example of cases like *Erlanger v New Sombrero Phosphate Co*[95] and *O'Sullivan v Management Agency and Music Ltd*[96] and require the claimant to make counter-restitution in value terms instead.[97]

That the interdependency of the parties' mutual performances may carry over into the realm of subsequent mutual restitutionary claims was already acknowledged in the late nineteenth-century decision of *Valentini v Canali*, where Lord Coleridge CJ said: 'When an infant has paid for something and has consumed or used it, it is contrary to natural justice that he should recover back the money which he has paid.'[98] Let us now look again at *Pearce v Brain*.[99] It will be recalled that the claimant there was a minor who had exchanged his motorcycle for the defendant's car and was trying to recover the motorcycle or its value. He was willing to return the car, but that had meanwhile broken down and was therefore in a damaged state. Assuming that judges deciding future cases like *Pearce v Brain* were willing to dispense with the need for a total failure of consideration, should the defendant nevertheless have won against the backdrop of Lord Coleridge's words in *Valentini v Canali*? The parties in *Pearce* had agreed for the purposes of the transaction that the motorcycle and the car were to be valued at £30 each, but the jury found that the car was in fact only worth £15.[100] Is it not right that the claimant be denied recovery of the motorcycle, at any rate so long as he does not offer to make up the full value of the car[101] in addition to returning the wreckage?

Such a conclusion would be rash, however. Leaving aside the specific problem that, on the facts of *Pearce v Brain*, the reason why the car had

[95] *Erlanger v New Sombrero Phosphate Co* (1878) 3 App Cas 1218 (HL), especially 1278–79 (Lord Blackburn).

[96] *O'Sullivan Management Agency and Music Ltd* [1985] QB 428 (CA).

[97] Burrows (n 19) 571–72; Birks (n 83) 227–28; *Goff & Jones* (n 19) [31-10]–[31-12]; Virgo (n 19) 25–27. See also *Halpern v Halpern* [2007] EWCA Civ 291; [2008] QB 195, especially [61]–[75].

[98] *Valentini v Canali* (1890) 24 QBD 166 (QBD) 167. The result in this case is questionable, however, as the infant was trying to recover the purchase price for some furniture which he had used for only a few months. In holding that counter-restitution was impossible (because '[h]e could not give back this benefit or replace the defendant in the position in which he was before the contract'), the Court took an extremely narrow view of the *restitutio in integrum* requirement: see the criticism by *Goff & Jones* (n 19) [24-23]; Virgo (n 19) 387.

[99] *Pearce v Brain* [1929] 2 KB 310 (KB), already discussed in the text accompanying nn 19–21.

[100] ibid 310–11.

[101] In the restitutionary context considered here, this would have to be measured by reference to the car's real economic value (£15), not its contractually agreed value (£30).

broken down was that the back axle was defective,[102] the strict insistence on counter-restitution *in specie* or in monetary terms takes no account of the claimant's minority. Yet a powerful argument can be made in support of the proposition that where the claimant is a minor and the defendant's performance is lost, damaged or destroyed in the claimant's hands, the claimant ought in principle to be able to recover without rendering (full) counter-restitution.

Again, there is a plethora of US case law and literature on precisely this kind of issue.[103] One well-known case lending support to the proposition advanced here is *Halbman v Lemke*,[104] where the facts were similar to those in *Pearce v Brain*. The claimant had purchased a car from the defendant for $1,250, paying part of the price in cash and the rest in instalments. Five weeks later, when a total of $1,100 had been paid, a connecting rod on the vehicle's engine broke. A dispute arose about the cost of repair and the claimant sought to disaffirm the contract.[105] The defendant initially counterclaimed for the remaining $150, but on appeal only insisted that the claimant make good the car's diminution in value.[106] The Supreme Court of Wisconsin held that:[107]

> Where there is misrepresentation by a minor [as to age[108]] or willful destruction of property, the vendor may be able to recover damages in tort ... But absent these factors, as in the present case, we believe that to require a disaffirming minor to make restitution for diminished value is, in effect, to bind the minor to a part of the obligation which by law he is privileged to avoid.

102 *Pearce v Brain* (n 99) 310. The jury found that the defendant had not given any warranty as regards the car's condition (at 311). Had such a warranty been given or had it—nowadays—been implied into a consumer contract by virtue of s 14 of the Sale of Goods Act 1979 (UK), this fact alone should have been a reason for making the defendant bear the risk of the defect materialising. For a comparable case in German law, see BGH (9.10.1980) BGHZ 78, 216.

103 See, eg, the overviews provided by Goodfellow (n 35) 142–47; *Williston on Contracts* (n 44) § 9:16, 134–59; WE Shipley, 'Infant's Liability for Use or Depreciation of Subject Matter, in Action to Recover Purchase Price upon His Disaffirmance of Contract to Purchase Goods' (1967) 12 *American Law Reports 3d* 1174.

104 *Halbman v Lemke* 99 Wis 2d 241; 298 NW 2d 562 (1980).

105 After disaffirmance, the vehicle was vandalised beyond salvage while parked at a garage and later at the house of Mr Halbman Senior, pending the resolution of the dispute between the claimant and the defendant.

106 The latter counterclaim related to the car's diminution in value *before* disaffirmance and was measured by reference to the repair bill (over $600).

107 *Halbman v Lemke* (n 104) Wis 2d 250; NW 2d 567. Rejecting decisions from other US jurisdictions which imposed on the rescinding minor an obligation to make up for the loss or depreciation of the defendant's performance, the Court said (at 251): 'Because these cases would at some point force the minor to bear the cost of the very improvidence from which the infancy doctrine is supposed to protect him, we cannot follow them'. The reasoning underlying this approach is summarised as follows in *Williston on Contracts* (n 44) § 9:16, 153: 'The same lack of prudence that leads the infant into the contract in the first instance causes the minor to dissipate the proceeds, and to hold her to an accounting for use and depreciation would be to require of her a degree of discretion in the use of the article that she was not required to have in obtaining the article originally.'

108 Wisconsin does not recognise an estoppel in such a case, but allows a tort claim: see n 37 and the accompanying text.

This sentiment is also reflected by the German courts, which normally apply a concept known as *Saldotheorie* where reciprocal contracts are being unwound.[109] In an ordinary case, this allows them to offset the parties' mutual enrichment claims in order to prevent a party who cannot restore what he or she has received from relying on the disenrichment defence, while at the same time reclaiming the entirety of his or her own performance.[110] The *Saldotheorie* is said to reflect the 'factual reciprocity' between the parties' respective performances.[111] Its practical effect is to make each contract partner bear the risk of his or her own disenrichment. Thus, if the object received by the claimant has perished in his hands, the right to recover his own performance from the defendant is adjusted or reduced accordingly.[112]

However, in line with virtually unanimous academic opinion,[113] German judges refuse to apply the *Saldotheorie* as against minors. In its seminal decision, the Federal Supreme Court (*Bundesgerichtshof*) reasoned as follows:[114]

> Application of the *Saldotheorie* has the effect that the correlation between performance and counter-performance which the contracting parties intended when concluding the contract remains intact even in the context of unwinding ineffective reciprocal contracts through the law of unjustified enrichment. If one were to apply it [ie, the *Saldotheorie*] to reciprocal contracts with persons lacking (full) legal capacity, then this would have the consequence that the bond of reciprocity which the intended contract was not able to bring about due to its ineffectiveness

[109] See, eg, G Dannemann, *The German Law of Unjustified Enrichment and Restitution: A Comparative Introduction* (Oxford, Oxford University Press, 2009) 141–45; Häcker (n 88) 71–77, especially 73–75; R Zimmermann and J du Plessis, 'Basic Features of the German Law of Unjustified Enrichment' (1994) 2 *Restitution Law Review* 14, 40–42.

[110] Precisely that would be the outcome if one regarded the parties' mutual restitutionary claims as wholly independent of one another, as the conventional so-called 'two claims theory' would have it.

[111] Leading cases propounding this analysis are BGH (14.10.1971) BGHZ 57, 137, 150, a translation of which is provided by Dannemann (n 109) 237–42 (case 6—'wrecked car', *cf* at 240: 'The *Saldotheorie* is therefore the logical application of the legal notion expressed in § 818 III [disenrichment defence] to reciprocal contracts in which the performance and return performance lie in one relationship of exchange (synallagma), a factor which must also be considered when reversing void contracts according to the law on enrichment'); BGH (26.10.1978) BGHZ 72, 252, 256. See also BGH (9.10.1980) BGHZ 78, 216, 223; BGH (10.2.1999) NJW 1999, 1181, 1181–82; BGH (20.3.2001) BGHZ 147, 152, 157–58.

[112] Assuming that the dispute in *Pearce v Brain* (n 99) had occurred amongst adults and was governed by German law, the *Saldotheorie* would hold that there was at all times notionally only a one-sided claim to restitution to the extent of £15 (the value of the motorcycle transferred minus the value of the car received in exchange). This claim is entirely unaffected by the claimant's subsequent 'disenrichment' through the car breaking down. In order to recover the motorcycle (worth £30), the claimant would have to pay the defendant for the car (worth £15) or alternatively return the car's wreckage and make up the difference in value.

[113] For further references, see eg S Lorenz in *J von Staudingers Kommentar zum Bürgerlichen Gesetzbuch: Buch 2, Recht der Schuldverhältnisse, §§ 812–822* (Munich, CH Beck, 2007) § 818 [42] (at 339); M Schwab in *Münchener Kommentar zum Bürgerlichen Gesetzbuch, Band 5: §§ 705–853*, 6th edn (Munich, CH Beck, 2013) § 818 [216], [269]–[271].

[114] BGH (4.5.1994) BGHZ 126, 105, 108–09, repeated in BGH (29.9.2000) NJW 2000, 3562. See also BGH (20.3.2001) BGHZ 147, 152, 158; BGH (17.1.2003) NJW 2003, 3271.

based on § 105 BGB[115] would be imported into the context of its unwinding. Such a result would be incompatible with the overriding protection afforded to minors and other people lacking (full) legal capacity. According to the statutory value judgement, this group of persons may not be even factually held to an invalid contract. But such would be the case if the contract partner lacking legal capacity had to make an allowance for the value of the (perished) counter-performance in the context of his own enrichment claim, thereby 'paying' for it [the counter-performance].

...

It is true that disapplication of the *Saldotheorie* can in the end result lead to the defendant enrichee and supposed contact partner of the person lacking legal capacity having to bear the adverse consequences flowing from the latter's dispositions over what he has received. But the person lacking (full) legal capacity ought to be protected against [these dispositions], too, and not merely against being contractually bound. This is because, due to the lack of full legal capacity, that group of persons does not truly accept the risk of the object which they have received without legal ground perishing amongst their own assets...

Even the US *Restatement Third: Restitution and Unjust Enrichment*, which takes the line that in principle a minor claiming restitution from his contract partner must make counter-restitution either *in specie* or in value terms,[116] acknowledges that: 'Notwithstanding the [minor's unjust enrichment at the contract partner's expense], restitution may be limited or denied if it would be inconsistent with the protection that the doctrine of incapacity is intended to afford in the circumstances of the case.'[117]

[115] § 105 BGB is the provision which renders declarations of intention by persons lacking legal capacity invalid.

[116] See American Law Institute, *Restatement Third* (n 46) vol 1, 527 (comment *a* on § 33): 'Where there has been performance on both sides, the parties' dispute involves both restitution claims at once. For example, a case might begin with a claim by an incapacitated buyer seeking to avoid the contract and to recover a price already paid. This claim by the incapacitated buyer (a claim in restitution within § 16) will be met by the claim of the seller under [§ 33] to recover the property previously transferred or its value. The obligation of the incapacitated party to restore what was received is described ... as part of the substantive liability in unjust enrichment involved in such a case. The same mutual restoration is often described as a requirement or condition of the rescission remedy.' See also § 16(3) of the *Restatement Third*.

[117] This is the wording of § 33(3) of the *Restatement Third* (n 46) vol 1, 526. Although § 33 is framed in terms of a one-sided unjust enrichment claim by an adult contract partner against a minor, comment *a* (at 526–27) makes clear that it also applies where the parties have mutual restitutionary claims. The operation of § 33(3) is discussed in illustration 9 (at 532) as well as in the Reporter's Note (at 541), which explains: 'The only difficult cases ... are those in which the incapacitated party has dissipated or consumed the fruits of the other party's performance, with the result that a liability in restitution requires the payment of money in exchange for performance—albeit at market value, as opposed to the contract price. The archetype is the case of the infant who buys a car on credit and wrecks it. The case is difficult because it is hard to be confident of the extent to which the infant was enriched by the value that has now been dissipated; and because the resulting liability in restitution (treating the dissipated value as benefit to the infant) so closely resembles the contractual responsibility from which—it might be thought—the doctrine of incapacity is designed to shield him. The solution proposed by this section [§ 33] is to adopt a broad rule of liability for benefits received, while recognising

If comparative reasoning is anything to go by, the upshot of all this is that English lawyers should think long and hard before allowing a defence of 'counter-restitution impossible' to the defendant or insisting that the minor provide counter-restitution in the same way as an adult would have to do.[118] At least where the claimant's minority—his lack of experience and prudence—lies at the heart of the unjust inquiry,[119] the claimant should arguably only have to return to the defendant that part of the defendant's performance which he retains and/or by which he is still enriched. It is debatable whether this special privilege ought to be confined to cases where the minor's inability to make counter-restitution is 'accidental' as opposed to being the result of a deliberate act on his part (eg, in destroying the subject matter received), but that is essentially a question about the proper ambit of the change of position defence.[120] What the present suggestion does mean as a minimum is that a defendant like the one in *Pearce v Brain* should not be allowed to resist the minor's claim for restitution of the motorcycle or its value by pointing to the much deteriorated condition of the car for which it was exchanged.

In a nutshell, with the possible exception of cases where the claimant minor has fraudulently led his contract partner to believe that he was of full age[121] and—subject to what will be said below—conceivably also where he

that the policy underlying a party's incapacity may justify a narrower measurement of benefits conferred in a particular case.' For a critical take on this approach, see CB Preston and BT Crowther, 'Minor Restrictions: Adolescence Across Legal Disciplines, the Infancy Doctrine, and the Restatement (Third) of Restitution and Unjust Enrichment' (2012) 61 *Kansas Law Review* 343, especially 348–53.

[118] But *cf Goff & Jones* (n 19) [24-21], writing with respect to *Steinberg v Scala (Leeds) Ltd* (n 19): '[W]e consider that the question in *Steinberg* should not have been whether the basis for the payments had totally failed, but whether the claimant could have made *restitutio in integrum*. A minor who cannot restore the status quo ante should be unable to avoid the contract; but if he has restored the status quo, then he should be able to avoid the contract and recover benefits conferred thereunder. Moreover, ... the courts should always take a flexible approach to the question whether counter-restitution is possible, allowing claimants to pay the money value of goods and services received without insisting on precise counter-restitution *in specie*.' Similarly, Virgo (n 19) 387 states that 'the restitutionary claim should not be barred simply because the claimant cannot make exact counter-restitution to the defendant. It should be sufficient that the claimant can restore the *value* of any benefit received to the defendant without necessarily having to restore the actual benefit received. This means that in a case such as *Valentini v Canali* [(n 98)], the claimant would have been able to rescind the contract and recover the money paid to the defendant, if he had made counter-restitution by paying the defendant the reasonable price for hiring the furniture.' However, elsewhere in their textbooks, the authors actually advocate a generous operation of the change of position defence in favour of the minor: see n 134 and the accompanying text.

[119] If incapacity itself were recognised as an unjust factor, but conceivably also in undue influence cases.

[120] The extent to which minors can rely on change of position is considered in section 3.3 below.

[121] See the estoppel argument discussed in section 2.1 above as well as in the text accompanying n 174 below.

intentionally puts it out of his power to give back what he has received,[122] the risk of counter-restitution *in specie* becoming impossible and the minor being thereby disenriched is better borne by the defendant than the claimant.

3. MINOR AS DEFENDANT

This takes us straight to cases where the unjust enrichment claim is brought against the minor. Rather than pleading the minor's inability to make *restitutio in integrum* in defence to an action brought *by* the minor, the other party is here in the position of the claimant actively seeking restitution *from* the minor. This may be because the claimant has entered into and rendered advance performance under a contract which the minor is now refusing to comply with (typically by invoking its voidability or unenforceability). Alternatively, the claimant may simply have overpaid the defendant minor by mistake or may have mistakenly rendered the same performance twice over.

It is worth noting at the outset that there is no problem about title passing from an adult claimant to the minor. Whether or not a minor is rightly considered capable of effecting valid conveyances,[123] he is certainly capable of receiving them. This is, for instance, evident from *Stocks v Wilson*, where Lush J expressly held that the delivery of goods to a minor with the relevant intent was effective to vest the property in him, notwithstanding the fact that the underlying contract of sale was void under the Infants Relief Act 1874 (UK).[124] It is also presupposed by section 3 of the Minors' Contracts Act 1987 (UK), giving courts a power to require the defendant minor to transfer to the claimant 'any property *acquired by the defendant* under the contract'.[125]

3.1. Incapacity as a Complete Defence?

There are suggestions in the case law that incapacity can operate as an almost complete defence to unjust enrichment claims in the contractual sphere. In *Cowern v Nield*,[126] the defendant minor had agreed to sell to the claimant some clover and hay, receiving payment up-front. When he tendered the goods, they were rotten and the claimant rightly refused to take delivery of them. The claimant thereupon sought damages for breach of contract, or failing that, recovery of the purchase price. He lost on the first

[122] See the text accompanying nn 120 and 182.
[123] See the text accompanying nn 14–17.
[124] *Stocks v Wilson* [1913] 2 KB 235 (KB) 246–47.
[125] Emphasis added. The provision is discussed in section 3.2 below.
[126] *Cowern v Nield* [1912] 2 KB 419 (KB).

count because the contract was unenforceable;[127] on the second count, his action for money had and received was held to be sustainable only insofar as 'the substance of the action is that the infant has obtained the money ex delicto', not where the defendant was in substance to be held liable 'ex contractu'.[128] *R Leslie Ltd v Sheill* is in a similar vein. There the defendant had induced the claimant money-lenders to advance £400 to him by deceiving them as to his age. The Court of Appeal refused to let the claimants recover this amount because to do so would in effect 'be nothing but enforcing a void contract'.[129] Lord Sumner explained:[130]

> To money had and received and other indebitatus counts infancy was a defence just as to any other action in contract ... Further, under the statute [the Infants Relief Act 1874] the principle, which at common law relieved an infant from liability for a tort directly connected with a voidable contract, namely, that it was impossible to enforce in a roundabout way an unenforceable contract, equally forbids Courts of law to allow, under the name of an implied contract or in the form of an action quasi ex contractu, a proceeding to enforce part of a contract, which the statute declares to be wholly void.

This type of reasoning has rightly been criticised as based on the 'implied contract fallacy'.[131] Holding the defendant liable in unjust enrichment is not the same as holding him to an unenforceable or void contract. This becomes

[127] The Infants Relief Act 1874 (UK) only governed cases were goods were supplied *to* the minor, not where they were supplied *by* him: Treitel (1957) (n 12) 196. See also *Cowern v Nield* (n 126) 420, 422, 424.

[128] *Cowern v Nield* (n 126) 423–25. The case was referred back for a new trial to determine whether or not the defendant had obtained the money by defrauding the claimant. Depending on what sort of fraud the judges had in mind, this may be seen as partly at odds with *Stocks v Wilson* (n 124), handed down less than a year later. In *Stocks v Wilson* at 245, Lush J distinguished *Cowern v Nield* by saying that: 'The fraud suggested there was committed, if at all, in the course of carrying out the contract.'

[129] *R Leslie Ltd v Sheill* [1914] 3 KB 607 (CA) 619 (Lord Sumner). Similarly, Kennedy LJ said at 624: '[T]here is no case in which I can find that a Court of Equity has given judgment against an infant in circumstances like the present, that is to say, in which it has interfered on the ground of the fraud of the infant, whereby he induced the making of the contract of loan, to order the infant to pay the plaintiff a sum equal to the sum borrowed under the void contract, *and so, in effect, to the amount of the principal lent, to give validity as against the infant to a void contract*' (emphasis added).

[130] ibid 613. He drew support for this observation from the 'closely analogous case' of *Sinclair v Brougham* [1914] AC 398 (HL). AT Lawrence J, who was sitting with Lord Sumner and Kennedy LJ in *R Leslie Ltd v Sheill* (n 129), observed in a similar fashion (at 626): 'I do not think that it is correct to say that the action for money had and received is wholly independent of contract. It arises wherever money has been received which ex æquo et bono belongs to the plaintiff. In such case the law implies a promise to pay it to the plaintiff, but where the express promise to repay the money is by statute "absolutely void" it is impossible to imply a promise to repay the same money ... To do so would be to (in large part) defeat the policy of the statute, and would violate the well-established principle that where there is an express promise no other like promise can be implied.'

[131] Burrows (n 19) 582; *Goff & Jones* (n 19) [34-04]; Virgo (n 19) 727–28; E Bant, 'Incapacity, Non Est Factum and Unjust Enrichment' (2009) 33 *Melbourne University Law Review* 368, 382.

clear when one considers that the claimants in *R Leslie Ltd v Sheill* had in the first instance actually tried to recover £475, consisting of the principal of £400 plus £75 as (apparently contractual) interest.[132]

The better approach is that already adopted by the 1937 US *Restatement of Restitution*, namely that: 'Incapacity to enter into a contract or to incur liability in tort is not in itself a defense in an action for restitution.'[133] Modern English commentators are widely agreed that it is sufficient to afford minors a generous change of position defence, taking account of their age and lack of contractual capacity.[134] The requisite or potential modifications to that defence will be explored further below.[135] For the time being, it is worth noting that we actually have a number of old equity cases which would seem to fit quite well with this suggestion,[136] though most concerned situations where the minor had fraudulently misrepresented his age to the other party or at any rate concealed his minority.[137] Their ratio was either that 'a representation by an infant that he was of full age gave rise to an equitable liability resulting from the fraud'[138] or 'the principle that an infant shall not take advantage of his own fraud'[139] more broadly conceived.[140] In *Stocks v Wilson*, where the defendant was held liable to account in equity

[132] See *R Leslie Ltd v Sheill* (n 129) 608, 620–21, 625, although they later described their claim as resting on the tort of deceit (this argument was abandoned) or as being for money had and received.

[133] American Law Institute, *Restatement of the Law of Restitution: Quasi Contracts and Constructive Trusts* (St Paul, MN, American Law Institute Publishers, 1937) § 139. The recent *Restatement Third* firmly maintains this stance: *Restatement Third* (n 46) vol 1, 528 (comment *c* on § 33) and 540 (corresponding Reporter's Note).

[134] *Goff & Jones* (n 19) [34-05]–[34-06], [34-16]–[34-17], [34-29]; Virgo (n 19) 728; Birks (n 83) 225, 261–63. See also Burrows (n 19) 582, who writes: 'Instead of a blanket infancy defence, minors would have been adequately protected by affording them a defence of change of position.' But note that he does not add any qualifications with respect to the operation of the change of position defence.

[135] See section 3.3, especially the text accompanying nn 159–62, 179–82.

[136] Discussed further in *Goff & Jones* (n 19) [34-18]–[34-20]. See also PS Atiyah, 'The Liability of Infants in Fraud and Restitution' (1959) 22 *MLR* 273, especially 286–90.

[137] *Lemprière v Lange* (1879) 12 Ch D 675 (Ch), where the defendant minor was said to have made an 'implied representation' to the effect that he was of full age, shows that the equitable notion of 'fraud' was rather vague and flexible, and certainly wider than the common law understanding of the term.

[138] *Levene v Brougham* (1909) 25 TLR 265 (CA) (Lord Alverstone CJ). In that case, it had been suggested that a minor who had fraudulently misrepresented his age in order to obtain a loan was estopped from relying on the Infants Relief Act 1874 (UK) in defence to the money-lender's action on the promissory note he had signed. The Court of Appeal firmly rejected this argument. While it accepted that an equitable liability could sometimes arise from such a misrepresentation (see the quote set out in the text), this 'did not mean that the contract would be enforced, but that *some other [ie, non contractual] remedy* would be given' (emphasis added).

[139] *Clarke v Cobley* (1789) 2 Cox Eq Cas 173, 174; 30 ER 80 (Lord Arden MR).

[140] Beside the cases already mentioned in nn 137–39, see also *Re King, ex p The Unity Joint Stock Mutual Banking Association* (1858) 3 De G & J 63; 44 ER 1192; *Nelson v Stocker* (1859) 4 De G & J 458, 464; 45 ER 178, 180 (Turner LJ): 'Infants are no more entitled than adults are to gain benefits to themselves by fraud'; *Bartlett v Wells* (1862) 1 B & S 836, 841; 121 ER 924, 926 (Lord Cockburn CJ).

for the proceeds of some furniture, pictures and a collection of weapons which he had fraudulently obtained from the claimant and disposed of before reaching majority,[141] Lush J observed that although the defrauded vendor had no remedy at common law:[142]

> What the Court of Equity has done in cases of this kind is to prevent the infant from retaining the benefit of what he has obtained by reason of his fraud ... If the infant has obtained property by fraud he can be compelled to restore it; if he has obtained money he can be compelled to refund it.

That the supposed infancy defence can be recast more modestly, as a requirement of the defendant minor not being left out-of-pocket, is demonstrable even as far as the common law is concerned. In *R Leslie Ltd v Sheill*, where the claimant money-lenders' action to recover the advance of £400 as money had and received failed, Lord Sumner observed with respect to the old equity cases that 'restitution stopped where repayment began'.[143] What he meant is that the minor could not be liable to make restitution beyond his surviving enrichment. As AT Lawrence J remarked:[144]

> There are no doubt many cases in which equity will give relief against frauds perpetrated by infants. Wherever the infant requires as a plaintiff the assistance of any Court, it will be refused until he has made good his fraudulent representation. *Wherever the infant is still in possession of any property which he has obtained by his fraud he will be made to restore it to its former owner.* But I think that it is incorrect to say that he can be made to repay money which he has spent, merely because he received it under a contract induced by his fraud.

On the facts of *R Leslie Ltd v Sheill*, it was evidently assumed that the defendant minor had squandered the loan advanced to him. Distinguishing *Stocks v Wilson*, Lord Sumner said:[145]

> In the present case there is clearly no accounting. There is no fiduciary relation: the money was paid over in order to be used as the defendant's own *and he has so used it and, I suppose, spent it. There is no question of tracing it, no possibility of restoring the very thing got by the fraud*, nothing but compulsion through a personal judgment to pay an equivalent sum out of his present or future resources, in a word nothing but a judgment in debt to repay the loan.

In the days before English law had openly und unequivocally recognised a defence of change of position,[146] it is understandable that allowing a restitutionary claim for 'money had and received'—literally measured by reference

[141] The defendant minor had sold a part of the goods for £30 and had granted a bill of sale of the residue to secure a loan of £100, thus realising a total of £130 from the disposition.

[142] *Stocks v Wilson* (n 124) 242–43.

[143] *R Leslie Ltd v Sheill* (n 129) 618.

[144] ibid 626 (emphasis added).

[145] ibid 619 (emphasis added).

[146] By virtue of the seminal House of Lords decision in *Lipkin Gorman* (n 74).

to the amount received—should have looked a little like enforcing the void contract. However, today incapacity as such ought never to function as a complete defence to claims in unjust enrichment.

3.2. Defences and Section 3(1) of the Minors' Contracts Act 1987

When the regime of the Infants Relief Act 1874 (UK) was ended by the Minors' Contracts Act 1987 (UK) and the traditional common law trichotomy between valid, voidable and unenforceable contracts was restored,[147] a provision was introduced which was intended to broaden the circumstances under which a claimant can obtain restitution from a defendant minor.[148] Section 3 of the Minors' Contracts Act 1987 reads:

(1) Where—
   (a) a person ('the plaintiff') has after the commencement of this Act entered into a contract with another ('the defendant'), and
   (b) the contract is unenforceable against the defendant (or he repudiates it) because he was a minor when the contract was made,

   the court may, if it is just and equitable to do so, require the defendant to transfer to the plaintiff any property acquired by the defendant under the contract, or any property representing it.

(2) Nothing in this section shall be taken to prejudice any other remedy available to the plaintiff.

Sub-section (1) provides a discretionary remedy in cases like *Cowern v Nield*,[149] where the minor accepts the claimant's performance under an unenforceable contract, but fails to render the promised counter-performance in return. It is irrelevant for this purpose whether or not he has acted fraudulently. The old line of equity cases granting relief for fraud is expressly preserved by sub-section (2),[150] and—following the argument set out above—one could even maintain that there exists in parallel to section 3(1) a generalised claim to restitution for the defendant's unjust enrichment at the claimant's expense based on total (or even partial) failure of consideration.[151]

[147] See the text accompanying nn 9–13.

[148] This is evident from the Law Commission Report which preceded the 1987 Act: Law Commission (1984) (n 54) paras 1.10 and 4.16–4.23.

[149] See n 126 and the accompanying text.

[150] For a comparison of the two bases of liability, see *Treitel on Contract* (n 9) [12-045].

[151] Birks (n 83) 225: 'It may now never be decided whether ... the modern extrapolation from the confused common law would be that the minor remained liable to the extent of his abstractly surviving enrichment, or, in other words, that, with heavily modified rules on disqualification, he remained liable in unjust enrichment subject to a defence of disenrichment.' There are also suggestions to this or a similar effect in Burrows (n 19) 582–83; *Goff & Jones* (n 19) [34-17], [34-29], [34-30].

Be that as it may, for present purposes the crucial question is what role defences play in the context of section 3(1). The legislature has here granted courts the power to order a retransfer, imposing no duty to do so, and circumscribing the use of this power by reference to an extremely open-textured kind of judicial discretion. Unfortunately, the provision appears never to have been tested in litigation, but its wording strongly suggests that most issues normally considered at the 'defences' stage of an unjust enrichment inquiry would simply be factored into the exercise of the court's discretion. So, for example, if the claimant had paid the defendant minor to commit a crime and the latter had subsequently failed to perform according to plan,[152] the illegality of the scheme should easily lead a judge to hold that it is not 'just and equitable' to require the defendant to make restitution of the money to the instigator.

With respect to the defence of disenrichment or change of position, it is notable that section 3(1) only envisages the court ordering the defendant to transfer to the claimant 'any property acquired by the defendant under the contract, or any property representing it'. The provision thereby confines the claim to the enrichment specifically or traceably surviving in the defendant's hands. The Law Commission, on whose recommendations the provision is based, had initially wanted to grant the remedy as of right, but restrict the claimant to recovery *in specie*.[153] It later opted for the discretionary approach and at the same time extended the remedy to traceable proceeds.[154]

[152] Note that it may nowadays be insufficient if the plan is simply frustrated and not carried into effect at all: see the comment in n 68.

[153] Law Commission (Working Paper, 1982) (n 54) para 6.8: 'If the adult's remedy were to be allowed to extend beyond recovery of specific articles obtained by the minor, but yet not to include a right to damages for breach of contract, then that remedy could be based only upon the concept of tracing, or upon that concept modified by some provision for discretionary relief. We do not think this would be desirable. In our view, if the limit of the adult's remedy is set at recovery of specific articles, the rule is clear and simple; and such a rule is preferable to the complications of tracing, with or without discretionary relief. This applies equally where the minor has exchanged the contract goods for other goods, but refuses to pay for the original goods. It can be argued that the adult should at least be entitled to the goods which the minor has received in exchange. But we believe that cases of straightforward exchange are rare and that, if the adult were allowed a remedy in respect of goods which the minor has obtained as a result of part exchange, that remedy would once again become unacceptably complex.' Note that, at this stage in its deliberations, the Law Commission still envisaged that a minor who was unable to return the property *in specie* should be liable to pay for it unless he could prove that he did not dispose of it to defeat the supplier's claims (at paras 6.9–6.10, 13.14), but this proposal was later abandoned.

[154] Law Commission (Report, 1984) (n 54) 35 (point 3 of the 'explanatory notes' to clause 3 of the proposed bill): 'The court's power is limited to ordering the transfer of property acquired under the contract, or property representing it. Thus, if the minor has sold or exchanged the goods acquired under the contract, he can be compelled to pay over the price, or hand over the goods received in exchange. But if he has consumed or otherwise 'dissipated' the goods or their proceeds, he cannot be required to pay to the seller a sum equivalent to the purchase price, or to the value of the goods.' The reasons for the Law Commission's change of approach are set out in paras 4.16–4.23 of the Report.

It might be asked how a judge is meant to apply the provision where the defendant minor retains the claimant's original performance or a traceable substitute, but where he is disenriched in abstract terms (for example, by spending money to celebrate the receipt).[155] There are two possible answers. One is that this is something for the court to take into account when exercising its statutory discretion. The other is that such a scenario is actually quite hard to envisage. In the contractual context, genuine reliance on one's receipt is typically dependent on having rendered the promised counter-performance. Until then, even the minor on the Clapham omnibus expects his acquisition to be in some way 'conditional'. This practically rules out 'reliance-mediated' changes of position not affecting the subject matter of what was received (where the link between the enrichment and the disenrichment is purely in the defendant's mind), simply because causation is exceedingly difficult to establish.[156] Hence, virtually all relevant disenrichments will affect the claimant's actual performance *in specie* or its traceable proceeds.

The fact that section 3(1) of the Minors' Contracts Act 1987 envisages the minor returning the (specifically or traceably) surviving enrichment, but no more, lends support to the view advanced above that a minor in the role of claimant should only have to make counter-restitution to the extent that he still retains the other party's performance.[157] After all, the requirement of *restitutio in integrum*—or a monetary approximation of it—is in essence simply a reflection of the contract partner's claim to restitution for unjust enrichment against the minor.

3.3. The Minor's Reliance on Change of Position

Let us now look a little more closely at how the change of position defence normally operates where minors are concerned as defendants. We have already touched on the issue in the contractual scenario,[158] but we also need

[155] The editors of *Goff & Jones* (n 19) [34-31] ask the converse question (not addressed here), namely about the case where the claimant's performance does not survive either *in specie* or traceably, but where the defendant's overall wealth is nevertheless still swollen by the value received. They suggest that the minor should then be made to disgorge that value by a personal claim to restitution for unjust enrichment, but this seems impossible under s 3(1) as drafted on account of the provision's clear and restrictive wording. Resort to the common law may therefore be necessary to achieve this end. See also their observations at [34-07].

[156] In this respect, the present scenario may differ from cases where the minor obtains cash and where—as a result of the receipt—he is (or feels) in a position to incur expenditure which he would not otherwise have been able to afford: see n 161 below.

[157] See the text accompanying and following n 118. It also suggests that minors should be relieved of their restitutionary liability quite irrespective of whether they have accidentally been disenriched or deliberately put it out of their power to make specific restitution (see the text accompanying nn 120 and 122).

[158] In the context of discussing the impossibility of a claimant minor making counter-restitution (see section 2.4) and of the discretionary award against defendant minors under s 3(1) of the Minors' Contracts Act 1987 (UK) (see section 3.2).

to consider under what circumstances minors may invoke the defence in their favour where they have received a mistaken overpayment or have been otherwise enriched outside the bargaining framework.

It was suggested above that it is preferable to protect minors via a generous change of position defence than to afford them a 'blanket' incapacity defence.[159] Of those commentators who have floated the idea, Professor Birks did so most rigorously, and he is the only one to hint at its broader implications. Taken to its logical conclusion, the argument that minors should not be disqualified from the change of position defence quite as easily as adults led him to postulate that all disenrichments causally connected with their initial enrichment should count.[160] This means, for instance, that an under-age defendant who has received a mistaken double payment ought not to be held liable for the full overpaid amount where he has squandered a part of the money,[161] although he may have been well aware of the claimant's error. And one who has knowingly received and consumed fungible luxury goods intended for someone else should be excused altogether from making restitution. On this view, even the most deliberate acts of disenrichment—such as the wanton destruction of the other party's performance—are not necessarily imputable to minors and should hence relieve them of their liability to make restitution (or counter-restitution, as the case may be).[162]

In a landmark 1971 decision, the German Federal Supreme Court had occasion to ponder over the appropriate disqualification threshold for children.[163] § 818(3) BGB excludes a defendant's liability to make restitution insofar as he is no longer enriched. In its statutory context, the provision is deemed inapplicable as soon as the defendant becomes aware that he is not entitled to keep what he has obtained.[164] The case concerned a 17-year-old who had somehow managed to board a Lufthansa flight from Hamburg to New York without a valid ticket.[165] His prank came to light after the US

[159] See n 134 and the accompanying text.

[160] Birks (n 83) 218, discussing in general terms 'policy-motivated deviations' from the 'bad faith' disqualification standard: '[I]n rare cases a defendant may be allowed the defence even in circumstances which would normally disqualify him. A minor's contracts are voidable at his option. The minor cannot, however, retain surviving enrichment. That proposition restricting his liability to surviving enrichment, taken with the underlying protective policy, *must entail allowing him, without inquiry into his honesty, all the disenrichments caused by his enrichment*' (emphasis added, footnote omitted).

[161] In a mistaken payment case, it may just be possible to establish a causative link between the defendant's receipt of specific cash on the one hand and his spending of other money (ie, money otherwise at his disposition) despite the lack of genuine reliance: see n 156 and the accompanying text. But *cf* also Bant (n 131) 387–88.

[162] See already the text accompanying nn 120 and 122 above.

[163] BGH (7.1.1971) BGHZ 55, 128, more fully reported in NJW 1971, 609. A partial translation of the decision is provided by Dannemann (n 109) 242–49 (case 7—'underage flyer').

[164] This is inferred from §§ 818(4) and 819(1) BGB.

[165] The defendant had flown from Munich to Hamburg as a regular passenger. After a stopover there, he joined the transit passengers and re-boarded the aeroplane without anyone noticing that he was not in possession of a boarding pass.

authorities denied him entry for want of a visa. Having flown him back to Germany, Lufthansa demanded, inter alia, payment of the ordinary ticket price for the journey to New York.

The Federal Supreme Court explained that neither a contractual nor a delictual claim could be maintained under the circumstances.[166] As far as the defendant's liability in unjust enrichment was concerned, it rejected the argument that the defendant was never enriched in the first place, effectively holding that (what an English lawyer would call) 'subjective devaluation' at the receipt stage was subject to the same disqualifying criteria as subsequent disenrichments.[167] The Court then turned to consider these criteria. It noted that commentators disagreed over whether disqualification should always depend on the state of mind of the minor's parents/guardians[168] or whether the minor's own knowledge and awareness counted as soon as he was mature enough to appreciate the situation.[169] The Federal Supreme Court itself opted for a middle way between these rival approaches:[170]

> As far as the protective aim underlying the restricted capacity of minors requires, it is necessary to look to the knowledge of the legal guardian in the context of § 819 BGB [the provision governing the liability of *mala fide* enrichees which implicitly denies recourse to the disenrichment defence in § 818(3) BGB]. This would seem to be particularly true where transactions entered into by minors without full capacity are to be unwound. Otherwise one would end up with cases where the minors' liability in unjustified enrichment leads to a state of affairs against which the law specifically intended to protect him ... However, the protective

[166] The minor's parents had refused to ratify any transaction he may have entered into (as required under § 108 BGB if it was to be validated retroactively), and the principles governing contracts arising implicitly from so-called 'typical social conduct' (*sozialtypisches Verhalten*)—developed to cater for modern public transport with its mass-character and anonymity—were held not to apply to travel by aeroplane, where every passenger is individually registered by name. Nor could the defendant be held liable in delict, since the claimant airline, whose plane was not fully booked, could not demonstrate that it had suffered any loss.

[167] BGHZ 55, 128, 134–35; NJW 1971, 609, 611: 'Yet if ... the law prevents an enrichee who knows of the lack of a *causa* at the moment of receipt from invoking in his defence the fact that his initial enrichment has subsequently disappeared, then it is hard to understand why, under similar conditions, he should be allowed to deny that he was ever enriched. That, at any rate, must be the case where—as here—the enrichment consists of saved expenditure for extravagances which the enrichee would not otherwise be willing or even able to afford. If the enrichee knows of the lack of a *causa*, then it can make no difference whether he first incorporates what he receives into his patrimony and subsequently spends it again, or whether the receipt itself is part and parcel of satisfying his extravagance. The decisive factor is that the enrichee has actually obtained something, knowing that it lacked a *causa*, for which he has to make restitution in value terms ... when it is no longer there.'

[168] Since parental or guardian consent is necessary to conclude or ratify a contract to which the minor is a party (§§ 106 ff BGB), so the reasoning runs, it should be the parents' or guardians' state of mind which matters when it comes to unwinding unjustified enrichments obtained by the minor.

[169] As explained in n 73, German law holds minors aged 7–17 responsible for causing delictual damage to others if (and only if) they had sufficient insight and understanding to appreciate their responsibility.

[170] BGHZ 55, 128, 136–37; NJW 1971, 609, 611–12.

> aim underlying the restricted capacity of minors comes to an end in the realm of delict. The law of delict circumscribes the responsibility of adolescents for damage caused by them by reference to other criteria, quite independently of the extent to which they are able to undertake contractual obligations. If, therefore, a minor is—in one way or the other—not wholly shielded from the negative consequences of his own behaviour, then there is at any rate no reason to spare him the stringent liability regime of § 819 BGB if and to the extent that he has obtained the enrichment by an intentional delict. In such a case, there is no good reason for assessing his behaviour according to any different criteria in the context of unjustified enrichment than are relevant in the context of the law of delict.

Since the 17-year-old defendant in the litigation at hand had sneaked onboard the aeroplane without a boarding pass and since it was found that he appreciated what he was doing, he was debarred from arguing that the trip to New York was a luxury which he would never have been able or willing to pay for. He was thus held to have been enriched by the full value of the flight, measured by reference to the ordinary ticket price.

This result closely aligns with the view that in a performance-based claim (so-called *Leistungskondiktion*), a minor should only be disqualified from invoking the disenrichment defence where his parents or other legal guardians were aware of his lack of entitlement, while in non-performance-based claims, especially if the defendant had obtained the enrichment by infringing some absolute right of the claimant (so-called *Eingriffskondiktion*), disqualification should turn on his own state of mind when viewed against the background of his moral and intellectual maturity.[171]

Given that English law—unlike German law—does not make the validity of contracts entered into by minors depend on the consent of their parents or guardians, it is hard to see how the latter's knowledge should have any relevance to the change of position inquiry on the English model of unjust enrichment. However, at least for claims which are based not on a defect in the performing party's consent (as in a typical mistake claim), but instead on the defendant's unilateral arrogation of the enrichment (such as in an 'ignorance' case, if one accepts this rather contentious unjust factor),[172] the Federal Supreme Court's decision might provide some food for thought. It is certainly worth considering whether, in appropriate cases,

[171] See, eg, Schwab in *Münchener Kommentar* (n 113) § 819 [8]. For a critical take on this approach, see Lorenz in *Staudinger* (n 113) § 819 [10].

[172] See, eg, Burrows (n 19) ch 16, especially 403–09, referring to *Holiday v Sigil* (1826) 2 Car & P 176; 172 ER 81 and to *Neate v Harding* (1851) 6 Exch 349; 155 ER 577 as examples of two-party 'ignorance' cases. In A Burrows, *A Restatement of the English Law of Unjust Enrichment* (Oxford, Oxford University Press, 2012) ss 16–17, Burrows lists 'want of authority'/'lack of consent' besides 'ignorance'/'powerlessness'. See also *Goff & Jones* (n 19) [8-01]–[8-14]. But contrast the critical discussions by Virgo (n 19) 11–17, 152–56; WJ Swadling, 'Ignorance and Unjust Enrichment: The Problem of Title' (2008) 28 *OJLS* 627.

the disqualification threshold for minors ought to be assimilated to the threshold of tortious liability.[173]

The editors of *Goff & Jones* go even further than this. They tentatively envisage generally withholding the benefits of a liberal change of position regime to fraudulent or otherwise 'dishonest' minors.[174] The attraction of their view is that it fits quite well with the estoppel argument floated above (concerning minors who deliberately misrepresent their age in order to induce a performance)[175] and with the need to hold deceitful parties tortiously liable in such a scenario.[176] On the other hand, if one reinterprets *R Leslie Ltd v Sheill* as a disenrichment case,[177] then its outcome would seem to indicate that even a fraudulent minor need never disgorge more than his (specifically or traceably)[178] surviving enrichment in a performance-based claim. But what this reading of *R Leslie Ltd v Sheill* illustrates, at any rate, is that 'bad faith' in the sense of a mere awareness that an enrichment ought or might have to be returned to the claimant should not necessarily disqualify a defendant minor from relying on change of position.

What is sorely needed—and what the suggestion in *Goff & Jones* may pave the way for—is a more general debate about the meaning of 'bad faith' and 'dishonesty', and in particular about the applicability of such criteria to minors. It would have to be a discussion spanning both tort law and the law of unjust enrichment. Once we know the exact conditions under which minors may be held liable in tort,[179] we can better decide whether all under-age defendants should be excused from making restitution to the extent that they are causally disenriched by their receipt, irrespective of their

[173] But note that, under English law, a number of the torts in question are strict liability wrongs triggered quite independently of the defendant's fault (eg, conversion or trespass to land), so that the scope for adjustments of the disqualification threshold would be much smaller in English than in German law.

[174] *Goff & Jones* (n 19) [34-17]: '[W]e believe that the best mechanism ... would be to allow claims to recover the value received by a defendant minor, but to allow the minor to rely on the change of position defence in a wider set of circumstances than would normally be permitted, so that he can escape liability for that portion of the value which he has consumed or otherwise disposed of by the time of the action, even if he was aware of the circumstances entitling the claimant to restitution. This would mean, for example, that the minor would not be prevented from relying on the defence by the fact that he knew that the claimant was unaware of his minority (*although there is an argument that he should not be allowed the defence where he has committed a fraudulent misrepresentation or has been dishonest in some other way*)' (emphasis added, footnote omitted).

[175] See section 2.1. If a minor who has fraudulently misrepresented his age is estopped from relying on his minority in order to recover his performance (and is thus effectively treated as if he were of full age), he should also be estopped from relying on his minority to invoke the change of position defence in circumstances where an adult would be unable to do so.

[176] See n 54 and the accompanying text.

[177] See the text accompanying nn 143–46.

[178] This is suggested by the wording Lord Sumner used in *R Leslie Ltd v Sheill* (n 52) (quote in the text accompanying n 145), but the defendant's abstractly surviving enrichment should arguably be enough to warrant restitution in value terms: see n 155.

[179] See the text accompanying nn 66–67.

state of mind,[180] or whether those who have committed an intentional tort in obtaining the enrichment (such as deceit)[181] and/or whose subsequent actions smack of tortious conduct (such as where the defendant deliberately destroys the object received)[182] should be denied reliance on change of position.

4. CONCLUSION

English law still has important choices to make when it comes to defining what impact a party's minority has on the operation of defences within the law of unjust enrichment. Adjusting the restitutionary regime to the interlocking contractual and tort law principles will be one of the main challenges. This chapter has sought to raise some of the most pertinent issues, taking stock of the case law and academic literature and outlining various possible solutions. In order to better assess the range of options in their broader context, it has sporadically drawn on US and German material, where courts and commentators have already had to answer questions which are still either unasked or—more often—as yet unsettled under the evolving English law of unjust enrichment.

The main points can be summarised as follows:

4.1. Situations where the Minor is in the Position of Claimant

a) If and when English law finally jettisons the total failure of consideration requirement in allowing a claimant minor to recover his performance under an 'unenforceable' or voidable contract, it could—but need not—recognise an estoppel defence in cases where the minor has fraudulently misrepresented his age in order to induce the contract.
b) For the purposes of the illegality defence, the parties are not *in pari delicto* unless the minor can be held legally responsible for his conduct and his fault is comparable to that of the defendant.

[180] As proposed by Birks: see n 160 and the accompanying text.

[181] See the text accompanying nn 121 and 174. Excluding minors who have fraudulently obtained a performance by misrepresenting their age would not seem to be a realistic option so long as English law continues to afford them a special immunity from liability in the tort of deceit: *cf* the discussion following n 49.

[182] See the text accompanying nn 120 and 122. The difficulty about such a disqualifier is that the defendant commits no tort where he wantonly destroys an asset belonging to himself (eg, a chattel which the claimant has conveyed to him). Nor is it easily possible to rely on a *hypothetical* tort (ie, a wrong that the defendant *would* have committed had the asset still belonged to the claimant, onto whom—after all—the change of position defence forces all of the risks normally connected with 'ownership') because the strict liability nature of many property torts makes an unsuitable criterion in the disenrichment context: *cf* comment in n 173.

c) Although the adult defendant's ability to rely on change of position has the effect of shifting the risk of his disenrichment onto the claimant minor, the defence should on balance not be excluded or restricted vis-à-vis the minor.
d) The impossibility of counter-restitution by a claimant minor ought to be a defence to the extent that the minor no longer retains the defendant's performance (or its traceable proceeds), at least where the minor has not been fraudulent in obtaining the enrichment and where his disenrichment came about 'accidentally'.

4.2. Situations where the Minor is in the Position of Defendant

a) Incapacity as such is not, and should not be, a defence to restitution for unjust enrichment.
b) Where discretionary relief is provided under section 3(1) of the Minors' Contracts Act 1987, the question of defences is merged into the cause of action inquiry.
c) Minors should not be disqualified from pleading change of position merely because they were aware of their restitutionary liability, but there may be instances of 'tortious' conduct where the disqualification threshold ought to be appropriately aligned.

10

Defences to Restitution Between Victims of a Common Fraud

ANDREW KULL

THE CLASSIC SCENARIO begins when Swindler obtains money from Victim 1, borrowing on the security of property he does not own. When V1 demands repayment, Swindler repeats his successful fraud—borrowing again on the same security, inducing V2 to repay V1 to discharge the imaginary prior lien. V2 sues V1 in restitution; the question is whether V1 has a defence. (Similar issues are presented when the agent of two principals first embezzles from P1, then embezzles from P2 to cover his shortage with P1.) A modern variation of this old story appears in the aftermath of a Ponzi scheme. Some residual assets have been found, clearly the product of the fraud, but nothing permits any particular victim to identify his property or trace it through Swindler's accounts. Victims' competing claims will normally yield a rateable distribution—a rule of no priority between fraud victims, a rule so intuitive it is scarcely perceived as a rule. The case is complicated, however, because some earlier, more fortunate victims have previously withdrawn funds from the scheme and because any funds withdrawn were necessarily obtained from subsequent victims of the same fraud. Resolution of all such cases requires an adjudication of what are, implicitly or otherwise, restitution claims between fraud victims inter se. Victims have a prima facie claim to recover their money from anyone to whom it was paid over; the question is whether prior victims have a defence. The conventional view is that they can keep earlier withdrawals, though only to the amount of their original investment. That defence yields a priority between victims rather like the rule in *Clayton's Case*—first in, first out—and often just as arbitrary.

This result is the consequence of the liberal defence allowed to anyone who receives a mistaken payment as a 'creditor/payee'. By the standard rule in US law, restitution of a mistaken payment is unavailable against a payee who took the claimant's money in satisfaction of a third party's pre-existing debt, without notice of the circumstances underlying the claim to restitution. In England, this is the rule of *Aiken v Short*,[1] where the claimant had paid to discharge a pre-existing lien on property in which the claimant believed (wrongly) that it had acquired an interest, and of *RE Jones Ltd v Waring & Gillow Ltd*,[2] where the claimant had been tricked into paying a swindler's pre-existing debt to an earlier creditor. In the US, it is moreover the most widely accepted explanation of *Price v Neal*,[3] where a drawee paid the innocent holder for value of a forged bill; of all cases like *Chambers v Miller*[4] and *Barclays Bank v WJ Simms*,[5] in which a bank pays a cheque while overlooking a problem with insufficient funds or a timely stop order; and of recent cases in which wire transfers are directed by mistake to the bank accounts of creditors, or in which health insurers pay hospitals before realising that the discharged patient had no coverage.[6]

The precise contours in modern US law of this defence of 'bona fide payee',[7] alias 'bona fide creditor', alias 'discharge for value',[8] are not the topic to be pursued here. Nor is the question whether and to what extent some version of the same defence, *sub nom* 'good consideration', is part of English restitution law.[9] The latter question is tempting, because to a US observer the answer is a reasonably clear 'yes'. The defence was originally identified by nineteenth-century American commentators largely on the basis of English cases,[10] and when Robert Goff J later summarised the

[1] *Aiken v Short* (1856) 1 H & N 210; 156 ER 1180.

[2] *RE Jones Ltd v Waring & Gillow Ltd* [1926] AC 670 (HL). The US analogue is *Concord Coal v Ferrin* 71 NH 33 (1901).

[3] *Price v Neal* 3 Burr 1354 (1762).

[4] *Chambers v Miller* (1862) 13 CB (NS) 125; 143 ER 50.

[5] *Barclays Bank v WJ Simms & Cooke (Southern) Ltd* [1980] QB 677 (QBD).

[6] For examples, see A Kull, 'Defenses to Restitution: The Bona Fide Creditor' (2001) 81 *Boston University Law Review* 919.

[7] American Law Institute, *Restatement Third, Restitution and Unjust Enrichment* § 67 (St Paul, MN, American Law Institute Publishers, 2011) (hereinafter 'R3RUE').

[8] American Law Institute, *Restatement of the Law of Restitution: Quasi Contracts and Constructive Trusts and Unjust Enrichment* § 14 (St Paul, MN, American Law Institute Publishers, 1937).

[9] For reasons for thinking it might not be, see A Burrows, 'Is There a Defence of Good Consideration?' in C Mitchell and W Swadling (eds), *The Restatement Third: Restitution and Unjust Enrichment* (Oxford, Hart Publishing, 2013) 165, 166–73.

[10] Reflecting on the various justifications offered for the rule in *Price v Neal*, William Keener observed: 'Many of the cases doubtless where a recovery is denied of money paid under mistake as to the genuineness of the drawer's signature could be put simply on the principles suggested in Aiken *v.* Short, 1 H. & N. 210; Chambers *v.* Miller, 13 C.B. N.S. 125; Southwick *v.* National Bank, 84 N.Y. 420; Merchants Ins. Co. *v.* Abbott, 131 Mass. 397,—namely, that where a party having certain rights receives from the plaintiff money in extinguishment thereof, he is in a position to say that he surrendered value for the money received, and should not therefore be required to return the money so paid.' WA Keener, *A Treatise on the Law of Quasi-Contracts* (New York, Baker, Voorhis & Co, 1893) 157.

same cases to the same effect, we thought we already knew what he was talking about.[11]

The question of defences between fraud victims inter se depends importantly on the reasons for allowing this defence (whatever we might call it) to creditor/payees generally. Disinterring the origins of the creditor/payee's defence reveals an interesting but largely forgotten story, in which a new defence came to life to supplement the existing ones—principally change of position. The new defence was significant precisely in those cases where the creditor/payee had not evidently changed position, and it was developed to handle such cases. It was the product of a momentous struggle within nineteenth-century commercial law, in which proponents of a 'mercantile' rule, protecting the finality of financial transactions, succeeded in displacing the former 'equitable' rule, by which a payee who could not show a detrimental change of position was liable to restore a mistaken payment. The crux of this battle was the contested status of 'antecedent debt' as a source of the 'valuable consideration' necessary to make the transferee a protected purchaser. Because change of position was acknowledged to be a good defence, the cases of 'valuable consideration' worth arguing about were naturally those in which the antecedent debt was essentially worthless. Once antecedent debt was recognised as 'value', no questions asked, the innocent creditor/payee had acquired an immunity to restitution with no need to demonstrate a change of position.

Powerful reasons support the finality of payment to someone who receives it bona fide on account of a valid obligation. The creditor/payee shelters behind three overlapping, cumulative layers of protection against liability. These are, successively, the protection afforded a defendant who changes position on receipt of a benefit of any kind; the broader protection afforded a bona fide purchaser of anything for value; and the still broader protection afforded a payee/purchaser of money. For the past two centuries, the visible and consistent policy of the law has been to expand these defences

[11] From the US viewpoint, the critical passage from *Barclays Bank v WJ Simms* was simply an acknowledgment of the creditor/payee's established defences to restitution, familiar in all respects but one: '(2) [A claim to recover a mistaken payment] may however fail if ... (b) the payment is made for good consideration, in particular if the money is paid to discharge, and does discharge, a debt owed to the payee (or a principal on whose behalf he is authorised to receive the payment) by the payer or by a third party *by whom he is authorised to discharge the debt*.' *Barclays Bank* (n 5) 695 (emphasis added). The proposition that there is no discharge of a debt without the debtor's authorisation is not only inconsistent with the US cases, it is one that American lawyers find mystifying. The practical result—that the bank can recover a payment where it overlooked a stop order (*Barclays v Simms*), but not where it mistook the balance of its customer's account (*Chambers v Miller*)—seems untoward. All such mistakes by the bank would be located by US courts somewhere within 'the rule of *Price v Neal*', which in its current (statutory) formulation protects an unintended payee 'who took the instrument in good faith and for value or who in good faith changed position in reliance on the payment or acceptance'. Uniform Commercial Code, s 3-418(c) (rev 1990).

wherever they serve commercial convenience. The consequences of allowing this defence include windfalls and unjust enrichments of the most obvious kind. But so long as the claim is between victim and creditor, and payment is received in the ordinary course of creditor's business, the case against restitution has long since carried the day.

Just possibly the victim v victim cases occupy another category, because V1 (the restitution defendant) occupies a dual role: he is simultaneously repaid creditor and fellow fraud victim. As creditor, he defeats the restitution claim and keeps V2's money, but as victim of a common misfortune, his entitlement is to a rateable distribution with V2. Courts are pulled one way or the other by their inclination to see the defendant primarily as creditor or primarily as victim. One reason for the judicial dilemma, and for the awkward reasoning in the cases, is that the result is all-or-nothing either way. If the defence is allowed, V1 keeps the money and V2 takes the loss. If the defence is denied, the result is reversed. Neither outcome seems especially fair. Instead of allowing restitution or denying it—leaving the whole loss on one side or the other—victim v victim restitution would ideally recover an asset subject to the joint claims of both victims.

Recent US decisions allocating assets (and losses) in the aftermath of Ponzi schemes have ignored basic rules of property—let alone defences to restitution—to impose a sharing of losses where courts have seen an opportunity to do so. Equalising outcomes to eliminate the effects of luck is not something the law normally attempts to do, and one question is why judges have taken this approach to restitution between fraud victims. Part of the answer is surely practical. Typically, the assets to be allocated between victims are already in the possession of the court (or its receiver) and it is easier to adjust accounts by withholding a distribution than by imposing a levy. A further explanation, and the one chiefly pursued in the following discussion, is that the creditor/payee's usual defence to restitution lacks both commercial justification and equitable force when asserted by one fraud victim against another.

1. THE CREDITOR/PAYEE'S DEFENCE

R3RUE describes a capacious affirmative defence for the 'bona fide payee'. A payment that would otherwise be subject to restitution—typically by reason of fraud or mistake—may be retained if it was taken, without notice, in satisfaction or reduction of a valid obligation.[12] Most of R3RUE's treatment of 'bona fide payees' was inherited from the original *Restatement of Restitution*, where the rule was somewhat obliquely called 'discharge for value'.[13]

[12] R3RUE, § 67.
[13] *Restatement of the Law of Restitution* (n 8) § 14.

The case for taking R3RUE's 'bona fide payee' as an accurate rule for these cases is not that it is universally applied—it is not—but that it marks the logical end-point of an unmistakable legal evolution. That evolution has seen the progressive displacement of an equitable rule (allowing a defence to restitution to a person who can show that restitution would be inequitable) by a commercial one (promoting the finality of money payments without regard to individual equities). In US law, the triumph of the commercial rule is essentially complete, at least for the 'ordinary course' transactions that the rule was developed to protect.[14]

The defence normally allowed to creditor/payees combines separate strands that the decisions have gradually woven together. As the original focus on countervailing equities gradually gave way to commercial or 'mercantile' objectives, the creditor/payee's defence to restitution was steadily supplemented and augmented. The equitable idea of change of position is as good a defence as it ever was, and it is still available to anyone, creditors included. What then of the creditor/payee who has not changed position in any significant way? After initial hesitation, the law protected him as well: first by reasoning that he gave 'valuable consideration', then by fiat, declaring that money and instruments are taken for 'value' even when the consideration given for them (if any) is almost certainly worthless. Evolution along these lines drew implicit support from the rules governing ownership of money and instruments. The argument is a fortiori. If the creditor/payee would be entitled to keep the money if it had been stolen from the claimant, presumably he can keep it when it was paid to him as a result of fraud or mistake. Simply put: if the old rule of *Miller v Race*[15] (to the effect that a purchaser for value without notice acquires good title to stolen money or instruments) is combined with the pivotal commercial fiat (to the effect that antecedent debt constitutes 'value', no questions asked), that combination affords an impenetrable defence to restitution to any creditor/payee who needs one. Because this ultimate form of the rule subsumes its intermediate stages, there is normally no need for a creditor/payee to justify a defence in any other terms.

The protection extended to creditor/payees has been part of the landscape for so long that its rationale, long a subject of vigorous debate, is something many lawyers would have a hard time explaining—beyond a trite reference to 'finality'. To prepare the ground for the proposition that victim v victim cases invite a different approach, it is worth recalling how the creditor/payee's defence came to be what it is.

[14] The formula adopted in § 67 of the R3RUE, which omits any limitation to ordinary-course transactions, reveals in this respect an oversight by the Reporter for the American Law Institute.

[15] *Miller v Race* (1758) 1 Burr 452.

2. THE MERCANTILE RULE

Defences to restitution started with the idea of countervailing equity. Just as the gist of the action was 'that the defendant, upon the circumstances of the case, is obliged by the ties of natural justice and equity to refund the money', so the defence was 'every thing which shews that the plaintiff, *ex aequo & bono,* is not intitled to the whole of his demand, or to any part of it'.[16] The most natural way to make the necessary equitable showing, then and now, is to point to a change of position on the part of the defendant—ideally, a change of position in response to the transaction the claimant seeks to reverse—making it impossible to right one injustice without inflicting another. So stated the defence sounds generous, but the test is one that a creditor/payee who takes money or instruments in payment of (or as security for) an antecedent debt may not be able to meet. The necessary showing becomes more elusive when we bear in mind how easily many changes of position can be reversed.

The competing 'mercantile rule' for these questions only required a name so long as it represented a departure and something worth debating. The essence of the departure was the proposition that a person who took money or instruments in payment of an antecedent debt—or even just as security for such a debt—gave 'valuable consideration' entitling him to protection against third party claims. The rule was controversial because it was clear from the outset—this was why the rule was developed—that neither the satisfaction nor the securing of antecedent debt necessarily involved giving up anything, or any other change of position, on the part of the creditor/payee. The eventual triumph of the mercantile rule marked a critical expansion of the available defences to restitution, since the third party claims cut off by treating antecedent debt as value are all restitution claims of one sort or another.

The rule about antecedent debt was no part of the law of restitution at the outset. A hard-headed commercial judge like Lord Mansfield was fully prepared to find that a creditor/payee who could not show a prejudicial change of position was not entitled to a defence. The plaintiff insurer in *Buller v Harrison*[17] had promptly paid a claim in the amount of £2,100, 'thinking the loss was fair'. Payment was made to defendant as agent of the insureds, who were 'resident at New York'. Discovering shortly thereafter that in fact 'it was a foul loss', the insurer sued the agent to recover the money. The agent's defence was that the insureds, at the time of the payment, had been indebted to the agent to the amount of £3,000 and that it had credited the

[16] *Moses v Macferlan* (1760) 2 Burr 1005, 1010, 1012.
[17] *Buller v Harrison* (1777) 2 Cowp 565; 98 ER 1243.

insurer's £2,100 against this antecedent debt. Lord Mansfield rejected the defence in memorable terms:[18]

> [S]hall a man, though innocent, gain by a mistake, or be in a better situation than if the mistake had not happened? Certainly not. In this case, there was no new credit, no acceptance of new bills, no fresh goods bought or money advanced. In short, no alteration in the situation which the defendant and his principals stood in towards each other on the 20th of April. What then is the case? The defendant has trusted Ludlow and Co. and given them credit. He trafficks to the country where they live, and has agents there who know how to get the money back. The plaintiff is a stranger to them and never heard of their names. Is it conscientious then, that the defendant should keep money which he has got by their misrepresentation, and should say, though there is no alteration in my account with my principal, this is a hit, I have got the money and I will keep it?

The law did not long remain in this position, but the equitable rule remained the point of comparison from which the mercantile rule was attacked and defended throughout the nineteenth century. After the mercantile rule emerged victorious, the competing positions tended to disappear from view. Those who recalled the debate sometimes suggested that one rule was only a version of the other: the American legal realist quip of the 1930s was that 'the defense of purchase for value may be nothing more than an instance of change of position grown doctrinaire'.[19] Approaching the subject today, with only the Uniform Commercial Code as a guide, a lawyer would not even recognise that he stood on an old battlefield, let alone what the fight had been about.

The place to start is the landmark New York case of *Coddington v Bay*, decided in 1821 by Chancellor James Kent and affirmed on appeal.[20] *Coddington* placed the law of New York in the direct line of Lord Mansfield's decision in *Buller v Harrison*, and New York held that ground for a century—supported by courts in only a handful of states—in opposition to the rising commercial tide.

[18] ibid 568.

[19] H Cohen, 'Change of Position in Quasi-Contracts' (1932) 45 *Harvard Law Review* 1333, 1342 (citing an anonymous note at (1923) 36 *Harvard Law Review* 858). For more earnest statements of the same idea, see SI Langmaid, 'Quasi-Contract—Change of Position by Receipt of Money in Satisfaction of a Pre-existing Obligation' (1933) 21 *California Law Review* 311, 319 ('The significant point is that the doctrine of purchaser for value, whether at law or in equity, rests upon and is merely a branch of a more general doctrine of change of position'); HW Ballantine, 'Purchase for Value and Estoppel' (1922) 6 *Minnesota Law Review* 87, 121 ('The rule as to cutting off equities has been crystallized into an artificial and technical doctrine by courts which have not clearly analyzed the "obvious equity" and policy of it. These are found in a kind of estoppel which generally exists, even if there is no inquiry in each particular case as to misreliance on ostensible ownership').

[20] *Coddington v Bay* 20 Johns 637 (NY 1822), affirming *Bay v Coddington* 5 Johns Ch 54 (NY Ch 1821).

Bay, residing in Hudson, NY, owned the schooner *Express*. He engaged agents Randolph & Savage in New York City to sell her on credit, instructing them to take 'unexceptionable paper'. The agents sold *Express* for $3,875, taking negotiable notes which (on a flimsy pretext) they delayed sending to Hudson. Eight days after the sale, the agents ceased paying their creditors. They assigned various assets (including Bay's notes) to Coddingtons, the defendants, to secure them against contingent 'responsibilities'. Coddingtons were almost but not quite creditors of the agents at this point: they were accommodation endorsers of some of the agents' unmatured notes. But as the notes would fall due in the coming weeks, and as the agents were now known to be insolvent, it was understandable that Coddingtons were eager to have security for the agents' impending obligations to them. Coddingtons sold some of Bay's notes a few days later and it was agreed that they had no notice that the notes belonged to someone else. Bay discovered what had happened and sued to recover the notes and their proceeds.

Unlike *Buller v Harrison*, the claim was not for money had and received, but to vindicate equitable ownership; accordingly, the defence was not 'change of position', but 'purchase for valuable consideration'. Yet just as we can see that the restitution claims in the two cases are essentially the same—the problem of involuntary transfer—so it is with the payees' defences. The defendants in *Coddington* argued that they were entitled to the same protection allowed to innocent purchasers of money and instruments. Chancellor Kent's opinion began by recalling the well-known authorities on which that defence was based:[21]

> In *Miller v Race,* (1 *Burr.* 452.) a bank note was stolen and came to the hands of the plaintiff, and he was held entitled to it. But the Court of *K. B.* considered bank notes as cash, which passed as money in the way of business; and the holder, in that case, came by the note, for a full and valuable consideration, by giving money in exchange for it, in the usual course of his business, and without notice of the robbery, and on those considerations he was entitled to the amount of the note. So, in *Grant v Vaughan,* (3 *Burr.* 1516. 1 *Black. Rep.* 785.) a bill of exchange payable to bearer, was lost, and the finder paid it to a grocer, for teas, and took the change. There the Court laid stress on the facts, that the holder came by the bill *bona fide,* and in the course of trade, and for a full and fair consideration, and that though he and the real owner were equally innocent, yet he was to be preferred, for the sake of commerce and confidence in negotiable paper. Again, in *Peacock v Rhodes,* (1 *Doug.* 633.) a bill of exchange, with a blank endorsement, was stolen and negotiated to a person who took it in the way of his trade, for cloth sold and cash for the balance, and he was held entitled to hold it. Lord *Mansfield* placed reliance on the circumstance that it was received in the course of trade.

Coddingtons, by contrast, 'were not holders for a valuable consideration within the meaning or within the policy of the law'. A valuable consideration

[21] *Bay v Coddington* (n 20) 57–58.

for this purpose—that is, a consideration sufficiently weighty to cut off prior equities—involved the sort of change of position that Lord Mansfield had required in *Buller v Harrison* and that the defendants here could not show:[22]

> In short, I have not been able to discover a case in which the holder of negotiable paper, fraudulently transferred to him, was deemed to have as good a title, in law or equity, as the true owner, unless he received it not only without notice, but in the course of business, and for a fair and valuable consideration given or allowed on his part, on the strength of that identical paper. It is the credit given to the paper, and the consideration *bona fide* paid on receiving it, that entitles the holder, on grounds of commercial policy, to such extraordinary protection, even in cases of the most palpable fraud. It is an exception to the general rule of law, and ought not to be carried beyond the necessity that created it.

The defendants appealed to New York's Court for the Correction of Errors, which affirmed Chancellor Kent by a vote of 22–7.[23] The published opinions emphatically approved and largely repeated Kent's authorities and reasoning, while adding two arguments that would become hallmarks of New York law on the subject—henceforth, 'the rule of *Coddington v Bay*'. One was to refute the contention that a creditor/payee's change of position might be inferred or presumed if one looked hard enough; in particular, that a payee who had not actually done anything on receipt the claimant's funds or paper might nevertheless have been 'lulled into inactivity'.[24] In New York, a change of position would not be inferred, at least when the facts of the case made it so unlikely:[25]

> It was suggested, that they might have lost the benefit of some other security, had they not taken these notes; but of this there is no proof or probability. It is not shown, or pretended, that *Randolph and Savage* had any other security to give; and it cannot be presumed, that they would have committed such a flagrant breach of faith, if they had any other available funds in their hands.

The second contribution made by the Court for the Correction of Errors was to underscore Lord Mansfield's equitable bottom line. Would a liability

[22] ibid 58–59.

[23] *Coddington v Bay* (n 20) 658. Under the New York Constitution of 1777, the members of the state's highest court included the president and members of the Senate, as well the Chancellor and the judges of the Supreme Court.

[24] Counsel for the defendant in *Buller v Harrison* had tried to argue that their client considered the money as his property at the time it was paid 'and for eleven days after', and that 'under this idea he was lulled into security, and did not take any means during that interval, to get the money from New York'. *Buller* (n 17) 1245. Lord Mansfield ignored this suggestion. The idea that a change of position might be presumed from a defendant's failure to act was frequently mentioned as one of the reasons to protect a creditor/payee. Following the decision in *Cocks v Masterman* (1829) 9 B & C 902, 908–09; 109 ER 335, it became one of the most prominent explanations of the rule of *Price v Neal*.

[25] *Coddington v Bay* (n 20) 650 (Spencer Ch J).

in restitution, under the circumstances of the case, leave the creditor/payee worse off than if the challenged transaction had never occurred?:[26]

> It would be inequitable, unreasonable and unjust that the benefit derived by the party claiming to hold, without correspondent injury if he could not hold, should be sufficient not only to countervail, but prevail over, the unmerited injury which the owner is to sustain by his consequent loss. The true test I take to be, that when the holder is left in as good a condition, after a retransfer, as he would have been had no transfer taken place, there the title of the owner shall prevail. This allows the rule, so far as it is dictated by commercial policy, to have its full effect, while it protects the owner of negotiable paper, necessarily intrusted, in the course of business, to the care of agents, from an injury revolting to every principle of moral equity.

Logically, such a 'but for' comparison merely paraphrases the equitable test of change of position, but it does so in a way that makes it intuitive and unmistakable. The equitable objection, thus stated, is one that a non-relying creditor/payee can never meet, and the mercantile rule that now developed in contradistinction to the equitable rule did not attempt to meet it. The rationale of the creditor/payee's defence, in its mercantile form, was not equitable at all.

The landmark on the opposite side of the question was *Swift v Tyson*, which was decided by the US Supreme Court in an opinion by Justice Joseph Story.[27] *Swift v Tyson* remains a famous case in US law, though it is known today for an altogether different point: namely, its clear statement of the rule that in deciding questions of general commercial law, the US federal courts were not bound by the judge-made law of the courts of the several states, but were free to follow their own view of the authorities and of the relevant principles of law and equity. This collateral issue of federal jurisdiction required some attention before the Court could reach the commercial question at the heart of the lawsuit. The case originated in New York, and one of the parties was arguing that it should be decided in accordance with New York law—the rule of *Coddington v Bay*—even though the suit was in federal court. Justice Story was determined to announce a contrary rule about the 'valuable consideration' needed to validate a transfer of commercial paper. As a necessary prelude, he ruled—more emphatically than the Supreme Court had previously had occasion to do—that the federal courts

[26] ibid 656–57 (Senator Vielie). All three opinions emphasised this point. See ibid 647–48 (Woodworth J) ('If the notes became effectual in their hands, then so much was gained; if not, they remained in *statu quo*'); ibid 650 (Spencer Ch J) ('If they have to account to the respondent for these notes, their situation is exactly as it would have been had the notes not been transferred to them').

[27] *Swift v Tyson* 41 US (16 Pet) 1 (1842).

were not bound to follow New York commercial law in deciding a New York case.[28]

Norton, a swindler in Maine, purported to sell land to Tyson, a victim in New York, misrepresenting both the attributes of the land and the state of his title. Tyson paid Norton for the land by accepting a draft at six months, drawn by Norton on Tyson and payable to Norton. Swift, one of Norton's creditors, held an overdue note on which Norton was liable. To redeem the defaulted note, Norton gave Swift several items of negotiable paper, including the draft that had been accepted by Tyson. Swift had no notice of any defect in the transaction between Norton and Tyson. On discovery of the facts, Tyson repudiated the fraudulent land deal with Norton and refused to honour the draft. Swift sued Tyson, claiming that as purchaser of the draft for a valuable consideration, he held it free of prior equities.

What made the case interesting was the assumption on all sides—not actually tested in this litigation—that Swift would not have been able to enforce the draft against Tyson in New York, where Tyson resided, because Swift had not given 'valuable consideration' within the rule of *Coddington v Bay*. Justice Story stated a broad rule to the contrary: that a transfer of a negotiable instrument either as payment of an antecedent debt, or as security for payment, is a transfer 'in the usual course of trade and business' and for a valuable consideration—entitling the transferee to the same protection against prior equities that was allowed to the innkeeper in *Miller v Race*. The part about a transfer for security was pure dictum, since it was unnecessary to the decision, but (as we shall see) it was actually the key feature of the commercial rule that Story intended to adopt for the federal courts.

[28] The federal Judiciary Act of 1789 provided 'that the laws of the several states ... shall be regarded as rules of decision, in trials at common law, in the courts of the United States, in cases where they apply'. The question was whether 'the laws of the several states' in that context referred only to state constitutions and statutes, or whether the phrase included the rules of judge-made law that might be followed in a particular state—for example, the extent of the 'valuable consideration' needed to qualify as a protected holder of commercial paper. According to Story: 'It has never been supposed by us, that the section did apply, or was designed to apply, to questions of a more general nature ... and especially to questions of general commercial law.' *Swift v Tyson* (n 27) 18–19. In this, Story was probably correct, both about what had previously been supposed and about what had been intended in 1789. When nineteenth-century lawyers spoke of 'the rule in *Swift v Tyson*', they were talking about antecedent debt, not 'rules of decision'. But unanticipated consequences of the original reading of the Judiciary Act eventually became intolerable. Once there had developed, at a few critical points, a significant divergence between 'federal common law' and the common law of a particular state, a plaintiff with access to both state and federal courts might select the law governing his case—and determine its outcome—by choosing the court in which to sue. The Supreme Court eventually responded to this problem of 'forum shopping' by holding that the Judiciary Act of 1789—assuming that it meant what Story said it meant—had been in that respect unconstitutional: *Erie R Co v Tompkins* 304 US 64 (1938). The result is that federal courts decide non-federal questions by applying the law of the state in which they sit. To a modern lawyer, 'the rule in *Swift v Tyson*' means only 'the rule that was overruled in *Erie v Tompkins*'.

The reasons given in *Swift v Tyson* are interesting for what they leave out: they make no reference whatever to the parties' competing equities. After explaining that the federal courts would not take their law from the courts of New York, Story reached the heart of the matter:[29]

> It becomes necessary for us, therefore, upon the present occasion, to express our own opinion of the true result of the commercial law upon the question now before us. And we have no hesitation in saying, that a pre-existing debt does constitute a valuable consideration, in the sense of the general rule already stated, as applicable to negotiable instruments ... And why, upon principle, should not a pre-existing debt be deemed such a valuable consideration?

We interrupt briefly to consider Story's rhetorical question.

Tyson (or any other defendant in his position) was obliged to present himself as a purchaser 'for a valuable consideration' not because it was an intuitive description of his situation, but because it was on that basis that the foundational decisions by Lord Mansfield (*Miller v Race*, *Grant v Vaughn*, *Peacock v Rhodes*) allowed the innocent taker of money or instruments to keep them against the restitution claim of a prior owner. The idea that a purchaser for value would be protected, whereas a donee would not, had been taken over from familiar equitable rules about bona fide purchase of trust property. An innocent purchaser who actually surrendered something of value had a change of position and a countervailing equity. A purchaser for 'present value' obviously qualified, and Lord Mansfield's payees had all been in this category.

It is less obvious that a creditor who accepts payment of a debt in stolen money has necessarily given anything of value or changed position. If payment is reversed, the debt is revived, and the creditor is possibly left where he started. Of course, the inconvenience to the repaid creditor might in fact be significant; the question of change of position would be burdensome to determine in individual cases, and there are other good reasons not to adopt such a rule. But what of the creditor who acquires someone else's property merely as security for debts already contracted and who can show no further advances, no forbearance and no previous security surrendered? If the lien is avoided, there is no prejudice to the creditor; if it is enforced, the creditor enjoys a windfall. There are reasons to recognise the validity of the pre-existing creditor's lien, but change of position and countervailing equity are plainly not among them. Nor did Justice Story assert that they were:[30]

> It is for the benefit and convenience of the commercial world, to give as wide an extent as practicable to the credit and circulation of negotiable paper, that it may pass not only as security for new purchases and advances, made upon the transfer

[29] *Swift v Tyson* (n 27) 19–20.
[30] ibid 20.

> thereof, but also in payment of, and as security for, pre-existing debts. The creditor is thereby enabled to realize or to secure his debt, and thus may safely give a prolonged credit, or forbear from taking any legal steps to enforce his rights. The debtor also has the advantage of making his negotiable securities of equivalent value to cash. But establish the opposite conclusion, that negotiable paper cannot be applied in payment of, or as security for, pre-existing debts, without letting in all the equities between the original and antecedent parties, and the value and circulation of such securities must be essentially diminished ...
>
> What, indeed, upon such a doctrine, would become of that large class of cases, where new notes are given by the same or by other parties, by way of renewal or security to banks, in lieu of old securities discounted by them, which have arrived at maturity? Probably, more than one-half of all bank transactions in our country, as well as those of other countries, are of this nature. The doctrine would strike a fatal blow at all discounts of negotiable securities for pre-existing debts.

The emphasis, somewhat unexpectedly, is on the less obvious proposition: that a taking for security (without a contemporaneous advance) is a purchase 'for valuable consideration'. Recall that this part of the rule was unnecessary to a decision of the case, since Swift had taken Tyson's paper in payment of Norton's debt, not as security. Consider, moreover, how awkward it is to explain that a creditor 'gives' anything—let alone 'valuable consideration'—if he merely takes collateral security for a pre-existing debt. These incongruities offer a hint that the central concern of *Swift v Tyson* is not what appears at first glance. The facts made it a case of owner v creditor. On such facts, the effect of the mercantile rule is that the creditor takes free of the owner's rights. He is 'unaffected with the equities between the antecedent parties'[31] and (given *Miller v Race*) he takes free of legal ownership as well. Let these results expand to fill their natural boundaries and ignore the differences between cash, instruments, bank transfers and what not, and the result is to give the innocent creditor/payee an affirmative defence to the owner's claim in restitution. Such precisely is the *Restatement*'s rule of 'bona fide payee'. But it is merely a consequence rather than the principal object of the rule of *Swift v Tyson*.

Justice Story's real concern is not with the restitution case of owner v creditor, but with the strictly commercial case of *creditor v creditor*. The critical function of the mercantile rule, in other words, was not to cut off the rights of 'antecedent parties' such as defrauded owners, but to confirm the validity of a transfer between 'immediate parties'—typically a bank and its customer. The transactions that Story is describing boil down to this. Customer delivers negotiable notes to his banker to serve as collateral security for outstanding loans and future advances. If Customer's loans are of longer

[31] ibid 19.

maturity than his collateral, Customer will eventually have to provide substitute collateral—probably in the form of more notes. Does the banker acquire a valid security interest in the substitute collateral? Once in a great while, the person challenging the banker's lien might be a defrauded prior owner, as in *Coddington v Bay*. More often the problem would be a challenge by Customer's unsecured creditors, upon Customer's insolvency, to the validity of the bank's lien.[32] The system of credit that Story describes could survive the occasional case like *Coddington v Bay*—the New York banks do not appear to have suffered appreciably from the New York rule. The 'fatal blow at all discounts of negotiable securities for pre-existing debt' would have been to tolerate any doubt about the validity of the pledge between the bank and its customer.

Cases like *Miller v Race* had already made it clear that a full-fledged purchaser for a valuable consideration—a payee who gave something valuable for what he received—was protected against adverse claims to the money, legal as well as equitable. The new mercantile rule expanded this protection to cases in which the element of exchange might not be readily apparent. But the older cases had already pointed the way to a more commercial way of thinking about the problem. The reason for protecting the innocent transferee of money or instruments, Lord Mansfield had suggested, was not really (or not only) his likely change of position, but rather 'upon account of the currency of it': the fact that—were the rule otherwise—'if a man paid to goldsmith 500*l.* in banknotes, the goldsmith could never pay them away'.[33] But if the reason for protecting the payee is the *currency* of money and money-substitutes, it is impossible to maintain a distinction between a goldsmith whose £500 is received in a cash sale and a goldsmith who takes the same notes in payment of his customer's account. In the same way, it was commercial usage—not countervailing equities—which required that a banker's lien be valid, whether the advances it secured were past, present or

[32] Story J relied on a number of English cases arising in this context, where the question was the extent to which bankers had given 'valuable consideration' when they took negotiable paper as collateral security for present and future advances to their customer, later a bankrupt. For example, in *Bosanquet v Dudman* 1 Stark (1814) 1, Lord Ellenborough was reported as saying that 'whenever the acceptances exceeded the cash balance, [the bankers] held all the collateral bills for value'. But Story J had not limited himself to stating a rule for the validity of the bankers' lien as against unsecured creditors. (He could not do so, given the facts of the case before him.) Of the English decisions, he said instead: 'They directly establish, that a *bona fide* holder, taking a negotiable note in payment of or as security for a pre-existing debt, is a holder for a valuable consideration, entitled to protection against *all the equities between the antecedent parties.*' *Swift v Tyson* (n 27) 22 (emphasis added). English authority on questions of commercial law commanded great respect, and the New York judges were immediately at pains to demonstrate that Story had misrepresented it. See *Stalker v McDonald* 6 Hill 93, 100–11 (NY 1843).

[33] *Miller v Race* (n 15) 457, 459; *cf Peacock v Rhodes* (1781) 2 Doug 633, 636; 99 ER 402 ('An assignee must take the thing assigned, subject to all the equity to which the original party was subject. If this rule applied to bills and promissory notes, it would stop their currency').

future. In both instances, the protected parties were called 'purchasers for a valuable consideration' not because this was an apt description, but because it was the accepted usage describing the intended legal result.

The New York courts indignantly rejected the result in *Swift v Tyson*, though they accepted Story's point about the market for commercial paper. Consideration that might be 'good' or 'sufficient' to validate a transfer between the immediate parties—a debtor's payment on account, or his pledge to secure past or future advances—was not the consideration of 'actual value' required 'to protect the holder of a negotiable security which has been passed to him in fraud of the rights of others'.[34] New York thus distinguished the commercial case of creditor v creditor, where the issue was the validity of a conveyance between the immediate parties, from the restitution case of owner v creditor, where the issue was cutting off 'prior equities'.[35] Such a distinction seems plausible enough, but most courts preferred to adopt a single rule for both cases. Ultimately the Bills of Exchange Act (1882) put an end to the discussion:

> Valuable consideration for a bill may be constituted by,—
>
> (a) Any consideration sufficient to support a simple contract;
> (b) An antecedent debt or liability. Such a debt or liability is deemed valuable consideration whether the bill is payable on demand or at a future time.[36]

The Act encouraged the use of the word 'value' as a relatively colourless substitute for 'valuable consideration'[37]—facilitating the understanding that the expression was really a term of art and that 'consideration' in this context need not be 'valuable' in any literal sense. In the US paraphrase that followed soon after, the Bills of Exchange Act became the Negotiable Instruments Law (NIL)—promulgated in 1896 as the first of the 'uniform laws' proposed (by a newly formed commission) for adoption by the legislatures of the several states:[38]

> Value is any consideration sufficient to support a simple contract. An antecedent or pre-existing debt constitutes value, and is deemed such whether the instrument is payable on demand or at a future time.

New York adopted the NIL in 1897, but 10 years later, the New York Court of Appeals was still enforcing the rule of *Coddington v Bay*.[39] As the Court

[34] *Stalker v McDonald* (n 32) 99–100.

[35] To cut off prior equities, a defendant had to show 'something more than a good consideration, a consideration which would be sufficient as between the parties to the transaction ... [Rather,] the consideration must be valuable and actually paid, and ... the defendant must have parted with value upon the faith of the purchase'. *Weaver v Barden* 49 NY 286, 291 (1872).

[36] Bills of Exchange Act (1882) 45 & 46 Vict ch 61, s 27(1).

[37] ibid s 2 ('"Value" means valuable consideration').

[38] Negotiable Instruments Law, § 32 (1896). The original text of the NIL (restyled 'Uniform Negotiable Instruments Act') is reproduced at 5 *Uniform Laws Annotated (Part 1)* (1943).

[39] See *Bank of America v Waydell* 187 NY 115, 120 (1907).

later explained: 'The New York rule was so well established that the inertia of *Coddington v Bay* carried it along for some distance before the external force of the Negotiable Instruments Law acted upon it.'[40]

The subsequent evolution of US law on this point is readily inferred from the text of the present-day Uniform Commercial Code (UCC). The list of circumstances in which 'value' is given for a negotiable instrument includes a transfer 'as payment of, or as security for, an antecedent claim against any person, whether or not the claim is due'.[41] An even more generous definition of 'value' protects the purchaser of goods, the secured lender, and everyone else within the scope of the Code.[42] Nor is there much doubt about how this came to be. Reflecting on his own work in drafting the UCC—under the direction of its Chief Reporter, Karl Llewellyn—Grant Gilmore recalled:[43]

> One of the ideas I took from Llewellyn's bounteous store was that the good faith purchaser is always right and that the story of his triumph was not only one of the most fascinating episodes in our nineteenth-century legal history (which it was), but was also one of continuing relevance for our own time (which, I have belatedly come to believe, it is not). That attitude, which was shared by almost all—perhaps all—the people who became involved in the Code's drafting, explains a great deal about the Code's treatment of third-party rights.

The old controversy about antecedent debt remains critical to the modern law of restitution because it is only two short steps from the rule of *Swift v Tyson* to a rule that allows creditor/payees a general defence. If antecedent debt is valuable consideration for transactions in instruments, then creditors paid in instruments defeat the prior owners of the instruments with which they are paid. Cash cannot be less negotiable than commercial paper, and other forms of payment are not going be treated differently in restitution from cash and paper, so the defence will eventually be made available to repaid creditors generally. And if the creditor's defence is good in cases of fraud or theft, as it was in its inception, then a fortiori it is good where the restitution claim alleges a possibly milder form of involuntary transfer, such as payment by mistake. It follows that if we accept the starting proposition about antecedent debt, a creditor who is repaid in someone else's money will not be liable to make restitution of the payment. This is what R3RUE calls the rule of 'bona fide payee'.

[40] *Kelso & Co v Ellis* 224 NY 528, 536–37 (1921) (C Pound J).

[41] UCC, s 3-303 (rev 1990).

[42] UCC, s 1-204 (rev 2001).

[43] G Gilmore, 'The Good Faith Purchase Idea and the Uniform Commercial Code: Confessions of a Repentant Draftsman' (1981) 15 *Georgia Law Review* 605. 'As a general rule', Gilmore observed on another occasion, 'anything—including negotiability—which was good enough for Lord Mansfield was good enough for Llewellyn. That attitude, unfortunately, carried through to the drafting of Article 3 [on negotiable instruments] of the Code, which can be described as the N.I.L. doubled in spades or negotiability *in excelsis*.' G Gilmore, 'Formalism and the Law of Negotiable Instruments' (1979) 13 *Creighton Law Review* 441, 460–61.

3. VICTIM v VICTIM

The first systematic account of the modern law of restitution, published by the American Law Institute in 1937, treated the mercantile rule for creditor/payees as one of its most basic propositions. Chapter 2 on 'Mistake, Including Fraud' included among its 'Definitions and General Rules' a standard version of bona fide purchase whereby:[44]

> A person who has entered into a transaction with another under such circumstances that, because of a mistake, he would be entitled to restitution from the other,
>
> (a) is not entitled to restitution from a third person who has received title to or a legal interest in the subject matter either from the other or from the transferor at the direction of the other, and has given value therefor without notice of the circumstances.

This was immediately followed by a partial definition of the term 'value'—mostly the part about antecedent debt:[45]

> § 14. Discharge for Value.
>
> (1) A creditor of another or one having a lien on another's property who has received from a third person any benefit in discharge of the debt or lien, is under no duty to make restitution therefor, although the discharge was given by mistake of the transferor as to his interests or duties, if the transferee made no misrepresentation and did not have notice of the transferor's mistake.

In their published notes on these sections, the American Law Institute's Reporters—Warren Seavey and Austin Scott of the Harvard Law School—dismissed the naïve idea that the rules of purchase for value reflected any concern with equitable outcomes. A purchaser from a thief obtained no protection, while the same purchase from an 'embezzling trustee' might yield good title:[46]

> In neither case is there a moral issue involved. The question is one of legal mechanics, or the operation of rules which determine who, as between equally innocent persons, is entitled to the subject matter ...
>
> It becomes clear, therefore, that as a new matter and from the standpoint of justice the result reached in any particular case might equally well be opposite to the result now reached under the rules. In other words, the rules as to bona fide purchase are not, as are the rules normally applicable to questions involving restitution, based upon the balance of justice between the parties, but merely upon technicalities.

[44] *Restatement of the Law of Restitution* (n 8) § 13.

[45] ibid § 14. The wording is awkward, since it is the transferee who gives the discharge (and the value), but the meaning is apparent.

[46] WA Seavey and AW Scott, *Notes on Certain Important Sections of Restatement of Restitution* (St Paul, MN, American Law Institute Publishers, 1937) 7–8.

The Reporters seem to be saying that in an important subset of cases, lying very close to the core of the subject, the law of restitution is unconcerned with equitable outcomes. This was a vast overstatement, if only because a purchaser for valuable consideration has normally changed position in some significant way. But their idea might be restated in less provocative terms. Without question, a rule that treats creditor/payees as purchasers for value will yield results that are inequitable in particular cases. (The most objectionable outcomes are probably those whereby a loss is fortuitously shifted from the party who would appropriately bear it to a party whose relation to the loss-making transaction is that of an innocent bystander.) Moreover, it is true that the rules of purchase for value—to the extent that they diverge from change of position—appear essentially amoral on this point, and it is true, finally, that courts will frequently tolerate inequitable outcomes for the sake of mercantile objectives that they consider more important than 'the balance of justice between the parties'.

Conceding all this, the cases in which the claimant and the defendant are successive victims of the same fraud still do not fit neatly with the others. It is not that these victim v victim cases all come out the other way, but when this element is added to the facts, otherwise uniform authority is suddenly divided, confidence wavers and reasoning is visibly perplexed.

To explain the scope and meaning of 'discharge for value', Seavey and Scott first offered five garden-variety illustrations of owner v creditor claims—cases in which the availability of the creditor/payee's defence is undisputed. They set the tone with a version of *Aiken v Short*:[47]

1. A, believing that he is devisee of B, mortgages his share in B's estate to C who, in order to sell the subject matter, pays D who has a prior mortgage thereon. In fact A is not B's devisee and has no share in B's estate. C is not entitled to restitution from D.

After four more illustrations much like this one, the atmosphere changes abruptly:[48]

6. A steals an automobile and mortgages it to B who lends him $500 thereon. A then borrows $700 from C, telling C of B's mortgage. In accordance with his agreement with A, C pays B $500 to discharge B's mortgage and gives A $200, taking a mortgage for $700. The owner of the car reclaims it. C is not entitled to restitution from B.
7. Purporting to be the owner of Blackacre A borrows $5000 from B, forging a note and mortgage in the name of the record owner of Blackacre. A then borrows $10,000 on a similarly forged mortgage of Blackacre from C who pays B $5,000 to discharge B's forged mortgage and to surrender the forged note, and pays A the remaining $5,000. C is not entitled to restitution from B.

[47] *Restatement of the Law of Restitution* (n 8) § 14, Illustration 1.
[48] ibid Illustrations 6–7.

By juxtaposing the owner v creditor and successive-fraud illustrations without a word of transition, the Reporters were implying that the cases were fundamentally the same. Their notes show that they knew better:[49]

> In Illustrations 6 and 7 ... the difficulty is that the payee never had a claim which was of substantial value ... Because of this, Mr. Patterson and Mr. Thurston, of the Advisers, believe that the payee had, in substance, lost his money when he originally lent the money to the thief or forger ... [Yet] the results in Illustrations 6 and 7 are consistent with the reasons for the doctrine of bona fide purchaser, since the payee acquired title to the money and surrendered something of technical value. In both of these cases the forger has defrauded both parties; the fact that the payee would have suffered had the technical rules as to bona fide purchaser not applied, is immaterial since this is frequently true in such cases ... The cases clearly support the results of Illustrations 1-5. *Upon Illustrations 6 and 7 the cases in point are neither numerous nor unanimous.*

In fact, the victim v victim cases are surprisingly numerous, and their very marked division of authority would allowed the Reporters, within the ordinary usages of the American Law Institute, to state the opposite outcomes for Illustrations 6 and 7.

To distinguish the successive fraud cases from the run of the mill, it would have been necessary to acknowledge that—*at least as between successive fraud victims*—the surrender of merely 'technical value' (in other words, of antecedent debt that was manifestly worthless) could not constitute the 'valuable consideration' that the doctrine of bona fide purchase purports to require. Reasons to resist such a distinction are not hard to reconstruct. To suggest that 'value' sometimes has to be actually valuable would seriously complicate the definition. It would imply the existence of different categories of cases—more or less mercantile, more or less concerned with 'the balance of justice'—whose differentiation would inevitably be a matter of difficulty. More generally, it would surrender some of the ground that had been steadily gained for the mercantile approach over the century following *Swift v Tyson* by acknowledging—contrary to the Reporters' professed convictions—that the rules of purchase for value were sometimes concerned with equity after all.

The Reporters' tactical decision made the law simpler to restate, but it made their Restatement of this point simpler than the reality. 'Discharge for value', followed too uncritically by R3RUE's 'bona fide payee', describes the result for the vast majority of ordinary-course commercial transactions, but the judicial response to the victim v victim scenario is more complex. Unable to escape the inherited formulation of the problem, the decisions for and against restitution pursue an old debate about the status of antecedent debt as 'value', while the most telling objection to restitution in victim v victim

[49] Seavey and Scott (n 46) 8–9 (emphasis added).

cases is rarely acknowledged. The real problem is that—when the parties are fellow victims of the same fraud—granting restitution does not obviously do any more for the balance of justice between the parties than denying it.

The facts of the classic successive-fraud cases are more entertaining than their schematic paraphrase (the Restatement's Illustrations 6 and 7), and the authorities were divided in a way that the Reporters did not acknowledge, but the arguments on either side were mostly predictable. Judges who favoured restitution saw a classic mistaken payment by V2 to V1, with no change of position and no 'value' given in exchange:[50]

> We are disposed to agree that an irrevocable change of position by defendant, so that a recovery will result in a loss to him, that is, put him in a worse position than he would have occupied had the money never been paid him, is a good defense to a recovery ... [But in] the case at bar we are unable to see that defendant, by receiving payment of his mortgage from plaintiff, and giving up the evidences of the supposed debt ... lost anything of value. The precise claim in this regard is that, had the payment not been made, defendant, when the mortgage became due, would have discovered that the mortgage was a forgery, and would have received payment from O'Donnell, who had not yet absconded, but was still doing business in Duluth. This claim is too uncertain and speculative. The evidence as to the dealings of O'Donnell warrant no inference that he would have paid the mortgage, but, on the contrary, convince us that he would either have forged a new mortgage in renewal of the old; or, if he feared discovery of his crimes, would have left the country, as he did do later. He was not in the business of paying his debts, but of obtaining money through forgery and fraud, and it is not shown that he could have been forced to pay. We conclude that the only reasonable inference is that, had plaintiff not paid defendant, he would be to-day the holder of a forged note and mortgage, but of nothing else in the way of satisfaction for the money O'Donnell procured of him through fraud.

[50] *Grand Lodge, AOUW of Minnesota v Towne* 136 Minn 72, 81—82 (1917). The dissenting opinion in *Walker v Conant* 69 Mich 321, 330–31 (1888), was to the same effect: 'Mrs. Conant, by releasing her mortgage, did not release her debt against Van Riper. Her claim still remains as good as it ever was against him. Mr. Walker never received anything from her, or any one else, for the money he let her have. The mortgage she discharged was the only thing she parted with for it, and that was worthless and void. Under such circumstances, to permit Mrs. Conant to withhold the money she received from Mr. Walker would not only be inequitable and unjust, but would be allowing her to reap the fruits of the crime committed by young Van Riper ... It is said by my Brother MORSE, in regard to Mrs. Conant's giving up her note and mortgage: "Her situation is changed, and without her fault, beyond all possible return or restoration." If by this it is meant she has given up for destruction a forged note and mortgage which she received for a loan of money made, it is true; but if by it is meant that her legal or equitable rights are changed, in the event she is obliged to return the money she received of Mr. Walker, I confess my inability to discover such change.' (Sherwood CJ). The same Morse and Sherwood JJ were the authors of the competing opinions in *Sherwood v Walker* 66 Mich 568 (1887), the most famous example of mutual mistake in American contract law. The case involved the sale of a purebred Aberdeen-Angus cow, Rose 2d of Aberlone, believed at the time of sale (by the seller at least) to be infertile, but discovered shortly thereafter to be with calf.

Judges who denied the claim sometimes began by arguing, disconcertingly, that V2 was not entitled to restitution because the funds he paid to V1 were not his money. Even when V2 paid V1 directly, he was acting at Swindler's direction and thus as Swindler's agent, with the result that the money belonged 'in legal contemplation' not to V2, but to Swindler himself.[51] This tortured notion is so unpersuasive that we can assume the real objections lay elsewhere. The standard arguments about antecedent debt were duly rehearsed. There had been at least a theoretical change of position through loss of recourse, even if the debtor was finishing his career in the penitentiary; a defendant who surrendered a forged note and mortgage 'has been damnified to some extent—how much cannot be told—if she has to lose the money paid to her'.[52] There had been at least 'technical value'; in other words, so long as the law refused to permit any examination of what an antecedent debt was actually worth. The underlying reason to deny restitution between victims, on this approach, was to avoid unsettling the protection of creditor/payees in the standard commercial setting:[53]

> She received [payment] in good faith, in satisfaction of a just and equitable claim, and when it was due, on honour and in conscience. And the authorities are uniform that where the money is received in good faith, and in the ordinary course of business, and for a valuable consideration, it cannot be recovered back because the money was fraudulently obtained of some other person by the payor. To hold otherwise would be to put every man who receives money in the due course of his business upon inquiry, at his peril, as to the manner in which such money was procured by the payor.

The implicit proposition—that the goal of assuring finality of payments or 'security of receipt' supersedes our usual interest in equitable outcomes—is more readily acceptable today than it was a century ago, and for many observers it will suffice. Both then and now, however, the special case of victim v victim restitution seemed to attract further reasoning or second thoughts. The argument for restitution was that Swindler should not be permitted to shift V1's loss to V2 by a further fraud:[54]

> [T]he defendant had been deceived and cheated out of his money, and had taken worthless notes therefor, and there would seem to be no reason for holding that he should be indemnified in the result of a like fraudulent deception practiced by the same impostor upon the plaintiff.

[51] See, eg, the majority opinion in *Walker v Conant* (n 50) 327; *Russell v Richard & Thalheimer* 6 Ala App 73 (1912).

[52] *Walker v Conant* (n 50) 326.

[53] ibid 329 (citations omitted).

[54] *Strauss v Hensey* 9 App DC 541, 547 (1896). *cf National Shawmut Bank of Boston v Fidelity Mutual Life Insurance Company* 318 Mass 142, 150 (1945) ('Before the plaintiff even considered making the payment to the defendant, the defendant had already lost its money, although it did not realize the fact').

But if equities were equal, there was no more reason for a court to shift the loss in the other direction, by ordering restitution:[55]

> If we look at this case from a purely equitable viewpoint, the result to which we must come will not be different than that above announced ... if respondent was innocent, so was the appellant. The equities in favour of the respondent are not less great than those running with the appellant. We think the judgment of the trial court [denying restitution] was right, and it is affirmed.

Between two victims are identically situated, the question comes down to this: whether the inability to demonstrate a superior equity is more harmful to the cause of action for unjust enrichment or to an innocent recipient's defence. Judicial views were plainly divided and either answer—indeed, the question itself—seems unsatisfactory.

If the task is to decide, as courts on either side of the question have routinely assumed, 'which of the innocent parties must bear a loss caused by the forgery and fraud'[56] and, moreover, if there is no equitable reason to shift a loss either one way or another, then the affirmative defence in victim v victim cases may be simply a matter of inertia. The accepted formulation of the problem, in which a claim to recover a mistaken payment is met with some sort of defence, to be judged good or bad, leaves no room for the obvious equitable response: that between victims identically situated the loss should be shared. Is it possible to recast the claim of victim v victim to make sharing an accessible alternative?

4. JESSEL'S BAG IN REVERSE

Recent decisions in the US federal courts, dealing with the allocation of losses in the aftermath of various Ponzi schemes, have imposed sharing between victims by ignoring the law that would ordinarily stand in the way. The setting is the one described at the outset in which a receiver—charged with the duty to make an equitable distribution—weighs the competing claims of victims to whatever residual assets it has been possible to marshal. The universal and unquestioned starting assumption of the courts in these cases is that equality is equity and that equality between fraud victims means rateable allocation in proportion to the investments they were originally tricked into making.

[55] *Gaffner v American Finance Co* 120 Wash 76, 81; 206 P 916, 918 (1922). The court appears to be momentarily confused about which party was the appellant (since the trial court had denied restitution to V2), but here too the intended meaning is clear: 'if the claimant was innocent, so too was the defendant'.

[56] *National Shawmut Bank* (n 54) 143.

Two circumstances potentially obstruct a rateable distribution on this basis. The first is the possibility that the assets of some claimants remain identifiable in the wreckage of the scheme—for example, because one victim's securities have been left untouched in Swindler's desk drawer, while those of the other victims were all sold and commingled. Ordinary property rules allow the defrauded owner to retake identifiable assets, thereby unsettling the incidence of losses between victims in a way that is purely fortuitous. A recent line of US cases resolves this difficulty by refusing to respect the usual boundaries of ownership. If allowing an owner to retake identifiable property produces inequitable consequences, then the baseline of ownership can be redrawn—by a judicial decree (in effect) that all victims lost their property when it first left their hands.[57] So radical a recharacterisation would be unthinkable if the doctrines affected were closer to the immediate concerns of contemporary judges, but a complete indifference to traditional authority has allowed these courts to decide old problems as if they were new.

The second potential obstacle to a rateable distribution is the one that has been the focus of this chapter: the defence to restitution normally allowed to a creditor/payee. Many recent US Ponzi decisions confront the question of how to account for prior distributions from the scheme, by which earlier victims have been partially repaid with funds obtained by fraud from subsequent victims. In a conventional analysis, this is the problem just rehearsed, turning on the presence or absence of change of position and on whether V1 gives 'value' when he takes payment in reduction or discharge of his claims against Swindler—such as they are. The orthodox answer is that prior withdrawals are immune from restitution to the extent of each recipient's

[57] In the first of a recent line of cases, *SEC v Elliott* 953 F2d 1560 (11th Cir 1992), victims 'loaned' their securities to swindler, delivering registered certificates with stock powers attached. Most of the securities entrusted in this way had been sold and the proceeds lost; some had been left untouched, still registered in the names of the victims who had 'loaned' them. The receiver (with the approval of the district court) refused to restore these securities to their previous owners. Doing so 'would create inequitable results, in that certain investors would recoup 100% of their investment while others would receive substantially less' (ibid 1569). The Eleventh Circuit agreed: 'Legally, these investors occupy the same position as the other investors whose securities were sold. All investors were defrauded. All investors were cleverly persuaded to part with their securities' (ibid). In *United States v Durham* 86 F3d 70 (5th Cir 1996), the funds of 13 victims had been commingled in swindler's bank account, which had a remaining balance of $83,000 when the scheme was halted. The sequence of deposits and withdrawals was such that one of the last victims was able to identify $70,000 of this balance as the product of its own contribution, based on 'uncontroverted evidence' and orthodox tracing rules. Finding that this claimant's ability to trace its funds was 'the result of the merely fortuitous fact that the defrauders spent the money of the other victims first', the lower court 'elected in the interest of equity to distribute the $83,000 pro rata'. Affirming this decision, the appellate court declared that it would not 'chain the hands of the court in Equity to do what is right under the circumstances' (ibid 71, 73). For a fuller account of these developments, see A Kull, 'Ponzi, Property, and Luck' (2014) 100 *Iowa Law Review* 291.

original investment.[58] The repaid victim has given 'value' to the extent that his inchoate restitution claim against swindler was thereby reduced—no questions being asked about the liquidation value of that claim—so the effect of a withdrawal is the same as if he had invested a smaller amount in the first place.

The courts in recent cases have been increasingly uncomfortable with this result, since the obvious effect of allowing V1 to reduce his net loss by prior withdrawals is to increase the net loss of V2 and every other victim. A purely rateable allocation, on the other hand, would require the denial of any affirmative defence in victim v victim restitution—and the courts have been understandably reluctant to ask that prior withdrawals be repaid. All repaid victims would assert (and many could demonstrate) a change of position in reliance on their withdrawals, giving them a good defence even if 'antecedent debt' is entirely disregarded. Given the cost of making the necessary determinations, there are many cases in which the assets recovered for rateable distribution could never justify the expense of recovering them. It is far easier to adjust a payment error by altering future distributions than by pursuing restitution of what was paid by mistake.

Recent innovations in post-Ponzi administration have been greatly facilitated by the fact that—unlike the judge in the case of V2 v V1—the receivers whose objective is rateable recovery have assets in their hands for future distribution. Confronted with the problem of prior withdrawals, they have discovered that it is possible to go some distance towards equalising net losses by adjusting the victims' 'distributive shares'—that is, without asking that any victim put his hand in his pocket to restore a payment previously received. The result, while apparently a product of sheer improvisation, actually achieves a compromise of some elegance.

The decisions do not frame the issue as a matter of claims and defences in restitution. They describe instead a choice between methods for achieving an equitable distribution: principally, the 'net loss method' v the newly developed (and obscurely named) 'rising tide method'. 'Net loss' is the orthodox rule of bona fide payee: it allows V1 to keep what he has withdrawn, reducing his net loss to that extent, and to claim a rateable distribution (based on all victims' net losses) of whatever assets have been marshalled. 'Rising tide' is a composite in which—while V1's prior withdrawals are not required to be repaid in cash—they are nevertheless counted (i) as part of the assets theoretically available for distribution and (ii) against V1's rateable share of those assets. Analysed in conventional restitution terms, the effect of 'rising tide' is to disallow V1's defence as creditor/payee while adopting a countervailing presumption that V1 has changed position on receipt of any repayment.[59]

[58] See R3RUE, § 67, Comment *f*, and cases cited in the Reporter's Note *ad loc.*
[59] See Kull (n 57) 306–12.

There may be an easier way to put it. If we accept the starting premise about victims' relative entitlements, a victim who has received a prior distribution from the scheme resembles a trust beneficiary who has received more than his share of income. An attractive analogy for 'rising tide' distribution may thus be found in the trust doctrine of 'adjustment' or 'recoupment'. When a trustee has overpaid one of several beneficiaries and there remain trust assets for future distribution, the authorities recognise a rule by which (i) the overpaid beneficiary may or may not be affirmatively liable to restore the overpayment—certainly not, if he has changed position—but (ii) the amount of the overpayment may at any rate be recouped, as far as possible, by deduction from his share of future distributions.[60] 'Rising tide' as a formula for adjustment between Ponzi victims has not been explicitly justified by reference to this doctrine (or any other), but the equitable intuition that guides the response to the two situations appears to be one and the same.

If rateable recovery represents justice between Ponzi victims, it should be justice between V2 and V1 as well. Accepted methods of restitution cannot achieve this result. A binary, all-or-nothing approach that either protects the repaid earlier victim as a purchaser for value or else denies protection on the ground that value has not been given will either shift the loss or leave things alone. Accepting this limitation leads quickly to the unattractive proposition, endorsed by the 1937 *Restatement*, that these cases are decided by technical rules to which considerations of justice are irrelevant.

In the Ponzi aftermath, where funds contributed by individual victims are normally untraceable, there may be no practical alternative to treating whatever can be marshalled as a commingled fund in which victims share rateably. By contrast, V2 can show exactly what happened to his money: it was paid to V1, often by V2 himself. Existing rules tell us only that this money belongs to one victim or the other. To share losses in these cases as well, it would be necessary to recharacterise the ownership of *both* victims' funds. The necessary rule is one by which assets entrusted to Swindler—whether by V1, V2 or V*n*, and whether traceable or not—become from that moment part of a commingled fund belonging to all victims in proportion to their contributions.

Equitable division between victims of a common fraud would thus implicate a significant change in property rules. Such a change is radical, but no longer unthinkable. Courts that refuse to allow Ponzi victims to retake even property identifiable *in specie* have been applying new rules for some

[60] See, eg, *Lewin on Trusts*, para 42-010 (19th ed 2015); *Snell's Equity*, para 30-049 (33rd ed 2015); *Restatement Second, Trusts* § 254 (1959); 4 *Scott & Ascher on Trusts* s 25.2.4 (5th ed 2007) (absent change of position, 'there is no reason why the [overpaid] beneficiary should be permitted to profit at the expense of the other beneficiaries'). I am indebted for this observation to the Hon Sir Launcelot Henderson.

time—though without acknowledgment, because the courts do not see what they are doing in traditional terms.[61]

Reaching such results plainly requires that a great deal of law be ignored or remade. Yet the problem arises in an area where ownership already depends, in important instances, on equitable variations of legal rules. Suppose that V2's funds—instead of being paid over to V1—are paid instead into Swindler's bank account, where there is a substantial pre-existing balance. Swindler withdraws and dissipates half. By legal logic, V2's interest in Swindler's account could only be an undivided fraction of the whole and his funds must therefore have been diminished *pari passu* by Swindler's dissipation. Of course, the result is otherwise, but only because the ordinary logic of ownership has been modified, by main force, to do justice between a wrongdoer and his victim.[62] A rule by which assets contributed by fraud victims become from that moment part of a commingled fund would be like 'Jessel's Bag' in reverse—a 'commingling fiction' instead of a 'tracing fiction'—and designed, in this instance, to do justice between the wrongdoer's victims inter se. Decisions to this effect may be impossible to square with previous authority, but they are arguably no more radical than *Re Hallett's Estate*.

[61] See n 57.

[62] See *Re Hallett's Estate (Knatchbull v Hallett)* (1879) 13 Ch D 696 (CA).

11

Bona Fide Purchase as a Defence in Unjust Enrichment

SONJA MEIER*

THE SUBJECT OF this chapter is the role of the defence of bona fide purchase within the law of unjust enrichment and the law of restitution. After *Lipkin Gorman v Karpnale*,[1] it is widely accepted that bona fide purchase can be raised as a defence to a personal claim for the value of property received by the defendant, although there is controversy as to whether the successful claim in that action was a claim in property, restitution or unjust enrichment. There also seems to be widespread acceptance today that bona fide purchase is not merely a subspecies of change of position.[2] In *Lipkin Gorman*, both defences were treated separately. The requirements regarding the defendant's state of mind may not be the same. Change of position is said to work *pro tanto*, only so far as is necessary to prevent the defendant from sustaining a loss if he is obliged to return the

* I am grateful to Charles Mitchell for his valuable comments at the conference.

[1] *Lipkin Gorman v Karpnale Ltd* [1991] 2 AC 548 (HL).

[2] Lord Goff in *Lipkin* (ibid) 580 f; K Barker, 'After Change of Position: Good Faith Exchange in the Modern Law of Restitution' in P Birks (ed), *Laundering and Tracing* (Oxford, Clarendon Press, 1995) 195 ff; K Barker, 'Bona Fide Purchase as a Defence to Unjust Enrichment Claims: A Concise Restatement' [1999] *Restitution Law Review* 86; W Swadling, 'Restitution and Bona Fide Purchase' in W Swadling (ed), *The Limits of Restitutionary Claims: A Comparative Analysis* (London, United Kingdom National Committee of Comparative Law, 1997) 100, 103; P Key, 'Bona Fide Purchase as a Defence in the Law of Restitution' [1994] *Lloyd's Maritime and Commercial Law Quarterly* 422 ff; R Nolan, 'Change of Position' in P Birks (ed), *Laundering and Tracing* (Oxford, Clarendon Press, 1995) 186 f; P Millett, 'Restitution and Constructive Trusts' in WR Cornish, R Nolan, J O'Sullivan and G Virgo (eds), *Restitution—Past, Present and Future, Essays in Honour of Gareth Jones* (Oxford, Hart Publishing, 1998) 209; A Burrows, *The Law of Restitution*, 3rd edn (Oxford, Oxford University Press, 2011) 575 f; A Burrows, *A Restatement of the English Law of Unjust Enrichment* (Oxford, Oxford University Press, 2012) 133, 135 f and ss 23, 27; G Virgo, *The Principles of the Law of Restitution*, 2nd edn (Oxford, Oxford University Press, 2006) 660, 714; C Mitchell, P Mitchell and S Watterson (eds), *Goff & Jones: The Law of Unjust Enrichment*, 8th edn (London, Sweet & Maxwell, 2011) [29-10] (hereinafter *Goff & Jones*); *cf* the different view by P Birks, 'The English Recognition of Unjust Enrichment' [1991] *Lloyd's Maritime and Commercial Law Quarterly* 490 f; P Birks, *Restitution—The Future* (Sydney, Federation Press, 1992) 132 ff.

benefit received.[3] In contrast, bona fide purchase is an absolute defence, protecting not only the individual defendant but also third parties who have received the property from him. Bona fide purchase plays, if at all, only a limited role in restitution or unjust enrichment. It seems to be widely accepted today that its application is restricted to cases where the defendant has acquired property under a contract with a third party.[4]

Underlying these differences are the different functions of the defences. Change of position protects the individual defendant from sustaining a loss in case he has to return the benefit received. Bona fide purchase, by contrast, is said to protect the defendant's reliance on his exchange transaction with a third party.[5] However, the exact ratio and the scope of application of this defence are far from clear. This chapter will look at these questions, also with some comparison of the English position to German law, although it has to be borne in mind that there are fundamental differences concerning the law of property between English and German law which make a comparison particularly difficult.

1. BONA FIDE PURCHASE AS A MEANS OF ACQUIRING TITLE

In both English and German law, bona fide purchase plays a role in the law of property. It constitutes an exception to the general principle of *nemo dat quod non habet*: nobody can give a better title than he himself has. In exceptional circumstances, the principle of bona fide purchase enables a transferee to acquire good title from a transferor who had no such title to give. The question whether and to what extent the law should allow a bona fide purchase is a policy decision which has to balance the competing interests of security of ownership and security of transactions. It is therefore not surprising that the requirements of a bona fide purchase vary considerably in different legal systems.

In English law, the main cases of bona fide purchase seem to be the following:[6] (i) at common law, where money has been received for value and

[3] This is true only if one does not follow Peter Birks' argument that a court will, when applying the change of position defence, not inquire into the value of the consideration: P Birks, *Unjust Enrichment*, 2nd edn (Oxford, Oxford University Press, 2005) 241 f. Another difference mentioned by Barker, 'Good Faith Exchange' (n 2) 195, namely that bona fide purchase is applicable even in cases where value has been given to the third party before receipt, may turn out not to exist after all if it is accepted that change of position covers acts in reliance of an anticipated receipt which takes place afterwards; see Birks, *Unjust Enrichment* (ibid) 211 f; Burrows, *Restitution* (n 2) 532 ff; Virgo (n 2) 701 f.

[4] Barker, 'Good Faith Exchange' (n 2) 198 ff; Barker, 'Bona Fide Purchase' (n 2) 79, 87 ff; Swadling, 'Bona Fide Purchase' (n 2) 94 f, 101 f; Millett (n 2) 209; Burrows, *Restitution* (n 2) 580.

[5] Swadling, 'Bona Fide Purchase' (n 2) 103 f; Barker, 'Bona Fide Purchase' (n 2) 86; Virgo (n 2) 657; *Goff & Jones* (n 2) [29-11].

[6] Swadling, 'Bona Fide Purchase' (n 2) 82 ff; *Goff & Jones* (n 2) [29-03] ff; D Fox, *Property Rights in Money* (Oxford, Oxford University Press, 2008) [8.20] ff.

in good faith, the transferee will get good title to it even where the transferor has no title to give; (ii) a bona fide purchaser of a legal estate for value without notice of the equitable proprietary rights of third parties acquires the property free of such equitable rights; (iii) whereas rescission of a contract (or a deed of gift) for misrepresentation, duress, undue influence or non-disclosure can revest legal title in the transferor or create an equitable title to the property transferred, rescission does not affect the position of a third party having acquired a legal or equitable interest in the property bona fide and for value; (iv) there are also some statutory cases of bona fide purchase, in particular sections 24 and 25 of the Sale of Goods Act 1979 (UK) (sellers and buyers in possession). In equity, a bona fide purchase requires value to be given, not merely promised.[7] The giving of value and the transfer of property need not be simultaneous, provided that, at the latest date, the purchaser was still in good faith or not fixed with notice.

German law, which does not distinguish between law and equity, has only one type of ownership. A bona fide acquisition of movables from a non-owner requires: (i) an agreement between the transferor and the transferee that ownership shall pass; (ii) the delivery of the property to the transferee, or similar events making the transferee a possessor; and (iii) good faith of the transferee, meaning that he had no knowledge of the lack of title and was not grossly negligent.[8] However, ownership will not pass if the property was stolen or lost by the owner, except in the case of money.[9] In the case of land, bona fide acquisition is only possible if the transferor has been incorrectly identified as the owner of the land in the official land register.[10] Whereas German law necessarily requires an agreement between the transferor and the transferee about the passing of ownership, the underlying contract (in most cases a contract of sale) need not be valid.[11] The biggest difference to English law is that value need neither be promised nor given: even a donee can in good faith acquire title from a non-owner.[12]

Returning to English law, the question is whether, and in what cases, bona fide purchase can work as a defence in unjust enrichment and/or restitution

[7] See, eg, Barker, 'Bona Fide Purchase' (n 2) 83; Fox (n 6) [8.39] ff. This requirement may not exist at law; *cf Goff & Jones* (n 2) [29-06]; D Sheehan, *The Principles of Personal Property Law* (Oxford, Hart Publishing, 2011) 250; Fox (n 6) [8.33] ff.

[8] BGB (Civil Code), §§ 932–34. For accounts in English, see C Zülch, 'Bona Fide Purchase, Property and Restitution: Lipkin Gorman v. Karpnale in German Law' in Swadling (ed), *The Limits of Restitutionary Claims* (n 2) 108 ff; B Häcker, *Consequences of Impaired Consent Transfers* (Tübingen, Mohr Siebeck, 2009) 52 f, 217 f; S van Erp and B Akkermans, *Cases, Materials and Text on Property Law, Ius Commune Casebooks for the Common Law of Europe* (Oxford, Hart Publishing, 2012) 931 ff.

[9] BGB, § 935.

[10] BGB, § 892.

[11] See, in English, Zülch (n 8) 122 ff; as to the German principle of abstraction, see Häcker (n 8) 49 f, 58 ff; van Erp and Akkermans (n 8) 931 ff.

[12] J Oechsler in FJ Säcker (ed), *Münchener Kommentar zum Bürgerlichen Gesetzbuch*, Vol 6, 6th edn (Munich, CH Beck, 2013) § 932 [33].

law. It is controversial whether bona fide purchase applies in the law of unjust enrichment,[13] or in restitution outside unjust enrichment,[14] or only in the law of property.[15] The answer mainly depends on how the terms 'unjust enrichment', 'restitution' and 'proprietary rights' are defined.

2. BONA FIDE PURCHASE AND PROPRIETARY REMEDIES

2.1. Pure Proprietary Claims

The claimant C may assert a pre-existing title in property held by D, ie, he may assert that he had legal or equitable title before the events giving rise to the claim, that he never lost his title and that the title relates to the exact property held by D, with no tracing or rescission involved. A case at law is where a third party T steals C's car or banknote and gives it to D. In contrast to the civil law, there is no general vindication of property at common law; instead, C may sue D in conversion. In some cases, C may have the property returned to him. An example in equity is the case where T transfers shares which he holds on trust for C to D. C may assert a continuing equitable title towards D; this may take the form of demanding that the legal title is transferred to him. In all these cases, where C's remedy depends on him still having title to the property held by D, D can defend the action by establishing that the requirements of a bona fide purchase were met when he acquired the property from T.

Although the remedy by virtue of which C can recover the property may be called 'restitution', there seems to be general agreement today that C's rights against D are not based on unjust enrichment.[16] C's claim is based on its pre-existing title, not on an enrichment on the part of D. C is 'vindicating' (not necessarily in the technical sense) his continuing property, in some cases with the help of tort law. Bona fide purchase is important here as a defence because change of position seems to be no defence against such 'pure proprietary' claims.

The role of bona fide purchase in these cases may be a defence in the broad sense of the term insofar as it is for the defendant to establish its

[13] Birks (n 3) 240 ff; Burrows, *Restitution* (n 2) 574 ff; Burrows, *Restatement* (n 2) 131 ff; Barker, 'Good Faith Exchange' (n 2) 211 ff; Barker, 'Bona Fide Purchase' (n 2) 78; L Smith, 'Unjust Enrichment, Property and the Structure of Trusts' (2000) 116 *LQR* 427 f; *Goff & Jones* (n 2) [29-09].

[14] Virgo (n 2) 656, 714.

[15] Key (n 2) 425 ff; Swadling, 'Bona Fide Purchase' (n 2) 92 ff; *Papamichael v National Westminster Bank plc (No 2)* [2003] EWHC 164 (Comm); [2003] 1 Lloyd's Rep 341 [253] (Judge Chambers QC).

[16] Birks (n 3) 27, 36, 64 f; Burrows, *Restitution* (n 2) 122, 169, 432; Virgo (n 2) 11 f; *Goff & Jones* (n 2) [8-15], [8-77].

elements. However, it seems to be no defence in the narrow sense of being a fact that is able to extinguish an otherwise given cause of action.[17] A pure proprietary claim requires a still-existing title on the part of the claimant. Where the requirements of a bona fide purchase are met at the moment that the defendant receives the asset from the third party, he acquires a good title, free of any pre-existing legal or equitable rights on part of the claimant. The claimant will no longer be able to assert his proprietary rights against the defendant. Thus, bona fide purchase simply removes the main requirement of the claim. A similar position can be found in German law. There, a bona fide purchase extinguishes the claimant's ownership, thus defeating the possibility of vindicating the property.

2.2. Proprietary Claims Involving Tracing or Rescission

In some cases where C claims to have an existing legal or equitable title to property held by D, he has to rely on the rules of tracing into substitutes in order to establish this title. Examples at law are the case where T steals a banknote from C, uses it to buy a car and transfers the car to D, who still holds the car (exchange before receipt), or the case where T steals a banknote from C and gives it to D, who uses it to buy a car which he still holds (exchange after receipt). Similarly, in equity, T may misappropriate trust money to buy a car which he then transfers to D, or he may, in breach of trust, give trust money to D, who uses it to buy a car for himself. If C now claims to have a proprietary right in the car held by D, D can successfully defend the action by establishing that the requirements of a bona fide purchase were met at the moment he acquired the money or the car from T.

There is controversy as to whether these kinds of claims depend on an unjust enrichment. For some authors, there is no difference to the abovementioned cases of 'pure' proprietary rights: The claimant merely vindicates his property rights, which can be traced from the original asset into the substitute in the defendant's hands.[18] This transfer of property rights is part of the law of property; rights *in rem* cannot be generated by unjust enrichment. This position was endorsed in *Foskett v McKeown*.[19] Others, by contrast,

[17] As to the difference between defences and denials, see J Goudkamp and C Mitchell, 'Denials and Defences in the Law of Unjust Enrichment' in C Mitchell and W Swadling (eds), *The Restatement Third: Restitution and Unjust Enrichment* (Oxford, Hart Publishing, 2013) 133.

[18] Virgo (n 2) 11 ff, 571 ff; W Swadling, 'Ignorance and Unjust Enrichment: The Problem of Title' (2008) 28 *OJLS* 627 ff; RB Grantham and CEF Rickett, 'Property and Unjust Enrichment: Categorical Truths or Unnecessary Complexity?' [1997] *New Zealand Law Review* 678; *Trustee of the Property of FC Jones & Sons v Jones* [1997] Ch 159 (CA) 168 (Millett LJ).

[19] *Foskett v McKeown* [2001] 1 AC 102 (HL) 108 (Lord Browne-Wilkinson), 115 (Lord Hoffmann), 127 ff (Lord Millett).

maintain that the power of the claimant to revest his property can only be explained by the unjust enrichment following from the unauthorised substitution. The resulting remedy *in rem* by C against D can then be seen as a restitutionary proprietary right created in response to an unjust enrichment.[20] An alternative view is to say that the remedy *in rem* is a vindication that does not depend on unjust enrichment, but that the proprietary rights which are vindicated are generated by unjust enrichment.[21]

The same controversy exists in cases where the claimant, having lost his legal title, asserts a right *in rem* based on an equitable title, which is arguably only created as a response to the circumstances of the loss of legal title,[22] or where the claimant's title to the property held by the defendant depends upon a rescission of a contract. Some say that this is a proprietary remedy generated by unjust enrichment, while others speak of the claimant simply vindicating his property rights.

Irrespective of whether these kinds of proprietary rights belong to the law of property or to unjust enrichment, it is clear that they can be defeated by a bona fide purchase for value.[23] The classification is relevant, however, in relation to the defence of change of position. If these claims belong to the law of property where change of position has no role to play,[24] the defence of bona fide purchase will be far more important than it would be if the claims were characterised as restitutionary proprietary claims against which the defence of change of position was available.[25]

The classification may also be relevant for answering the question whether bona fide purchase is a defence or rather a denial. For those who regard these claims as belonging to the law of property, bona fide purchase works as a denial in the same way as described above: it simply removes the main requirement of any claim *in rem*, namely the right to assert a title or a power *in rem*. It may be different for those who regard restitutionary proprietary claims as generated by unjust enrichment. Seen in this way, the defendant, holding a benefit which is a traceable substitute of a property of

[20] A Burrows, 'Proprietary Restitution: Unmasking Unjust Enrichment' (2001) 117 *LQR* 412; Burrows, *Restitution* (n 2) 118 f, 122, 168 ff, 432 f; *Goff & Jones* (n 2) [8-17] ff, [8-74] ff; L Smith, *The Law of Tracing* (Oxford, Clarendon Press, 1997) 292 ff, 300; Sheehan (n 7) 252 ff.

[21] Birks (n 3) 32 ff, 65 f, 68 f, 180 ff.

[22] *cf Chase Manhattan Bank v British-Israel Bank* [1981] Ch 105 (Ch D).

[23] *Banque Belge pour l'Etranger v Hambrouck* [1921] 1 KB 321 (CA) 324 ff, 328 ff (Bankes and Scrutton LJJ); *In Re Diplock* [1948] Ch 465 (CA) 522; *Agip (Africa) v Jackson* [1990] Ch 265 (Ch D) 287 (Millett J); *Eagle Trust v SBC Securities* [1993] 1 WLR 484 (Ch D) (Vinelott J); *Polly Peck International v Nadir (No 2)* [1992] 4 All ER 769 (CA); *Foskett* (n 19) 108 f, 127, 129.

[24] Virgo (n 2) 572, 709 f; *Foskett* (n 19) 129 (Lord Millett); *cf Boscawen v Bajwa* [1996] 1 WLR 328 (CA) 334 (Millett LJ).

[25] Nolan (n 2) 176 ff; Smith (n 20) 384 f; Birks (n 3) 209 f; Burrows, *Restitution* (n 2) 122, 547; *Goff & Jones* (n 2) [27-55]; Sheehan (n 7) 254; see also the contribution of R Chambers in ch 6 of this volume.

the claimant, is enriched at the claimant's expense. Since the claimant did not consent to the substitution, the enrichment is unjust. A response may be to give the claimant a power to assert a proprietary right over the asset. In the event that the defendant is a bona fide purchaser for value, the claim will be defeated, although all elements of the cause of action are given.

3. BONA FIDE PURCHASE AND PERSONAL CLAIMS BASED ON RECEIPT

3.1. Personal Claims at Law

In *Lipkin Gorman*, bona fide purchase was held to be a possible defence to a personal claim for value received (even though, on the facts of the case, the defendant could not establish its existence). It is therefore widely accepted that bona fide purchase can be a defence against a personal claim of the *Lipkin Gorman* type.[26] The nature of this claim, however, is controversial. Its essence is that the defendant receives property from a third party which, at the time of receipt, is the property of the claimant, or a traceable substitute of it, and that the claimant did not consent to the transfer. It is a personal claim for the value of the asset at the moment of receipt.[27] It does not depend on whether the asset still exists or whether the claimant still has a title or a power *in rem*.[28] The simplest case is where the claimant has a pre-existing title, as where T takes C's banknote and gives it to D. More difficult is the case where the title of the claimant depends on tracing or on another operation of law, as where T takes C's car, exchanges it for a banknote and gives the banknote to D. In *Lipkin Gorman*, Cass (the third party) acquired legal title in the money he drew from the partnership account. The judgment was based on the assumption that this money, as well as the money received by the defendant club, was a traceable substitute of the firm's chose

[26] Birks (n 3) 86 f, 156, 240; Burrows, *Restitution* (n 2) 415, 574 f; Swadling, 'Bona Fide Purchase' (n 2) 96 f; Virgo (n 2) 661; Barker, 'Good Faith Exchange' (n 2) 202, 212; Nolan (n 2) 186 f; see *Clarke v Shee and Johnson* (1774) 1 Cowp 197, 200; 98 ER 1041 (Lord Mansfield); *Thomson v Clydesdale Bank Ltd* [1893] AC 282 (HL); *Phillips v Brooks Ltd* [1919] 2 KB 243 (KBD); *Banque Belge* (n 23) 331 ff (per Atkin LJ); *Nelson v Larholt* [1948] 1 KB 339 (KBD) (Denning J); *Barros Mattos Junior v MacDaniels Ltd* [2004] EWHC 1188 (Ch); [2005] 1 WLR 247 [17] (Laddie J).

[27] See, in addition to the cases cited in the foregoing footnote, *Marsh v Keating* (1834) 1 Bing NC 198; 131 ER 1094; *Calland v Loyd* (1840) 6 M&W 26; 151 ER 307; *Litt v Martindale* (1856) 18 CB 314; 139 ER 1390; *Reckitt v Barnett, Pembroke and Slater Ltd* [1929] AC 176 (HL); *OEM plc v Schneider* [2005] EWHC 1072 (Ch) [47]–[48].

[28] See, however, L Smith, 'Simplifying Claims to Traceable Proceeds' (2009) 125 *LQR* 338, according to whom the claim may better be regarded as a common law claim to vindicate equitable interests in the form of a personal claim for the value of substitute assets received and traceably retained.

in action against the bank and that the firm therefore had a power to assert title in the money received by the club.

According to some authors, the claimant in *Lipkin Gorman* was simply vindicating his property rights.[29] The claim, although personal, is based on the receipt of property that belongs to someone else. Since title did not pass, the defendant is not enriched. The cause of action is thus interference with another's property, not unjust enrichment.

For other authors, the *Lipkin* claim is a restitutionary claim based on unjust enrichment.[30] The requirement that it has to be the claimant's property that the defendant receives serves to establish that the enrichment is at the claimant's expense. The general rule is that only immediate recipients can be liable in unjust enrichment. If D receives an asset in which C does not have any title or power *in rem*, C has, in principle, no claim in unjust enrichment. C therefore has to show, through title and tracing rules, that property transferred by T to D was C's legal or equitable property.[31] The problem of an enrichment without title passing is approached in different ways.[32] According to Peter Birks, the claimant renounces his title if he elects to proceed in unjust enrichment.[33] Others maintain that enrichment is assessed factually rather than in terms of legal entitlement and that title passes by operation of law after the defendant has satisfied the claim.[34] The enrichment is unjust because the claimant was ignorant of it,[35] or did not consent to it or authorise it,[36] or because, due to the lack of consent, there was no basis for the enrichment.[37]

The answer to the question whether bona fide purchase is a defence in unjust enrichment therefore seems to depend upon the classification of the *Lipkin Gorman* claim. If this is unjust enrichment, bona fide purchase has a role to play in unjust enrichment. However, those who regard it as a claim

[29] Swadling, 'Bona Fide Purchase' (n 2) 97 ff; Swadling (n 18) 627 ff; Grantham and Rickett (n 18) 678 ff; Virgo (n 2) 11 ff, 570 ff, 585, 645; Fox (n 6) [9.25].

[30] Birks (n 3) 66–68; Burrows, *Restitution* (n 2) 128, 410 ff, 574; *Goff & Jones* (n 2) [8-34] ff; E McKendrick, 'Restitution, Misdirected Funds and Change of Position' (1992) 55 *MLR* 377 ff; Smith (n 13) 416 ff.

[31] Birks, 'English Recognition' (n 2) 476 ff; Birks (n 3) 86; Burrows, *Restitution* (n 2) 75 f, 128 ff, 574; Birks, *Restatement* (n 2) ss 8(2)(a), 9; Smith (n 13) 417 f; but see also *Goff & Jones* (n 2) [6-40] ff, [8-23], [8-35] f.

[32] *cf* Swadling, 'Bona Fide Purchase' (n 2) 94 f, 100; Swadling (n 18) 642 ff.

[33] Birks (n 3) 27, 66.

[34] Burrows, *Restitution* (n 2) 194 ff, 408; see also D Fox, 'Legal Title as a Ground of Restitutionary Liability' [2000] *Restitution Law Review* 465, 486 f; Fox, *Property Rights* (n 6) [9.26] ff; *Goff & Jones* (n 2) [5-17], [8-35].

[35] Birks, 'English Recognition' (n 2) 482 f; Burrows, *Restitution* (n 2) 404 ff; McKendrick (n 30) 380 ff.

[36] *Goff & Jones* (n 2) [8-33] ff.

[37] Birks (n 3) 155.

vindicating property rights maintain that bona fide purchase is not applicable in the law of unjust enrichment.

3.2. German Law Compared

It is difficult to 'translate' the *Lipkin Gorman* claim and the discussion about its classification into German terms. A claim for value received, without title having passed, does not exist in German law.[38] Nor can the claimant unilaterally renounce his title. As long as he is the owner, he can bring a *vindicatio* for return of the thing.[39] A claim in unjustified enrichment for the value of the thing is only possible if the claimant, in one way or another, has lost his title.[40] If D receives C's wine and drinks it, C will have a claim in unjustified enrichment for the amount of D's enrichment.[41] If D receives C's brick and builds it into his wall, or if D receives C's cloth and makes a dress with it, C will lose title and have a claim in unjust enrichment for the value instead.[42] If D mala fide sells the property to X who is a bona fide purchaser, C loses his title, but can claim the purchase price or the value from D in unjustified enrichment.[43] If the bona fide purchase by X fails for

[38] There may be a *condictio* regarding possession, which is, however, directed towards restitution of the possession and/or of the use value, not towards restitution of the value of the thing: K Larenz and CW Canaris, *Lehrbuch des Schuldrechts*, vol II/2, 13th edn (Munich, CH Beck, 1994) 174; M Schwab in FJ Säcker (ed), *Münchener Kommentar zum Bürgerlichen Gesetzbuch*, vol 5, 6th edn (Munich, CH Beck, 2013) § 812 [326]; S Lorenz, '§§ 812–822' in *Staudingers Kommentar zum Bürgerlichen Gesetzbuch* (Berlin, Sellier-de Gruyter, 2007) § 812 [73]; in English, P Schlechtriem, 'Unjust Enrichment by Interference with Property Rights' in E von Caemmerer and P Schlechtriem (eds), *International Encyclopedia of Comparative Law, Vol X: Restitution–Unjust Enrichment and Negotiorum Gestio* (Tübingen, Mohr Siebeck, 2007) ch 8, s 14; L Smith, 'Property, Subsidiarity and Unjust Enrichment' in D Johnston and R Zimmermann (eds), *Unjustified Enrichment: Key Issues in Comparative Perspective* (Cambridge, Cambridge University Press, 2002) 588, 594; L Smith, 'Tracing' in A Burrows and Lord Rodger of Earlsferry (eds), *Mapping the Law, Essays in Memory of Peter Birks* (Oxford, Oxford University Press, 2006) 120, 132.

[39] BGB, § 985.

[40] See, in English, Häcker (n 8) 219 ff; BS Markesinis, W Lorenz and G Dannemann, *The German Law of Obligations, Vol 1: The Law of Contracts and Restitution: A Comparative Introduction* (Oxford, Clarendon Press, 1997) 743 ff; G Dannemann, *The German Law of Unjustified Enrichment and Restitution: A Comparative Introduction* (Oxford, Oxford University Press, 2009) 92 ff.

[41] BGB, § 812 I 1 Var 2; see Larenz and Canaris (n 38) 172; Schwab (n 38) § 812 [253 a]; in English R Zimmermann and J du Plessis, 'Basic Features of the German Law of Unjustified Enrichment' [1994] *Restitution Law Review* 29.

[42] BGB, §§ 951, 812. See BGHZ 55, 176 (1971), English translation in Markesinis, Lorenz and Dannemann (n 40) 786 ff, in Dannemann, *German Law of Unjustified Enrichment* (n 40) 233 ff and in J Beatson and E Schrage (eds), *Cases, Materials and Texts on Unjustified Enrichment, Ius Commune Casebooks for the Common Law of Europe* (Oxford, Hart Publishing, 2003) 351 f; Schwab (n 38) § 812 [278]; in English Zimmermann and du Plessis (n 41) 29.

[43] BGB, § 816 I 1; see Schwab (n 38) § 816 [1–8]; Lorenz (n 38) § 812 [25]; in English, Schlechtriem (n 38) s 16; Zimmermann and du Plessis (n 41) 28.

some reason (eg, because the thing had been stolen from C), C can ratify the transfer, thereby losing title, but acquiring an enrichment claim against D.[44]

In result, where a defendant receives the claimant's property from a third party in circumstances where title does not pass, the defendant's liability in unjustified enrichment will not arise at the moment of receipt, but (if at all) only at a later point when the claimant loses his title. Assuming in the *Lipkin Gorman* situation that Cass stole a banknote from the claimant and handed that very banknote to the defendant club (tracing is, in principle, not permitted under German law)[45] and assuming further that title did not pass to the club (eg because it knew of the theft), the club will not be liable in unjustified enrichment for the value as long as the claimant can follow and vindicate its banknote. However, in nearly all cases, the claimant will lose his title shortly after, eg, if the club gives the money to its bank or if it spends the money, enabling the recipient to acquire title by bona fide purchase. This is the closest German law comes to the receipt-based *Lipkin Gorman* claim in English law. The claim is considered to be a claim in unjustified enrichment which, in a wider sense, protects ownership, as it takes the place of the lost *vindicatio*. Unjust enrichment and the protection of ownership are not seen as incompatible.[46]

However, what happens if the defendant acquires title in the property transferred by the third party by virtue of a bona fide purchase? In this case, if the claimant has any enrichment claim at all, it will arise at the time of the defendant's receipt, as this is the moment where the claimant loses its title. The problems described in the last paragraph do not arise. But is there really an enrichment claim? Or is the defendant protected by his bona fide purchase? The answer depends on whether he acquired the title for value or gratuitously.

If the defendant is a bona fide purchaser for value, he is not only protected against a proprietary claim but also against a claim in unjust enrichment by the former owner.[47] The claimant can only sue the transferor (the third party) in unjustified enrichment and recover the purchase price.[48] The outcome will be different if the defendant is a donee. As mentioned before, it is possible for even a donee to acquire title from a non-owner in good faith. But this does not affect his liability in unjustified enrichment: he is required to redeliver the property and re-transfer the title or to pay its value

[44] BGB, § 185 (2). See Larenz and Canaris (n 38) 182; Schwab (n 38) § 816 [33]; Lorenz (n 38) § 816 [9]; in English, Zimmermann and du Plessis (n 41) 28; Markesinis, Lorenz and Dannemann (n 40) 748; Smith (n 38) 132 f.

[45] See, in English, Markesinis, Lorenz and Dannemann (n 40) 756 ff.

[46] Larenz and Canaris (n 38) 130, 170; Schlechtriem (n 38) s 9; Häcker (n 8) 44 f. For a similar argument relating to English law, see Fox (n 34) 488 ff.

[47] *cf* Schwab (n 38) § 816 [8].

[48] BGB, § 816 (1) 1. If the transferor acted wrongfully and was at fault, the former owner will also be able to claim damages in tort. See, in English, Zülch (n 8) 113 ff.

to the former owner.[49] A bona fide purchaser for value is therefore protected from enrichment liability, while a bona fide donee is not. Bona fide purchase *for value* can thus, at least in an untechnical sense, be regarded as a defence in unjustified enrichment or as a legal basis entitling the recipient to keep the benefit.[50]

In order to establish a bona fide purchase for value, value need not have been given; it is sufficient that value has been promised. This is generally accepted where value has been promised under a valid contract, which includes normal gaming contracts that are merely unenforceable and not void.[51] There is a dispute as to whether bona fide purchase for value is possible if the contract between the transferor and the defendant is void, or whether this case should be treated as if the defendant were a donee. In a case concerning a void gaming contract, comparable to *Lipkin Gorman*, the Federal Court chose the second alternative,[52] whereas the majority of commentators strongly favour the first solution.[53]

3.3. Personal Claims in Equity

Returning to English law, personal claims for the value of an asset received by the defendant are well known in equity. However, bona fide purchase for value has no role to play as long as the courts stand by their position that personal claims can only arise in the context of knowing receipt or constructive trusteeship, requiring a certain degree of fault.[54] In contrast, Peter Birks has always maintained that receipt-based liability in equity should be strict, as it is at law, subject only to a defence of change of position.[55] Cases where the defendant has given value and was held not liable could then be explained by an application of bona fide purchase for value, whereas a

[49] BGB, § 816 (1) 2. See Larenz and Canaris (n 38) 184; in English, Zimmermann and du Plessis (n 41) 28; Markesinis, Lorenz and Dannemann (n 40) 748 f; Häcker (n 8) 221–24.

[50] Larenz and Canaris (n 38) 138 f, 181; Häcker (n 8) 223 fn 34.

[51] BGB, § 762.

[52] BGHZ 37, 363 (1962); *cf* BGHZ 47, 393 (1967).

[53] Larenz and Canaris (n 38) 184, 211 f; Schwab (n 38) § 812 [59]; Lorenz (n 38) § 816 [16] ff. See, in English, Zülch (n 8) 125 ff.; Schlechtriem (n 38) s 93.

[54] *Selangor United Rubber Estates Ltd v Cradock (No 3)* [1968] 1 WLR 1555 (Ch D) (Ungoed-Thomas J); *Carl Zeiss Stiftung v Herbert Smith & Co (No 2)* [1969] 2 Ch 276 (CA); *Re J Leslie Engineers Co Ltd* [1976] 1 WLR 292 (Ch D) (Oliver J); *International Sales and Agencies Ltd v Marcus* [1982] 3 All ER 551 (QBD) (Lawson J); *In Re Montagu's Settlement Trusts* [1987] Ch 264 (Ch D) (Sir Megarry VC); *Eagle Trust* (n 23) (Vinelott J); *Polly Peck* (n 23); *El Ajou v Dollar Land Holding Plc* [1993] 3 All ER 717 (Ch D) (Millett J); [1994] 2 All ER 685 (CA); *Bank of Credit and Commerce International (Overseas) Ltd v Akindele* [2001] Ch 437 (CA).

[55] P Birks, *An Introduction to the Law of Restitution* (Oxford, Clarendon Press, 1989) 441 ff; P Birks, 'Persistent Problems in Misdirected Money: A Quintet' [1993] *Lloyd's Maritime and Commercial Law Quarterly* 218; Birks, *Future* (n 2) 26 ff; Birks (n 3) 156 f.

donee could, contrary to some decided cases, only escape liability by establishing a change of position. According to a number of authors, while this may not be the law as it stands, it should at least be the direction into which the law should go.[56]

4. THE POSSIBLE RATIONALE OF BONA FIDE PURCHASE AS A DEFENCE AGAINST PERSONAL CLAIMS

There is further no agreement about the reason why some personal receipt-based claims can be defeated by the defence of bona fide purchase. The ratio of the defence is important for the question whether it should have any scope of application beyond the cases described above.

4.1. Requirements of Claim not Given

An explanation may be that a bona fide purchase simply negates one of the essential elements for establishing the claim, in the same way as a bona fide purchase extinguishes pure proprietary claims. Assuming he gave value before the receipt of the property, the defendant acquires title at the moment of receipt. Following the vindication model, it could be argued that he does not receive the claimant's property and thus does not interfere with the claimant's property rights.[57] Following the unjust enrichment model, it might be said that, while the usual type of unjust enrichment claims applies where title has passed to the defendant, this is a special case: since the defendant receives the property from a third party, the enrichment claim requires a proprietary connection between the claimant and the defendant, which is cut off by the bona fide purchase.[58] Or it could be argued that the defendant's enrichment is not at the claimant's expense, for the bona fide purchase vests a fresh title in the defendant, which is not derived from the claimant, but from the third party.[59]

However, it is not the acquisition of title as such that protects the defendant from a restitutionary claim. Assuming T steals a brick from C and builds it into D's house, D will acquire property in the brick. But this will not

[56] There might be a strict liability based solely on receipt on the one hand and the equitable wrong of knowing or dishonest receipt on the other hand. *cf* P Millett, 'Tracing the Proceeds of Fraud' (1991) 107 *LQR* 71, 82; Lord Nicholls, 'Knowing Receipt: The Need for a New Landmark' in Cornish et al (n 2) 231–45; Burrows, *Restitution* (n 2) 424 ff; Virgo (n 2) 651 ff; Barker, 'Good Faith Exchange' (n 2) 208 f; *Goff & Jones* (n 2) [8-50] ff, [8-63] ff; Häcker (n 8) 238 ff. But see the powerful arguments by Smith (n 13) 430 ff.

[57] Virgo (n 2) 657, 661; Smith (n 20) 370 f, 388.

[58] *cf* Nolan (n 2) 186; Birks (n 3) 87.

[59] Swadling, 'Bona Fide Purchase' (n 2) 100.

necessarily mean that D is immune from restitutionary liability, in particular if he is mala fide. In case of a bona fide purchase, the defendant is protected, not because he acquired the title, but because of the reason why he acquired the title, namely the bona fide purchase for value without notice.[60]

4.2. Stultification

The function of bona fide purchase as a defence against personal claims is therefore widely considered to be to complete the protection of a bona fide purchaser granted by property law.[61] Bona fide purchase is thought to strike a balance between the sanctity of property and the security of receipt. If the requirements of a bona fide purchase are met, the transferee's interests prevail over those of the owner. This policy decision would be undermined if a personal restitutionary claim were allowed against the bona fide purchaser. Bona fide purchase thus has to be extended to restitutionary personal claims in order to avoid its stultification.

If this ratio is taken seriously, the defence will have to be synchronised with its counterpart in property law. It will have to be restricted to cases where the defendant acquired title in a property received from a third party by way of bona fide purchase.

4.3. Sanctity of Contract Between the Defendant and the Third Party

A competing strategy is to cut off the defence from its proprietary roots. Bona fide purchase could be regarded as a general defence against personal restitutionary claims, based on the protection of the valid contract between the defendant and the third party.[62] Where the defendant receives property under a contract with the claimant, he is protected against any restitutionary claim as long as the contract is valid and not terminated. It could be argued that the defendant needs similar protection if he receives the benefit under a contract with a third party. A court shall not undermine that contract unless the defendant was dishonest or had notice of facts entitling the claimant to restitution.

There is, however, an immediate objection to this approach. If the defendant receives a benefit under a contract with the claimant, there is no doubt that the claimant must abide by that contract. Yet it is not clear why the claimant should be bound or disadvantaged by a contract to which he is not

[60] Smith (n 13) 427.

[61] Birks (n 3) 242 ff; Swadling (n 18) 657; *Goff & Jones* (n 2) [29-01]; Burrows, *Restatement* (n 2) 133.

[62] Barker, 'Good Faith Exchange' (n 2) 211 ff; Burrows, *Restitution* (n 2) 577 ff.; see also Häcker (n 8) 247 ff.

privy. Where the particular requirements of a bona fide purchase are not met, the defendant does not acquire good title and is subject to proprietary rights of the claimant, despite there being a valid contract with the third party.[63] Why should the law of restitution or unjust enrichment respect a contract which the law of property does not respect?

5. THE RELATIONSHIP BETWEEN BONA FIDE PURCHASE AS A MEANS OF ACQUIRING TITLE AND BONA FIDE PURCHASE AS A DEFENCE AGAINST PERSONAL CLAIMS

At this stage, it may be helpful to consider in which cases a defence of bona fide purchase against personal restitutionary claims could differ from its counterpart in property law, in order to see whether there should be a difference or whether bona fide purchase should be applied in the same way throughout. The requirements of a bona fide purchase defence against personal claims might be stricter or less strict than the requirements of a bona fide purchase in property law. Thus, two groups of cases are conceivable: (i) a defendant acquires title by way of bona fide purchase, but is nevertheless subjected to personal restitutionary liability; (ii) a defendant did not acquire title by way of bona fide purchase, but is nevertheless protected against personal liability by a defence of bona fide purchase. The first case is widely held to be impossible in English law, while the same is true of the second in German law.

5.1. Personal Restitutionary Liability of a Bona Fide Purchaser?

The position that a defendant who has acquired title by way of bona fide purchase and is thus immune from a claim *in rem* should nevertheless be subjected to a personal claim in restitution has been advocated by Key: according to him, and contrary to what was said in *Lipkin Gorman*, bona fide purchase is no defence against personal claims, which can only be defeated by change of position.[64] Thus, if T uses C's banknote of 100 to buy a bicycle worth 70 from D who had no notice, D acquires title to the banknote, but incurs restitutionary liability to pay 30 to C. The vast majority of authors reject this position. Bona fide purchase as an exception to *nemo dat quod non habet* would be undermined if the recipient were nevertheless liable to a personal restitutionary claim. Such a result would be absurd, contradictory or self-defeating.[65]

[63] Birks (n 3) 243 f.

[64] Key (n 2) 426 f.

[65] See, eg, Birks (n 3) 242; Barker, 'Good Faith Exchange' (n 2) 213; Birks, 'Bona Fide Purchase' (n 2) 78; Burrows, *Restatement* (n 2) 133 f.

The position taken in German law is different. The bona fide acquirer is only protected from restitutionary liability if he was a bona fide purchaser for value, which in German law means that the property was acquired under a contract providing for consideration.[66] The bona fide purchaser for value does not merely acquire title; he is also entitled to retain the property free from any claims. Yet there is no such parallelism between property and enrichment law where the defendant is a donee. As mentioned before, in property law, even a donee can acquire title from a non-owner in good faith. Enrichment law, however, requires him to return the property (re-transfer the title) or the value to the former owner.

Underlying this apparent contradiction are the different functions of property and unjustified enrichment in German law. The German rules on the acquisition of ownership pay particular attention to the interests of third parties. The rules on good faith acquisition do not merely protect the bona fide purchaser, but also third party transferees of the property.[67] The rules therefore have to be clear and simple. Allowing a bona fide purchase by a donee is not meant to protect the donee; rather, its purpose is to ensure that third parties to whom he transfers the property do not have to inquire into whether he promised or gave value to the original owner. This is regarded as an element of the internal relationship between the donee and the person having transferred the property to the donee. However, when it comes to the law of unjustified enrichment, the interests of third parties no longer have to be taken into account, since the remedies are merely personal. The bona fide donee will be forced to give up his enrichment, which may take the form of re-transferring the title to the claimant. Third parties are not affected by this: in the event that the defendant has already transferred the property to them, they have acquired title from an owner and are therefore safe.

It could thus be said that, in German law, the defence of bona fide purchase is wider in property law, where it covers every case of bona fide acquisition, than in enrichment law, where only a bona fide purchase for value is relevant. The reason behind this apparent dichotomy is the attention German property law pays to third parties. The situation is different in English law, where only a bona fide purchaser for value can acquire ownership from a non-owner. These rules seem to focus on the circumstances and the interests of the individual bona fide purchaser, while the protection of third parties is only an indirect effect. If this is true, it will be a reasonable step to extend the protection afforded by property law to an immunity against personal claims. The decision to protect the individual defendant has been made (contrary to German law) in the law of property and its effect should indeed not be stultified by allowing a personal restitutionary claim.

[66] See above, section 3.2.

[67] *cf* Oechsler (n 12) § 932 [3]; W Wiegand in *Staudingers Kommentar zum Bürgerlichen Gesetzbuch*, §§ 925–984 (Berlin, Sellier-de Gruyter, 2011) Intro §§ 932–36 [3]; Häcker (n 8) 223 f.

5.2. Defence of Bona Fide Purchase Without an Acquisition of Title by Way of Bona Fide Purchase?

The opposite situation is the case where the defendant did not acquire title by way of bona fide purchase. The question here is whether bona fide purchase can be raised as a defence against personal liability, thus having a function independent of property law, or whether bona fide purchase has no role to play because there is no danger of undermining property law. The answer may depend on why the defendant did not acquire title by bona fide purchase.

5.2.1. The Defendant Cannot Acquire Title Because the Requirements of a Bona Fide Purchase are not Met

The reason why the defendant cannot become the owner of property transferred to him by a third party may be that the requirements of a bona fide purchase are not met. Under English law, this is the case where the defendant receives property other than money that belongs to the claimant. If T sells and delivers the claimant's bicycle to D, D cannot acquire legal title, even if he has no notice of T's lack of title. The same is true in German law if the bicycle was stolen from C; the transfer to D does not extinguish C's title.

In these circumstances, German law does not protect the defendant from restitutionary liability even if he has acquired the property in good faith and for value. As long as he retains the property in its original form, the claimant can vindicate it. As mentioned above, liability in unjustified enrichment for the value arises when the vindication is lost, for example, when the claimant consumes the thing, disposes of it or becomes its owner by rules of accession or specification.[68] The defence of change of position is generally applicable, with one remarkable exception: the purchase price or consideration paid to the third party transferor will not be taken into account.[69] Thus, German law seems to treat the defendant less favourably than English law.

The reason is that the liability in unjustified enrichment takes the place of the lost *vindicatio*.[70] As long as the defendant has the property in his hands, the claimant can vindicate it, ie, demand its return, without the defendant being able to point to the purchase price he paid to the third party as a defence. This risk allocation should not change merely because the claimant lost his title due to consumption, accession or specification. Where the

[68] Above, section 3.2.

[69] BGHZ 55, 176 (1971), English translation in Markesinis, Lorenz and Dannemann (n 40) 786 ff, Dannemann (n 40) 233 ff and Beatson and Schrage (n 42) 351 f; Larenz and Canaris (n 38) 302 f; Schwab (n 38) § 816 [53], § 818 [136].

[70] BGHZ 55, 176, 179 f; Larenz and Canaris (n 38) 170, 181, 302 f; Lorenz (n 38) § 812 [62].

defendant buys a brick stolen from the claimant, the claimant can vindicate it without having to take account of the purchase price paid by the defendant. The purchase price should continue to be irrelevant if the defendant now builds the brick into his wall, so that the claimant can recover only the value. As described above, liability in enrichment arises only at the moment that the claimant loses his title. This is also the point in time for valuing the benefit, with rules of subjective devaluation similar to those in English law. Therefore, the defendant's liability in unjustified enrichment will generally not be more detrimental than his duty to return the thing *in specie* in case of a *vindicatio*.

The basic position in German law is that, where the defendant receives the claimant's property from a third party for value, neither the contract nor the defendant's good faith, nor the giving of value protects the defendant from personal liability as long as the requirements of a bona fide purchase in property law are not met. The same position is advocated by a number of authors for English law. According to Peter Birks, where the recipient does not come within the terms of a bona fide purchase under the rule of property law, he must be liable in the same way as anyone who takes another's property.[71] If this were the law, a defendant having received the claimant's property could not raise a defence of bona fide purchase against personal claims that went beyond the proprietary defence. However, it is not clear whether this position is generally accepted. In its favour, it can be argued that the law of restitution or unjust enrichment should follow the decisions made in other areas of law. If the defendant cannot acquire the title by way of a bona fide purchase, he is holding the claimant's property and should, in principle, be liable for its return. If he assumes ownership over the property, he will be liable in conversion. It seems to be consistent to hold that the defendant should also be liable for the property's value in the even that he is unable or unwilling to return it to the claimant. Any injustice this position might cause to the defendant could be mitigated by a liberal assessment of his enrichment and by the defence of change of position.

A different picture presents itself when the personal liability of third party recipients in equity is considered. A donee who, in good faith and without notice, receives property which belongs to the claimant in equity cannot acquire the property free from equitable titles. Since the purchase was not for value, an essential element of a bona fide purchase is lacking. The claimant can therefore assert a proprietary interest in an asset held by the defendant. Nevertheless, the courts are generally not prepared to subject the defendant to personal liability to account for the value received. Thus, his protection is stronger against personal liability than it is against liability

[71] Birks, *Introduction* (n 55), 447; see also Barker, 'Good Faith Exchange' (n 2) 213; Barker, 'Bona Fide Purchase' (n 2) 82; Burrows, *Restatement* (n 2) 133 f.

in rem. Functionally, it could be said that there is a defence of bona fide acquisition applicable in relation to personal claims, which is wider than its proprietary counterpart in that it does not require the giving of value.

The reason for the courts' attitude seems to be the lack of a defence of change of position before 1991. Granting a proprietary remedy while excluding personal liability was a way of protecting those defendants who had lost their enrichment. Since the rules of tracing allowed the claimant to assert proprietary interests in substitutes, the value received could be traced until it was lost by the defendant. The claim *in rem* was, however, only an imperfect instrument to protect the defendant. A defendant who used the money received to pay for a journey which he would otherwise have financed by a loan was protected despite being enriched, while the defendant who, in reliance on the receipt, gave some other money to charity while retaining the money received was liable, although he was arguably no longer enriched. The defence of change of position, recognised in 1991, seems to be a better means to fine-tune the interests of the parties. This is the position of a number of authors who argue that, in principle, there should be a strict receipt-based liability in equity, subject only to the change of position defence.[72] If the law were to go into this direction, this would remove the oddity of immunising a defendant from personal liability while at the same time asserting that he received and handled property of the claimant.

5.2.2. *The Defendant Need not Acquire Title by Way of Bona Fide Purchase Because the Third Party Transferor had Good Title*

The defendant may receive property from a third party who has good title to the property, despite the fact that the third party has received the property from the claimant under circumstances giving rise to a claim in unjust enrichment. This is the case where the claimant transfers the property to the third party under a mistake not preventing title from passing, or where there is a failure of consideration and the third party transfers the property to the defendant. The defendant, acquiring title from a transferor who himself had good title, does not have to rely on a bona fide purchase in property law. Is there nevertheless a need for such a defence against personal claims?

It may be argued that *Lipkin Gorman* itself belongs to this category, since the transferor Cass was said to have legal title in the money he took from the claimant and gave to the defendant club. It may be said that the concept of bona fide purchase was not required here on the proprietary level, but only as a defence against personal liability.[73] However, the judgments were based

[72] See nn 55–56.

[73] *cf* Barker, 'Good Faith Exchange' (n 2) 212; P Birks, 'Direct and Indirect Enrichment in English Law' in D Johnston and R Zimmermann (eds), *Unjustified Enrichment: Key Issues in Comparative Perspective* (Cambridge, Cambridge University Press, 2002) 519; Birks (n 3) 95 f.

on the assumption that the money received by the club was the traceable substitute of a chose of action belonging to the claimant, and that the claimant had the power to assert its title to this money.[74] It seems, therefore, that there was indeed a proprietary base entitling the claimant at least to revest its title, with the consequence that the club would face a proprietary remedy if it still held the specific banknotes in its cashbox. A bona fide purchase for value by the club, if it had been accepted by the judges, would not only have protected the club from personal liability but also have destroyed this proprietary base and made the club immune from any claims *in rem*.

Turning to cases where there is no proprietary connection between the claimant and the defendant, the general rule is that the claimant does not have any claim in unjust enrichment, since the defendant is merely an indirect enrichee. This rule is applied strictly in German law, with its clear separation of personal rights and rights *in rem*, where it is argued that the defendant as a third party must not be affected by events concerning merely the personal rights between the claimant and the first recipient.[75] However, there seems to be a similar rule in English law.[76] Whether a defence of bona fide purchase may be applicable will therefore depend on whether exceptions to the rule are recognised or, as Peter Birks has said, whether leapfrogging is allowed.

Birks himself thought that leapfrogging should in principle be permitted unless there was a valid contract between the claimant and the first recipient.[77] If this view were correct, there would be room for a defence of bona fide purchase against personal claims with no proprietary counterpart.[78] However, it is not clear whether this view is supported by authority. If C pays money to T under a void contract and T uses the same money to buy a car from D, it is by no means clear whether C should have a claim in unjust enrichment against D at all.

The case for liability of an indirect recipient is stronger where the indirect recipient received the benefit gratuitously. In German law, an indirect recipient who gave no value can exceptionally be liable in unjustified enrichment if the liability of the direct recipient (the third party transferor) is excluded due to a change of position made up of this transfer.[79] It is a kind

[74] *Lipkin* (n 1) 572 ff (Lord Goff).

[75] Larenz and Canaris (n 38) 135 f, 200; in English, Schlechtriem (n 38) s 92; Birks (n 73) 513.

[76] See Burrows, *Restitution* (n 2) 69 ff; Burrows, *Restatement* (n 2) 48 f; A Tettenborn, 'Lawful Receipt—A Justifying Factor?' [1997] *Restitution Law Review* 1; Virgo (n 2) 105 ff; Millett (n 56) 77 ff; *Agip* (n 23) 272 f (Millett J); *cf* Birks (n 73) 493 ff; *contra Goff & Jones* (n 2) [6-18] ff.

[77] Birks (n 73) 512 ff; Birks (n 3) 94; to a similar effect, see *Goff & Jones* (n 2) [6-18] ff; S Watterson, 'Direct Transfers in the Law of Unjust Enrichment' (2011) 64 *Current Legal Problems* 435.

[78] Birks (n 73) 514; Häcker (n 8) 247 ff.

[79] BGB, § 822. See Larenz and Canaris (n 38) 136, 195; Lorenz (n 38) § 822 [1]; in English, Zimmermann and du Plessis (n 41) 28; Häcker (n 8) 225 f.

of subsidiary liability of a donee. In England, a similar reasoning could be used to explain the personal liability of the charities in *Re Diplock*,[80] which was held to be subsidiary to the liability of the representatives (instead of explaining the result with the equitable title of the claimant beneficiaries).[81] It could be argued that all indirect recipients are liable in unjust enrichment unless they can show a bona fide purchase for value. But this does not seem to represent the law as it stands. The liability of indirect recipients who receive the property gratuitously is regarded as an exception (and therefore subsidiary) in both Germany and England. The consequence of this is that it is not the defendant who is required to prove a bona fide purchase, but rather the claimant who has to show why this exception shall apply.

5.2.3. The Defendant Receives the Asset from the Claimant Albeit under a Contract with a Third Party

In a third group of cases, the defendant need not rely on bona fide purchase in property law because he receives the asset directly from the claimant who transfers his title to the defendant. However, the defendant receives the property under a contract with a third party. It has been argued that bona fide purchase may play a role in these cases: the defendant has a defence against a claim in unjust enrichment if he can show that he received the payment (or another asset) under a valid contract with the third party, which the courts will not undermine unless the defendant was dishonest or had notice of facts entitling the claimant to restitution.[82]

A possible example is the case of the *Trident Beauty*,[83] where the creditors of the claimants had assigned their claims to the defendants. The claimants, having paid the defendants, were held not to be able to recover from the defendants for failure of consideration. It is possible that the result would have been the same if the claimants had based their restitutionary claim on mistake, eg, because they had not realised that their contract was void. A claimant may also pay directly to the defendant because he was instructed by his contract partner to do so, eg, a bank paying the defendant on account of an order of its client. If the claimant then brings a claim in unjust enrichment against the defendant, eg, because he had not realised that he was

[80] *Diplock* (n 23) 479 ff; *Ministry of Health v Simpson* [1951] AC 251 (HL).

[81] *cf* L Smith, 'Three-Party Restitution: A Critique of Birks's Theory of Interceptive Subtraction' (1991) 11 *OJLS* 481, 498 ff; Smith (n 13) 437 ff; Burrows, *Restitution* (n 2) 73, 82 f.

[82] Barker, 'Good Faith Exchange' (n 2) 204 f; see also A Burrows, 'Restitution from Assignees' [1994] *Restitution Law Review* 52, 55 f; Barker, *Restitution* (n 2) 577 ff; *Goff & Jones* (n 2) [29-21].

[83] *Pan Ocean Shipping Co Ltd v Creditcorp Ltd (The Trident Beauty)* [1994] 1 WLR 161 (HL).

actually not liable towards his creditor, can the defendant point to his valid contract with the third party (the claimant's contract partner) in defence?[84]

The better view, it is submitted, is that the claimant should indeed not be able to recover from the defendant in these cases. However, the reason for this is not the valid contract between the defendant and the third party. The claimant should not be able to recover because, by paying the defendant, he knowingly follows an instruction of his contract partner (the third party) either in the form of a direct order or an assignment. He should therefore recover from his contract partner, not from the defendant. In other words, the case should be treated as if the third party itself had paid to the defendant.[85]

The important point is that the defendant will not have a defence if the claimant does not follow any instructions given by the third party. This was the case in *RE Jones v Waring and Gillow*.[86] The defendants were entitled to the money received from the claimants under a contract with Bodenham and thought that the claimants, by paying, were following Bodenham's instructions. In reality, however, the claimants paid because they wanted to discharge an obligation they owed to International Motors, which they identified with the defendants. The House of Lords allowed restitution for mistake. The contract with Bodenham did not help the defendants because the claimants did not pay on the instruction of Bodenham.

It is therefore not the contract with the third party that confers upon the defendant the right to retain the benefit; something more is required. The reason for the claimant being obliged to pay the defendant is his relationship with the third party. The third party may have ordered him to pay the defendant or may have assigned its claims to the defendant. In both cases, the claimant pays because of his contract with the third party and should look to him for restitution.[87] A valid contract with a third party is a good defence to restitutionary claims by that third party. But it is difficult to see, as a matter of principle, how it can shield the defendant from restitutionary liability towards the claimant, thereby affecting the position of a person who was not privy to the contract.[88]

5.2.4. Summing Up

There seems to be no place for a defence of bona fide purchase beyond the cases where the claimant acquired title by way of bona fide purchase.

[84] This seems to have been the opinion of Lord Goff in *Pan Ocean* (ibid) 166.

[85] The argument is more fully developed in S Meier, 'Mistaken Payments in Three-Party Situations: A German View of English Law' [1999] *CLJ* 567, 599 ff.

[86] *RE Jones v Waring and Gillow* [1926] AC 670 (HL).

[87] *cf Goff & Jones* [3-62] ff, 77 ff; Barker, 'Bona Fide Purchase' (n 2) 88.

[88] To the same effect, see Swadling (n 18) 656 f.

Where the defendant cannot acquire title because the requirements of bona fide purchase are not met, he should not be protected from personal liability. This view should ultimately prevail even in equity. Where the defendant receives property from a third party having good title, a defence of bona fide purchase is arguably not required because the defendant is, in principle, not liable anyway. Where the defendant receives property from the claimant under a contract with a third party, it is the fact that the claimant knowingly pays for the third party rather than the contract between the defendant and the third party that protects the defendant from liability towards the claimant.

If this is correct, the role of bona fide purchase is merely to exclude personal liability where a defendant has acquired title by way of bona fide purchase. The ratio of the defence is rather the prevention of stultification than the sanctity of the contract between the defendant and a third party.

6. THE REQUIREMENT OF A VALID CONTRACT

In *Lipkin Gorman*, the defendant club received the money under a gaming contract and provided consideration by paying out the winnings. Reversing the Court of Appeal's decision on this point,[89] the House of Lords held that this was not enough to establish a defence of bona fide purchase for value.[90] The business was lawful, but the gaming contracts were void. The payment of the winnings was said to be of no value in the eyes of the law; it could only count as a change of position in the amount of the sum paid. It is therefore said that the defence of bona fide purchase requires the contract underlying the receipt of the property and the giving of value to be valid.[91] However, if the defence is not based on the sanctity of the contract between the defendant and the third party, it is not obvious why this should be so.[92]

Take the case of T, who buys a bicycle from D with C's money. D will clearly be a bona fide purchaser for value if the contract of sale between T and D is valid. Why should the outcome be different if the contract is, unbeknownst to the parties, void? It could be argued that the void contract cannot entitle D to retain the money. However, this result can be avoided by allowing the transferor T to bring a restitutionary claim in unjust enrichment, founded on the void contract which establishes a mistake or an absence of basis. Bona fide purchase for value is no defence in a two-party relationship. It requires the defendant to have received the property under

[89] *Lipkin Gorman v Karpnale Ltd* [1989] 1 WLR 1340 (CA) 1362 ff.

[90] *Lipkin* (n 1) 560 ff, 575, 577; to the same effect, see Nicholls LJ in the CA (n 89) 1382 ff.

[91] Birks (n 3) 156, 240 f; Burrows, *Restitution* (n 2) 574 f; Fox (n 6) [8.29].

[92] In *Clarke* (n 26), where the defence was denied, the contract was illegal and not merely void.

a contract with a third party other than the claimant, which is not the case with T's restitutionary claim. If this is accepted, D will have a bona fide purchase defence against C, but not against T. Faced with T's restitutionary claim, D can claim counter-restitution, so that he will not have to return the money without getting the bicycle, or its value, back. Furthermore, he will not be liable towards T where the usual bars apply, for example, where T paid the money despite knowing that the contract was void, where there was a representation by T amounting to an estoppel or where T's claim is time-barred.

In contrast, if bona fide purchase required the validity of the underlying contract, D would be subjected to a restitutionary claim by C. The fact that he gave the bicycle as consideration for the money received could only establish a change of position. The value of the bicycle would have to be calculated and deducted from the sum of C's claim, and even this would not be certain if D had transferred the bicycle before payment. Any defences relating to D's relationship with T (knowledge, estoppel, limitation) would not apply to C's restitutionary claim. This worsening of D's position would be solely due to the fact that the contract between D and T was void, a factor that exclusively concerns the relationship between D and T.

The defence of bona fide purchase for value protects the defendant where he has given value in an exchange transaction with a third party. It is not the contract with the third party as such, but the bona fide giving of value that overrides the protection of the claimant's property. The fact that the defendant has given value is independent of the validity of the underlying contract. The better view therefore seems to be not to regard the validity of the contract as a requirement for a bona fide purchase for value.[93]

7. CONCLUSION

Bona fide purchase is a means of acquiring good title from a transferor who had no such title to give. It shields the defendant from any right *in rem*, whether it is a pure or a restitutionary right. Bona fide purchase can be raised as a defence against personal claims founded on the receipt of the claimant's property by the defendant, irrespective of whether these claims are characterised as claims in unjust enrichment, restitution or vindication of property rights. As a defence against personal claims, bona fide purchase cannot simply be explained by the fact that the defendant acquired title; rather, the defence complements the protection afforded to a bona fide purchaser by the rules of property law. Unlike in German law, the acceptance

[93] See, to the same effect, Swadling, 'Bona Fide Purchase' (n 2) 96, fn 56; McKendrick (n 30) 383 f; Burrows, *Restatement* (n 2) 132. The authority of *Lipkin* (n 1) could be restricted to the special case of gaming contracts.

of a bona fide purchase in English property law constitutes a policy decision to protect the individual defendant from any liability. This policy decision must not be undermined by the law of restitution.

Apart from cases of a bona fide acquisition of title, there seems to be no place for a defence of bona fide purchase. Where the defendant could not acquire title because the requirements of a bona fide purchase are not met, he should arguably not be protected from personal liability. The contrary view of the courts in respect of receipt-based claims in equity can only be explained by the lack of a defence of change of position until 1991. Where the third party transferor had good title, the defendant transferee will arguably not be liable in unjust enrichment, thus removing the need of a defence of bona fide purchase. This is true irrespective of whether an exceptional subsidiary liability of donees is accepted or not. Where the defendant receives the property from the claimant himself, albeit under a contract with a third party, he can rely on this contract as a defence only if the claimant was consciously acting for the third party, so that it is not the contract as such that protects the defendant. The defence of bona fide purchase cannot be based on the sanctity of the contract between the defendant and the third party simply because the claimant was not privy to it. It is therefore doubtful whether there is, or should be, a requirement that this contract has to be valid. The sole justification of the defence seems to be the need to prevent an undermining of the rules of property law. If this is correct, then bona fide purchase does not perform any independent functions in the law of unjust enrichment.

12

Counterfactual Arguments Against Woolwich *Liability*

CHARLES MITCHELL*

1. INTRODUCTION

IN *WOOLWICH EQUITABLE Building Society v IRC*,[1] the claimant paid money in response to a tax demand issued under regulations that were ultra vires. The claimant disputed the validity of the regulations, but paid to avoid penalties and unfavourable publicity. The Revenue repaid the capital sum, but purported to do so ex gratia and refused to pay interest from the date of receipt. To recover this interest, the claimant had to show that it was legally entitled to restitution of the capital sum, although it had made no mistake and had not acted under duress. The House of Lords held that it was so entitled. One reason given by Lord Goff was that an action for restitution of money paid as tax that is not due is needed to give full effect to the principle in Article 4 of the Bill of Rights 1689, which states that the Crown may not levy taxation without parliamentary authority. Another reason implicit in their Lordships' speeches was that public bodies must respect the rule of law and must not exceed the limits of their authority.[2]

Consistently with both reasons, the courts have held that *Woolwich* mandates the recovery of money paid as tax under legislation that is incompatible with EU law. For example, in *Littlewoods Retail Ltd v HMRC*,[3]

* I thank the editors and the other participants at the seminar on which this book is based, the members of the UCL Private Law Group who also discussed a draft of this chapter at a work-in-progress seminar, and Steven Elliott, Julius Grower, Jeff King, Rick Rawlings, and Joanne Scott.

[1] *Woolwich Equitable Building Society v IRC* [1993] AC 70 (HL).

[2] J Beatson, 'Restitution of Taxes, Levies and Other Imposts: Defining the Extent of the *Woolwich* Principle' (1993) 109 *LQR* 401, 409–18.

[3] *Littlewoods Retail Ltd v HMRC* [2014] EWHC 868 (Ch); [2014] STC 1761. See also *Deutsche Morgan Grenfell Group plc v IRC* [2006] UKHL 49; [2007] 1 AC 558; *Sempra Metals Ltd v IRC* [2007] UKHL 34; [2008] 1 AC 561; *Test Claimants in the FII Group Litigation v HMRC (No 1)* [2012] UKSC 19; [2012] 2 AC 337. There was no appeal from the part of Henderson J's decision in *Littlewoods* with which this chapter is concerned, but other parts of his decision were affirmed by the Court of Appeal: [2015] EWCA Civ 515.

Henderson J ordered HMRC to repay the use value of money paid as VAT that was not due. Consistently with the second reason, the courts have also held that *Woolwich* mandates the recovery of money paid to public bodies other than tax authorities as charges and fees that were not due. For example, in *Waikato Regional Airport Ltd v AG of New Zealand*,[4] the Privy Council awarded restitution of money improperly charged for the provision of border control services, and in *Hemming (t/a Simply Pleasure Ltd) v Westminster CC*,[5] the Court of Appeal ordered the defendant to repay money improperly charged as sex shop licence fees.

In addition to the fact that they all concerned *Woolwich* claims, these cases have another common feature, which they also share with *Lady & Kid A/S v Skatteministeriet*,[6] where the European Court of Justice ordered restitution of money paid as tax levied under legislation that was contrary to EU law. In each case, the defendant argued that its liability should be reduced to the extent that the claimant would have incurred and paid a valid legal obligation to the defendant had the claimant not paid the defendant to discharge a non-existent liability. This argument does not purport to justify the defendant's enrichment on the ground that the claimant was liable to the defendant on the facts as they happened. It concedes that the money was not due on the facts as they happened, but contends that if the money had not been paid, other events would have occurred, as a result of which the money would have become legally due.

In the cases under consideration, the defendants have presented this argument as though it were simply a matter of common sense. They have not sought to express the argument in clear legal terms, either as a denial that the claimant has failed to establish a recognised ingredient of his action or as a recognised defence which accepts that the claimant has made out a prima facie case, but asserts another reason why he should not be entitled to restitution.[7] One reason may have been counsel's unfamiliarity with the conceptual structure of claims in unjust enrichment and the answers that can be made to them. The unfortunate result is that the legal relevance of the defendants' argument in the cases under consideration is rather obscure, and this makes it hard to assess its merits. Nevertheless, this chapter will

[4] *Waikato Regional Airport Ltd v AG of New Zealand* [2003] UKPC 50; [2004] 3 NZLR 1.

[5] *Hemming (t/a Simply Pleasure Ltd) v Westminster CC* [2013] EWCA Civ 591; [2013] PTSR 1377; partly reversing [2012] EWHC 1260 (Admin); [2012] PTSR 1676. There was no appeal from the part of the Court of Appeal's decision with which this chapter is concerned, but another part of its decision was reversed, and a reference made to the CJEU, by the Supreme Court: [2015] UKSC 25; [2015] 2 WLR 1271.

[6] Case C-398/09 *Lady & Kid A/S v Skatteministeriet* [2012] CMLR 14 (ECJ). See also Case C-331/13 *Nicula v Administraţia Finanţelor Publice a Municipiului Sibiu* [2015] 1 CMLR 33 (ECJ).

[7] For the distinction between denials and defences, see J Goudkamp and C Mitchell, 'Denials and Defences in the Law of Unjust Enrichment' in C Mitchell and W Swadling (eds), *The Restatement Third, Restitution and Unjust Enrichment: Critical and Comparative Essays* (Oxford, Hart Publishing, 2013).

attempt such an assessment after a more detailed account has been given of the cases in sections 2 and 3. The merits of counterfactual arguments against *Woolwich* liability will be examined from a public law perspective in section 4. They will then be considered from a private law perspective in section 5, where it will be asked how such arguments might be framed in legal terms and what responses might be made to them, depending on how they have been pleaded.

2. THE CASES IN MORE DETAIL

2.1. *Waikato Regional Airport Ltd v AG of New Zealand*

Under the New Zealand Biosecurity Act 1993, certain airports could not operate international flights without border control services provided by the Ministry of Agriculture and Fishery (MAF). The cost of these was partly met from central government funding, and section 135 of the Act required and empowered the Director-General of Agriculture and Forestry to recover the balance by charging service users. He adopted a policy of charging regional, but not metropolitan, airports. This policy was successfully challenged in judicial review proceedings by the claimant, which then sought to recover its payments. Speaking for the Privy Council, Lord Nicholls and Lord Walker held that the case fell within the scope of the *Woolwich* principle, although MAF's charges had not constituted a tax. Nor did it matter that the claimant had received services in exchange for its money, since these had not been of commercial benefit. Nor (probably) would it have mattered if they had been of commercial benefit, following *South of Scotland Electricity Board v British Oxygen Co Ltd*,[8] where the court had ordered restitution of excessive charges for electricity supplies by a provider with statutory charging powers.

It followed that the claimant in *Waikato* was entitled to restitution. At first instance, however, Wild J had held that it would be:[9]

> unjust not to allow MAF to retain a reasonable portion of [the claimant's] payments to it (reasonable based on a proper s 135 assessment). Section 135 was enacted specifically to enable MAF to recover any shortfall in Crown funding appropriated for the enforcement of the Biosecurity Act. It follows that … it would be unjust for [the claimant] to succeed on a claim for full repayment.

This finding was affirmed in the Privy Council. Lord Nicholls and Lord Walker held that the claimant could recover no more than 'the excess over what would have been a fair and proportionate charge'.[10]

[8] *South of Scotland Electricity Board v British Oxygen Co Ltd* [1959] 1 WLR 587 (HL).
[9] *Waikato Regional Airport Ltd v AG of New Zealand* [2001] 2 NZLR 670 (NZHC) 713.
[10] *Waikato* (PC) (n 4) [84].

2.2. *Lady & Kid A/S v Skatteministeriet*

The Danish government abolished employer social security contributions in order to stimulate growth and develop employment. To pay for this measure, it introduced a new business tax named the employment market contribution (*arbejdsmarkedsbidrag*, known as the 'Ambi'). The Ambi was charged on the full sale price of imported goods on their first sale in Denmark. The European Court of Justice then ruled that the Ambi was incompatible with EU law, and so the Danish government enacted legislation arranging for repayment of the Ambi that had been unlawfully levied.

The applicant retailers sought restitution of their Ambi payments. The Danish tax authorities rejected their applications on the ground that if the Danish government had known that the Ambi was contrary to EU law, then it would not have abolished employer social security contributions. Although the applicants had made Ambi payments which had not been due, the value of these had been less than the value of the employer social security contributions which they would otherwise have had to pay. The applicants brought proceedings for restitution in the Danish courts, which made a reference to the European Court of Justice to determine (among other things) whether it was open to Denmark to provide that payments of money as tax levied in breach of EU law could not be recovered if the payer had made a saving as a result of the concomitant abolition of another (legally valid) tax.

The European Court of Justice held that the recognition of such a defence under Danish law would be contrary to EU law. This precludes a Member State from:[11]

> refusing reimbursement of a tax wrongfully levied on the ground that the amounts wrongly paid by the taxpayer have been set off by a saving made as a result of the concomitant abolition of other levies, since such a set-off cannot be regarded, from the point of view of European Union law, as an unjust enrichment as regards that tax.

The court's reference to an 'unjust enrichment as regards that tax' was to a defence that is more familiar to English unjust enrichment lawyers as the passing on defence (although the same language is used in section 80(3) of the Value Added Tax 1994 (UK)). The point made by the court was that apart from reasonable limitation defences, there is only one argument that EU law permits public authority defendants to make in reply to claims for restitution of money paid as tax levied in breach of EU law, namely that the claimant has passed on its loss to a third party.[12] Thus, the court stated that

[11] *Lady & Kid* (n 6) [26].

[12] Case C-192/95 *Société Comateb v Directeur Général des Douanes et Droits Indirects* [1997] STC 1006 (ECJ) [27]–[28]; Case C-147/01 *Weber's Wine World Handels-GmbH v Abgabenberufungskommission Wien* [2004] 1 CMLR 7 (ECJ).

'the direct passing on of the tax wrongly levied on the [claimant] constitutes the sole exception to the right to reimbursement of tax levied in breach of EU law'.[13]

The counterfactual argument made by the defendant in *Lady & Kid* did not purport to say that the claimants had passed on their losses to third parties. Hence it was not a valid argument under EU law.

2.3. *Hemming (t/a Simply Pleasure Ltd) v Westminster CC*

The applicant paid money to the defendant council as fees for sex shop licences. The fees included sums that reflected the costs to the council of enforcing the licensing regime by prosecuting unlicensed sex shop operators. The applicant brought judicial review proceedings arguing that these costs should not have been included in the fees following the implementation in the UK of a European Directive which provides that charges for such authorisation schemes must not exceed the cost of authorisation procedures and formalities. This argument succeeded before Keith J, whose decision was affirmed by the Court of Appeal.

It followed that the applicant was entitled to restitution. However, the applicant accepted that he could not recover the whole of the sums paid, and only claimed the difference between the sums paid and whatever would have constituted reasonable licence fees. Keith J described this as a 'concession' which had properly been made in light of the findings in *Waikato* that have been set out above, and awarded the amount sought.[14] The Court of Appeal upheld this result, but stated that the applicant had had no choice whether to 'concede' the point, since he had not been legally entitled to claim the full amount of his payments.

Beatson LJ stated[15] that English authority for this proposition could be found in Lord Goff's observation in *Woolwich* that:[16]

> money paid to a person in a public or quasi-public position to obtain the performance by him of a duty which he is bound to perform for nothing or for less than the sum demanded by him is recoverable to the extent that he is not entitled to it.

Lord Goff had based this statement of the law on cases in which public officials acting under colour of their office had illegitimately demanded too high a fee for their services, and recovery had been limited to the amount

[13] *Lady & Kid* (n 6) [20].
[14] *Hemming* (Admin) (n 5) [47].
[15] *Hemming* (CA) (n 5) [110].
[16] *Woolwich* (n 1) 164–65.

by which the sums paid had exceeded a legitimate fee.[17] Beatson LJ thought that this approach:[18]

> has the practical attraction of entitling the person who overpaid in circumstances in which the public authority is able to levy the fee or part of it lawfully to recover only the excess. In this way it reflects the economic reality of what happened notwithstanding the public law flaw in the circumstances of the original payment.

Beatson LJ also noted that in the *Waikato* case, Wild J had considered that 'it would be unjust for [the airport] to succeed on a claim for full repayment',[19] but that:[20]

> [neither] he nor the Judicial Committee, which reinstated his order, expressly considered whether the mechanism for the partial restitution ordered was that it was assumed that the lawful amount had in fact been determined but that must be the position. It was therefore not the entire payment that was due back 'forthwith' with the attendant consequences for interest, but only that to which the payee, the Director General, could not be entitled.

The *Hemming* case was appealed to the Supreme Court, which partly reversed the Court of Appeal's decision and made a reference to the Court of Justice of the European Union on the question whether aspects of the defendant's charging process were compatible with EU law. The Supreme Court did not consider the lower courts' findings in connection with the defendant's restitutionary liability.

2.4. *Littlewoods Retail Ltd v HMRC*

The claimant companies undertook catalogue-based home shopping businesses, making sales through agents who earned commission on third party purchases. This was payable in cash or in further goods. For many years, the claimants accounted for VAT on the basis that 100 per cent of the cash

[17] *Steele v Williams* (1853) 8 Ex 625, 630–31; 155 ER 1502, 1504–05 (Parke B): a parish clerk could keep money legitimately demanded as a fee for searching the parish register, but had to repay money illegitimately demanded as a fee for copying entries; *Great Western Railway Co v Sutton* (1869) LR 4 HL 226, especially 249 (Willes J): 'when a man pays more than he is bound to do by law for the performance of a duty which the law says is owed to him for nothing, or for less than he has paid, there is a compulsion or concussion in respect of which he is entitled to recover the excess by *condictio indebiti*, or action for money had and received'; *South of Scotland Electricity Board v British Oxygen Co Ltd (No 2)* [1959] 1 WLR 587 (HL), where industrial consumers of electricity claimed that the Board's tariffs unduly discriminated against them contrary to statute, and at 596, Viscount Kilmuir LC said that they could 'recover whatever sum they may be able to prove was in excess of such a charge as would have avoided undue discrimination against them'.

[18] *Hemming* (CA) (n 5) [110].

[19] *Waikato* (NZHC) (n 9) [177].

[20] *Hemming* (CA) (n 5) [128].

commission and 80 per cent of the goods commission was consideration for services provided by the agents. HMRC then conceded that this treatment had been incorrect and that VAT should have been payable on the basis that the commission operated as a discount on goods supplied by the claimants to their agents. It followed that HMRC had been paid money as VAT that had not been due.

HMRC repaid this money under section 80 of the Value Added Tax Act 1994 (UK), along with simple interest under section 78. However, the claimants said that this was insufficient to give effect to their right under EU law to a full indemnity, and that EU law required that they should be given a common law right against HMRC to recover compound interest because this represented the use value of the money received by HMRC. Among various answers which HMRC made to this claim, they argued that any restitutionary liability they had incurred should be reduced to reflect the fact that if the claimants had not made the relevant VAT payments, their profits would have been correspondingly larger and so they would have incurred and paid a larger corporation tax liability than they had actually incurred and paid.

Henderson J allowed the claim and rejected HMRC's counterfactual argument. He held as a matter of EU law that HMRC were prohibited from making this argument by *Lady & Kid*.[21] But even if EU law had not been in play, he would have held that the argument was a bad one.[22] He gave several reasons for this, which are considered in sections 4 and 5 below. HMRC won leave to appeal from various parts of Henderson J's judgment, but his decision was subsequently affirmed by the Court of Appeal. HMRC did not seek leave to appeal from the judge's findings on their counterfactual argument. They may have calculated that an appellate court would uphold his analysis of the EU law issue, making it pointless for them to challenge his rejection of the argument as a matter of English law.

3. THE EUROPEAN DIMENSION

The focus of this chapter is on counterfactual arguments against *Woolwich* liability under English law. It is not intended to undertake a detailed discussion of the reasons why the European Court of Justice has radically curtailed the range of answers which defendants can make to claims for restitution of money paid as tax levied in breach of EU law. However, it seems useful to summarise these briefly.

In essence, the Court has held this curtailment to be required by the EU law principle of effectiveness. Where money is paid to discharge a liability imposed by a Member State in breach of EU law, EU law requires that the

[21] *Littlewoods* (Ch) (n 3) [421]–[425].
[22] ibid [426]–[434].

money should be repaid, that the payor should therefore be given a remedy by the domestic law of the Member State[23] and that this remedy should not be made ineffective by the operation of defences under the Member State's domestic law. Reasonable limitation defences apart, passing on is the only argument that the Court allows Member States to make available as a reply to claims in unjust enrichment to recover money paid as tax levied in breach of EU law. And in the form of the passing on argument allowed under EU law, even this may not excuse defendants, since it is essentially an argument that the defendant should make restitution to the person to whom the claimant has passed on his loss. If this person can be identified, the defendant may have to repay the money on the basis that it will be channelled back to him by the claimant.[24]

4. PUBLIC LAW PERSPECTIVES

Woolwich claims have a hybrid character. They are private law claims whose function is to implement public law goals and whose elements derive from both bodies of law. This point has been well made by Rebecca Williams,[25] who has additionally argued that in principle, claimants seeking restitution of money paid to public bodies acting ultra vires should be confined to a *Woolwich* claim and should not be permitted to rely on other grounds of recovery such as mistake. In her view, this rule would have the beneficial effect of enabling the courts to recognise that such claims have a public law aspect and that the appropriate mechanisms for resolving the policy issues in play can be found in the body of law concerning judicial oversight of administrative action. The significance of this body of authority might be

[23] English lawyers commonly call this the '*San Giorgio* principle', after Case 199/82 *Amministrazione delle Finanze dello Stato v SpA San Giorgio* [1983] ECR 3595. But *San Giorgio* was not the first ECJ decision to recognise the principle—see Case 68/79, *Hans Just I/S v Danish Ministry for Fiscal Affairs* [1980] ECR 501—and the ECJ itself does not accord the *San Giorgio* case any special significance.

[24] For the points made in this paragraph, see M Bhandari, 'Unjust Enrichment and Section 80(3) VAT Act 1994' [2004] *British Tax Review* 620; R Williams, '*Lady & Kid A/S v Skatteministeriet (C-398/09)* and *Ministre du Budget, des Comptes Publics et de la Fonction Publique v Accor SA (C-310/09)*: Unjust Enrichment and the Court of Justice of the European Communities, a Loss of National Competence and Principle?' [2011] *British Tax Review* 631; C Mitchell, P Mitchell and S Watterson, *Goff & Jones: The Law of Unjust Enrichment*, 8th edn (Sweet & Maxwell, 2011) ch 32; M Schlote, 'The Principle of Effectiveness and Restitution of Overpaid Tax' in S Elliott, B Häcker and C Mitchell (eds), *Restitution of Overpaid Tax* (Oxford, Hart Publishing, 2013); M Schlote, 'The *San Giorgio* "Cause of Action"' [2014] *British Tax Review* 103.

[25] R Williams, *Unjust Enrichment and Public Law* (Oxford, Hart Publishing, 2010) especially chs 2 and 3, reprised in R Williams, 'Overpaid Taxes: A Hybrid Public and Private Approach' in Elliott, Häcker and Mitchell (n 24).

overlooked or marginalised if the claimant were allowed to frame his action as though it were a purely private law claim founded on, eg, mistake, for the purposes of which the only significant issue is the vitiation of the claimant's intention to benefit the defendant.

As Williams recognises, English law does not have such a rule[26] and, in fact, the House of Lords held the exact opposite in *Deutsche Morgan Grenfell Group plc v IRC*,[27] where the court refused to confine the claimant to its *Woolwich* claim and held that it was free to bring a mistake claim if it wished to do so. Nevertheless, in a case where money has been paid as tax that was not due and a claim in unjust enrichment is made that is founded on a ground of recovery other than the *Woolwich* ground, it is still open to the court to treat the public character of the defendant as a relevant factor when adjudicating the claim and assessing the merits of arguments made by the defendant to resist liability.[28] Even where a claim has been pleaded as a mistake claim, therefore, and certainly where it has been pleaded as a *Woolwich* claim, the court can and should take note of any public law (including tax law) principles that bear upon the legitimacy of such arguments—including counterfactual arguments of the kind that are discussed in this chapter.

Several such principles will now be considered.

4.1. No Taxation Without Parliament

Self-assessment has become an increasingly prevalent feature of the UK tax system, but whatever mechanism is used to calculate a taxpayer's liability, it remains the case that HMRC's entitlement to charge and receive tax arises only in situations identified by the tax legislation and is additionally subject to compliance with rules governing administrative procedures, time

[26] But *cf Kingstreet Investments Ltd v New Brunswick (Department of Finance)* [2007] SCC 1; [2007] 1 SCR 3 [33]–[35] (Bastarache J): under Canadian law, claims to recover money paid as tax which was not due are a *sui generis* type of restitutionary claim 'based on the constitutional principle that taxes should not be levied without proper authority'; such claims raise 'important constitutional principles which would be ignored by treating the claim [as a private law restitutionary claim founded on unjust enrichment or wrongdoing]'.

[27] *Deutsche Morgan Grenfell* (n 3). Note also that the logic of Williams' argument suggests that the limitation rule governing *Woolwich* claims should be the three-month rule applicable to proceedings for judicial review rather than the six-year rule applicable to actions for unjust enrichment, yet the latter rule has been held to apply: *Hemming* (CA) (n 5) [138] (Beatson LJ); *Investment Trust Companies (In Liquidation) v HMRC* [2015] EWCA Civ 82; [2015] STC 1280 [23] (Patten LJ, giving the judgment of the court); *Littlewoods* (CA) (n 3) [8] (Arden LJ, giving the judgment of the court).

[28] *cf Test Claimants in the FII Group Litigation v HMRC (No 2)* [2014] EWHC 4302 (Ch); [2015] STC 1471 [316]–[341], where Henderson J discussed without deciding whether the policy reasons that might justify debarring HMRC from raising a change of position defence in answer to a *Woolwich* claim might also debar them from relying on the defence in answer to a mistake claim.

limits, etc. Taxpayers owe no obligation to pay tax and HMRC have no corresponding right to receive tax, except in the situations defined by this body of law.

This principle was applied in *Bowles v Bank of England*,[29] which concerned the Revenue's former practice of levying taxes on the basis of Commons resolutions pending the enactment of the annual Finance Act. Parker J held this to be illegal, with the result that the Bank of England had no legal authority to deduct income tax at source from payments due to the claimant prior to the enactment of the Finance Act for the relevant year. It made no difference that the claimant would have become liable to pay the tax at the end of the tax year once the statute had been enacted.

It is true that in the context of some taxes, eg, VAT, mechanisms exist to correct overcharging mistakes by reducing the taxpayer's liability by the amount of the excess in the next tax year, and it might be said that these mechanisms effectively justify the receipt by HMRC of sums to which they are not entitled in the tax year when they are paid, because the parties are in an ongoing relationship constituted by the taxpayer's liability to account for and pay tax year after year, so that the account between them runs on from one year to the next and is not finally settled on an end-of-year basis. Nevertheless, the general principle is well established, and the reason for it is not hard to find. Obligations to pay tax are substantively different from most obligations arising in private law, owing to the significant power imbalance between the parties. HMRC can deploy the coercive power of the state to take taxpayers' property, and taxpayers are vulnerable to abuses of that power. That is why Article 4 of the Bill of Rights, invoked by Parker J in *Bowles*,[30] insists that this power can only be exercised with parliamentary sanction, even where it is predictable that this sanction will be granted in the future with retrospective effect. That is also why the courts should not lightly deem HMRC to have acted within the limits of their power when in fact they have not done so.

What are the implications of this for an argument by HMRC that they could and would have validly charged the claimant for tax that would have become due if he had not paid them money to discharge a non-existent tax liability? Does it matter that this argument requires the court to assume in HMRC's favour that they would have complied with all the rules governing the exercise of their valid charging power, including time limits, although in fact they never complied with them because in fact they never sought

[29] *Bowles v Bank of England* [1913] 1 Ch 57 (Ch D); discussed in J Jaconelli, 'The "Bowles Act"—Cornerstone of the Fiscal Constitution' (2010) 69 *CLJ* 582.

[30] *Bowles* (n 29) 84–85: 'The Bill of Rights still remains unrepealed, and no practice or custom, however prolonged, or however acquiesced in on the part of the subject, can be relied on by the Crown as justifying any infringement of its provisions.'

to exercise the power? In *Littlewoods*, the claimant argued that this does matter, but Henderson J disagreed. He held that: 'No constitutional principle is engaged by the making of counterfactual assumptions.'[31] The claimant's argument and Henderson J's response were as follows:

> [S]ince the [corporation] tax was never in fact levied or paid, [the claimants] say that to take it into account would offend the constitutional principle that tax cannot be recovered without the authority of Parliament. In substance, submit the claimants, the Revenue are attempting to collect a tax, or interest on a tax, which is not and never has been due ... I can rapidly dispose of [this objection]. I agree with [HMRC] that taking account of the corporation tax saved by the claimants would not offend against any constitutional principle. The Revenue are not attempting to levy the tax which has been saved, but simply arguing that any realistic assessment of the actual benefit to the Government from the overpayments of VAT must make due allowance for the hypothetical extra corporation tax which would have been paid by the claimants.

Some support for this stance might be drawn from cases which hold that compensatory damages for tort or breach of contract, which are not themselves taxable, should nevertheless be reduced to reflect the fact that tax would have been payable on the victim's lost income, although ex hypothesi there will have been no compliance with legal rules governing the imposition of the tax because the victim will never receive the income.[32] However, there is a difference between quantifying loss wrongfully caused by one private individual to another and quantifying gain unlawfully received by a public body from a taxpayer, and it may be illegitimate to draw an analogy between the two classes of case if one gives rise to constitutional (and wider rule of law) concerns while the other does not.

Do such concerns arise where HMRC purport to keep money paid as tax that was not due on the ground that they would have validly collected the money as tax by another mechanism if the claimant's actual payment had not been made? In my view, HMRC's argument is more problematic than Henderson J recognised in *Littlewoods*. If it justifies HMRC keeping money which they were not entitled to receive, then this is not very different from saying that it justifies HMRC taking money which they are not entitled to take. Yet in *Bowles*, Parker J held, with good reason, that the tax authorities cannot justify taking a taxpayer's money without parliamentary authority by saying that they could alternatively have taken the money in an authorised way.

[31] *Littlewoods* (Ch) (n 3) [429].

[32] eg, *British Transport Commission v Gourley* [1956] AC 185 (HL); *Parsons v BNM Laboratories Ltd* [1964] 1 QB 95 (CA). These and other cases are discussed by Ramsey J in *BSkyB Ltd v HP Enterprise Services UK Ltd (No 2)* [2010] EWHC 862 (TCC); (2010) 131 Con LR 42.

4.2. Equality of Arms Between Taxpayers and HMRC

Taxpayers are not obliged to arrange their affairs so that they incur the maximum possible amount of tax liability.[33] They are 'entitled to arrange their affairs to avoid payment of tax if they legitimately can'.[34] When a taxpayer does this, HMRC must take him as they find him. But when a taxpayer fails to arrange his affairs in the most tax-efficient way, HMRC are entitled to tax him according to the state of his affairs as they are, and not as they might have been. In this case, the taxpayer cannot complain that he has paid 'too much' tax, because he has no right to be treated as though he has arranged his affairs to minimise his tax liability. As Monica Bhandari has written:[35]

> If his tax liability were really a 'windfall' to the Revenue, then that would suggest that whenever a taxpayer arranged his affairs in a way that exposed him to a greater tax liability than the minimum he could have achieved with more careful planning, the Revenue should not be allowed to keep the difference. If that were the rule then administration of the tax system would be significantly more burdensome and expensive, taxpayers would have no incentive to set out their affairs in a sensible manner from the outset, and tax advisers would effectively be given the benefit of hindsight and carte blanche to change transactions so as to minimize tax liability.

If taxpayers are unable to escape a tax liability by saying that they would have arranged their affairs differently had they known that this would reduce their liability, then HMRC should be unable to charge more tax by saying that taxpayers would have incurred an additional tax liability if their affairs had been arranged differently. Were HMRC permitted to make such an argument, this would contradict the premise on which all tax is collected, that HMRC take taxpayers as they find them, and there is no justification for allowing HMRC to make an argument that contradicts this premise while denying taxpayers the right to do the same thing.

4.3. Flawed Exercise of Valid Powers

In some of the cases under review, such as *Littlewoods*, the defendant had no valid power to charge the claimant under legislation which it mistakenly

[33] *IRC v Duke of Westminster* [1936] AC 1 (HL); *Ensign Tankers (Leasing) Ltd v Stokes (Inspector of Taxes)* [1992] 1 AC 655 (HL).

[34] *Re Slocock's WT* [1979] 1 All ER 358 (Ch D), 363 (Graham J). Their scope for taking such action has been greatly reduced by anti-avoidance legislation, but this does not alter the basic point made in the text.

[35] M Bhandari, 'Undoing Transactions for Tax Purposes: The *Hastings-Bass* Principle' in Elliott, Häcker and Mitchell (n 24) 163–64.

believed to cover the case. Hence, the essence of the defendant's counterfactual argument was that if the claimant had not paid its non-existent liability, the claimant's affairs would have played out differently and the case would have fallen within the scope of different legislation under which the defendant could validly have made a different charge. Other cases, such as *Waikato*, are different: the defendant had a valid statutory power to charge the claimant, but its exercise of the power was flawed. Hence the essence of the defendant's counterfactual argument was that if it had not used the wrong process, then it would have used the right process and would therefore have exercised its power to make the same kind of charge in a valid way.

On one view, the courts should not make assumptions in the defendant's favour in either class of case, but it is understandable why a court might think it easier to do this in the second class of case than in the first. The reason is that less counterfactual hypothesising is needed. In the second class of case, the defendant correctly identifies the source of its charging power and complies with many of the rules governing the exercise of this power (including time limits), but exercises the power in a flawed way (eg, because it invalidly treats the claimant differently from other chargees). So a court which decides to allow the defendant's argument only needs to make one assumption in its favour, namely that it would have exercised its power in a valid way had it known there was a problem. In contrast, the defendant in the first class of case fails to identify the source of its valid charging power, fails to comply with any of the rules governing the exercise of this power (including time limits) and, indeed, fails to exercise the power at all. So the court may have to make many assumptions in the defendant's favour before the argument can work.

The argument that the courts should not make assumptions in the defendant's favour where the defendant has exercised a valid power in an invalid way is premised on the idea that good process is a desirable end in itself and hence that a flawed process is deplorable even where it produces outcomes that could have been reached by valid means. This has frequently been stated in the context of actions for judicial review of administrative decision making, where the courts have cautioned against 'the notion that when the rules of natural justice have not been observed, one can still uphold the result because it would not have made any difference'[36]—albeit that they have also said that they will not award a remedy where compliance with good process

[36] *R v Ealing Magistrates Court ex p Fanneran* (1996) 160 JP 409 (QBD) (Staughton LJ). *cf R v Tanbridge DC ex p Al Fayed* (1998) 80 P&CR 90, 94 (Schiemann LJ): 'Once it is apprised of a procedural impropriety the court will always be slow to say, in effect, "no harm has been done". That would involve arrogating to itself a value judgment which Parliament has left to others.' See too Lord Woolf, J Jowell and A Le Sueur (eds) *De Smith's Judicial Review* (London, Sweet & Maxwell, 2007) 471–74.

would inevitably have led to the same decision being made.[37] An example is *R (Lumba) v Secretary of State for the Home Department*,[38] where it was no answer to the argument that the Home Secretary had acted unlawfully when ordering the applicant's detention pursuant to a secret policy that she would have made the same decision if she had followed her published policy.[39]

4.4. Tax Cases and Service Charge Cases

Another point of difference between the cases is that in *Littlewoods*, the claimant paid money as tax, while in others, such as *Waikato* and the service charge cases cited by Lord Goff in *Woolwich*, the claimant paid money as a fee for the defendant's services. The difference between taxes and service charges by public bodies is not particularly clear, but for a levy to be classified as a charge rather than a tax, a benefit must usually be provided directly to the payor, and the amount charged must be calculated by reference to the cost of providing the benefit rather than some other criterion, eg, the payor's means or the value of his property.[40] But laying to one side the rather abstract issue of how the charge made by the defendant in each of our cases should be classified,[41] the question arises whether it affects our understanding of the cases that in some the defendant performed services for the claimant and in others it did not, save in the larger sense that taxes fund public services for everyone?

[37] A test that has recently—and controversially—been watered down by s 84 of the Criminal Justice and Courts Act 2014 (UK), inserting a new provision into the Senior Courts Act 1981 (UK) which requires the court to refuse relief where 'it appears to the court to be highly likely that the outcome for the applicant would not have been substantially different if the conduct complained of had not occurred'.

[38] *R (Lumba) v Secretary of State for the Home Department* [2011] UKSC 12; [2012] 1 AC 245. See too *Kambadzi v Secretary of State for the Home Department* [2011] UKSC 23; [2011] 1 WLR 1299; *Bostridge v Oxleas NHS Foundation Trust* [2015] EWCA Civ 79; [2015] Med LR 113.

[39] Although it followed from this that the Home Secretary had committed the tort of false imprisonment, the Supreme Court controversially declined to award substantive damages as it held that on a 'but for' basis, the applicant had suffered no loss. This has left the law governing tort liability for unlawful detention in some disarray, although the decision can be defended from a policy perspective on the basis that 'a range of public interests are in play [in such cases] which do not outweigh a person's claim to liberty but may outweigh a claim to damages for loss of liberty': D Feldman, 'Error of Law and Flawed Administrative Acts' [2014] *CLJ* 275, 300–01.

[40] *Daymond v South West Water Authority* [1976] AC 609 (HL). It is no objection to categorisation as a charge that a levy results in the public body making a reasonable profit: *Minister of Justice for the Dominion of Canada v City of Levis* [1919] AC 505 (PC (Can)). For general discussion of taxes and charges, see J Tiley and G Loutzenhiser, *Revenue Law*, 7th edn (Oxford, Hart Publishing, 2012) 3–7.

[41] The distinction has some practical consequences—eg, the rule that taxpayers can stand on a strict and literal construction of tax legislation does not apply to statutes which give a power to charge for services: *Pryce v Monmouthshire Canal & Railway Cos* (1879) 4 App Cas 197 (HL) 202–03.

This can make no difference to those who hold that constitutional (and wider rule of law) principles are not threatened by allowing defendants to make counterfactual arguments: they would allow defendants to make such arguments in both types of case. But it could make a difference to those who think it desirable to incentivise public bodies not to exceed their powers by forbidding them from keeping improperly collected money, although some or all of it would have been properly collected if the defendant had done the right thing. Those who take this stance might make an exception for cases where the claimant receives the benefit of services, particularly if he knows that the defendant expects to be paid for them. The point would be to stop the claimant keeping a benefit to which he was not entitled unless he paid for it.

This line of argument prompts the question whether a clear line can be drawn between 'personal' benefits received by claimants in exchange for fees and 'public' benefits received by all taxpayers in exchange for their taxes? An associated question is whether a distinction can be drawn between services that claimants choose to receive because they want them, and services that claimants are required to receive whether they want them or not. The border control services supplied by the defendant in *Waikato* were services which the claimant was obliged to receive as a condition of operating its airport. So was the defendant's work of administering the sex shop licensing system for which the claimant paid the licence fee in *Hemming*. In cases of this kind, there is less force in the argument that the claimant should pay for benefits which it sought from the defendant.

4.5. Summary

The discussion in this section has identified some principles of public law (including tax law) that might affect a court's assessment of whether a public body defendant should be able to use counterfactual reasoning to escape *Woolwich* liability. Some principles suggest that such arguments should generally be disallowed, for example, the rule that there should be no taxation without Parliament and the desirability of incentivising good process in administrative decision making. However, there may be good reasons to distinguish between different classes of case and it may be that the courts will wish to engage in a balancing exercise that takes various factors into account when considering the merits of counterfactual arguments on the facts of individual cases. More work is needed to identify and assess the criteria by reference to which such an exercise might be undertaken, for example, whether the defendant's error of law was egregious or excusable, whether it resulted in the breach of an essential procedural requirement, whether awarding a remedy would have a chilling effect on the defendant experimenting with fairer and more efficient methods of tax collection, and whether the claimant received a personal benefit in exchange for his money.

5. PRIVATE LAW DIMENSIONS

In each of the cases discussed in section 2, the defendant made a bare counterfactual assertion that it should escape liability because events would have occurred if the claimant's payment had not been made, as a result of which the claimant would have incurred a valid liability to pay the defendant. Assertions of this kind are not legal arguments, in the sense that they use counterfactual reasoning to disprove an identified element of the claim or prove that the defendant has an identified defence. To understand their legal relevance to the outcome of *Woolwich* claims, we must therefore consider the possible ways in which a defendant might conceivably use counterfactual reasoning to support a legal argument against liability.

The discussion is divided into two sections. The first section examines some legal arguments which probably cannot be supported by counterfactual reasoning because they can only plausibly work in cases where the claimant was liable to the defendant on the facts as they happened. The second section looks at some other legal arguments, which are more promising for defendants in the sense that it is enough for the purposes of the argument that the claimant would have become liable on the facts which would have happened if the claimant had not paid the defendant.

5.1. Arguments that Cannot Be Supported by Counterfactual Reasoning

5.1.1. Presence of Legal Ground

Many cases establish that a claim in unjust enrichment will not lie to recover benefits which the defendant is legally entitled to receive by statute.[42] However, a defendant can only resist liability by invoking this principle where the relevant statute rendered the claimant liable to pay on the facts as they happened and not on the facts as they would have happened if the claimant had not paid its non-existent liability.

5.1.2. Counterclaim/Set-Off

For the same reason, a defendant cannot use counterfactual reasoning to show that it has a counterclaim for the amount of a valid liability owed by the claimant, which should be set off against the amount of defendant's restitutionary liability. The defendant can only have a counterclaim if the claimant incurred a valid liability to the defendant on the facts as they happened. Henderson J made this point in *Littlewoods* when he observed that HMRC 'never had an actual claim for the additional corporation tax. It was

[42] *Goff & Jones* (n 24) ch 2.

always a hypothetical claim, in a counterfactual world where the VAT had not been overpaid. There can therefore be no question of an actual set-off'.[43]

5.1.3. Counter-restitution

In *Littlewoods*,[44] Henderson J suggested that the same problem may also prevent the defendant from arguing that the claimant should make counter-restitution of a benefit that it received in exchange for its money, namely the release of a valid legal liability owed by the claimant to the defendant. This argument would run as follows. The law requires a claimant to make counter-restitution of benefits he has received from a defendant as a precondition for restitution. This rule applies where a claimant pays a tax liability which is not due, but owes a different, valid liability from which he is released following his payment, so that he is enriched at the defendant's expense.[45]

Henderson J seems to say that this argument can only work if the claimant has escaped a valid liability which arose on the facts as they happened. Could a defendant overcome this objection by arguing that a claimant can relevantly be enriched, although no liability actually arose on the facts, because a liability would have arisen if the claimant had not paid the invalid liability, and the claimant is better off to the extent that he has not had to pay this liability? There are some cases which might support this proposition, discussed in *Goff & Jones* under the heading 'Pre-Emptive Liabilities'.[46] Examples are *Metropolitan Police District v Croydon Corp*[47] and *AMP Workers Compensation Services (NSW) Ltd v QBE Insurance Ltd*.[48] These cases hold that a defendant is unjustly enriched at a claimant's expense when a third party chooses to recover a loss from the claimant in such a way that the defendant never becomes legally liable to the third party for the same loss, although as between the claimant and the defendant, the defendant is the 'right person' to pay the third party. However, this line of authority is not strong and the situation it addresses is quite far removed from the case in issue.

43 *Littlewoods* (Ch) (n 3) [434].

44 ibid.

45 For the rule that a defendant is enriched at a claimant's expense if the claimant releases him from a liability, see *Gibb v Maidstone and Tunbridge Wells NHS Trust* [2010] EWCA Civ 678; [2010] IRLR 786, especially [30] (Laws LJ): there is no difference between 'a benefit consisting in money paid and a benefit consisting in a claim foregone'. This principle was considered in *Investment Trust Companies* (n 27) [30], but was held not to apply on the facts of that case.

46 *Goff & Jones* (n 24) paras [4-22]–[4-26].

47 *Metropolitan Police District v Croydon Corp* [1956] 1 WLR 1113 (QBD), overruled [1957] 2 QB 154 (CA).

48 *AMP Workers Compensation Services (NSW) Ltd v QBE Insurance Ltd* [2011] NSWCA 267; (2001) 53 NSWLR 35.

The rule that a claimant seeking restitution must make counter-restitution of benefits received from the defendant was considered by Hobhouse J in *Kleinwort Benson Ltd v Sandwell BC*.[49] This concerned an interest rate swap contract that had been performed for more than six years before the parties discovered that the contract was void and the claimant bank brought proceedings to recover the value of its money. The question arose whether the bank should have to make counter-restitution of payments received more than six years previously, given that an independent claim by the defendant council to recover these payments would be time-barred. Hobhouse J held that all payments both ways should be taken into account when quantifying the claim, proceeding on the basis that, as payments went back and forth between the parties, there was only ever a single enrichment consisting in the difference between the value of the parties' performances. It followed that all of the parties' payments to one another should be taken into account when quantifying the bank's claim, which was for the net amount that the bank was owed following the most recent payment under the contract (made within the limitation period).[50]

The significance of this decision has been disputed. In Andrew Burrows' view, it simply shows that a defendant 'normally has a set-off defence for counter-restitution of reciprocal benefits conferred on the claimant by the defendant'.[51] However, my own view is that Hobhouse J's decision introduces a rule into English law that resembles the 'difference theory' (*Saldotheorie*) advocated by German scholars who contend that where benefits go back and forth under a contract, a claim lies against the party who received the greater value on the basis that he is enriched by the difference between what he received and what he gave, and the other party is not enriched at all.[52] If that is right, the reason why *Sandwell* requires that enrichments which have gone back and forth between the parties should be netted off is that this method of unwinding their dealings best reflects their mutual reciprocity. In other words, the law holds that one benefit should be set off against another when the parties' dealings are unwound because they agreed that one benefit should be given in exchange for another. On this view, the key factual feature of *Sandwell* was that the bank and the council *agreed* that their payments out would be made in exchange for payments in. Their contract was void, but this did not alter their shared understanding of why the payments and counter-payments were made.

If Burrows' interpretation of *Sandwell* is correct, then it is just another set-off case and there is nothing more to be said about this way of framing a

[49] *Kleinwort Benson Ltd v Sandwell BC* [1994] 1 WLR 938 (CA).

[50] ibid 941.

[51] A Burrows, *A Restatement of the English Law of Unjust Enrichment* (Oxford, Oxford University Press, 2012) 128.

[52] *Goff & Jones* (n 24) para [31-22].

defendant's argument against *Woolwich* liability than has already been said in section 5.1.2. However, if my reading of *Sandwell* is correct, it embodies a special rule that applies only where benefits have gone back and forth between the parties by agreement. This suggests an additional reason why the rule could not be invoked by a public authority defendant wishing to rely on the fact that the claimant was benefited by his escape from the imposition of a putative liability, viz that there was no agreement between the parties that the claimant would receive this benefit in exchange for his payment.

This analysis is consistent with Henderson J's finding in *Littlewoods*[53] that HMRC could not gain any support from *Sandwell* because the facts of *Littlewoods* were less closely analogous to the facts of *Sandwell* than they were to the facts of another swaps case, *Kleinwort Benson Ltd v South Tyneside MBC*.[54] In that case, there were five different contracts between the parties and because each was an independent transaction Hobhouse J refused to recognise any right of set-off or aggregation as between one contract and another.[55] Note, however, that one reason why Henderson J thought *South Tyneside* rather than *Sandwell* was the more closely analogous case was that in *Littlewoods*, it could not be said that the invalid VAT liability and the putative corporation tax liability 'arose out of the same underlying transaction, or that there was anything akin to a single running account between the parties'.[56] This leaves open the possibility that a defendant might make a counter-restitution argument in a case where this *can* be said of the parties' relationship, as it might be said eg, where a claimant is assessed for VAT on an invalid basis, but could have been assessed for VAT on a different, valid basis on the facts as they happened.

5.1.4. Bona Fide Purchase/Good Consideration

This is a fourth version of the defendant's argument that is most probably not viable unless the claimant incurred a valid liability on the facts as they happened, although again the cases on 'pre-emptive liabilities' might possibly support an argument that the claimant was benefited when he escaped a liability that would have arisen had the facts played out differently. In this version, the defendant would say that it should escape liability to the extent that it gave 'value' or 'consideration' for the claimant's money when it released the claimant from a valid liability.

In *Lipkin Gorman v Karpnale Ltd*,[57] the House of Lords accepted that bona fide purchase can operate as a defence to personal claims in unjust

[53] *Littlewoods* (Ch) (n 3) [431]–[432] and [434].
[54] *Kleinwort Benson Ltd v South Tyneside MBC* [1994] 4 All ER 972 (QBD).
[55] ibid 979.
[56] *Littlewoods* (Ch) (n 3) [434].
[57] *Lipkin Gorman v Karpnale Ltd* [1991] 2 AC 548 (HL).

enrichment, although it was not available on the facts of the case. Lord Templeman also said that:[58]

> An innocent recipient of stolen money may not be enriched at all; if [A] paid £20,000 derived from [B] to a car dealer for a motor car priced at £20,000, the car dealer would not have been enriched. The car dealer would have received £20,000 for a car worth £20,000.

This suggests that a good faith defendant who gives value in exchange for a benefit can argue that he is not enriched to the extent that his net position remains the same.

Furthermore, when calculating the defendant's 'net position', the court will ask only whether he gave all the consideration that was agreed with the transferor. This is the point of Lord Templeman's additional remark that 'an innocent recipient of stolen money will be enriched if the recipient has not given full consideration', taken in combination with Lord Goff's comment that 'where bona fide purchase is invoked, no inquiry is made (in most cases) into the adequacy of the consideration'.[59] This suggests that a good faith defendant who delivers a car worth £10,000 in exchange for £20,000 in stolen cash can still argue that he was not enriched at all. What generally matters (other than in cases of nominal consideration) is not the objective value of the consideration given by the defendant in exchange for the benefit he received, but whether he gave everything that he and the transferor agreed should be given.

Although bona fide purchase is widely described as a 'defence', Lord Templeman's analysis suggests that it is not a defence, but a denial of enrichment. However, no light has been cast on this question by later cases. It is also unclear whether the underlying point of the bona fide purchase defence is to track the rules of property law about the passing of title or to protect contracts of exchange.[60] And if the latter view of bona fide purchase is correct, it is unclear whether this leaves room for a discrete defence of 'good consideration'. Building on comments by Robert Goff J in *Barclays Bank Ltd v WJ Simms Son & Cooke (Southern) Ltd*,[61] Commonwealth courts have held that 'good consideration' is a defence to claims in unjust enrichment in both two-party and three-party situations.[62] In common

[58] ibid 560.

[59] ibid 580–81.

[60] *Goff & Jones* (n 24) paras [29-12]–[29-13].

[61] *Barclays Bank Ltd v WJ Simms Son & Cooke (Southern) Ltd* [1980] QB 677 (QBD) 695.

[62] eg, *Australia and New Zealand Banking Group Ltd v Westpac Banking Corp* (1988) 164 CLR 662 (HCA); *David Securities Pty Ltd v Commonwealth Bank of Australia* (1992) 175 CLR 353 (HCA); *Lloyds Bank plc v Independent Insurance Co Ltd* [2000] QB 110 (CA); *Ovidio Carrideo Nominees Pty Ltd v The Dog Depot Pty Ltd* [2006] VSCA 6; *Stiassny v Commissioner of Inland Revenue* [2012] NZCA 93, affirmed [2012] NZSC 106; [2013] 1 NZLR 453; *Hills Industries Ltd v Australian Financial Services and Leasing Pty Ltd* [2014] HCA 14; (2014) 253 CLR 560 [113] ff; [2014] HCA 14; (2014) 307 ALR 512 [100]–[102].

with Andrew Burrows, however, my own view is that 'good consideration' should not be regarded as a discrete defence to claims in unjust enrichment under English law, as it does no different work from bona fide purchase and/or the principle that claims in unjust enrichment will not lie to recover benefits which the recipient was contractually entitled to receive.[63]

If a defendant argues that it has a bona fide purchase defence or (if different) a good consideration defence to a *Woolwich* claim, basing itself on the fact that the claimant received value or consideration in the form of a release, the claimant could reply that these defences both presuppose that the parties *agreed* that the defendant would confer the relevant value or consideration in exchange for the benefit he receives. It is not enough for the defendant simply to show that he conferred a benefit on the claimant, even if there was a causal link between this conferral and his receipt of a benefit from the claimant.[64] Defendants in *Woolwich* cases are generally unlikely to be able to show that there was a relevant agreement. In a typical case, the claimant pays the defendant on the shared understanding that this will discharge a liability that both parties erroneously believe to exist. The claimant's payment is not typically made on the shared understanding that it will discharge a liability that has not actually arisen, although it would have arisen if the parties had appreciated their common error and acted differently.

5.2. Arguments that might be Supported by Counterfactual Reasoning

5.2.1. No Enrichment

It is trite law that a claim in unjust enrichment cannot lie unless the defendant has been enriched.[65] However, it is unclear whether English law allows defendants to use counterfactual reasoning to disprove enrichment. Burrows believes that it does, writing that 'it is possible that even the receipt of money is, overall, not beneficial to the defendant' and giving this example to illustrate this point: 'C pays D by mistake. As a result, a third party does not pay D the £100 she would otherwise have paid them.'[66]

[63] *Goff & Jones* (n 24) paras [29-15]–[29-22]; A Burrows, 'Is There a Defence of Good Consideration?' in C Mitchell and W Swadling (eds), *The Restatement Third, Restitution and Unjust Enrichment: Critical and Comparative Essays* (Oxford, Hart Publishing, 2013); A Burrows, 'Good Consideration in the Law of Unjust Enrichment' (2013) 129 *LQR* 329.

[64] *David Securities* (n 62).

[65] *Deutsche Morgan Grenfell plc v IRC* [2005] EWCA Civ 78; [2006] Ch 243 [294]; *Sempra* (n 3) [28]; *Gibb* (n 45) [32].

[66] Burrows, *Restatement* (n 51) 43. No cases are cited to support Burrows' view that counterfactual reasoning can be used to disprove enrichment.

Applying this reasoning to the facts of *Littlewoods*, HMRC should have been able to escape liability to the extent that they were not enriched by receipt of the invalid VAT payments because they would have become entitled to valid corporation tax payments if the VAT payments had not been made. Interestingly, though, Henderson J seems to have denied this, stating that:[67]

> If the additional corporation tax were to be netted-off, it could only be on the basis of a general principle of considerable width and uncertainty which may have a place in the quantification of damages for wrongs, but seems to me to be at odds with the essentially subtractive nature of an unjust enrichment claim. The Government was undoubtedly enriched by the overpayments of VAT as and when they were received. The benefit of the payment of that money may not be strictly incontrovertible, but the presumption that the Government was thereby enriched by the full amount of the receipts must be a very strong one. That is the benefit which needs to be restored to the claimants, and the justice of the claim to restitution is not in my opinion affected by the probability that, but for the overpayments, the Government would subsequently have received larger amounts of corporation tax than it did in fact receive.

Henderson J's comments were not made in response to an explicit legal argument by HMRC that they had not been enriched by the claimant's invalid VAT payments to the extent that they would otherwise have received corporation tax payments. If he meant to hold that counterfactual reasoning cannot generally be used to disprove enrichment, then that is a proposition for which there is no other judicial authority and so the point cannot be regarded as decisively settled.

5.2.2. *Subjective Devaluation*

Whether subjective devaluation is conceptually different from the 'no enrichment' argument considered in the previous subsection depends in part on whether one adheres to Lord Clarke's or Lord Reed's version of the subjective devaluation argument in *Benedetti v Sawiris*.[68] This is explained below.

In *Littlewoods*, Henderson J held that HMRC's counterfactual assertion did not 'fall within, or even close to, the principles of … subjective devaluation as they are currently understood'.[69] The judge had no help on this point from HMRC, which did not attempt to express their argument in the language of subjective devaluation. Contrary to Henderson J's view, however, it would have been conceptually possible for HMRC to put their argument in this way. Even if they had been objectively enriched by the value of the claimant's money, they should have been able to argue that they had not

[67] *Littlewoods* (Ch) (n 3) [434].
[68] *Benedetti v Sawiris* [2013] UKSC 50; [2014] AC 938.
[69] *Littlewoods* (Ch) (n 3) [434].

been subjectively enriched, because they could have obtained the same benefit for free by enforcing the valid legal rights that they would have acquired against the claimant if the invalid VAT payment had not been made—and HMRC would have chosen to do this had they known that they had the choice.

The quantification of money benefits received by public bodies was discussed in *Sempra Metals Ltd v IRC*[70] and *Benedetti v Sawiris*.[71] In *Sempra*, the majority of the court held that the Revenue had been enriched by the acquisition of an opportunity to use money prematurely paid as corporation tax.[72] The minority denied that a claim in unjust enrichment lies to recover the value of such an opportunity, holding that this is a 'wholly conceptual' benefit, and that a defendant who has received money can only be sued for the face value of the money (which was not claimed in *Sempra*) or for the face value of an 'actual benefit' derived from his use of the money, meaning some secondary gain such as the profits of lending the money to somebody else.[73] However, the majority stressed that the 'time value of money', by which they meant the opportunity to use the money quantified by reference to the saved cost of borrowing, 'is to be distinguished from the value of the benefits a defendant actually derived from the use of the money' and that the latter were 'not in point in the present case'.[74] They also held that the value of the Revenue's saved borrowing costs should be quantified by identifying the rate which would have been charged to the government by a lender, which was lower than the rate which a lender would have charged a commercial enterprise.[75]

The *Sempra* majority seem to have thought that this followed from the application of the principle (termed 'subjective devaluation' by Lord Nicholls)[76] that a good faith defendant should not have to repay the objective market value of a benefit if he would not have chosen to pay that amount for it. They reasoned that the objective value of the opportunity to use the money was the commercial borrowing rate, but that the government would not have chosen to pay so much for this benefit because it would have been able to obtain the same benefit by paying a lower rate. Subsequently, the members of the Supreme Court in *Benedetti* all agreed that the *Sempra* majority could have arrived at the same result by holding that the lower rate was itself the objective value of the government's saved borrowing costs. They reasoned that the objective value of a benefit should be determined

70 *Sempra* (n 3).
71 *Benedetti* (n 68).
72 *Sempra* (n 3) [32]–[33] (Lord Hope), [102] (Lord Nicholls) and [154] (Lord Walker).
73 ibid [145]–[146] (Lord Scott) and [231] (Lord Mance).
74 ibid [117]–[118] (Lord Nicholls).
75 ibid [43]–[49] (Lord Hope), [116]–[119] (Lord Nicholls) and [154] (Lord Walker).
76 ibid [119], adopting terminology used in P Birks *An Introduction to the Law of Restitution* (Oxford, Oxford University Press, 1985) 413.

by reference to market rates where there exists a market for the benefit, but that account should be taken of the fact that the price charged in the market may vary with the individual characteristics of buyers. There is an individuated market rate for government borrowing which is less expensive than the rate for borrowing by less creditworthy commercial borrowers, and this lower rate is therefore the objective value of the opportunity to use money paid to the government as tax which is not due.[77]

Putting that to one side, the more important point for present purposes is that the *Sempra* majority and the *Benedetti* court all considered that a good faith defendant who would not have chosen to pay the market price for a benefit received from a claimant should not be ordered to make restitution of the market value of the benefit. In *Benedetti*, Lord Clarke followed Lord Nicholls' analysis in *Sempra* and said that the reason for this was that the defendant could 'subjectively devalue' the benefit, ie, he could say that he did not subjectively value the benefit at the market price.[78] Lord Reed disagreed, holding that for the purposes of a claim in unjust enrichment, the only yardstick against which the value of benefits should be measured is the objective market price. Thus, he preferred to say that the reason why a claimant should not be ordered to pay this amount where he would not have chosen to do so is that this would be unjust.[79]

Whichever approach is correct, their Lordships agreed that a defendant should not be deprived of his freedom to choose how to spend his resources and that in order to protect this freedom, the law would reduce his restitutionary liability to the amount which he would have chosen to pay for the relevant benefit. In *Littlewoods* and the other cases discussed in section 2, the defendant could have invoked this principle to say that it would not have chosen to receive money from the claimant, the value of which it was liable to repay to the claimant, and which was therefore effectively worth nothing, if it could instead have had received money to which it was legally entitled by enforcing the valid rights it would have acquired against the claimant if the invalid payment had not been made.

5.2.3. Not at the Claimant's Expense

A defendant's enrichment must have been gained at the claimant's expense.[80] There are two aspects to this requirement: first, the claimant must show that he has suffered loss of a kind that the law deems relevant; and, second, he

[77] See especially *Benedetti* (n 68) [22] (Lord Clarke) and [126]–[138] (Lord Reed).
[78] ibid [12]–[26].
[79] ibid [110]–[117].
[80] *Banque Financière de la Cité SA v Parc (Battersea) Ltd* [1999] 1 AC 221 (HL) 227; *Investment Trust Companies* (n 27) [26].

must show that this loss is relevantly linked to the defendant's enrichment. Neither rule is well understood; indeed, the courts do not often recognise that they are two distinct rules and tend to subsume discussion of the first within discussion of the second. In principle, however, they are distinct and in principle either aspect of the requirement might conceivably be disproved with the use of counterfactual reasoning.

So, for example, on the facts of *Littlewoods*, HMRC might conceivably have argued that the claimant had suffered no loss to the extent that it would in any case have suffered a loss when paying the corporation tax liability that would have arisen if it had not made the VAT payments. Alternatively, HMRC might have conceded that the claimant suffered a loss when making the VAT payments, but might have argued that this loss was not relevantly linked to HMRC's gain to the extent that HMRC would otherwise have received corporation tax payments. Whether these arguments would have been sustainable as a matter of law depends on two questions: first, whether the law of unjust enrichment defines a claimant's loss in a way that allows defendants to use counterfactual reasoning to disprove that a loss occurred; and, second, whether the law defines the necessary link between a claimant's loss and a defendant's gain in a way that allows defendants to use counterfactual reasoning to disprove that such a link existed.

The first question has not been directly considered by the English courts, but *Kleinwort Benson Ltd v Birmingham CC*[81] bears on the issue. The claimant bank sought to recover money paid to the defendant local authority under a void interest rate swap contract. The defendant replied that its enrichment had not been gained at the claimant's expense because the claimant had passed on its loss to a second bank with which it had entered a back-to-back hedging contract, under which it had recouped the value of its payments to the defendant. The Court of Appeal rejected this for two reasons: first, because the payments received by the claimant under the hedge contract were not relevantly connected with the payments made by the claimant to the defendant under the swaps contract;[82] and, second, in Saville LJ's words, because:[83]

> The expression 'at the payer's expense' ... [does not justify] the importation of concepts of loss or damage with their attendant concepts of mitigation, for these have nothing whatever to do with the reason why our law imposes an obligation on the payee to repay to the payer what he has no right to retain.

The first of these reasons was essentially a finding of fact that the claimant had not relevantly passed on its loss to its counter-party under the hedge contract and if that was the ground for the court's decision, then its second,

[81] *Kleinwort Benson Ltd v Birmingham CC* [1997] QB 380 (CA).
[82] ibid 399 (Morritt LJ).
[83] ibid 395.

legal reason for denying the defence was not the ratio of the case.[84] This second reason was essentially a finding of law that for the purposes of a claim of unjust enrichment, the type of loss which must be established differs from the type of loss which must be established for the purposes of a claim in tort, at least to the extent that the defendant cannot argue for a reduction of his liability on the basis that the claimant should have mitigated his loss, but failed to do so. This suggests that claims in unjust enrichment may have a more absolute quality than tort claims, which makes them more closely resemble claims in debt. This would be consistent with a rule that counterfactual reasoning cannot be used to disprove the claimant's loss and it would also be consistent with Henderson J's finding in *Littlewoods*, noted in section 5.2.1 above, that such reasoning cannot be used to disprove the defendant's enrichment.

Turning to the question of whether counterfactual reasoning can be used to disprove the required connection between a claimant's loss and a defendant's gain, the view that it can gains support from Arden LJ's statement in *Test Claimants in the FII Group Litigation v HMRC (No 1)*[85] that the 'test of causation for unjust enrichment is the "but for" test'—although her Ladyship's analysis was weakened by her failure to distinguish clearly between the question of whether the claimant's mistake had caused its decision to benefit the defendant and the question of whether the claimant's resulting loss was connected with the defendant's resulting enrichment.[86] More recently, Arden LJ returned to this question in *Relfo Ltd (In Liquidation) v Varsani*, where she seems to have accepted the proposition that 'liability in unjust enrichment requires more than a "but for" test to be satisfied where the claimant, as in this case, contends that the defendant was enriched at the claimant's expense through the intervention of third parties'.[87]

Taken together, these dicta suggest that a defendant's enrichment is not relevantly gained at a claimant's expense if the claimant's loss and the defendant's gain are not causally connected on a 'but for' basis. And this suggests that counterfactual reasoning can be used by the defendant to show that there was no relevant connection between the two. However, the law in this area is far from clear and in several recent cases, including *Relfo*, the Court of Appeal has declined to lay down a general test for determining when the parties' gain and loss are relevantly connected.[88] Possibly some

[84] As noted in M Rush, *The Defence of Passing On* (Oxford, Hart Publishing, 2006) 39.

[85] *Test Claimants in the FII Group Litigation v HMRC (No 1)* [2010] EWCA Civ 103; [2010] STC 1251 [182]; not considered on appeal: [2012] UKSC 19; [2012] 2 AC 337.

[86] See *Goff & Jones* (n 24) paras [6-06]–[6-08].

[87] *Relfo Ltd (In Liquidation) v Varsani* [2014] EWCA Civ 360; [2015] 1 BCLC 14 [72].

[88] See also *Menelaou v Bank of Cyprus UK Ltd* [2013] EWCA Civ 1960; [2014] 1 WLR 854; *Investment Trust Companies* (n 27).

light will be shed on this question when the Supreme Court decides the appeal in another case where this issue arose, *Menelaou v Bank of Cyprus UK Ltd*.[89]

5.2.4. Change of Position

In *Sempra*, Lord Nicholls suggested that there may be an overlap between cases where defendants can make 'subjective devaluation' arguments and cases where they can invoke the change of position defence.[90] Consistently with this, and following on from the discussion in section 5.2.2, a defendant might frame a counterfactual argument against *Woolwich* liability by saying that it changed its position to its detriment when it failed to enforce a valid liability that the claimant would have owed if he had not paid the defendant in respect of an invalid liability.

Three possible objections might be made to this. First, there are English cases which hold that a defendant cannot invoke the change of position defence unless he relied on his receipt of the relevant benefit from the claimant.[91] A defendant cannot be said to have forgone his rights against a claimant in reliance on his receipt of the claimant's money where he is unaware that these rights exist. To meet this objection, the defendant would have to persuade the court that reliance should not be required, provided that there is a causal link between receipt and detriment, and in fact there are judicial dicta to this effect[92] and good reasons in principle for believing this to be the preferable rule.[93]

A second objection might be that foregone opportunities to make a gain do not constitute detriment for the purpose of the defence, according to Potter LJ in *National Westminster Bank plc v Somer International (UK) Ltd*, where he said that 'the defence of "change of position" only protects the actual reduction of the transferee's assets ... [and a] transferee who, in reliance upon a receipt, forgoes a realistic and quantifiable opportunity to increase his assets is not apparently protected'.[94] However, dicta in other cases say the opposite,[95] and the point remains unsettled.

A third objection might be that as a matter of general policy, public authority defendants should not be allowed to invoke the change of position

[89] *Menelaou* (n 88).
[90] *Sempra* (n 3) [119].
[91] *Streiner v Bank Leumi (UK) plc* (unreported, QBD, 31 October 1985); *Credit Suisse (Monaco) SA v Attar* [2004] EWHC 374 (Comm) [98].
[92] *Scottish Equitable plc v Derby* [2001] 3 All ER 818 (CA) [30]–[31]; *Cressman v Coys of Kensington (Sales) Ltd* [2004] EWCA Civ 47; [2004] 1 WLR 2774 [41].
[93] Discussed in *Goff & Jones* (n 24) paras [27-27]–[27-28].
[94] *National Westminster Bank plc v Somer International (UK) Ltd* [2001] EWCA Civ 970; [2002] QB 1286 [47].
[95] eg, *Scottish Equitable plc v Derby* [2001] 3 All ER 818 (CA) [32] (Robert Walker LJ) and other cases in *Goff & Jones* (n 24) para [27-21].

defence in answer to *Woolwich* claims. In the most recent round of the FII group litigation, Henderson J espoused this view, holding that:[96]

> to allow scope for the defence would unacceptably subvert, and be inconsistent with, the high principles of public policy which led to recognition of the *Woolwich* cause of action as a separate one in the English law of unjust enrichment, with its own specific 'unjust factor'.

Against this a defendant might say that Henderson J stated his rule against allowing the defence in *Woolwich* cases too broadly and that permitting defendants to rely on it would be less objectionable in some cases than in others. Where the detriment relied on to support the defence is not expenditure of public funds, but the release (or at least the foregoing) of a valid right against the claimant, the same objections to allowing the defence do not arise.

5.3. Summary

In this section, an attempt has been made to identify the legal arguments against *Woolwich* liability which might plausibly be supported by counterfactual reasoning. Various arguments have been considered and some have been found more apt for the defendant's purposes than others. The value of the exercise has been threefold. First, it has helped us to assess the legal merits of counterfactual arguments against *Woolwich* liability. Second, it should help the parties to draft their pleadings with greater exactitude in future cases where the point arises. Third, it has forced us to think carefully about the legal content of claims in unjust enrichment and the defences that can be raised against them. It is only by identifying the exact legal content of such claims and defences that we have been able to assess whether counterfactual reasoning can aptly be used to defeat them.

6. CONCLUSION

This chapter has identified an argument which public authority defendants have made with varying degrees of success in answer to *Woolwich* claims. People's intuitions about the merits of the argument vary: some believe it is obviously right, while others believe that it is not. The discussion points towards the conclusion that it is more plausible in some types of case than in others. The argument has not often been pleaded in clear legal terms and this has hampered the courts' efforts to address it. Various ways in which

[96] *FII (No 2)* (n 28) [315].

the argument might be framed in legal terms have been examined and some have been found to be a better fit than others with the law and with the facts of the cases in which the argument might typically be made. It is hoped that this work will make it easier for litigants and the courts to identify and analyse the policies and legal principles in play when the argument is made.

Three questions of particular interest for the general law of unjust enrichment have been identified: can counterfactual reasoning be used to disprove enrichment; can it be used to disprove loss; and can it be used to disprove the required connection between gain and loss? None of these questions has been clearly and decisively answered in the case law, but much turns on them for our understanding of claims in unjust enrichment, their operation, their conceptual structure and their normative underpinnings.

13

Theory and Practice

ROBERT REED*

WHEN I WAS appointed to the Supreme Court, I commented to my colleague Lord Brown that the library seemed to me to be rather weak in some areas.[1] He responded by asking me if I knew what Lord Diplock was reputed to have said when the newly appointed Lord Brandon made a similar comment: 'Books? You don't need books. All you need is the Appeal Cases and your own intelligence.' That attitude changed during the time of Lord Goff, who was a former teacher of law and author of academic writings, as several later members of the House of Lords and the Supreme Court have also been. He insisted on being referred by counsel to the relevant academic literature, and this practice is now firmly established in difficult cases. The court may indeed have become more demanding: in the case of *AIB v Redler*,[2] for example, although we were referred to academic work, it emanated almost exclusively from present or former members of a single law school and tended to reflect a particular point of view. My request to be referred to a more diverse range of material resulted, as Lord Toulson noted in his judgment, in our being provided with some 900 pages of academic commentary from around the world. It is indeed possible to have too much of a good thing.

As that anecdote illustrates, appellate judges appreciate the help that they can derive from academic scholarship. To an extent which academics may not always appreciate, most appellate judges are on a remorseless treadmill of cases, with limited time to devote to their judgments. Particularly at the level of the Court of Appeal, there has been a tendency for court administrations to focus on minimising the delay before cases are heard, with correspondingly less priority given to allowing the judges time for research and writing. So judges are grateful for the work done by others who have thought about the same problems and have considered the arguments. But

* I am grateful to Frederick Wilmot-Smith for commenting on an earlier version of this chapter. The usual disclaimer applies.

[1] A matter which has since been addressed.

[2] *AIB Group (UK) plc v Mark Redler & Co Solicitors* [2014] UKSC 58; [2014] 3 WLR 1367.

doctrinal scholarship is not a substitute for the analysis of the law by the judges themselves. It can influence that process, but it cannot replace it. Unlike in a civil law system, the writings of jurists are not, in English law, sources of law.

That is why I was slightly concerned by the methodology adopted in counsel's submissions in a number of recent cases, including *Benedetti v Sawiris*,[3] *FHR European Ventures v Cedar Capital Partners*[4] and *AIB v Redler*. The focus of some of the arguments was so much upon the views of academic authors that it almost seemed as though the court was being invited to conclude that because a number of distinguished academics took a particular view of a problem, that must therefore be the answer which the court should adopt. In the absence of a Law of Citations,[5] however, the court must grapple with the issues for itself.

My expression of these thoughts to my colleagues led to my being encouraged to put pen to paper in *Benedetti*. Some may think that I was hoist by my own petard. But the experience of reading a great deal of academic writing during the process of writing a judgment led me to reflect on the value of doctrinal scholarship to judges, particularly at the appellate level, and on the ways in which my approach to the problem at hand differed from that of the academic writers whose work I was reading.

In that regard, I was struck, when reading some of the material, by the relatively abstract character of the discussion and the absence of much sense of social or historical context. Some scholars wrote as if legal questions have (and have always had) a correct solution, which can be reached by applying principles that are open to inspection by those with clear minds, even if they remain obscure to everyone else. The implicit message appeared to be that legal truths are not discovered without mental effort, but that once the necessary thinking has been done, the legal principles emerge from their hiding places and hand themselves in. I was also struck by the somewhat dogmatic tone of some of the writing (for example, when criticising jurisdictions where the earlier Birksian approach has not been followed) in a field where much of the case law pre-dates the modern development of unjust enrichment as a category, and lacks the clarity and coherence of scholars' explanatory theories.

It occurred to me, in relation to the present volume and the conference which preceded it, that it might be of some interest if I were to share my thoughts about some differences between the approach to the law required by the judicial enterprise, as I see it, and the approach adopted in some (but by no means all) academic scholarship. This is terrain which has been

[3] *Benedetti v Sawiris* [2013] UKSC 50; [2014] AC 938.

[4] *FHR European Ventures LLP v Cedar Capital Partners LLC* [2014] UKSC 45; [2015] AC 250.

[5] *Codex Theodosianus*, I.iv.3–5.

traversed by a number of academic writers,[6] but less so by judges.[7] I should make it clear at the outset that I am expressing a purely personal view.

The strength of the common law, as I see it, is derived from its casuistic nature, and the consequent scope which it allows to judges—in particular, appellate judge—to develop the law, usually incrementally, so as to adapt it to the current needs of society as they see them. Judicial decisions thus reflect not only an inherited tradition but also a particular conception of how the law ought to regulate relationships and behaviour here and now. This might be contrasted with the more abstract and putatively universal conception of legal relationships characteristic of Roman law and systems strongly influenced by it. Judges' conceptions of how relationships and behaviour should be regulated can of course vary from one area of life to another,[8] are constantly evolving and are often in tension with one another. Their answers to questions about these matters can depend on the specific context and the potential consequences. As it seems to me, the living connection between the common law and life as it is lived thus depends on the willingness of judges to particularise, and to accept the contingency of their (and their predecessors') convictions. It has to be acknowledged that there are concomitant uncertainties and conflicts within and between their convictions, which are often impossible to resolve.

Some academic work brings out these aspects of the common law. As a student, I was greatly impressed by the lectures on 'Recent Cases in Contract and Tort' given by John Davies, a fellow of Brasenose. A lecture might be devoted to a single recent decision of the House of Lords. Davies explained the legal background to the case and how the authorities were marshalled by each side in support of their competing analyses of the law. He made clear a fact which is all too often overlooked when cases are read with the benefit of hindsight: that the losing side had at least a reasonable argument, which might have been accepted by other judges or at another time. He then examined the speeches and brought out the differences between them, explaining the implications which the adoption of one approach or another might have for the future development of the law.

[6] See, eg, N Duxbury, *Jurists and Judges: An Essay on Influence* (Oxford, Hart Publishing, 2001); and K Stanton, 'Use of Scholarship by the House of Lords in Tort Cases' in J Lee (ed), *From House of Lords to Supreme Court: Judges, Jurists and the Process of Judging* (Oxford, Hart Publishing, 2010).

[7] Two exceptions are Lord Goff and Lord Rodger of Earlsferry: see, eg, the former's Maccabean Lecture, 'In Search of Principle' (1983) 69 *Proceedings of the British Academy* 169, 186, and the latter's John Kelly Memorial Lecture, 'Savigny in the Strand' (1993–95) 28–30 *Irish Jurist* 1. Another is Sir Jack Beatson: see 'Legal Academics: Forgotten Players or Interlopers?' in A Burrows, D Johnston and R Zimmermann (eds), *Judge and Jurist* (Oxford, Hart Publishing, 2013).

[8] They may also, of course, vary from one judge to another—hence the importance of having final appeals decided by a majority of a relatively large panel.

This is a model which I have borrowed when lecturing students. I particularly like to speak to them about cases in which judgment has not yet been given. A lecture of this kind makes especially clear to them that legal thinking in a common law system is based on respect for an inherited tradition, but is nevertheless dynamic; that the derivation of answers to difficult legal problems from the existing law is not a mechanical process or a matter only of technical legal reasoning, let alone of logic, but one which calls for creativity and judgment as to the approach which is likely to work best; and that the law is therefore not fixed, but a range of possibilities, constantly rolling forward. This sort of lecture may lead the best students to question whether the conceptual structures and principles taught to them by their teachers are as definitive as they might have appeared.

John Davies' lectures provided a good foundation for practice at the Bar. If the textbooks provided an apparently clear answer to the question arising in a case, and that answer was against you, you did not necessarily shrug your shoulders and advise your client that the case was hopeless. You read the authorities supposedly vouching the proposition and asked yourself what the judge was really deciding. What arguments were presented to him and what cases were cited to him? If he indeed decided that the law was as stated in the textbooks, and if he considered and rejected the argument which you would wish to advance, was his decision influenced by the particular circumstances in which the point arose or the social and intellectual context of his times? At what level was he sitting? How highly respected is he? How well does his decision now sit with the decisions of other judges in other cases? Even if the argument you wish to advance appears unlikely ultimately to prevail, is it nevertheless sufficiently strong to be worth running in order to bring your opponent to a settlement?

Although John Davies' lectures taught his students how to deconstruct appellate decision making and analyse it critically, much written academic work is less likely to focus explicitly on the dynamic aspect of the common law or on what I have described as the contingent nature of judicial decision making. The most important contribution made to the common law by academic scholarship is to my mind the descriptive analyses to be found in the leading textbooks on different subjects, such as *Dicey, Morris and Collins on the Conflict of Laws*, *McGregor on Damages* and *Bowstead & Reynolds on Agency*: works which were at one time mostly produced by practitioners, but which are now usually written by academic lawyers. In a casuistic system, works of this kind, which order and analyse a mass of case law, are vital to any understanding of the law. It is impossible to imagine making sense of the law of contract, for example, in the absence of *Chitty*, *Anson* and similar texts, and, in the area of the law with which this volume is concerned, it is scarcely an exaggeration to say that the subject has been created by the authors of textbooks such as *Goff & Jones*.

However, for the reasons I have explained, it is impossible, even in theory, that a descriptive account of the common law can be definitive. The less interesting reason for this is that the law is constantly being developed by the courts, so that textbooks require to be updated from time to time as superseded decisions are weeded out and new decisions take their place. Of course, courts operating within a common law system apply a doctrine of precedent and are respectful of the tradition handed down to them. So the development of the law by the courts is usually incremental, and the current edition of a standard textbook will still be recognisably the same vessel as the previous edition, even if some of the timbers have been replaced. But one can be reasonably certain that some of the current timbers will have been replaced by the time of the next edition, and a skilled analyst may be able to judge which of them are candidates for replacement and to explain why. An account which undertakes that exercise provides a more realistic and useful description of the law than one which does not.

The more interesting reason why a descriptive account cannot be definitive is more fundamental. It is, as I have explained, because uncertainty is inherent in the common law, and tensions and conflicts between the ideas it espouses are an unavoidable aspect of its nature as a human response to particular problems thrown up by life at particular times and places. This aspect may not be considered in a descriptive account of the kind one generally finds in legal textbooks, but may be in other kinds of academic work, which undertake a more detailed analysis of specific legal problems or examine the historical background to a particular area of the law. The type of analysis I have in mind may be found in case notes: those of Tony Weir or Glanville Williams, for example, were especially valuable to the highest courts, as they contained acute analyses of specific current legal problems and often concerned the very cases which might then be awaiting a hearing before the House of Lords. Equally detailed and thoughtful analysis, across a wider field, can be found in articles such as those in the present volume or in the leading journals, and in monographs on particular aspects of the law or on legal history. Some of the most useful discussions of this kind, for the purposes of appellate judges considering the development of the law, are to be found in the reports and consultation papers published by the Law Commissions, which are often written by academic lawyers.

Generally, for the reasons I have explained, academic scholarship which adopts an abstract and universalising approach to legal problems seems to me to be less useful to a judge than scholarship which demonstrates an awareness that legal problems are situated at a particular time and place, and that they require an approach to their resolution which is concrete and particular. Equally, it seems to me that scholarship which insists on lucid rationality and consistency may at times be less realistic than scholarship which accepts that life sometimes requires the adoption of conflicting ideas, held simultaneously in tension with each other.

Appellate judges of course consider the likely implications of their decisions for the coherence and clarity of the law, as well as considering their other implications. They attempt to write lucid judgments and to state legal principles as clearly as they feel they can. Their function, however, is primarily to decide particular disputes, rather than to formulate general principles. Didactic judgments are sometimes necessary, but they are fraught with risk. Other things being equal, clarity and coherence are of course preferable to obscurity and inconsistency. But a degree of vagueness, and occasionally even inconsistency, is unavoidable in practice.

A legal proposition formulated by a court is often best expressed with a degree of indeterminacy, so as to be sufficiently flexible to be workable in practice or over the longer term, given the court's inability to foresee all the circumstances in which it may have to be applied. In much the same way, many of the provisions of continental codes of law are expressed in broad and general language, which the judge then has to apply creatively to the facts of the particular case before him. Even internal inconsistencies between, for example, concurring judgments in an appellate court[9] seem to me to be sometimes unavoidable in practice, as a means of reflecting disparate sentiments. If it is left to the lower courts to find an acceptable way through the inconsistencies in later cases, in reaction to the problems thrown up by their particular circumstances, this is not always or necessarily a bad thing.

Judges are also aware that the law is not always, or even generally, a logical body of rules deducible from general principles, but an untidy and historically situated body of judicial decisions and other materials, which were designed to resolve particular problems at a particular time and place, and whose interpretation is often difficult and uncertain.[10] The scholar who devises a logical analysis of the law may respond that he is not attempting to reflect the thinking of the judges who decided the cases, but to show the way to a clearer and more coherent future. That is of course a valuable aspect of the work done by legal academics. Valuable as it is, however, there are limits to the extent to which the courts may be able to follow the scholar down that path, particularly in an area of the law which is viewed as functioning as a residual basis for avoiding injustice.

The principal value of explanatory theories, such as one finds in the textbooks on unjust enrichment, is that the cases are analysed so as to identify the principles which they appear to establish, the points of divergence between them, and perhaps their strengths and weaknesses. Such texts are

[9] Or, sometimes, within a single judgment, as for example in some of the judgments of the Court of Justice of the European Union.

[10] As Oliver Wendell Holmes Jr remarked in OW Holmes, *The Common Law* (London, Macmillan, 1881) 1, 'the law embodies the story of a nation's development through many centuries, and it cannot be dealt with as if it contained only the axioms and corollaries of a book of mathematics'.

far more than an elaborate arrangement of pigeonholes into which the cases can be slotted. Indeed, although the labelling of pigeonholes matters, there is a tension between a focus on taxonomy and a recognition of the dynamic and contingent nature of judicial decision making. The characteristics of the law, as experienced in practice, which I have described make it inherently resistant to a static analysis. It is easier to dissect a corpse than a living body.

On a related point, elegance—by which I mean a structure which is simple, logical and economical—is another quality which has been viewed since William of Ockham as generally desirable in an explanatory theory, but I am inclined to doubt whether it is universally possible or desirable in the law. All other things being equal, a simple explanatory account of the law, rather than a more complex one, is of course preferable. But the most adequate explanation of the law is not always the simplest, and a legal system whose structure is more complex is not necessarily worse in its practical operation than one whose structure is simpler, or whose leading principles can be formulated at a higher level of generality. The law exists to meets the needs of society, and the standards by which its performance of that function should be assessed are not aesthetic. Unless society's needs are simple, logical and economical, it is unlikely that a legal system which meets its needs satisfactorily will exhibit those characteristics.

By way of illustration, the practical problems which resulted from the adoption of Lord Wilberforce's abstract formulation of the duty of care in *Anns v Merton LBC*[11] led to its abandonment only 13 years later,[12] and to the adoption in *Caparo*[13] of an approach that is less abstract, less clear and less elegant: an approach which is dependent on pragmatic judgments of what is 'fair, just and reasonable' in particular factual situations, but which has nevertheless been found to work better in practice. The point is that the law, in order to meet the needs of society, is sometimes better formulated in terms which are concrete and specific rather than abstract and general.

One final general point should be made. While the courts risk what might be termed temporal parochialism, if they fail to grasp that a current academic orthodoxy may be more ephemeral than its methodology might suggest, they risk a different sort of parochialism if they are unwilling to give careful consideration to the approaches adopted in other common law jurisdictions. The Supreme Court has said more than once in the recent past that it is highly desirable for the common law jurisdictions to learn from each other and at least to lean in favour of harmonising the development of the common law around the world.[14] Each of the cases in which that

[11] *Anns v Merton LBC* [1978] AC 728 (HL).

[12] *Murphy v Brentwood LBC* [1991] 1 AC 398 (HL).

[13] *Caparo Industries plc v Dickman* [1990] 2 AC 605 (HL).

[14] *FHR European Ventures LLP v Cedar Capital Partners LLC* (n 4) [45]; *AIB Group (UK) plc v Mark Redler & Co Solicitors* (n 2) [121].

was said provides an example of the Supreme Court's rejecting an approach favoured by many respected academic lawyers in this country in favour of an approach which was intended to bring English law into closer alignment with other major common law jurisdictions. Nor is it only common law jurisdictions which should be considered. Particularly at a time when steps have begun to be taken towards some degree of harmonisation of private law across the EU, it can sometimes be helpful to also consider civilian approaches.

This cannot be taken too far: as I have suggested, courts operate in a particular local context, and the UK, Canada and Australia, for example, have different histories and identities. There are many differences between their societies. However, there is also much that is shared, particularly in terms of legal traditions and values. The desire to harmonise the development of the common law, at the same time as recognising that the law has to be developed by the judges to meet the needs of their particular society, is perhaps a good example of the simultaneous holding of conflicting values.

Drawing these remarks to a close, it seems to me that although academic scholarship on the subject of unjust enrichment has developed impressively in recent years, the court should resist the temptation to lay down broad or inflexible rules at what is still an early stage in the evolution of this area of English law. The first edition of *Goff & Jones* was only published in 1966. As recently as 1977, Lord Diplock, no mean lawyer, stated that 'there is no general doctrine of unjust enrichment recognised in English law'.[15] The approach now generally prevailing amongst English academic lawyers is more recent still. The Canadian case law demonstrates a different approach to unjust enrichment. The Australian case law indicates another, arguably more traditional, way of approaching some of the same problems. There remains much to be judicially tested. For an essentially inductive system, such as the common law, it seems to me to be too early for the courts to attempt even a provisional general analysis. As Lord Walker of Gestingthorpe observed in *Deutsche Morgan Grenfell Group plc v Inland Revenue Commissioners*, 'it is of the nature of the common law to develop slowly, and attempts at dramatic simplification may turn out to have been premature and indeed mistaken'.[16]

[15] As distinct from 'specific remedies in particular cases of what might be classified as unjust enrichment in a legal system that is based upon the civil law': *Orakpo v Manson Investments Ltd* [1978] AC 95 (CA) 104.

[16] *Deutsche Morgan Grenfell Group plc v Inland Revenue Commissioners* [2006] UKHL 49; [2007] 1 AC 558 [156].

Index of Authors

Index

Printed by Libri Plureos GmbH in Hamburg,
Germany

9 781509 921102